Hope for Every Day

KEN PENNER

FriesenPress

One Printers Way
Altona, MB R0G 0B0
Canada

www.friesenpress.com

ISBN
978-1-03-830902-0 (Hardcover)
978-1-03-830901-3 (Paperback)
978-1-03-830903-7 (eBook)

1. RELIGION, CHRISTIAN LIVING, DEVOTIONAL

Distributed to the trade by The Ingram Book Company

Hope for Every Day

INTRODUCTION

The following 366 readings represent some of the accumulated newspaper articles I've had the privilege of writing over the course of ten years! As you read them, you'll notice a common theme: faith in God's inspired Word, the Bible, faith in Abba Father and trust in Jesus Christ, our Creator, Sustainer, and Saviour through the power of His Holy Spirit. My prayer is that these daily readings will be an encouragement to you as you read them and meditate on God and His Word! Sometimes the chronology may be a bit out of order, such as during the Easter season, which differs every year, but the principles remain the same for every day of the year! May you be encouraged in your faith and may your trust in God grow as you consider God's Holy Word and how it applies to your life!

DEDICATION

This book is dedicated to our children, grandchildren, and great-grandchildren, as well as to others as they grow up to become our next generation of leaders. May God grant you faith, wisdom, and discernment that only comes from following Him, as revealed through His Holy Word, the Bible!

May the daily meditations in this book bring *Hope for Every Day* to all who read it! And may you be encouraged to be set apart to grow in God's Kingdom, to *"love the Lord your God with all your heart, all your soul, all your mind, and all your strength" (Mark 12:30)*, until Jesus, our true Hope, comes to set up His Kingdom on earth!

January 1

Know-So Hope

Many years ago, when I was much younger, I was driving up the Salmo-Creston Highway in my 1952 Ford pickup when I ran into a mean snowstorm. Snowflakes the size of silver dollars were coming down with hardly any space between them. The road was steep, and I didn't want to spin out. My windshield wipers couldn't keep up, and I only had an area half the size of my fist to look out of.

As I opened the side window to look out, I realized I could only see twenty feet ahead of me. My thoughts raced through my mind. *What am I to do? Will I spin out, drive off the road? Is there a semi ahead? If I stop, some other vehicle might ram me from behind. I hope this snowstorm blows over. I hope the truck doesn't spin out. I hope I don't drive off the road. I hope God sees my predicament and helps me. God help me!*

What kind of hope did I have in this situation? My hope was in the weather changing, in my truck not spinning out, in nobody being stopped ahead of me, maybe in God possibly being there and hearing my desperate cry for help. I call this a hope-so hope. I wasn't sure, but I hoped it would turn out somehow. Have you ever found yourself in such a situation?

Since that time, I've come to realize that I can have a different kind of hope, a know-so hope. Through faith and trust in God, I realize that everything is in His hands. He created this whole universe by the command of His Word (Genesis 1:1; Hebrews 11:3). He designed the ecosystems and knows the storms we're going through. He made us and knows how many hairs are on our head (Matthew 10:30). He even knows our every thought (Psalm 139). He knows the beginning from the end. He has my future in His hands. Even if I die, He has a place for me in His presence forever (John 14:1, 2). I can trust Him no matter what happens.

What is your situation today? Does it seem desperate? My prayer is that you and I will be able to put our trust and hope in the Almighty God and say with the psalmist in the Bible, *"Why are you so downcast, O my soul? Why so disturbed within me? Put your hope in God, for I will yet praise Him, my Saviour and my God"* (Psalm 42:5, NIV).

In the Image of God

A few years ago while walking down a street in Vancouver, I came across a construction site. They had the sidewalk narrowed, so only one person could walk through. As I approached the narrowing, I noticed a beautifully dressed Asian lady approaching the same narrowing in the sidewalk from the opposite direction. As she came to the obstruction, she looked up, and her eyes caught mine. She immediately stepped aside and, with a serious look on her face, looked down. It was obvious she was giving me the right-of-way. I almost kept going, but something stopped me. *She's a woman created in God's image; she's someone's daughter. She's probably someone's mother, someone's wife*, I thought. *I will stop and give her the right-of-way.*

As I spoke to her and invited her to go first, her head lifted and her eyes lit up. She walked through and said "thank you" with a cheery voice as she passed by.

This to me was a special moment. It's a special moment whenever two people meet. Why is this? I'd never met this woman before. I didn't know her name. I didn't know where she lived, and I didn't know her country of origin. All that happened is that we met for a moment on the street.

Every human being is special because we're all created in the image of God. The Bible, God's Word, says, *"From one man He made all the nations, that they should inhabit the whole earth; and He marked out their appointed times in history and the boundaries of their lands" (Acts 17:26).* Every person is unique and stands apart from the rest of creation because we bear the image of God. The Bible says, *"So God created mankind is His own image, in the image of God He created them; male and female He created them" (Genesis 1:27, NIV).* Every person deserves respect.

This woman is also part of God's creation. She also carries in her the image of God that each person has. I was glad that I didn't take the right-of-way but rather let her go first.

Chance or Creation?

How did we get here? Where did we come from? This is a question most of us ask sometime in our lives.

As a youngster, I was taught in school that I came from a monkey or a monkey-type of being. They even showed pictures depicting a progression from some kind of amoeba to a chimp-like creature and finally to a human being. They called it evolution and said it all happened by chance over many, many years. In fact, it all started billions of years ago, they said. Maybe you've seen this type of description of our origins. They're still teaching it in most schools to this day.

I believed it at that time. *I came from a monkey*, I thought, so I acted like a monkey. Why not? It really didn't matter—no standard, no design, and therefore no real accountability, just chance.

As time went on, I came to see design all around us. The exact positioning of the earth on its axis, just the right distance from the sun. The complexity of the human eye and the process of the coagulation of our blood. The human brain, said to be the most complex organism in the universe. The amazing complexity of DNA. Plants that reproduce plants of the same kind. The thought patterns of people and social structure. This was amazing—clear evidence of design all around us! It's obvious that airplanes aren't made by throwing dynamite into a garbage dump. When we see a car, we don't in our wildest imagination think of how it evolved in the wilderness somewhere, and how long it took to slowly form there all by itself. No! We ask who designed the car, where, when was it made, and who is the manufacturer. It became very evident that chance could not be the reason for us being here. Where there's design, there's a designer.

The amazing complexity of everything all around us isn't our only evidence for a Creator, but we have an eyewitness account of our origins written down some 3,500 years ago. It was given to us by the eyewitness and Creator, God Himself. It is recorded in the Bible: *"In the beginning God created the heavens and the earth"* (Genesis 1:1, NIV). It goes on to reveal to us that God created this whole universe by speaking it into existence in six days, with evening and morning on each day. After each day of creation, God saw *"it was good."* On the sixth day, God created man and woman in His image, and on that day, He saw *"it was very good."*

I am convinced we didn't get here just by chance but are designed for a purpose. We have a reason to live, and that is to stand in awe and worship the One who made us!

What Will We Do with Jesus?

When we pick up the newspaper, we see the date, say 2013. This bears witness to a person. That person is Jesus Christ, the greatest person to have ever lived on earth. Some two thousand years ago, He lived a life of humility and compassion as no other man before or after Him. Yet He had a very difficult life here because He was rejected by the very men He came to save, even from the beginning of His ministry (see Luke 4:16–30).

"He was in the world and though the world was made through Him, the world did not recognise Him. He came to that which was His own, but His own did not receive Him" (John 1:10–11, NIV). By the end of His time here on earth, even the religious leaders of the day shouted to Pontius Pilate, *"Crucify! Crucify!" (John 19:6, NIV).* Furthermore, both of the thieves who were crucified with Him scorned Him (Matthew 27:44). Yet one thief changed his mind and called out, *"'Jesus, remember me when you come into your kingdom.' Jesus answered him, 'Truly I tell you, today you will be with me in paradise'" (Luke 23:4243, NIV).* Jesus was scorned and beaten. He was spit on and whipped; He was crucified and left to die on an ugly Roman cross.

Jesus proved that He had the power over death by rising from the dead three days later. While speaking to the people after the resurrection, Peter said, *"You killed the author of life but God raised Him from the dead" (Acts 3:15, NIV).* Death could not keep the Author of life in the grave!

Today Jesus is still rejected and despised. His name is often used in vain. Many, some even His followers, are afraid to mention His name in a public place, as they may be ridiculed. Many people don't hesitate to talk about God or religion, or even about moral issues, but Jesus is seldom spoken about in the public forum. As the Author of life, the Creator of all things, should He not be honoured and highly spoken about?

I used to take His name in vain. I didn't care if He ever lived, or even that He rose from the dead, but there came a time when He got a grip on my heart and gave me faith to trust in Him. I received Him as my Lord and Saviour; now I am a believer, a forgiven child of God, just like the thief on the cross.

My prayer is, "Lord, cause us to be faithful to you. May we never be ashamed of you. Empower us to live for you for all eternity and to worship you in spirit and in truth."

What will you do with Jesus?

"Yet to all who did receive Him, to those who believed in His name, He gave the right to become children of God ..." (John 1:12, NIV).

Is There Really Hope for Us?

It was hard to believe, seeing the reports of the bombs going off at the Boston Marathon on April 15, 2013, killing and maiming innocent people as they were watching the runners come to the finish line. More recently we were horrified by the brutal killing and murder of innocent people, including children, women, and elderly people, by the Hamas killers in Israel on October 7, 2023. How can human beings do this to other human beings?

As we watch the news, we see some terrible things happen closer to home on a daily basis, like racism, drunken brawls, spousal abuse, armed robbery, and murder, to name a few. As I look closer into my own heart, I'm sometimes appalled at things that I think, say, or do. Yet we have been created in the image of God. How could people created in the image of God do such things?

The Bible informs us in Genesis 3 that Adam and Eve, the first people God created, sinned against God by disobeying Him and choosing their own way instead of God's way. This resulted in their death both spiritually and physically. It was soon after this that their son Cain killed his brother Abel because he was jealous of him. Sin had entered the human heart, and every human being since that time has inherited this sinful nature—including you and me.

Is there hope for us? Can the human heart change? Some 2,600 years ago, God informed His people: *"I will give you a new heart and put a new spirit in you; I will remove from you your heart of stone and give you a heart of flesh. And I will put my Spirit in you and move you to follow my decrees and be careful to keep my laws." (Ezekiel 36:26–27, NIV).*

In the New Testament, He says, *"I will put my laws in their hearts, and I will write them on their minds ... their sins and lawless acts I will remember no more" (Hebrews 10:16–17, NIV).* How can this happen? It is accomplished through faith in Jesus Christ, who came to save us from ourselves, from our desperate state of rebellion against Him. *"Yet to all who did receive Him, to those who believed in His name, He gave the right to become children of God" (John 1:12, NIV);* *"For God so loved the world that He gave his one and only Son, that whoever believes in Him shall not perish but have eternal life" (John 3:16, NIV);* *"And this is His command: to believe in the name of His Son, Jesus Christ, and to love one another as He commanded us" (1 John 3:23, NIV).*

JANUARY 6

Focus

While driving through the Prairies, we encountered a swarm of bugs, which splattered all over our windshield. In a short time, it was very difficult to see past them and keep my eyes on the road ahead. I had to concentrate to keep my focus off of the mess on the windshield and on to where I was going so I wouldn't run into the ditch. I'm sure you've experienced the same thing to a greater or lesser degree. (This was very extreme; the windshield was almost covered in bugs. We had to pull over at the nearest opportunity and clear them off, only to hit another swarm a little farther down the road!)

Life is often like this. Many "bugs" come along that distract us from the path we should be on. On the negative side, it could be that unkind remark, the car that wouldn't start, the bank account that's empty, an unexpected bill that needs to be paid, the rust on the old car, or the eyesight that's not as good as it used to be. Sometimes even things that we think are positive take our attention from the really important things in life, such as spending too much attention on my hobby at the expense of my family, or eating my favourite flavour of ice cream cone without watching my waistline. Maybe it's making sure I'm blessed without thinking how I can be a blessing to others, when Jesus tells us it's more blessed to give than to receive (Acts 20:35). *Splat!* Another bug has hit and is obstructing my view. What am I to do? Should I focus on the distraction? If I do, I'll become disoriented and my true sense of direction will be impaired at best, or even completely lost. The only way to stay on the path laid out for us is to keep our focus on where we should be going, on our goal.

Our Creator, God, has made a way for us. It's the only true way. This true way is through the person of Jesus Christ: *"I am the way, the truth, and the life. No one can come to the father except through me" (John 14:6).* We must keep our eyes focused on Him and the life He has for us. Then we'll have a true direction with eternal results, no matter how many "bugs" hit us along the way. *"We do this by keeping our eyes on Jesus, the champion who initiates and perfects our faith" (Hebrews 12:2).*

JANUARY 7

Whose Fault?

A mother once told me of a story about her young daughter who had just broken an ornament in their living room. When the daughter was confronted with the broken pieces and asked "Who did this?" she told her mom, "Daddy did it," even though Daddy was nowhere in sight. This would seem like a cute little story if it were only an isolated childhood incident, but we see this type of reaction happening on a daily basis all around us.

Why is it so easy to blame my wife for the dish that I broke (she shouldn't have left it on the edge of the counter)? Or for me being late for that important appointment (she should have had breakfast ready sooner)? Why is it usually the other guy we blame for the accident when I backed into his vehicle (he shouldn't have parked in that spot behind my vehicle)?

We're all inherently selfish. It seems that our primary task is to defend ourselves at any cost. We deflect the blame onto someone else by pointing our finger their way. The problem is, when I point my finger at others, there are three pointing back at me, and my thumb is pointing to God!

The book of Genesis, in God's Word, records the first time this ever happened (Genesis 3). The first human beings, Adam and Eve, soon after they were created by God, sinned. God confronted them on their transgression. First, He spoke to Adam, and Adam pointed his finger at Eve, blaming her. He even blamed God for putting him in this situation. When the focus was on Eve, she pointed her finger at the serpent, blaming him. Nobody wanted to take responsibility for their actions. We've been blaming each other and God ever since.

It's only when we take responsibility for our own actions that we can change. The Bible addresses the problem of finger pointing: *"You may think you can condemn such people, but you are just as bad, and you have no excuse! When you say they are wicked and should be punished, you are condemning yourself, for you who judge others do these very same things" (Romans 2:1).* God is the one who will judge sinful humanity, but if we take responsibility for our own sins and confess them to Him, He is willing to forgive us: *"If we claim we have no sin, we are only fooling ourselves and not living in the truth. But if we confess our sins to Him, He is faithful and just to forgive us our sins and to cleanse us from all wickedness" (1 John 1:8–9).* Should we not want this for ourselves and all those around us?

JANUARY 8

Who's Driving?

Years ago while driving down the highway, we came across a van in the ditch. Someone had crossed the centreline and hit a deep ditch, which had put a quick stop to their travels! It was obvious by the deep ruts made in the shoulder of the road that they had previously attempted to get out of the ditch and back onto the road, but to no avail.

I stopped to check if anyone was hurt. The windows were all steamed up, but I could make out an image of a person sitting in the driver's seat. I knocked on the window, and he cleared the water vapour with his hand. I could see he had been sleeping and there were at least another five people sleeping in the van. He was obviously very drunk. He rolled down the window and said, "Who's driving?" as he pulled the keys from the ignition and threw them somewhere into the back of the vehicle.

Though people under the influence don't usually make much sense, this man did have a good question for all of us: "Who's driving?"

Who's driving my life? Who's in control of what I do? Is it me and my addictions? Is it drugs or alcohol? Is it my selfish nature, or is it God, who controls my life?

God doesn't want us to be in the "ditch," but He wants us to give our lives to Him so we can be the people He created us to be. He has wonderful things in store for those who trust Him (Ephesians 3:20–21). On the other hand, if we're trying to control our own lives, in our own way, we will end up in the "ditch" sooner or later. *There is a way that appears to be right, but in the end it leads to death" (Proverbs 14:12, NIV).*

God has given us the choice. Will I surrender myself, my life, my everything to God and follow His direction, or will I try to live my way, end up in the "ditch," and be immobilized, embarrassed, and ashamed?

The apostle Paul, speaking of Jesus, wrote, *"As Scripture says, 'Anyone who believes in him will never be put to shame'" (Romans 10:11, NIV).*

May we have the same attitude as King David when he wrote: *"Now this I know: The Lord gives victory to His anointed. He answers him from his heavenly sanctuary with the victorious power of His right hand. Some trust in chariots and some in horses, but we trust in the name of the Lord our God. They are brought to their knees and fall, but we rise up and stand firm" (Psalm 20:6–8, NIV).*

JANUARY 9

Entropy

Have you ever noticed a truck driving down the highway with a load of flattened vehicles stacked one on top of the other, each flattened to about one or two feet high? As we think about it, they all were shiny and brand new once, on the parking lot with a salesman waiting for someone to make a purchase. What happened? How did these vehicles end up as scrap metal?

There's a process happening throughout the universe. In this process, everything is deteriorating and becoming less organized, less complex, and tending to become more disorderly; that's why cars rust, tires wear out, houses deteriorate, and people get old and frail. Scientists confirm that the whole universe is moving towards a state of disorder as time goes on. Given enough time, the whole universe would come to a complete state of disorder. This is expressed in the Second Law of Thermodynamics and is sometimes called entropy. As a law, there have been found no exceptions to this, or it would no longer be a law.

The universe was not created this way. When God completed His creation on the sixth day, He saw that *"It was very good" (Genesis 1:31)* The problems started when, back in the Garden of Eden, Adam rebelled and sinned against God. God said to him: *"Since you listened to your wife and ate from the tree whose fruit I commanded you not to eat, the ground is cursed because of you. All your life you will struggle to scratch a living from it. It will grow thorns and thistles for you, though you will eat of its grains. By the sweat of your brow you will have food to eat until you return to the ground from which you were made. For you were made from dust and to dust you will return" (Genesis 3:17–19).*

The whole universe began to deteriorate at that moment, and evidence of entropy was all around them. All because of their rebellion against God, death and disorder were the rule of the day.

Some people believe that things are getting more complex, that everything is progressing to a higher, more organized state. Given enough time, mutations, and chemical reactions, it will produce a better, more ordered world. Sometimes this is called the Theory of Evolution, but the evidence around us is that everything is deteriorating, just like the load of cars going by on the highway.

What will we believe, a Law that has no exceptions, or a theory that goes against all the evidence?

"By faith we understand that the entire universe was formed at God's command ..." (Hebrews 11:3).

JANUARY 10

Dust on the Scales

On the news we hear of Russia invading Ukraine and threatening to take over at least parts of the country, they say to protect their Russian-speaking people. It's nothing short of aggression against another country. Some call it a declaration of war. Others liken it to Germany slowly absorbing more territory before the Second World War. In the past, these regimes have had a record of ungodliness and persecution of those of faith.

Why do they do this? Why does one country want to invade another? I think it has a lot to do with control. They want to control the people around them and make them subservient to them. Their desire is to rule over others; their insecurity is shown in their aggression towards others. They do not consult with, or have respect for the Almighty God, so they take things into their own hands.

Yet God tells us in His Word, *"... for all the nations of the world are but a drop in the bucket. They are nothing but dust on the scales. He picks up the whole earth as though it were a grain of sand" (Isaiah 40:15)*. If the nations are but dust to God, then what of the personal problems and enemies of daily life that try to invade and rob us of our faith and our freedom to be all God wants us to be? We don't have the power to control these things, but God does! It's comforting to know that Ultimate Power is in the LORD God Almighty. We have nothing to fear when we put our trust in Him. Let us surrender to God and let Him have control in every area of our lives.

In God's Word, we are reminded: *"Only by your power can we push back our enemies; only in your name can we trample our foes ... You are the one who gives us victory over our enemies ..." (Psalm 44:5, 7)*.

What is your battle today? What seems impossible to you today? Does it seem the enemy has invaded and there's no hope? Rest assured that nothing is too big for the LORD to handle! Let us call on the Lord in our time of need!

"He giveth power to the faint; and to them that have no might He increaseth strength. Even the youths shall faint and be weary, and the young men shall utterly fall; But they that wait upon the Lord shall renew their strength; they shall mount up with wings as eagles; they shall run, and not be weary; and they shall walk, and not faint." (Isaiah 40:29-31 KJV)

JANUARY 11

YHWH

What's in a name? When my father taught us about finances, he said that he had built up his name in the community by always paying his bills. He didn't owe anybody any money. He could write a check and anybody in town would accept it. His warning to us was that we should not taint his name by not paying our bills. He wanted to be known for his honesty; we were to honour him by being honest as well.

When we mention someone's name, we think about their character, who they are. A mental image of what they look like can even come into our mind when we hear or read their name. Whether they were kind, mean, or honest can also come to mind.

God's Word, the Bible, calls God by many names, each one describing His character.

The name for God that we sometimes pronounce as "Jehovah" is mentioned over six thousand times in the Old Testament. Actually, this name was so holy that the scribes who copied the Scriptures, we are told, were to stop writing and wash their hands in a very special ceremony before actually writing that name. God was so feared that they would seldom mention the name. When they actually said the name, it would be pronounced Yahweh, and it was written YHWH. In some translations, it's translated as LORD, all in capital letters, and other times it's written as Jehovah. It was very serious to even mention the holy name of God, let alone approach Him in any way. It wasn't taken lightly. We couldn't live up to that name.

The New Testament explains to us how Jesus came to earth to reveal God to us in person (John 1:1–2). When He spoke to His Father in heaven, He often called him "Abba," which was a very intimate, endearing, and friendly expression, something like our present word "Daddy," which described His relationship with the heavenly Father. Jesus, tender and compassionate, came to forgive our sins and make it possible for us to become children of God (John 1:12) in whom the Spirit of God dwells. *"So you have not received a spirit that makes you fearful slaves. Instead, you received God's Spirit when He adopted you as His own children. Now we call Him 'Abba Father'. For His Spirit joins with our spirit to affirm that we are God's children/"* (Romans 8:15–16).

The Holy God of the universe wants us to turn to Him so we can have an intimate relationship with Him: *"The LORD is like a father to His children, tender and compassionate to those who fear Him"* (Psalm 103:13).

JANUARY 12

Worship God Alone!

What's important in our life? Is it our spouse? Our children? Sometimes I hear people say that the most important thing is that we're healthy. Often we hear politicians tell us that the economy or health care is most important.

One day a friend and I were having a discussion about something on the street in Smithers, BC, a town near our home. As we were speaking, my friend happened to lean lightly on a car that was parked beside him. Suddenly a woman started yelling at him: "Quit leaning on my car! That's my car! You might scratch it." Could it be that this woman was worshipping her car?

The word "worship" comes from the root words "worth-ship." The thing that is most important to us is that which has most worth to us, and that which is of most worth to us is that which we worship.

The first and second of the Ten Commandments say: *"You must not have any other god but me. You must not make for yourself an idol of any kind or an image of anything in the heavens or on the earth or in the sea. You must not bow down to them or worship them, for I the LORD your God, am a jealous God who will not tolerate your affection for any other gods." (Exodus 20:4).*

When Satan tempted Jesus, saying he would give him all the kingdoms of the world if Jesus would only bow down and worship him, Jesus answered, *"Get out of here Satan ... For the Scriptures say 'You must worship the LORD your God and serve only Him'"* *(Matthew 4:10).*

After Jesus rose from the dead, Thomas, one of the disciples, doubted the other disciples' testimony about Jesus' resurrection, but after touching the scars of the wounds in Jesus' hands and side, he proclaimed to Him, *"My Lord and my God!"* then Jesus told him, *"You believe because you have seen me. Blessed are those who believe without seeing me" (John 20:28–29).*

We are also told *"that at the name of Jesus every knee should bow, in heaven and on earth and under the earth, and every tongue confess that Jesus Christ is Lord, to the glory of God the Father" (Philippians 2:10).*

There is no question: we will all bow our knee in worship to God. But when will this happen? We can freely bow to Him and worship Him as our Lord and Saviour now, while He's extending grace and mercy to all who will call out to Him (Acts 10:42–43; 1 John 1:9), or we will be compelled to bow before Him when it's too late, and He judges all people for their unconfessed sins (Romans 2:16; 2 Peter 2:9–10).

JANUARY 13

Rescued!

Back in the early 1960s, my older sister and I went swimming in the Arrow Lakes on a hot summer day. I couldn't swim yet, so she warned me to stay near the shore. I found a piece of driftwood and discovered that I could hold on to the wood and kick my feet, thus propelling me around like those who could swim. In my attempt to stay near the shore, I would occasionally reach for the bottom of the lake with my feet. After some time, I drifted out into the deeper water. Sure that the bottom was near, I tried to touch the bottom with my feet. It wasn't there, and I slipped off the log and into the water, well over my head.

Panicking and gasping for breath, I inhaled a good volume of water. Up I went and down again. I was desperate. I couldn't even cry out for help. I thought I was done! Then a hand reached down and grabbed me. It was an older friend, Gordon Peters, who, with a firm grip, pulled me up out of the water, sputtering and gasping for air. To this day I'm thankful that he saved my life; had he not been there and fetched me out, I would have silently slipped into the water and drowned.

I needed a person to save my life; nothing else would do at that point. No principles, no advice, no lessons on swimming, not even the piece of driftwood was of any help. I was done without personal intervention.

Sometimes we think that our religion and philosophies will save us. "I am secure because I go to church, my parents are believers, or I know a lot about the Bible." It seems that we're doing well. Then reality hits and the bottom falls out; desperation and even death look us in the face. What do we do? Even all the religious things I do can't rescue me. I need someone to save me. Only a person will do. Jesus Christ is the only one who can save us (John 14:6; Acts 4:12).

Jesus said to the religious folks of His day, *"You search the Scriptures because you think they give you eternal life. But the Scriptures point to me! Yet you refuse to come to me to receive this life"* (John 5:39–40).

Jesus said, *"For it is my Father's will that all who see his Son and believe in Him should have eternal life. I will raise them up on that last day"* (John 6:40).

JANUARY 14

Resolutions

One more year is past. Some of us have made resolutions to change something in our life. We may seek to make an extra effort to quit smoking or rid ourselves from some other unhealthy vice. Other times we challenge ourselves to do something we've never done before. For me, many years ago I was determined to read through the Bible in a year, only to fail over and over again. Sometimes after just a few days! Disappointed, I determined to try harder! I seemed unable to meet this noble goal no matter how hard I tried.

Then I realized that when Jesus said *"For apart from me you can do nothing" (John 15:5),* He really meant it. Every heartbeat, every breath I take is given me by God. He's more interested in a relationship with me than in me reading through the Bible in a certain length of time! Then I surrendered Bible reading, as well as everything I could think of, even myself, to God.

Soon after recognizing my propensity to trusting in myself rather than Him, I realized that this surrender was essential on a daily and moment-by-moment basis for my relationship with Him to grow! Still today when I sense frustration, fear, anger, or anxiety in my life, I realize the need to surrender afresh to Him.

Then Jesus began to live His life through me in a fuller way. People, events, disappointments, and frustrations no longer had the same negative effect on my life as before! The desire to know this wonderful God began to grow from day to day; this, in turn, drew me to His Holy Word, the Bible. What a pleasure to read and learn of His will and His way for my life! To get to know Him, to spend time with Him, to grasp His mercy and grace became most important to me. His love, His acceptance, His care became more obvious as I surrendered my desires, anxieties, doubts, and fears to Him!

Since then, I've read through the Bible many times and can hardly wait to read it again—as a personal love letter from the Almighty God! It surely is a relationship with Him rather than resolutions that causes one to desire His will and His way in our life. Jesus said, *"Seek the Kingdom of God above all else, and live righteously, and He will give you everything you need" (Matthew 6:33); "Look! I stand at the door and knock. If you hear my voice and open the door, I will come in, and we will share a meal together as friends" (Revelation 3:20).*

JANUARY 15

Martin Luther King Jr.

January 15 marks a national holiday in the USA commemorating the birth and life of Martin Luther King Jr. Dr. King was a man who stood up for equal rights for every human being. His nonviolent campaigns, sit-ins, and speeches began to turn the tide of prejudice, hatred, and racism in the United States and the world. The truth of his vision of equality for every human being is rooted in the very first chapter of God's Word, the Bible: *"So God created human beings in His own image. In the image of God He created them; male and female He created them"* (Genesis 1:27).

Though Dr. King was not a perfect man by any means, he had a message that we all must take to heart every day of our lives. There's only one race, and that's the human race! Every person is created in the image of God and must be treated with dignity and respect! Let's not fool ourselves, *"If anyone says, 'I love God,' and hates his brother, he is a liar; for he who does not love his brother whom he has seen cannot love God whom he has not seen'"* (1 John 4:20, ESV).

Dr. King said, "I have chosen to stick with love, hate has too great a burden to bear." If we want to be instruments of God, showing His love and peace, we must take His Word to heart and allow the loving character of Jesus to rule our lives every day! In the words of Jesus, *"So now I am giving you a new commandment: Love each other. Just as I have loved you, you should love each other. Your love for one another will prove to the world that you are my disciples"* (John 13:34–35).

JANUARY 16

More Than Leverage

The power of a lever is amazing. Perhaps you've seen an otherwise seemingly immovable object such as a boulder, a machine, or even possibly a building move inch by inch once leverage is applied! Sometimes we think of prayer as a type of leverage in which we summon God to do whatever we'd like to see done. Though this may seem wise at first glance, upon further examination, we realize that prayer is much more than leverage! Most often when we use a lever, we're still in control; it is our will, our power, and even likely our object to move.

When we pray in Jesus' name, we call upon the Almighty, all powerful, all-knowing, ever-present God. He is the Creator, the Sustainer, the Saviour. He holds everything together (Colossians 1:15–17). We are surrendering our will to His will, our way to His way, our weakness to His power, our plan to His plan. We're surrendering the battle, the burden into His hands. We essentially give our worries, our cares, even ourselves over to Him! Surely He can handle it better than I can! What a relief when ultimately His love, His joy, His peace permeate our hearts and we praise Him with thankfulness!

Prayer is not a lever, trying to convince God to do our will, but prayer is to cry out to God: *"May your will be done on earth, as it is in heaven" (Matthew 6:10).*

Oh Lord Jesus, cause us to surrender to you from the depth of our heart, as you did to the heavenly Father before going to the cross to die for our sins: *"... I want your will to be done, not mine" (Matthew 26:39).*

JANUARY 17

Led

When I was a teenager, I was enamored with old cars. My first car was a 1950 Chevrolet two-door Fastback. Then followed a 1957 Plymouth, a 1956 Dodge Custom Royal, a 1960 Rambler, a 1952 Ford pickup, a 1951 Mercury Meteor coupe, and on and on. Wherever I saw on older or classic vehicle I would, if possible, stop to check it out! Car shows fascinated me! I followed the cars, but I didn't realize at the time that they were leading me! One of my key focuses and desires was to own these vehicles!

Yet there was also a deep-down draw in my inner self to be right with and know God. As I look back on it, it's clear that the desire of cars and my desire for God were in direct conflict with each other in my life. The time came when the draw of God on my life became so strong that I surrendered to Him. Since then, the desire for vehicles has diminished to the point of having only a slight curiosity. I can truly say I have little desire for them anymore. My desire to grow in my relationship with God has increased to the point that when I allow other desires to creep in, I very seriously miss the personal connection with Him. I miss reading His Word, communicating in prayer, and hearing His still small voice leading me in the way I should go.

What we most desire and are following is what we are led by. Jesus illustrated this very clearly: *"No servant can serve two masters; for either he will hate the one and love the other, or he will stand devotedly by the one and despise the other. You cannot serve both God and mammon [that is, your earthly possessions or anything else you trust in and rely on instead of God]"* (Luke 16:13, AMP)

As we examine our hearts, let's ask ourselves what we desire most. God is the only One who can truly satisfy!

When Change Happens

They bulldozed and burned our house. They cut down our fruit trees. They flattened my father's business and told us we had to move. Believe it or not, this happened in Canada, to our family and many other families, when the Hugh Keenlyside Dam on the Arrow Lakes near Castlegar, BC was built in the 1960s.

We lived in a beautiful community called Renata, BC on the Arrow Lakes, some twenty-five kilometres up the lake from the proposed dam site. We had land on which we grew our garden vegetables every year. We had walnut and hazelnut trees and orchards of peaches, apples, cherries, apricots, and plums. I grew up there, thinking somehow it would last forever. We had two houses and a cabin and a barn for the livestock. It seemed a bit like paradise to me.

Then the surveyors came and measured our land and houses. They also came with the news that a dam was being built and we would have to move. Dad said, "What if we don't move?" They told him that there would be forty feet of water over our property once the dam was built.

Everything changed as we watched people come with chainsaws and cut down the neighbours' fruit trees and bulldoze and burn their houses. They didn't compensate us enough to set up in a similar setting, but they did give us something, and we moved. Then they cleared our property and orchards—everything. I was bitter when I saw the stumps of the trees and the barren land.

We moved to the city. New school, all strangers, it wasn't easy. Many changes happened in a short time.

Maybe you have a similar story. Maybe your story is a lot different, but change is inevitable, for better or for worse.

What do we do when change comes our way? Is there something solid that we can trust in? Is there a strong foundation that will not move?

The Bible tells us there is One who never changes, and that is God: (*"I am the Lord and do not change" (Malachi 3:6)*; *"He never changes or casts a shifting shadow" (James 1:17)*; and again, *"Jesus Christ is the same yesterday, today and forever" (Hebrews 13:8)*.

When everything else fails, the wisdom given to us by God some three thousand years ago still stands today: *"Trust in the Lord with all your heart; do not depend on your own understanding. Seek His will in all you do, and He will show you which path to take" (Proverbs 3:5–6)*.

JANUARY 19

Dead Ends?

Ted Jefferson gave his testimony in the mid 1970s to a crowd of prisoners at Attica prison in the US. He shared how he had tried to find meaning in life through "the drug scene, the pimping scene, the alcohol scene, the armed robbery scene."[1] His pursuit of money, ladies, diamonds, and cars all led to dead ends. He was left with a dark void in his life. This path eventually led him to prison for shooting and killing his best friend in a drunken rage. All his pursuits had come to nothing, and he fell to the floor of his cell, a "heap of nothing." In desperation, he called out to Jesus. Jesus answered him (Romans 10:11–13).

It was like a light had come on in his prison cell. From that time forward, he started a completely new life. He shared with the prisoners how Jesus Christ changed his life and brought him hope, purpose, and meaning. Now he belonged to Jesus, the true-life giver. If there was hope for him, there's hope for others.

Though most of us don't have a past like Ted, we need life from God just as much as he did. Sometimes our "respectable" lifestyle keeps us from seeing our absolute need for God: *"There is a path before each person that seems right, but it ends in death" (Proverbs 14:12)*. God's Word, the Bible, teaches that we are all broken and desperately in need, really a "heap of nothing," without him (John 3:16–21; Romans 3:9–26, 6:23). Yet there is hope for all who call out and put their trust in Jesus: *"And this is what God has testified; He has given us eternal life, and this life is in His Son. Whoever has the Son has life; whoever does not have God's Son does not have life" (1 John 5:11)*.

Are we going to insist on our ways, which will eventually lead to dead ends, or will we take God at His invitation to trust Jesus and follow Him on the pathway of eternal life (John 7:37–38)?

Jesus said, *"My purpose is to give them a rich and satisfying life" (John 10:10)*.

---

1 Ted Jefferson's testimony from DVD *God's Prison Gang*, International Prison Ministry, Dallas, Texas.

JANUARY 20

Somebody's Daughter

I'm sure all of us have noticed the signs along Hwy 16 in northern British Columbia, the "Highway of Tears," warning women not to hitchhike. There are also pictures on billboards of women who have gone missing. What a tragedy. What a heartache. I can't imagine the pain in their mothers' hearts. This should not be. This should not happen, but it does, and it all starts in the hearts of people. It's a process of hardening of the heart. Men do not become predators overnight.

A man thinks, looking at a woman walking down the street, with lust in one's heart, *Just one look; it won't hurt, as long as I don't touch.* Buying a pornographic magazine and googling at the naked women, he thinks, *They offered their bodies for this, so it's OK* (see Matthew 5:28). Sin increases, the heart becomes harder, respect for women diminishes.

Would you want someone looking at your daughter in this way? One thing leads to another, and the heart becomes hardened to the fact that every one of these women are precious to their parents, their mothers, and to God. These precious daughters become just an object to abuse and discard at one's own perverted pleasure. Would we want people taking advantage of our daughters in this way? Of course not! Every right-minded and moral person would scream out, "Protect my child, no matter what situation you find her in!" Every man should be there to protect these women from predators and harm and not take advantage of them when they're vulnerable.

You who have abused women in this way, leave our daughters alone! You are going to have to answer for your evil actions one day. Every woman is not only somebody's daughter but also God's daughter, beautifully created by God in His image (Genesis 1:27). If we harm them, we seriously offend God. You'll have to answer to Him one day! He knows who you are, and He will take vengeance (Romans 12:19)! It's time to come clean and repent, admit the terrible sin for what it is to God, to the authorities, and to those who have been so deeply hurt.

"... God shows His anger from heaven against all sinful, wicked people who suppress the truth by their wickedness" (Romans 1:18).

Neither Death nor Life

I was with a friend waiting for his appointment at the radiation department at University Hospital of Northern BC in Prince George, British Columbia. There were many people there, some obviously very sad. Some were discouraged and distraught. One was sitting in his wheelchair, very thin and muttering curses as he waited for his treatment. Another said he had lost over fifty pounds in a month and a half. It was tough to see the disappointment on people's faces. Life had not worked out as planned. Disease had entered into the picture, threatening to consume the very life we hold so dearly. Many plans for the future were shattered. Questions came up. Would the treatment work? Would the cancer be eradicated, or would it come back? Would one feel better after the radiation, or would it make it worse? If I die, what will happen to me, to our loved ones?

There were others in the room who I'm sure had many of the same questions, yet they were very optimistic, even though they knew that if the cancer continued to grow, they would die. They knew there was a bigger plan. They knew they and their loved ones were in the hands of the God they trusted in, no matter what happened to them. They knew that even if they died, they had a place in heaven prepared for them. There would be no cancer there, no sickness, no death, no pain or sorrow. In conversation with these people, they expressed that the reason for their optimism was their faith in Jesus Christ. He would be with them through whatever would happen in their life, good or bad, even in death.

One morning before his treatment, my friend and I were reading the following verses from the Bible. *"Can anything ever separate us from Christ's love? Does it mean He no longer loves us if we have trouble or calamity, or are persecuted, or hungry, or destitute, or in danger, or threatened with death? ... No, despite all these things, overwhelming victory is ours through Christ who loved us. And I am convinced that nothing can ever separate us from God's love. Neither death nor life, neither angels nor demons, neither our fears for today nor our worries about tomorrow—not even the powers of hell can separate us from God's love. No power in the sky above or on the earth below—indeed nothing in all creation will ever be able to separate us from the love of God that is revealed in Christ Jesus our Lord." (Romans 8:35, 37–39).*

This reality, this confidence, can only be ours as we surrender in faith to Jesus Christ as our Lord and Saviour.

JANUARY 22

Contentment

The other day I saw a rainbow in the sky. It reached to a certain spot on the ground, it seemed. As I drove towards it, the rainbow moved, and the spot where it seemed to reach the ground moved with it. I'm sure you've noticed this too as you pursued that "pot of gold" at the end of the rainbow. Our search for contentment seems to be just as elusive as the "pot of gold" at the end of the rainbow.

During the gold rush, many men looked for the elusive yellow metal that was going to make them rich. Many of them found bitter cold and empty pockets and death, even before they reached the goldfields. When some of them found the gold, were they content?

Today the pursuit might look something like this: first we think a car will make us content, then a new car, then possibly a house with a big garage to park it in. Then maybe an airplane, then a landing strip, maybe a private airport and a jet, maybe an airline or a private little island where we could hide out. What would it take to make us content? Would we be content with one million dollars? Would we be content if there was peace between family members? What if there was peace in the world or equal distribution of the wealth in the world? It seems our pursuit of contentment is often a never-ending journey, where one rarely reaches the goal.

In the Bible we're told, *"Don't love money, be satisfied with what you have. For God has said, 'I will never fail you, I will never abandon you'"* (Hebrews 13:5).

When we fully trust in God, we'll be satisfied or content with whatever circumstances He has for us. He won't fail us or abandon us. He is near. He knows what's going on, and He's the one we really need. He will fill our hearts. He is our contentment.

"Yet true godliness with contentment is itself great wealth" (1 Timothy 6:6).

January 23

New Every Morning

Some say that New Year's resolutions are made to be broken. Why are they so frequently broken? Why is it so difficult to keep the commitment we've made? Why can we not rid ourselves of the things that plague us year in and year out? The answers to these questions become even more challenging when we tend to focus on the issues. It seems the harder I try to stop a certain behaviour, the more I indulge in it! There seems to be no hope. I am powerless to do what I know is right!

I've found myself in this predicament numerous times. Maybe you have too! New Year's resolutions just didn't do it because I was still trusting in my frail, fallen human nature. We wonder if there's anything we can bank on, any hope, or anyone we can truly trust.

Then I look to God! In His Word I see hope—powerful hope! *"The faithful love of the Lord never ends! His mercies never cease. Great is His faithfulness; His mercies begin afresh each morning. I say to myself, 'The Lord is my inheritance; therefore, I will hope in Him!'"* (Lamentations 3:22–23).

As I look to the Lord God Almighty, I'm overwhelmed that in His love and mercy He doesn't give me what I deserve. He took the penalty for me on the cross of Calvary! In His grace, He strengthens me by His Holy Spirit! He alone is my strength! He gives me every heartbeat, every breath. He gives me the will and the power to overcome, to live in victory!

As the old song says, "Turn your eyes upon Jesus. Look full in His wonderful face. And the things of earth will grow strangely dim, in the light of His glory and grace!"[2]

He is my resolve! He is my hope! He is my victory! Jesus and Jesus alone!

"For I can do everything through Christ, who gives me strength" (Philippians 4:13).

---

2 Written by Helen H Lemmel, 1864, public domain.

JANUARY 24

Facing Forgiveness

She was known as "Napalm Girl" because she had been so badly burned by napalm, which had been mistakenly dropped on her people by a South Vietnamese warplane during the Vietnam War on June 8, 1972. The haunting picture of her running down a road, screaming, the clothes burned off her body, soldiers behind her, with smoke and the scorching fires of napalm in the background, graphically depict to all the world the horrors of war.

Not expected to live due to the burns to much of her body, she miraculously survived, yet she still suffers from the effects of the burns. Though the physical pain was extreme, the mental, psychological, and spiritual pain was even worse. She became angry, bitter, and resentful towards those who had done this to her. It seemed there was no way out of this mountain of toxic pain and unforgiveness. Then, ten years later, she was touched by the words recorded in the Bible describing the pain that Jesus Christ suffered at the hands of evil men and His forgiveness towards those who had sinned against him. Kim received Jesus as her Lord and Saviour on December 24, 1982. Since then, she has become a powerful witness and proclaimer of forgiveness and healing to the world at large, especially to those who suffer similar pain as she did.

When Kim met Jesus, she met forgiveness face to face! Now through the power of the Holy Spirit, she boldly declares "My faith in Jesus Christ is what has enabled me to forgive those who have wronged me, no matter how severe those wrongs were."

Jesus said, *"Do not judge others, and you will not be judged. Do not condemn others, or it will all come back against you. Forgive others, and you will be forgiven"* (Luke 6:37).

Lord Jesus, rule my heart and empower me by your Holy Spirit to forgive those who have wronged me!

JANUARY 25

I Am Loved!

I have a few very special mugs. They are precious because they've been given to me by my grandchildren! They each have very special messages written on them. One even has custom personal artwork imprinted on it! Another one says "Grandfather" on the front. And on the back, it says "In addition to being grand, we think you are really great!" An even more touching message appears inside the lip of the mug: "You are loved." As I drink my coffee, I am constantly reminded how much my children and grandchildren love me!

One morning as I was tipping my cup and read "You are loved," the thought came: *I am loved.* This thought deeply touched me! My wife loves me, my children love me, my grandchildren love me, God loves me! As the Lord touched my heart, I realized that truly knowing I am loved is deeply profound. I sensed a more personal understanding of the love that they have for me! Though they can repeatedly say that they love me, it doesn't mean much until I receive that love and make it personal!

A well-known verse is written in the pages of God's Holy Word: *"For this is how God loved the world: He gave his one and only Son, so that everyone who believes in Him will not perish but have eternal life" (John 3:16).* Anyone who picks up a Bible or sees these words on a sign somewhere can read this wonderful truth expressed from the heart of God. Yet until we are touched in our heart and personally receive God and His love, they only remain words.

How does God's Word affect you today? Are they just words on a page, points of doctrine, or words memorized in Sunday school many years ago? Or have you received Jesus and His love? Have you allowed the Spirit of God to work in your heart to truly know, "I am loved"?

Reconciliation

Today in Canada we have much talk about reconciliation, especially with our First Nations people. Many attempts are being made to advance reconciliation through, among other things, political legislation, inquiries, court decisions, town hall discussions, and cultural awareness seminars. Though these efforts have some merit, why does reconciliation seem so distant? Is a key element being missed?

I have many precious First Nations friends. Some of my closest relationships are with First Nations brothers and sisters, yet interestingly, our relationship isn't based on us being First Nations or Colonial at all. I can think of many good times of fellowship and sharing when suddenly I realized I was the only White person in the room. Everyone present was respected and accepted on a much more significant basis than being from a certain culture or background! Firstly, we accept and respect each other because we recognize that we're all human beings created in the image of God!

Secondly, we're even more strongly bound together through a personal relationship with our Creator God! This relationship with God is made available by God for everyone who receives Him in faith, regardless of human culture or rank! It was purchased for us through Jesus Christ giving Himself as a sacrifice, shedding His blood for all who would believe in Him! Thus, our Creator Jesus Christ not only reconciled us to God but also to each other! Whenever we come together with our focus on our Lord and Saviour, we have sweet fellowship with each other! Can we be so presumptuous to think that we can extend reconciliation to others if we ourselves are not reconciled with our Maker? *"And all of this is a gift from God, who brought us back to Himself through Christ. And God has given us this task of reconciling people to Him. For God was in Christ, reconciling the world to Himself, no longer counting people's sins against them. And He gave us this wonderful message of reconciliation. So we are Christ's ambassadors; God is making His appeal through us. We speak for Christ when we plead, "Come back to God!" (2 Corinthians 5:18–20).*

Grinding Axes

When working as a surveyor delineating property lines, we'd often use an axe to clear brush and trees that were in our way. Before we used the axe, we'd use a grinder or a file to sharpen it so it would be a more efficient tool. It's a compact and useful instrument when used properly. If not used in a careful manner, however, it could become a lethal weapon of injury and destruction. One could hurt someone standing nearby, or even oneself if not careful!

I knew a fellow who built a house for his lover with an axe and a tool called an adze. He formed the rough logs into perfect beams to shape a beautiful dwelling. Though he has since passed away, the house still stands as a monument of his expression of heartfelt love for his sweetheart!

On the other hand, we don't have to look very far to find instances where the axe is used as a weapon of destruction. I could use it indirectly by making a trap intending to hurt an unsuspecting person—a trap that I might fall into myself! Or I could use it to directly hurt those around me, at times even to hurt my own family. Our words can be likened to an axe. This proverbial "axe" that we grind may be our destructive reaction in word or deed to an offence that has been done to us.

May we sharpen the tools the Creator has given us to bring true healing and reconciliation! How will we respond in a given situation? As a healer and builder of grace, mercy, and love? Or a destroyer of everything good? The tool is in our hands; the choice is up to us. How will we use it?

"Never pay back evil with more evil. Do things in such a way that everyone can see you are honorable. Do all that you can to live in peace with everyone.... Don't let evil conquer you, but conquer evil by doing good" (Romans 12:17–18, 21).

JANUARY 28

Real Leaders

With the 2020 election coming up in the US, a struggling minority government in Canada, a coalition arrangement in BC, and the current struggle for leadership among some First Nations people, the question of good leadership comes to the forefront. Thus, we examine the qualities we might want in a leader. Qualities like vision, morality, honesty, assertiveness, and sound character, among other things, come to mind. When we observe those who are clamouring for a leadership position, servanthood doesn't often stand out as a prerequisite.

When Jesus' disciples were vying for the highest positions, He exhorted them: *"In this world the kings and great men lord it over their people, yet they are called "friends of the people." But among you it will be different. Those who are the greatest among you should take the lowest rank, and the leader should be like a servant." (Luke 22:25–26).*

This is difficult for us to understand because we tend to think of a leader in a different light, especially when we want to be the leader!

Still, Jesus was emphatic that servanthood equals greatness in His kingdom! Jesus told them, *"For I am among you as one who serves" (Luke 22:27).* He set the example. As the Creator of all things, He lowered Himself to take on the form of humanity. He touched the untouchable, washed people's feet, and ultimately gave His life so those who didn't deserve it could have eternal life (Philippians 2:5–11)!

Because of our sinful nature, the only way we'll be able to truly follow Jesus' example is to humble ourselves in surrender to Him and allow Him to empower us to be the servant leaders He requires of us!

"And all of you, serve each other in humility for 'God opposes the proud but favors the humble.' So humble yourselves under the mighty power of God, and at the right time He will lift you up in honor" (1 Peter 5:5–6).

January 29

Corona Crisis

It's 2020 and our leaders tell us that we're in the middle of a pandemic! The stock markets are way down, whole countries are off limits, people are advised to practise social distancing. Those who have flu like symptoms are encouraged to self quarantine at home to protect themselves and others from possible serious illness and even death by the coronavirus. Is it really as dangerous as they say? Could this all be an overreaction? Only time will tell.

Though not as obvious to some, there's a much graver danger that eternally affects every one of us human beings. It is sin—our inherent rebellion against God in thought, speech, and deed that brings eternal spiritual death to each of us if not dealt with. Though we're all warned to keep from sin, it has already infected each of us! *"For everyone has sinned; we all fall short of God's glorious standard" (Romans 3:23)*. The Scriptures warn us of the consequences of this rebellion against God! *"For the wages of sin is death ..." (Romans 6:23)*. This death is an eternal separation from God—forever! God created us to have fellowship, a living and active life of obedience to Him. But we have all turned against Him and chosen to go our own way instead of His way. Sin has separated us from Him and put the death sentence on each of us!

The sentence is grim, but there is hope! *"This is good and pleases God our Savior, who wants everyone to be saved and to understand the truth. For, there is only one God and one Mediator who can reconcile God and humanity—the man Christ Jesus. He gave His life to purchase freedom for everyone" (1 Timothy 2:3–6); "... but the free gift of God is eternal life through Christ Jesus our Lord" (Romans 6:23)*.

A gift is not ours until it has been received! Have you received this precious gift of life?

JANUARY 30

Confidence

When I lost my car keys, it was distressing! I couldn't go anywhere and missed appointments. Even more distressing was when I lost my wallet. I had my keys but needed my driver's licence to legally operate the car. Plus, I wouldn't be able to buy anything without money or a credit card. If something happened and I needed medical attention, my medical card was in my wallet. I was anxious about these sudden changes! Our world can change in very short order. Losing keys, wallet, driver's licence, medical card, or, for that matter, our health, reminds us of how unstable our world really is. Small things that we take for granted and come to rely on could suddenly change and affect our whole life.

Our present state of affairs magnifies to us how quickly everything changes, even on a worldwide scale! Every person, every nation, and the whole world economy is brought to its knees by the reaction to the tiny coronavirus.

By nature, we as human beings like stability. We look far and wide to have permanency, especially when it comes to our personal lives. Our mobility, our security, our health are dear to us. Yet at one time or another, each of these will fail us! Dwelling on this causes anxiety to build within me—then a familiar chorus written by A.B. Simpson in 1890 begins to ring in my heart! "Yesterday, today, forever Jesus is the same! All may change but Jesus never! Glory to His name!"[3]

At that very moment, the Word of God, on which this song is based flooded my mind and brought calm and assurance to my soul! *"I will never fail you. I will never abandon you. So we can say with confidence, 'The Lord is my helper, so I will have no fear.' ... Jesus Christ is the same yesterday, today, and forever"* (Hebrews 13:5–6, 8, NLT).

This is where I will put my faith and confidence each and every day of my life!

---

3 A.B. Simpson, 1890, "Yesterday, Today, Forever," public domain.

JANUARY 31

Faith or Fear?

The other day I was talking with a man at the supermarket as we waited in line, six feet apart of course! He said fear was a worse enemy than COVID-19. I think he was right! God's Word often repeats the words "don't be afraid." A few of the instances of where God said this are:

To Abraham: *"Do not be afraid, Abram, for I will protect you, and your reward will be great" (Genesis 15:1).*

To Isaac: *"'I am the God of your father, Abraham,' he said. 'Do not be afraid, for I am with you and will bless you. I will multiply your descendants, and they will become a great nation. I will do this because of my promise to Abraham, my servant'" (Genesis 26:24).*

To Joshua: *"This is my command—be strong and courageous! Do not be afraid or discouraged. For the Lord your God is with you wherever you go!" (Joshua 1:9).*

To Joseph: *"Do not be afraid to take Mary as your wife. For the child within her was conceived by the Holy Spirit. And she will have a son, and you are to name him Jesus, for he will save his people from their sins" (Matthew 1:20–21).*

To the shepherds: *"'Don't be afraid!' he said. 'I bring you good news that will bring great joy to all people. The Savior—yes, the Messiah, the Lord—has been born today in Bethlehem, the city of David!'" (Luke 2:10–11).*

To the disciples: *"And the very hairs on your head are all numbered. So don't be afraid; you are more valuable to God than a whole flock of sparrows" (Matthew 10:30–31).*

In every circumstance mentioned above, God had a message for the people, people who were experiencing scary, often humanly impossible, daunting situations. He gave them the message to have faith in Him and not to fear!

This is the same message God has for us today! For if we trust Him and follow Him, we really don't have anything to fear!

"So don't be afraid, little flock. For it gives your Father great happiness to give you the Kingdom" (Luke 12:32).

FEBRUARY 1

Authority

We were in a hurry, late for an upcoming meeting. As I drove over the crest of a hill, I saw him coming towards us. I had no time to slow down. I noticed him turn around and put his lights on. I pulled over.

"You know you were speeding?" he asked. I wasn't sure how fast, but he told me it was 121 kph in a 100 kph zone. I didn't argue as my shaky hands pulled my driver's licence from my wallet.

Why should I stop when the red and blue lights come on? Because behind that police officer was the authority of the Province of British Columbia and the Government of Canada. He was enforcing laws that were written by the government. When the lights went on, it meant I was to stop and pay attention to what he said—no ifs, ands, or buts.

Just as the laws of the land have the authority of the government behind them, God's Word, the Bible, has His supreme authority behind it, which extends over all heaven and earth. God used the prophets and apostles to write down His inspired Word exactly as He wanted it to be written. Because He is the author of His Word, it carries His authority with it.

When we read the Bible and are convicted that we fall short of its standard, we should tremble at our sin and repent, calling for mercy from our gracious God. If we continue in our rebellion against God, we will surely cause harm to ourselves and those around us.

The Bible says we have all fallen short of God's requirements (Romans 3:23), and He is willing to forgive us when we come to Him with an honest and open heart (1 John 1:9; Romans 6:23). He will even empower us to live for Him through the power of His Holy Spirit (Galatians 5:16).

He wants us to surrender to His authority so we can be all He wants us to be. This brings honour and glory to His name. *"For the word of God is alive and powerful. It is sharper than the sharpest two-edged sword ... It exposes our innermost thoughts and desires. Nothing in all creation is hidden from God. Everything is naked and exposed before his eyes, and he is the one to whom we are accountable." (Hebrews 4:12–13).*

Waves

We were constantly inundated with reports concerning the COVID-19 "pandemic": variant stains, community spread, ventilator, death—all words that could easily instill fear in us. We had the second wave and predictions of a third wave. Some shared their concern for their elderly parents self-isolating in their house during this COVID "pandemic"! What should we do?

Considering this situation, I'm reminded of a storm that happened on the Sea of Galilee some two thousand years ago. Waves were threatening to sink the boat, and the disciples thought they would drown. They woke Jesus, who was sleeping in the boat: *"When Jesus woke up, He rebuked the wind and said to the waves, "Silence! Be still! Suddenly the wind stopped, and there was a great calm ... The disciples were absolutely terrified. 'Who is this man?' they asked each other. 'Even the wind and waves obey Him!'"* (Mark 4:39, 41).

The scriptures also record that He healed the sick, caused the blind to see, raised the dead, and even overcame His own death by crucifixion by rising to life after three days in the grave (Luke 7:21–23; John 20). He could do this because He is the Creator of everything (John 1:1–5; Colossians 1:15–17)!

Paul the apostle faced many difficulties during his life, including sickness (2 Corinthians 12:7–10), shipwrecks, floggings, and persecution (2 Corinthians 11:23–30), yet he proclaimed: *"And I am convinced that nothing can ever separate us from God's love. Neither death nor life, neither angels nor demons, neither our fears for today nor our worries about tomorrow—not even the powers of hell can separate us from God's love. No power in the sky above or in the earth below—indeed, nothing in all creation will ever be able to separate us from the love of God that is revealed in Christ Jesus our Lord."* (Romans 8:38–39).

Jesus didn't promise us an easy life but He did promise to be with us through it (John 16:33; Hebrews 13:5)! Have we put our trust in Him (Mark 4:40)?

Man of Sorrows

I read a book written by a doctor in which he explained through personal experience how he would attempt to extend his patients' lives at all cost. Through these efforts, people, including himself, didn't face the truth of their mortality and didn't prepare for the inevitable—death—that will come upon us all. These experiences, especially the death of his father, caused him to realize that facing death was an important element of life.

As we consider the coming of Jesus Christ to this earth and His brief lifetime and experience here, we see a much different picture! He came to suffer and bleed and die—not holding on to his life—so all those who would trust Him would be set free! It was prophesied of Him some seven hundred years before He came: *"He was despised and rejected—a man of sorrows, acquainted with deepest grief" (Isaiah 53:3)*. He knew before He came to live in a human body here on earth that He was coming to die a horrendous death at the hands of His own creation—all to make the payment for the very sins they and we commit against Him.

His attitude towards His inevitable death is described as: *"Because of the joy awaiting Him, He endured the cross, disregarding its shame" (Hebrews 12:2)*. He willingly faced His death so that we through faith in Him wouldn't have to fear death. Through faith in Him we can be assured of His promise: *"There is more than enough room in my Father's home ... When everything is ready, I will come and get you, so that you will always be with me where I am ... I am the way, the truth, and the life. No one can come to the Father except through me." (John 14:2–3, 6)*.

You and I do not need to fear death if we put our trust in Jesus, who prepared the way for us to experience eternal life!

Right Place—Right Time

Have you ever known the right thing to do but missed it because you hesitated, procrastinated, or doubted? It might have been something such as seeing an accident and not stopping, failing to encourage someone when you knew you should, or not showing up to help someone in need. It happens to all of us at one time or another.

This was never the case with Jesus. He recognized and showed up at exactly the time and place that was set for Him throughout His life. Early in His ministry, Jesus read this prophecy written about Himself by the prophet Isaiah approximately seven hundred years previously: *"The Spirit of the Lord is upon Me, for He has anointed Me to bring Good News to the poor. He has sent Me to proclaim that captives will be released, that the blind will see, that the oppressed will be set free, and that the time of the Lord's favor has come." Then He sat down and told them; "The Scripture you've just heard has been fulfilled this very day!"* (Luke 4:18–19, 21).

After He spoke to them about their doubts and unbelief, they became angry and tried to kill Him. Many people wanted to kill Him throughout His life, yet none succeeded—until it was His time to die on the Passover, some two thousand years ago!

The Passover was a time when the nation of Israel annually celebrated their deliverance from Egypt by offering an unblemished animal sacrifice to God. This is exactly when Jesus died and shed His blood on the cross at Calvary! He had come at exactly the appointed time to be the perfect sacrifice, fulfilling, replacing, and cancelling the previous sacrifices to become the only perfect sacrifice for sin for all time (Hebrews 10:17–18)!

"For God says, 'At just the right time, I heard you. On the day of salvation, I helped you.' Indeed, the 'right time' is now. Today is the day of salvation" (2 Corinthians 6:2).

We must turn to follow Him while there is still time! Tomorrow might be too late!

FEBRUARY 5

Hummingbird

A bright, crimson-red glimmer sparkled among the pieces of bark mulch under the window next to our house. At first I thought it was a fishing lure. As I took a closer look, it became obvious that it was a hummingbird that must have hit the window and died as a result. Each intricately woven feather of its ruby throat shone brightly in the sun.

We have quite a number of these birds darting back and forth and hovering next to our hummingbird feeder during the spring and summer. The tiny wings beating at sixty beats per second, the ability to hover in mid-air, fly backwards, and dart around, and the amazing energy of these miniature birds never ceases to amaze me. As they aggressively protect their spot at the feeder, I wonder how this would all play out if they were the size of a robin or an eagle?

More questions arise as I consider this wonderful little creation of God. How do they migrate? What are some of the difficulties they run into as they try to raise their young? How do they survive in such a ruthless world? Some don't, like the one I found under our window that day.

As I pondered all this, the words of Jesus, to His disciples, came to mind: *"Are not two sparrows sold for a penny? Yet not one of them will fall to the ground outside your Father's care. And even the very hairs of your head are all numbered. So don't be afraid; you are worth more than many sparrows"* (Matthew 10:29–31, NIV).

Jesus didn't promise that life on this earth would be easy; actually, He said there would be many hardships, even for those who believe in Him, but He encourages us to trust in Him even when difficulties arise (Hebrews 12:5–7).

Some of the difficulties we face, such as loneliness, sickness, weakness, financial crisis, persecution, or even imminent death will certainly instill fear, especially to those who live life without God.

God knows it all. He knew when that hummingbird fell to the ground. He knows every detail and situation in our lives. He even knows the day we will die. We're created in His image and are much more valuable to Him than the birds. We have no need to fear when we surrender to Him and put our complete trust in Him.

"Even though I walk through the valley of the shadow of death, I will fear no evil, for you are with me; your rod and your staff, they comfort me" (Psalm 23:4, ESV).

Human

In the late 1970s and early 1980s, my wife and I had two premature births in which both babies died in the womb before birth. Some called it a miscarriage; others called it a spontaneous abortion, but we definitely still grieve the loss. At the time, it seemed almost a taboo to talk about it much. We had the sense we were to just "suck it up" and get on with life.

The first baby we didn't see, as it was quickly taken from us before we had a chance to even observe if it was a boy or a girl. The second one, thanks to the nurse on duty at the time, I had the chance to see. It was a boy, perfectly formed. I looked in awe and wonder at his little hands, fingers, and toes—the intricate detail, every part, a little human being. The body of our little baby lay there in that jar! At that moment I became a staunch pro-lifer! No person, whether a scientist, doctor, politician, ethicist, or vicar can tell me what I saw there was not a human being!

We've learned a few things since and encourage those who experience similar circumstances to take time to grieve, take time to name the baby, take time, if possible, to have a little memorial or funeral for the little one to bring some closure. This is the right thing to do—a human life cut short needs to be grieved!

"You made all the delicate, inner parts of my body and knit me together in my mother's womb ... You saw me before I was born. Every day of my life was recorded in your book. Every moment was laid out before a single day had passed." (Psalm 139:13, 16).

FEBRUARY 7

Runaway

If you watch the news at all, you may be wondering what's happening in our world. Foundations of our society that we have come to see as secure are crumbling before our eyes. As we drive into town, we see billboards advertising recreational drugs, while others that say "Police matter" or advocate for the innocent unborn are vandalized. In town we observe some people injecting drugs into their arms in "safe injection sites." The list of young friends who have died from drug abuse is growing. Reports of shootings in the city are all too common. What is going on?

This reminds me of several runaway train incidents, the disaster at Lac-Megantic on July 6, 2013 being by far the worst of them. Certain essential protocols were overlooked, which led to forty-seven lives being taken and much of the town destroyed. Since then, rules, regulations, and protocols have been reviewed, reinstated, and implemented to hopefully prevent this type of incident from happening again.

As in the case with trains, certain rules must also be followed for a society to function properly. The mayhem we're seeing today is due to humanity forgetting the essential decrees that have been instituted by our Creator in His Holy Word. Even more disastrous is the fact that most people don't even recognize the Creator Himself. We've become comparable to a rail company that has not only ignored but thrown out the instruction manual and rule book! We've forgotten our God and the safety plan He put in place for our good! No wonder we're having problems! History teaches us that many nations experienced, to their demise, the same problems we have today. This should serve as a stark warning to us.

In His mercy, God exhorted King Solomon of Israel with the following instructions required for the healing of a runaway people: *"Then if my people who are called by my name will humble themselves and pray and seek my face and turn from their wicked ways, I will hear from heaven and will forgive their sins and restore their land"* (2 Chronicles 7:14).

May we turn to our Creator and seek Him and His will before it's too late!

FEBRUARY 8

Time Is of Essence!

Have you ever wondered why societies fall apart? Great civilizations lay in ruins, some buried under desert sands, such as ancient Babylon, and others overgrown by jungles, such as Inca and Mayan cities, abandoned and empty. Often the reason for this is that they abandoned certain principles, and their society fell apart from within. Becoming derelict, they couldn't sustain a proper and functional social order.

God's Word contains some important principles essential to personal and societal life. When we forget these, we wander from the purpose and direction He has created us for. In the next few articles, I'd like to briefly outline some of these principles from the first few chapters of God's Word.

The very first words of the Bible say *"In the beginning" (Genesis 1:1)*. This points to a beginning of time as we know it. Sometimes we flitter away with our everyday concerns, and days go by before we look at the really important things before us. There's a beginning and an end! We're all bound in the element of time! Lawyers sometimes say "time is of essence," and it is! The time we had today will never be available tomorrow! *"How do you know what your life will be like tomorrow? Your life is like the morning fog—it's here a little while, then it's gone" (James 4:14)*; *"For everything there is a season, a time for every activity under heaven. A time to be born and a time to die. A time to plant and a time to harvest" (Ecclesiastes 3:1–2)*.

God's Word teaches that time as we know it will culminate with a day of judgement. We will all be judged as to what we have done in this life. Our only hope is to turn to God for mercy and the purposeful life He offers!

The apostle Paul said, *"I have had one message for Jews and Greeks alike—the necessity of repenting from sin and turning to God, and of having faith in our Lord Jesus" (Acts 20:21)*.

In the Beginning, God!

Is there a God? If He exists, what is He like? What if there is a God but I don't recognize Him, or I have my own idea of what He's like. Does that change who He really is? Here in the West, evolutionists have replaced God with time. When I was in school, they taught that the universe was 2.5 billion years old. Now as we are discovering how extremely complex the universe is, it has been adjusted to 4.7 billion years—time will never replace God! In the East, God has been reduced to idols, millions of them, but idols of any sort or number will never replace God! Others have substituted the only true God with a state of being, of nothingness, but nothing will ever replace God! Since the beginning, humanity has tried to replace God with ludicrous, preposterous ideas: *"And they began to think up foolish ideas of what God was like. As a result, their minds became dark and confused. Claiming to be wise, they instead became utter fools" (Romans 1:21–22); "Only fools say in their hearts, 'There is no God'" (Psalm 14:1).* The Bible clearly proclaims God in the first verse! (Genesis1:1).

God through His Holy Word goes on to describe who He is, what He is like, and what His relationship is to humankind! The New Testament reveals that Jesus Christ is the very Word of God that in the beginning spoke the creation into being (John 1:1–5)! His virgin birth, His miracles, even raising others and Himself from the dead, and especially His sacrificial love proved who He is! The Sovereign of the universe has revealed Himself to us and is intimately acquainted with each of us!

What then will we do with Jesus? Will we surrender to and follow Him, or will we continue to follow our own wicked ways? Jesus said, *"I am the way, the truth, and the life. No one can come to the Father except through me" (John 14:6).* He is calling. Can you hear Him?

February 10

God Created

Some friends of mine came across an object that had been hidden in the bush for quite some time. Trees had grown around and through it. Rusty metal had remnants of paint on it. As they cleared away the foliage around it, they realized it was some sort of implement—made for a purpose. Upon further investigation, they found it was a grader, designed to be drawn by horses or a tractor. I can just imagine the intrigue as they made their discovery! This implement didn't just appear by accident or by chance; it was obviously made for a purpose! Should we have access to more details, we could discover the who, why, where, and when it was made!

As we observe the beautiful creation around us, from the multitude of stars in the sky to the smallest molecule, we're intrigued by the intricate, complex, awe-inspiring design, order, and purpose behind it all! Obviously, it was made for a purpose! The sunrise, the trees, the insects, the birds, the vast variety of animals, the people—you and me! Wouldn't it be absolutely absurd for my friends to come to the conclusion that this grader just happened to show up by chance! How much more ridiculous to think the creation around us, infinitely more complex, just happened! Where there is design, there is a designer! Where there is a creation, there is a Creator!

We have access to the ancient Scriptures, God's Holy Word, that reveal clearly how everything came to be! The very first verse of the first chapter of God's Holy Word says: *"In the beginning God created the heavens and the earth" (Genesis 1:1).*

Have we lost intrigue and purpose in our life? Have we forgotten our Maker? He is near! Let's seek Him while He may be found!

"You are worthy, our Lord and God, to receive glory and honor and power, for you created all things, and by your will they were created and have their being" (Revelation 4:11, NIV).

FEBRUARY 11

Fatal Decision

If God created everything, why is it so messed up? Why do natural disasters happen? Why do people kill each other? Where does racism come from? Why do we question our identity and insist that our own ideas are best? Why the conflict within my heart? The tension? The unrest? The constant vying for a position in society? Why do we die?

I'm sure that you've asked many if not all of the above questions at some time or another. Are there answers? God's Word, the Bible, gives us the answer in the first chapters of the book of Genesis. Though God had spoken a perfect creation into existence, He had warned Adam, the father of every human being, not to eat of one specific tree: the tree of the knowledge of good and evil. He and his wife, Eve, instead listened to Satan, thinking they knew better than God. Contrary to His instructions, they ate of that tree.

Instantly their relationship with God and each other died. God had to throw them out of the beautiful paradise He had created for them. Conflict, tension, self interest, and hate permeated their hearts. Everything around them, even the beautiful creation, changed and began to deteriorate. Their own firstborn son killed his brother in a fit of jealousy. Thorns and weeds grew up, and they had to work hard just to make ends meet. To this very day we experience the things mentioned above—all because we think we know better than God. Death has come upon each of us!

Yet God is a God of life, and He has made a way back to Him: *"Hear, O heavens, and give ear, O earth! For the Lord has spoken: "I have nourished and brought up children, And they have rebelled against Me;" ... "Come now, and let us reason together," Says the Lord, "Though your sins are like scarlet, they shall be as white as snow; though they are red like crimson, they shall be as wool" (Isaiah 1:2, 18, NKJV).*

Unglued

Have you ever seen a piece of plywood when the glue has failed? Possibly the glue was of inferior quality, was applied improperly, or wasn't applied at all and the plywood lost its strength and function—it became useless. The strength of plywood is in the glue.

Much in the same way, the strength and stability of our society depends on how God and His will are applied in our individual and corporate lives. We were created to live in a personal relationship with God. When we think we know better than God, when we ignore God, when we deny His existence and don't heed Him and His will for our life, we become unglued.

Consider what's happening in our culture today. We deny that we are created beings. We deny the inspiration of God's Holy Word. We want to go our own ways instead of His way. Rather than seek God and His will, we think we can save the earth through human rules and legislation, so governments restrict our freedoms and tell us what to do. We think we can determine our own sexuality, so we allow biological men who think they are women to take over the women's Olympics and use women's washrooms. We redefine God's holy institution of marriage (a union of a man and a woman) as a union between a man and a man, so we deny children the stable influence of a father and a mother. God's Holy Word says *"The human heart is the most deceitful of all things, and desperately wicked. Who really knows how bad it is? But I, the Lord, search all hearts and examine secret motives. I give all people their due rewards, according to what their actions deserve" (Jeremiah 17:9–10).*

Is there hope for humanity today? *"Then if my people who are called by my name will humble themselves and pray and seek my face and turn from their wicked ways, I will hear from heaven and will forgive their sins and restore their land" (2 Chronicles 7:14).*

The Desires of Our Heart

One time a high school friend of mine told me that his greatest desire was to have a date with Diana Ross of the Supremes. Another friend said her greatest desire was to have a ride in a brand-new Corvette. I lost track of the fellow who wanted the date with Diana Ross, but I am certain his desire was not fulfilled! As for the friend who wanted a ride in a Corvette, she may have since ridden in her favourite sports car, but I think fancy automobiles are the furthest thing from her mind right now. She's married to a Godly man; they have children, and her desire is to live a life pleasing to God.

Jesus said, *"If you remain in me and my words remain in you, you may ask for anything you want, and it will be granted" (John 15:7).* Does this really mean that I come to God with whatever I want, as in the case mentioned by my friend—a date with a celebrity? Should I just ask for what I want and expect that from God? Is God at my command? Can I just tell Him whatever I want—health, wealth, or fame—and expect him to give it? I think not! God is not a genie.

When we look at these words of Jesus in context, they take on a whole different meaning. One translation says, *"If you remain in Me and My words remain in you [that is, if we are vitally united and My message lives in your heart], ask whatever you wish and it will be done for you" (John 15:7, AMP).* This means He is the source of our very being; every thought, action, and motivation is from Him. Just as the life of a branch comes from the vine, our life comes from Him. Then He says *"and if my words remain in you …"* If He rules in our lives and we have a love for His Word, it will become an essential part of our lives. We won't want to utter any word or ask anything contrary to His Word or His will. Our life will be in tune with Him in all we think, say, do, or ask. His desires will become our desires. He will give us the strength to live out the rich, satisfying, abundant life He has already planned for those who trust Him (Ephesians 2:10; John 10:10).

Are we remaining, abiding, living in Him? Is He the boss of our life? Are His desires our desires?

He has great things in store for those who surrender to Him.

"Take delight in the LORD, and He will give you your heart's desires" (Psalm 37:4).

No Greater Love

Do you remember your first Valentine's card? We exchanged cards in elementary school. The card said something like "You are my Valentine" with hearts all over it. It was a nice message, but we knew the teacher had set it up so that everyone was given a card and everyone received one, so no one would be left out. The power of the message was greatly diminished because this was a compulsory exercise. Though there were hearts all over the card, there was no real love or heart behind it. Love is more than sentimental words or hearts drawn on a piece of paper.

Jesus told His disciples that *"There is no greater love than to lay down one's life for one's friends" (John 15:13).* This could have just been another quotation among many about love given by men. But the power of these words was soon confirmed by Jesus voluntarily dying on a cruel Roman cross to pay for the sins of all who would trust in Him!

What greater love can there be than this? It's called "agape" in the Greek. Only God can give this totally self-sacrificing love. Not only has He shown this love in His actions two thousand years ago, but He has given each person who receives Him that same kind of love (1 John 4:19)! So we don't have to settle for a false or second-rate love, but through His indwelling Holy Spirit we can love others, even our enemies, in the same way as He does.

Have you received forgiveness of your sins through faith in Jesus and His sacrificial death for you? Have you received the love that God has offered you? If you have, Valentine's Day, or any day for that matter, will take on a whole new meaning for you!

"God showed how much He loved us by sending His one and only Son into the world so that we might have eternal life through Him. This is real love—not that we loved God, but that He loved us and sent His Son as a sacrifice to take away our sins." (1 John 4:9–10).

FEBRUARY 15

True Love

I remember when I was very young, I received a Valentine's card from someone I liked a lot! It was very special to think someone had such cherished thoughts about me! Someone cared (I really think she did)! But soon after the cards were exchanged, everything returned to usual; the distance, the shyness, the prejudices, the walls came up again. The messages exchanged on that day were at best only a glimpse of what could have been, and in some cases, as mentioned yesterday, they were just words written on a piece of paper.

Can you imagine what it would be like for us to really live out a loving, open, honest, and transparent relationship one with another? Wars would cease; racism would be a thing of the past; marriages would thrive; children would all get along in the playground. Parliament would function in a civil manner, where MPs would complement each other for the good of the people! Could this actually happen, or is it only a dream that fades as fast as the message received on Valentine's Day?

Jesus prayed for all those who believed in Him: *"May they experience such perfect unity that the world will know that you sent me and that you love them as much as you love me" (John 17:23).* The apostle John wrote *"Dear friends, let us continue to love one another, for love comes from God ... But if we love each other, God lives in us, and His love is brought to full expression in us" (1 John 4:7, 12).*

When we truly commit ourselves to God, His Holy Spirit comes and dwells within us (Romans 8:11). As we submit our lives to God, the Holy Spirit produces His fruit in our lives. The first fruit of the Spirit mentioned by the apostle Paul to the Galatians is love (Galatians 5:22). So as we submit to God and surrender our lives to Him, we will produce love for our spouse, our families, our neighbours, even for our enemies (Matthew 5:44; Romans 12:20). This love is impossible by strictly human effort, but it's the will of God for all who trust in Him. May our desire be to allow God to have His way in our life so that we can truly love those around us in a way that pleases God—more than fleeting words on a Valentine's card, but in action and in truth (1 John 3:18).

"Three things will last forever—faith, hope and love—and the greatest of these is love" (1 Corinthians 13:13).

Planting and Harvesting

What a tragedy we've seen unfold in the US in the last while. What has gone wrong? How could violence break out in this way, first on the streets for months on end, then culminating on Capital Hill on July 6, 2020 with the governing authorities being held siege for a time? Yet this is nothing new. Violence, abuse, and hatred have been lurking within our hearts and manifested in our homes almost since the beginning of time, as families are torn apart, parents fight, and children are left abandoned. Sin emanates from within our own broken hearts. We struggle within ourselves, confusion reigns, and our world falls apart.

God's Word is very clear—we are born with a sinful nature (Galatians 5:19–21). This sinful nature within every human being, left unchecked, produces the very things mentioned above: *"Don't be misled—you cannot mock the justice of God. You will always harvest what you plant. Those who live only to satisfy their own sinful nature will harvest decay and death from that sinful nature" (Galatians 6:7–8).*

When I proudly think I am perfect and can do nothing wrong, I'm living out of that sinful nature and deceive myself (James 4:6). I'm in for a great fall (Proverbs 16:18). When I use God's Word to make myself look holy and righteous, when in fact my heart is far from God, I attempt to hide my sin and do whatever possible to cover it up, and I thus deceive myself. Without God we have turmoil in our hearts; racism is rampant, children are left fatherless, women are raped, preborn babies are sacrificed at the altar of our convenience, and our children are killed in the streets. What we plant, we harvest.

Our only hope is to humbly surrender ourselves to God, to give Him pre-eminence, to receive new life from Him and let His Holy Spirit control our lives! *"But the Holy Spirit produces this kind of fruit in our lives: love, joy, peace, patience, kindness, goodness, faithfulness, gentleness, and self-control. There is no law against these things!" (Galatians 5:22–23).*

New Motivation

We were stranded far from home; our car was at the wreckers, broken beyond repair. We found an attractive four-door Oldsmobile for sale with no visible rust. The motor appeared to run well when we took it for a spin. As it seemed to suit our needs, we bought it and headed home! I noticed it lacked power as it strained to get up the steeper hills. I checked the oil, and it was down, so we added more. This continued along the way. Someone suggested I put in some oil and fuel additives to "tune it up," yet nothing helped. When we got home, a mechanic friend told me that the motor was worn out. I had bought a lemon. I found a new motor and exchanged the old one with the new! The car had power! It didn't use oil, and it ran like a top! It was like we had a new car!

At one time I attempted to live a Christian life out of my old sinful nature. I thought if I tried harder, maybe read the Bible more, went to church, or kept my tongue from swearing, I'd be a good Christian. But I found this futile. I couldn't find it in me to live the life God required. It was very frustrating, and I almost gave up! Then at the end of myself, in desperation, I called to God to forgive me, to come into my life to change me so I could live for Him. And He did! He gave me a new life and new motivation to live for Him! Now though the hills are sometimes steep, He provides the power and motivation to persist and overcome! What was previously impossible, He does in and through me as I surrender to Him!

"... anyone who belongs to Christ has become a new person. The old life is gone; a new life has begun! And all of this is a gift from God, who brought us back to Himself through Christ" (2 Corinthians 5:17–18).

Who Is Right?

When we were little, our mothers helped us get dressed. Then as we became more independent, we'd try to dress ourselves. We'd be reminded to put the right shoe on the right foot, to have the label at the back of our t-shirts or jackets, and to have the proper button in its matching buttonhole. If we stubbornly insisted on having it our way, we'd walk around in discomfort or dysfunction. These are obvious, simple truths that we take for granted every day. They exist because they were included in the basic design of the garments to make life easier.

As adults we live by basic truths in life that seriously influence how we live. These principles come out of some of the most basic questions in life, for example: Is there a God? If we start with the premise that there is no God, then we must assume that we weren't created and that there is no absolute truth. Truth becomes subject to our own interpretation and no longer objective and something to be sought, learned, and followed! We become right in our own eyes! Claiming to be wise we become fools, walking around with our clothes on backwards!

The very first words in the Bible are, *"In the beginning God created the heavens and the earth" (Genesis 1:1).* When we ignore God and His Word to us, we think we know better than Him, and we become as the prophet of old proclaimed; *"My people are fools; they do not know me. They are senseless children; they have no understanding. They are skilled in doing evil; they know not how to do good" (Jeremiah 4:22, NIV).* On the other hand, we can trust God and proclaim; *"I am overwhelmed with joy in the Lord my God! For He has dressed me with the clothing of salvation and draped me in a robe of righteousness. I am like a bridegroom dressed for his wedding or a bride with her jewels" (Isaiah 61:10).*

FEBRUARY 19

Flaming Tongue!

It's absolutely heartbreaking to remember the toll in human lives and devastation caused by the raging northern California "Camp Fire" wildfire that occurred in November 2018. The death count was eighty-five due to this uncontrolled raging fire. The extremely dry conditions coupled with a growing suburbia encroaching on forest areas of the hinterland contributed to these horrific wildfires. The deadly wildfire is said to have started with sparks created by a faulty electrical short in a power line. The city of Paradise was almost completely destroyed by this ravenous inferno. Just a few sparks, a small flame, can under certain conditions have devastating, and even in this case, apocalyptic consequences.

In God's Word we are warned that the tongue can be just as destructive. It can cause untold damage to those around us, to our society, and even to ourselves. Reckless, demeaning, and hateful words can cause irreparable damage. We can fan into flames prejudice, racism, hate, discord, and dissention by speaking impulsively from our sinful nature.

"Likewise, the tongue is a small part of the body, but it makes great boasts. Consider what a great forest is set on fire by a small spark. The tongue also is a fire, a world of evil among the parts of the body. It corrupts the whole body, sets the whole course of one's life on fire, and is itself set on fire by hell." (James 3:5–6, NIV).

On the other hand, we can surrender ourselves to Jesus, our Creator God, and allow His Holy Spirit to give us words of wisdom and healing by speaking the truth in love (Ephesians 4:15). *"A gentle answer deflects anger, but harsh words make tempers flare" (Proverbs 15:1);*

"May the words of my mouth and the meditation of my heart be pleasing to you, O Lord, my rock and my redeemer" (Psalm 19:14).

One-Woman Man

Our wedding anniversary is just around the corner. In some ways it seems like yesterday that we met and got married. Yet when we look back on it, we've been together for well over half of our lives! Do I have any regrets? One may be that I should have spent more time at home and less on the road, but I don't ever regret having marrying and staying faithful to the one and only true love of my life.

I am a one-woman man. I had various dates many years ago, but I distinctly remember the day I looked into the church choir and was attracted to a redheaded gal singing to her heart's content. I asked a friend of mine who she was. Little did I know that in a few years she would become my wife!

I believe God brought us together, no doubt about it. I am thankful that we both had a strong Christian and biblical upbringing that taught us the Godly principles that have carried us through the storms of life. Through the temptations and trials of life, I often sensed the power and conviction of God that kept me a one-woman man. Has it always been easy? I would be lying if I said it was. Yet I know the trials we went through actually made us stronger, as we trusted God to carry us through.

I am so thankful that God didn't leave us here to our own devises. The Bible gives us clear instructions as to what He would want for our lives. In the beginning, God created Adam and Eve to be a couple, and He blessed them to have children and to fill the earth (Genesis 1:27–28).

Jesus confirmed the will of God concerning marriage when He said, "'Haven't you read the Scriptures?' Jesus replied. *'They record that from the beginning "God made male and female."' And he said, "This explains why a man leaves his father and mother and is joined to his wife and the two are united as one." Since they are no longer two but one, let no one split apart what God has joined together'"* (Matthew 19:4–6).

Men, I don't know where you are in your relationships in life, but I can tell you I am thankful God made the way for us to be faithful to our wives. No matter the past, when a man agrees with God, he can be empowered to be a one-woman man. God is faithful. And ladies, you too for that matter can be a one-man woman. It takes three to work this out: God, a man, and a woman.

Sacred Institution

Every time our anniversary comes around, I am especially thankful for the institution of marriage. What a wonderful partner God has given me to share life with! God has been gracious to give us numerous children and grandchildren!

Some people think marriage is an invention of humanity, but it was God's idea right from the beginning. In the very first pages of the Holy Scriptures, it says *"... male and female He created them ... and the two are united into one" (Genesis 1:27, 2:24)*. This is the created order; it is a sacred institution: one man, one woman for life. Any other type of marriage union people conjure up in their mind is outside of this sacred institution.

I didn't always think this way. At one time I thought we should be given our freedom to do as we want! What a lie that was. Thank God that He had mercy on me!

Marriage today is often taken very lightly, yet Jesus explains how important it is. *"And He said, 'This explains why a man leaves his father and mother and is joined to his wife, and the two are united into one. Since they are no longer two but one, let no one split apart what God has joined together'" (Matthew 19:5–6)*. The institution of family comes directly from this union. It should be a safe place for children to be raised and taught. When it's broken, it causes untold heartbreak and pain for both spouses and for the children. Many take this pain from family breakups to their grave. But it doesn't have to be so. No matter what situation we find ourselves in, no matter how broken we are from pursuing our own ways, God is always willing to forgive us and guide us into His truth when we honestly come to Him in faith, willing to let Him change us.

"The fear of the Lord is pure, enduring forever. The decrees of the Lord are firm, and all of them are righteous" (Psalm 19:9, NIV).

FEBRUARY 22

He Wept

February 22 1989, was the day my mother died. It still seems like just yesterday. I answered the phone. Dad was waiting for news, as Mom had gone to the hospital for tests, and some complications had ensued. "She is gone," were the words on the phone to me. Dad asked if she was OK. We hugged as I told him she was gone. She was no longer with us. We wept. He trembled and wept deeply and bitterly for days. We were concerned for his wellbeing. Then he saw a vision of her. She was young again, in a bright, white gown. She looked at him and smiled. Then she disappeared. After this he repeatedly told us, "I'm only crying for me; she is OK." Dad never was quite the same after his life partner was torn away that day, but he had hope because he knew she was in the hands of Jesus, the One who had died for her and all those who would put their trust in Him!

Jesus approached the tomb of his friend Lazarus, who had died four days earlier. He told Lazarus' sister, *"I am the resurrection and the life. Anyone who believes in me will live, even after dying. Everyone who lives in me and believes in me will never ever die. Do you believe this, Martha?"* (*John 11:25–26*). Jesus saw the anguish of His friends and all the people around Him as they grieved in deep sorrow. He was overcome with anger and emotions as He saw their desperate state. *"Then Jesus wept"* (*John 11:35*). In front of the tomb, ignoring protests, Jesus ordered the stone rolled away. *"Then Jesus shouted, 'Lazarus, come out!'"* (*John 11:43*). And Lazarus rose from the dead and came out of the tomb. *"Jesus told them, 'Unwrap him and let him go!'"* (*John 11:44*).

Have we put our trust in Jesus, *"the resurrection and the life"*? Jesus is our Maker, our Redeemer, our only hope for eternal life—even in the face of death. *Do you believe this?*

FEBRUARY 23

Dangerous Path

While driving past an area of the Bulkley River near Telkwa, BC, I noticed that someone had been cross country skiing on the ice over the river. Just downstream was open water. It's impossible for any human being to know where the weak spots are or where the currents have thinned out the ice. Only God knows the perils that lurk along this dangerous path. People have fallen through the ice, disappeared into the water under the ice, never to be seen again doing such foolish things as this!

In a similar way, we often travel the path of life to satisfy our own desires, not thinking of the dangers we might encounter. Pornography is a case in point. Some men, and even women, think they can tread the path of beholding the naked images of others' bodies for temporary pleasure without any consequences. Yet very real and lethal dangers lurk behind this façade. Participating in this sinful behaviour not only takes advantage of the people who have been exploited through this evil industry, but the images burned into one's mind hinder the sacred, God-ordained, intimate husband wife relationship and can create an insatiable, adulterous desire to act out physically, which can ultimately lead to death.

Jesus warned: *"... anyone who even looks at a woman with lust has already committed adultery with her in his heart. So if your eye—even your good eye—causes you to lust, gouge it out and throw it away. It is better for you to lose one part of your body than for your whole body to be thrown into hell."* (Matthew 5:27–28).

Though Jesus isn't advocating that one should actually gouge out one's eye, He is emphasizing the real, inherent death-trap in following this sinful, dangerous path. If we willingly follow God's ways as revealed in His Holy Scriptures, we will avoid untold pain, suffering, and even death: *"The teaching of your word gives light, so even the simple can understand ... Guide my steps by your word, so I will not be overcome by evil"* (Psalm 119:130, 133).

Final Justice

The 2018–2019 turmoil in the highest places of our Canadian federal government, involving even Prime Minister Justin Trudeau lobbying the then Attorney General Jody Wilson-Raybould to intervene in a criminal case against a very large Canadian corporation, SNC Lavalan, shows an amazing lack of ethics by our powers that be. They say they did this in an attempt to save many Canadian jobs, to keep Canada's economy strong, and to defend Canadian workers. It seems quite obvious that they are saying that the end justifies the means—sacrifice our justice system to save Canadian jobs. Thank God the Attorney General didn't give in to the pressure.

But the irony goes much deeper as we consider that these same people advocate, even promote, the killing of preborn human babies at any stage of gestation. Not one of them steps in to intervene in the genocide of 100,000 preborn Canadian babies every year. In fact, not one of them is even allowed to take such a stand, because their leadership has excluded pro-life individuals from running under their banner.

One day every person will have to answer to the true judge, the Almighty Creator of the earth, the One who has made each of us, including the preborn, in His image. There will be no lobbying then, no coercing, no pressuring, and no cover-ups. Even the powerful leaders who wield temporary power with supposed impunity will stand in fearful silence as they face the truth of their actions: *"... but they found no place to hide. I saw the dead, both great and small, standing before God's throne. And the books were opened, including the Book of Life. And the dead were judged according to what they had done, as recorded in the books."* (Revelation 20:11–12).

Final Justice will be served: *"... that at the name of Jesus every knee should bow, in heaven and on earth and under the earth, and every tongue declare that Jesus Christ is Lord, to the glory of God the Father"* (Philippians 2:10–11).

Yet there is still hope, as Jesus said, *"The Kingdom of God is near! Repent of your sins and believe the Good News!"* (Mark 1:15).

God have mercy on us and cause us to repent of our wicked ways. Forgive us our many sins and cause us to walk in your ways, Oh Sovereign Lord.

FEBRUARY 25

Children of God

My wife and I are very blessed to have the opportunity to see our grandchildren grow up! One of the most precious experiences is watching them as they begin to say "Daddy" or "Mommy" as they run into the arms of their respective parent!

When Jesus was in the Garden of Gethsemane praying to His Father, the Almighty God, He was in great agony as He anticipated what was about to happen to Him in the next few hours at the hands of the religious leaders and ruthless Roman soldiers. Mark records that Jesus, in His distress, addressed His heavenly Father as *"Abba"* (Mark 14:36). This is an Aramaic word used by a child towards his father, something like the word "Daddy" that we use today. Jesus' relationship to the heavenly Father was very intimate and personal. He spent much time with Him alone as He prayed and sought His will and strength for each moment of every day!

Even more amazing is the context of this word *"Abba,"* mentioned only two more times in the Bible. The apostle Paul tells the believers in Rome, *"So you have not received a spirit that makes you fearful slaves. Instead, you received God's Spirit when he adopted you as his own children. Now we call him, 'Abba, Father'"* (Romans 8:15), and again he reminds the Galatian believers, *"And because we are His children, God has sent the Spirit of His Son into our hearts, prompting us to call out, 'Abba, Father'"* (Galatians 4:6).

This intimate relationship is only available for God's children! Do you desire this kind of fellowship with the Almighty God? Do you desire to be a child of God? Have you received Jesus as your Lord and Saviour?

"Yet to all who did receive Him, to those who believed in His name, He gave the right to become children of God - children born not of natural descent, nor of human decision or a husband's will, but born of God" (John 1:12, NIV).

Clean Slate

When I turned the key, my trusty car wouldn't start. No matter what I tried, it wouldn't run. A number of experts informed me that the computer in the car was corrupted and needed to be cleared of all the junk that had interfered with its proper function. Once this was done, it started and has been running ever since.

In the same way, sin can corrupt our lives and cause us to be ineffective and immobilized in our spiritual walk with God. When this happens, we come to the end of ourselves; nothing we do seems to make sense. Life has lost its meaning, and there is nothing real to live for anymore. We, like my car, are unable to go any farther! Have you ever felt this way? I have, and it's a desperate state to be in, to say the least!

God's Word says that sin entangles us (Hebrews 12:1) and makes us ineffective, unable to be the people God created us to be, yet God's Word also gives us hope! *"But if we confess our sins to Him, He is faithful and just to forgive us our sins and to cleanse us from all wickedness" (1 John 1:9).* When God cleans our slate, it's truly clean, and we can be free to be all He wants us to be! Which would you rather be, dead in sin or truly free?

"Those who live only to satisfy their own sinful nature will harvest decay and death from that sinful nature. But those who live to please the Spirit will harvest everlasting life from the Spirit" (Galatians 6:8).

True Unity

Unity has been sought by humanity for thousands of years. This is reflected in names such as United Nations, United States, United Church, United Arab Emirates, etc. Yet do we see unity among, or even within, these countries, organizations, and individuals? Certainly simply adding the word to the title doesn't bring about the desired effect! When we desire unity, what are our terms of that unity? I'm sure the terms are different in every case and even with every individual involved. These individual pursuits of unity can often be the cause of disunity! No wonder we see very little, if any, true unity in our world today!

As we read the prayer of our Creator Jesus Christ in the Bible, just before He was dragged off to be crucified, we hear the desire of His heart: *"I am praying not only for these disciples but also for all who will ever believe in me through their message. I pray that they will all be one, just as you and I are one—as you are in me, Father, and I am in you. And may they be in us so that the world will believe you sent me." (John 17:20–21).*

He is speaking of relationship: His relationship with his Father, and His relationship with those who believe in Him. God is not divided. The only way we will have true unity is on His terms, under His authority!

God is calling us to a relationship with Him, where we in faith submit to Him, His authority, and His Word to experience true unity! Do you believe that Jesus is *"the way the truth and the life" (John 14:6, NIV)*? If you do, then *"Make every effort to keep yourselves united in the Spirit, binding yourselves together with peace" (Ephesians 4:3).*

Progressive?

Word plays of all sorts have been appearing more frequently in the media. One such moniker is "progressives," which generally speaks of people with a liberal ideology. We likewise hear some abortion rights people calling themselves "pro-choice." Yet these descriptives really couldn't be farther from the truth. Often those who are called progressives are people who have digressed from God's truth. An example of this digression is the pro-choice movement, which is really the pro-abortion movement. Typically, they like to call pro-life people anti-abortion, thus at least by inference disassociating themselves from abortion—when they are the ones who are actually promoting it! They say they are pro-choice, but what choice does the baby have? What choice is the woman making? We even have some political parties that allow only pro-choice candidates to run for their party, which in reality makes them a no-choice party! As we digress from the light of God's truth, we're not really being progressive but rather moving backwards into the darkness of human sin and rebellion.

It's obvious that human life is sacred and God given, begins at conception, and continues so until natural death (Psalm 139:13–16). The womb should be the safest, most protected place on earth for the baby, yet it has become the most dangerous place. If I don't speak out in defence of these, the most vulnerable, if our leaders don't speak out, who will? I choose to cast my vote for the preborn baby and only for a leader who will clearly do likewise!

"When Jesus saw this, He was indignant. He said to them, "Let the little children come to me, and do not hinder them, for the kingdom of God belongs to such as these. Truly I tell you, anyone who will not receive the kingdom of God like a little child will never enter it." And He took the children in His arms, placed His hands on them and blessed them" (Mark 10:14–16, NIV).

Got the Music?

When attempting to contact BC Hydro, a computer-generated voice said that the call was important to them but all operators were busy and they would answer as soon as one became available—then came the music! A notice interrupted the music from time to time saying that the call was important to them but all operators were busy and I should wait for one to become available. I was on hold with only music in my ear! Sound familiar?

While listening to the music, a scripture verse came into my mind: *"Because of Christ and our faith in Him, we can now come boldly and confidently into God's presence" (Ephesians 3:12).* Jesus, by dying on the cross, made the way that we can have a relationship with God, a relationship based on faith in Him, and we can have access in prayer to the Creator of the universe—any time, any place, anywhere (1 Timothy 2:5; 1 Thessalonians 5:17–18)! By faith in Him, we enter into fellowship with God, where we have uninterrupted access to Him. He is never too busy, never uncaring, but desires to hear our heartfelt prayers.

When was the last time you called on Him? Rest assured, He will not give a computer-generated regimen of music but will answer an honest prayer of faith: *"Call to me and I will answer you and tell you great and unsearchable things you do not know" (Jeremiah 33:3, NIV).*

MARCH 1

When Adding Takes Away

My friend had a rare, older farm machine that needed a part that was not readily available. After seeking for some time, he was told that an older fellow had such a machine in his back yard. When approached by my friend, the older fellow offered it to him completely free of charge, even though, because of its vintage and rarity, it was of considerable value. My friend found it difficult to receive the free gift and reached into his pocket, pulling out his last five dollars to give to the old man. The old man became very angry and told him to leave and never come back. He was greatly offended because he had generously offered the part for free, and the attempted payment had taken away from and cheapened his gracious offer.

In a much greater way, God the heavenly Father offered humanity His one and only Son, Jesus Christ, as the only payment for our sins. Through Jesus' death on the cross, the complete payment was made. When Jesus cried out *"It is finished"* He was in essence saying *"Paid in full."* Jesus took the death penalty for our sins, and nothing can be added to this complete payment for sins that God has offered to all who in faith receive it!

If we do add any work of our own, such as baptism (baptism is done because we are saved, not to save us), penance, or any gift or good deed to this finished and complete work of Jesus Christ, we actually take away from and cheapen the most amazing sacrificial deed done in the history of humanity. The prophet Isaiah says these *"righteous acts"* are like filthy rags to God in the light of His great mercy and grace (Isaiah 64:6)!

"For the wages of sin is death, but the free gift of God is eternal life in Christ Jesus our Lord" (Romans 6:23, ESV).

"But when the kindness and love of God our Savior appeared, he saved us, not because of righteous things we had done, but because of his mercy" (Titus 3:5, NIV).

MARCH 2

Signs and Wonders

When I was quite young, my neighbour friend and I decided to bake some pies to make a little extra money. I had watched my mother in the kitchen carefully make some tasty delicacies out of various ingredients, so we asked her for instructions. As Mom told us what to do, she specifically warned us to never confuse the salt for the sugar, because if we did, the pies would have to be thrown out. Though the two ingredients looked similar, the mixing up of the two would bring a fatal blow to our fledgling baking industry! Someone desiring to sabotage a bakery could easily do so by switching the two!

Today, some say signs and wonders are the fruit of God working in one's life. Healings, miracles, and supernatural manifestations are cited as the stamp of approval upon a true Christian. Yet Jesus warned us in the scriptures: *"A wicked and adulterous generation asks for a sign!" (Matthew 12:39, NIV); "For false messiahs and false prophets will rise up and perform great signs and wonders so as to deceive, if possible, even God's chosen ones" (Matthew 24:24)*.

On the contrary, Jesus said that we could tell the true from the false not by signs and wonders, but by their fruit (Matthew 7:15–20). This fruit, produced by God's Holy Spirit in the life of every true believer, cannot be counterfeited! *"But the Holy Spirit produces this kind of fruit in our lives: love, joy, peace, patience, kindness, goodness, faithfulness, gentleness, and self-control" (Galatians 5:22–23)*.

Rather than focusing on the miraculous, let us keep our eyes on Jesus and the truth of His Word so that we can, through faith in Him, produce a rich and fruitful life for Him! (Hebrews 12:1–2).

MARCH 3

Never Leaves Me

After another follow-up cystoscopy, I couldn't get the image of that tumour out of my mind. I saw it fill much of the monitor screen. I was hoping I would be cancer-free after having so many immunotherapy treatments. Lying there, glum and heading into a dark hole of discouragement, anxious thoughts raced through my mind. Another cancerous tumour, another surgery. *Will I die from this?* As I focused on all this, the outlook seemed grim indeed!

My heart cried out, *"Hear me as I pray, O Lord. Be merciful and answer me! My heart has heard you say, 'Come and talk with me.' And my heart responds, 'Lord, I am coming'"* *(Psalm 27:7–8).* So I talked with the Lord, and He spoke to me! I began to remember the promises from God's Word: *"I will never fail you. I will never abandon you" (Hebrews 13:5).* After a time, my attitude changed, and I began to praise Him! The thoughts of cancer, death, depression, and despair completely disappeared as I focused on the Lord—His awesome greatness, His faithfulness, and His overwhelming love and care for me! I knew that whatever happened, He would take care of me. He would never leave me!

On the way home, I met a wonderful First Nations couple, unfamiliar to me until this meeting. I felt to greet them in their language, and a brief but powerful conversation ensued! They too were Christians and encouraged me greatly. Hopefully I was also an encouragement to them! Had I remained in my discouraged state, had I focused on the problem rather than the Lord, I would have missed this wonderful fellowship with these special folks!

"I waited patiently for the Lord to help me, and He turned to me and heard my cry. He lifted me out of the pit of despair, out of the mud and the mire. He set my feet on solid ground and steadied me as I walked along. He has given me a new song to sing, a hymn of praise to our God. Many will see what He has done and be amazed. They will put their trust in the Lord. (Psalm 40:1–3).

MARCH 4

Riches

Today some of the richest people in the world include Jeff Bezos, Bill Gates, Warren Buffet, Bernard Arnault, etc. These men have somehow amassed tens and hundreds of billions of dollars. In view of this, I ponder my own privileged situation. I realize I am rich compared to most of the people in this world. What do these material things really add to my life? Comfort, security, power, and freedom might come to mind as we contemplate these matters. Somehow in our society we have this idea that people with money have more than those who have little or no possessions. Much weight is put on our earthly possessions. We tend to seek our security in the fleeting and temporary earthly things we possess.

Yet Jesus taught the opposite: *"Don't store up treasures here on earth, where moths eat them and rust destroys them, and where thieves break in and steal ... No one can serve two masters. For you will hate one and love the other; you will be devoted to one and despise the other. You cannot serve God and be enslaved to money"* (Matthew 6:19, 24).

He is encouraging a life of faith in God that will last forever! This begs the question: "What do I put my trust in? Do I trust God to take care of me here on earth and ultimately to give me eternal life? Or do I trust in the temporary fleeting things of life?" This is a question each of us must answer. Our response has everything to do with our eternal destiny!

"Life is not measured by how much you own ... a person is a fool to store up earthly wealth but not have a rich relationship with God" (Luke 12:13, 21).

MARCH 5

Attitude Adjustment

A friend of mine phoned after he heard that I might have cancer. Since he had been diagnosed with cancer some years ago, he had similar feelings as I. He shared how just the word "cancer" put fear in him. I could identify with him, as the possibility of cancer made me look at everything in a different light. I felt more temporary and vulnerable, thinking increasingly of my temporary time here on earth. The reality of my imminent death was right in front of me! Thoughts echoed through my mind: *How long will I be here? Will I go in pain and misery, or will I fall asleep in the night to wake up on the other side? How will my inevitable time for leaving this earth come? How will my loved ones cope without me here?*

Yet on the other hand is the promise of Jesus for those who trust in Him: *"Don't let your hearts be troubled. Trust in God, and trust also in me. There is more than enough room in my Father's home. If this were not so, would I have told you that I am going to prepare a place for you? When everything is ready, I will come and get you, so that you will always be with me where I am." (John 14:1–3).*

The possibility of cancer helped me to adjust my attitude to the reality of the temporary nature of my present time on earth and to consider the greater reality of an eternal home where we will live in the perfect Presence of Almighty God for ever and ever! In faith, with the apostle Paul, I can say, *"And I am convinced that nothing can ever separate us from God's love. Neither death nor life, neither angels nor demons, neither our fears for today nor our worries about tomorrow—not even the powers of hell can separate us from God's love" (Romans 8:38).* This is a sure promise for all those who trust in Jesus and the promises of God!

MARCH 6

Heart to Heart

Mavis Staples is very gifted rhythm and blues, soul and gospel singer. She started singing with her father and family when she was just eight years old. She's not shy about sharing that she is a Christian. She says that when she became a believer, the words to her songs had much more meaning than before. Now her request to the Lord is that she will keep her voice until she dies, so she can use her voice for Him.

Mavis' father, Pops Staples, became involved in the civil rights movement with Dr. Martin Luther King Jr., thus Mavis, a young girl at the time, sang with her family, expressing freedom for the African American people in a powerful but non-violent way. Pops impressed upon her that she had a voice that was a gift from God, and more important than the type of music she would sing, the notes, or whatever else, she should always remember that, and sing from the heart. He said if she sang from the heart, she would in turn speak to others' hearts.

I believe Pops was right on! God tells us in His Word, *"People look at the outward appearance, but the Lord looks at the heart" (1 Samuel 16:7, NIV)*. Jesus said, *"God blesses those whose hearts are pure, for they will see God" (Matthew 5:8); "For whatever is in your heart determines what you say" (Matthew 12:34)*. If we live our lives from a good heart, speak our words from the heart, sing from the heart, look at others with love in our hearts, we will touch their hearts also.

So how do we change the condition of our hearts so God can use us in this way?

This type of living originates from *"... a change of heart produced by God's Spirit" (Romans 2:29)*. As we allow the Holy Spirit to rule our heart, He will give us the ability to speak love, joy, and peace from our heart to others' hearts. Would the earth not be a better place if more people lived like this?

"Above all else, guard your heart, for everything you do flows from it" (Proverbs 4:23, NIV).

MARCH 7

Altar of Convenience

The news recently reported a concern that the medical establishment had about women from a certain ethnic group having disproportionally more boys than girls at birth. It seems some women are choosing to abort girls, because for cultural reasons it's more prestigious to have boys, especially as the firstborn. As a result, many more baby boys are born among this people group than baby girls: when the average natural birth rate is almost 50-50. The call was for legislation regulating this discrimination against women.

I absolutely agree that this is blatant discrimination against women, both born and preborn.Yet some question this whole line of reasoning. How can this be discrimination if preborn children are not human beings in the first place? If it's legal to kill a preborn baby, then why would it be illegal to chose if it were a boy or a girl? Isn't the more pressing issue that human preborn children are being killed, no matter what the gender?

The real problem here is that we humans have a warped bent towards doing what is right, or at least convenient, in our own eyes, turning a blind eye to God and His will. God's Word, the Bible, teaches us that all human life is sacred because we are created in the image of God (Genesis 1:27; Exodus 20:13). When we pick and choose to live our lives according to our own will, we do so at our own peril (Proverbs 14:12; Revelation 21:8).

This, at its root, is a heart problem because the human heart is basically selfish and corrupt (Jeremiah 17:9), thus human lives are being sacrificed on the altar of convenience. Jesus said, *"For from the heart come evil thoughts, murder, adultery, all sexual immorality, theft, lying and slander. These are what defile you"* (Matthew 15:18).

Our only hope is to surrender our life, our heart, and our will to God, to call out to Him for mercy. Only He can forgive us and give us wisdom and strength to live our lives according to His perfect will. *"But if we confess our sins to Him, He is faithful and just to forgive us our sins and to cleanse us from all wickedness"* (1 John 1:9); *"I will put my laws in their minds, and I will write them on their hearts. I will be their God and they will be my people"* (Hebrews 8:10).

MARCH 8

Yes, No, Wait.

One time a friend confronted me with the question of why God wasn't answering his prayer. He said his old truck was worn out and no longer working, and he needed a new one. He asked God for a new truck but he didn't get it. God wasn't answering his prayer, he said. Was God not listening? Did He not care? What was wrong?

After thinking about it for a while, I thought, *Maybe God is answering his prayer but not in the way he wanted or expected*. So I spoke to him again and mentioned that God might be answering "No" to his prayer, or maybe He was answering "Wait." Could it be possible that God knew better than him what was best for him?

When my children were younger, they would reach for the shiny knife on the counter, but I would say, "Wait until you're older. This is dangerous for you now, and you can't handle it yet." That was a good answer, was it not? While driving down the highway, my children wanted me to pass the car ahead of us when it wasn't safe. I said "No." That was also a good answer, was it not? When I wanted to buy that new car and asked Dad to co-sign for me, he said "No." Now I'm glad that he knew better.

Knowing even better than earthly parents, our heavenly Father sees the bigger picture when we only see a small part. He knows the beginning from the end. When He says "Wait," that is best, even though we may not understand why. When He says "No," He knows the possible dangers that our request would bring to us. When He answers "Yes," we smile.

The key here is to trust God and let Him have His way in our lives, no matter what. We ask and He answers with the best answer for us at the time. *"Trust in the LORD with all your heart, and do not depend on your own understanding. Seek His will in all you do and He will show you which path to take"* (Proverbs 3:5–6).

A few months later, my friend came up to me with a smile on his face. God had answered "Wait," and he waited, then eventually God provided him with another truck!

"The LORD has heard my plea, The LORD will answer my prayer" (Psalm 6:9).

MARCH 9

Never Die

The evangelist Billy Graham passed away on February 21, 2018, at nearly one hundred years of age. From some reports, he had spoken to more than 200 million people over his lifetime. He was quoted in Christianity Today as saying, "Someday you will read or hear that Billy Graham is dead. Don't you believe a word of it. I shall be more alive than I am now. I will just have changed my address. I will have gone into the presence of God." How could he say this? What was the basis of his confident belief in an afterlife with God in heaven? Was it because he somehow earned a standing with God? Was it because he obeyed God by speaking to millions about the hope there is in Jesus Christ? Was it because he had some kind of a superior understanding of the Bible? Was it because he somehow lived a sinless life? Billy would have been the first to say that he was a sinner and no matter how hard he tried, he couldn't be good enough or earn favour with God.

His confidence was based on his personal faith in Jesus Christ and the Good News Jesus offered to all who would trust in Him, as recorded in God's Holy Word, the Bible. The Good news is that our Creator Jesus Christ, because of His great love for us, voluntarily died by cruel crucifixion on the cross some two thousand years ago to make payment for the sins of all who would believe, receive, and put their trust in Him (John 1:12, 3:16). Jesus, true to His own words, rose from the dead three days later. The grave could not keep Him because He is the Author of life. He said, *"I am the resurrection and the life. Anyone who believes in me will live, even after dying. Everyone who lives in me and believes in me will never ever die" (John 11:25–26).*

Do you believe? Have you received Jesus and His payment for your sins? Are you confident that you will spend eternity with Him?

MARCH 10

Suppressing the Truth

Have you ever heard of the National Citizens Inquiry (NCI)? I've asked many people this question and most haven't even heard of it. NCI is a citizen-led inquiry into the effects of the establishment's response to COVID-19. This Inquiry has taken place throughout 2023 in major cities all across Canada. A number of select commissioners heard many people from various backgrounds whose rights and experiences have been suppressed. The mainstream media were invited, yet they didn't show up at a single event! Though they may not necessarily agree with everything that was said at the NCI, they reneged on their duty to report by refusing to cover this event, thus suppressing the witness of these concerned citizens, including many expert doctors, police, scientists, and reporters. History has shown that this type of censorship is commonly practised by dictatorships, oligarchies, and totalitarian regimes, rather than in free democratic societies such as Canada.

One example of such censorship is the former Soviet Union, which had an official publication called *Pravda* (a Russian word that ironically means "truth" when translated) that only reported the information approved by the state and ignored the truth of the suppressive actions of the dictators in power. They further supressed the truth by hunting down people who proclaimed the truth, even to the point of imprisoning and taking the lives of those who refused to be silenced! Bibles were forbidden and destroyed as they suppressed the truth with their lies. There was only one narrative allowed—that of the dictators who sought to control the populace. When the truth is suppressed, lies become the norm, the people are suppressed, chaos reigns, and the citizens become slaves in their own country! *"For the wrath of God is revealed from heaven against all ungodliness and unrighteousness of men, who by their unrighteousness suppress the truth"* (Romans 1:18, ESV).

Yet there is hope because the truth always prevails! Jesus said *"... and you will know the truth, and the truth will set you free"* (John 8:32, ESV). He didn't suppress those who questioned Him because He knew the truth would triumph. He proclaimed, *"I am the way, and the truth, and the life. No one comes to the Father except through me"* (John 14:6, ESV). Let us seek the truth at all cost, for only the truth will set us free!

MARCH 11

Forgiven

In July 2008, John and Eloise Bergen were brutally attacked by nine men when they were working in an orphanage in Kenya, Africa. John was almost beaten to death, and Eloise was raped and severely beaten. Eloise managed to find her husband in the dark of the night and miraculously got him into a vehicle and drove them to the hospital. Amazingly, they both survived and have, through the power of Jesus Christ, completely forgiven their attackers. John and Eloise could only forgive their attackers because of their relationship with Jesus. Furthermore, the forgiveness offered by John and Eloise could only be complete for the attackers if they received it. Then a relationship with them could be restored, and love, peace, and joy could replace guilt and shame. Forgiveness is not complete if it's offered but not received, just as a gift offered is not the recipient's until it's received.

Some two thousand years ago, Jesus Christ was scorned, beaten, whipped, and brutally nailed to an ugly wooden cross by those He'd created in His own image (Genesis 1:27; John 1:3,4; Colossians1:16–17). As they were doing this to Him, He said, *"Father, forgive them, for they don't know what they are doing" (Luke 23:34).* Jesus not only forgave those who killed Him but everyone who would trust in Him so that sin would no longer stand between them, and a relationship could be restored with them. He made provision for this by making payment for our sins by dying in our place on the cross.

Though the Bergens could only extend forgiveness for the attacks against them, Jesus, God in human flesh, has the authority to extend forgiveness for every sin we've ever committed. Will we remain in our sins, or will we receive the wonderful gift of forgiveness and the love, joy, and peace He has offered?

"For the wages of sin is death, but the free gift of God is eternal life through Christ Jesus our Lord" (Romans 6:23).

MARCH 12

Living Proof

A fellow once told me that he was so sure he could raise his deceased friend from the dead that he attempted to do this at his funeral. Needless to say, the body of the friend remained in the coffin, and the fellow attempting to do the raising was briskly escorted out! He obviously did not have the power to bring the dead to life!

Jesus prophesied that He would die by crucifixion and come back to life three days later (Matthew 16:21). He was indeed crucified on a Roman cross, and His death witnessed by many and confirmed by the Roman soldiers piercing His side with a spear. Blood and water came out, strongly indicating that He had water around His heart from congestive heart failure, and blood indicating that they had pierced His heart. His body was taken from the cross by Joseph and Nicodemus, two Pharisees who had previously been secret followers of His, and placed in Joseph's newly carved tomb. It was sealed up with a large stone over the entrance with Roman guards watching over it. Then on the third day, Mary Magdalene, Mary, and Salome encountered Jesus risen from the dead and spoke with Him. Later He appeared to the disciples and also to many people before He ascended into heaven to be seated at the right hand of God the Father (Matthew 27:32–28, 30; Luke 23:26–24, 49; John 19:16–21, 25).

How could this have happened? The Holy Scriptures indicate that Jesus was the Author of life (Acts 3:15) and the Creator of everything (John 1:2; Colossians 1:16–17). As all life came from and through Him, death could not keep Him! He proved who He was by rising from the dead, just as He predicted would happen!

All the disciples except John went on to die at the hands of persecutors for their faith in Jesus. There is no doubt Jesus has risen. He has risen indeed!

The words of the apostle Paul, who came to faith in Jesus after he had an encounter with the risen Lord (Acts 9:1–20), still ring out for us today: *"Believe in the Lord Jesus and you will be saved, along with everyone in your household" (Acts 16:31).*

MARCH 13

Exercise

It was a bit steep in places, but the hike was worth it! From this elevated vantage point, we could see the spectacular view of Fraser Lake below us, much of the town, and sprawling farmlands in the far distance.

As a family, we had repeatedly travelled past this spot on our way to some destination beyond. Yet on a trip back from Prince George, a good friend of mine insisted that we stop and take a little hike up Mouse Mountain trail at Fraser Lake, BC. I hesitated, being in a hurry and out of shape from lack of exercise through the winter, but I nevertheless took up the challenge! After huffing and puffing up the trail, the physical exercise was well worth it! At the summit, my eyes were opened a little more to the wonders of creation. My outlook of the area will never be the same!

Though physical exercise can benefit us temporarily, much more importantly, we can grow in our knowledge and faith in God by the spiritual exercises of prayer, worship, obedience, and meditation on God through his Holy Word, the Bible. Then we will gain a far greater and eternal perspective of life. We can experience an intimate relationship with Jesus our Creator, realize His peace, sense His amazing Presence, and know His wonderful eternal plan for us, each and every day! This makes the experience on Mouse Mountain pale in comparison!

"Physical training is good, but training for godliness is much better, promising benefits in this life and in the life to come" (1 Timothy 4:8).

Light of Life

We discovered an effective method of getting rid of weeds in our garden! A black plastic tarp over the weedy soil for a few months will kill the weeds and anything else under it. The black plastic blocks out all the sunlight, and the plants, absolutely dependent on the light, die for lack of the life-giving light. All of life on earth is in some way or another dependent upon light.

Just as the physical creation is reliant on light for life, so are we in need of Jesus for the true spiritual light of life. Without Him we all walk in spiritual darkness, which God spoke of through the prophet Isaiah: *"So there is no justice among us, and we know nothing about right living. We look for light but find only darkness. We look for bright skies but walk in gloom" (Isaiah 59:9).* In this fallen state, death and darkness reign, and we're left with no earthly hope. In this darkness we are deceived. We can't see until the light of Jesus shines through the darkness to reveal our true condition. The killing of our unwanted preborn babies, suicide, euthanasia, and the redefinition of family and marriage are just a few of the deceptive evil deeds of darkness that, though sometimes presented as good, actually bring spiritual and even physical death upon us. Jesus said, *"I am the light of the world. If you follow me, you won't have to walk in darkness, because you will have the light that leads to life" (John 8:12).*

We have before us to either continue to walk in darkness and death, or to let Jesus into our lives to give us the light of life that we need to live transparent lives in the light of true love, joy, and peace!

MARCH 15

Recreational Drugs?

It's very important to take some time for recreation, to get away from the everyday workload, to refresh ourselves and get some peace in the middle of the storms of life. A walk in the park, a ride on the bicycle, hiking in the hills, a quiet time at the lake, maybe a good read in a book, meditating on God's goodness to us—something to give us a change of pace, a natural way of dealing with built-up stress.

Yet today we hear that the government is approving the use of recreational cannabis, or marijuana. I have a relative who has been diagnosed with terminal cancer; he has been prescribed medical marijuana pills to help him sleep, and he says it works! He's near the end of his days, and it has been a great help to him in his struggle with cancer. Does this mean we should be using it recreationally?

My doctor tells me there's a side effect for every drug we take. Some of the side effects for marijuana use are memory loss, paranoia, psychosis, hallucinations, panic, lowering of IQ, impaired brain development, and the list goes on and on. Is this what we've come to in our attempt to cope with life and find peace by taking drugs? Prescription drugs are one thing, but recreational drugs? When the time comes that one might need drugs, let the doctor prescribe the proper remedy.

All of creation has been made for us to enjoy; nature even provides many cures for diseases and ailments, but to take drugs for recreational purposes is ridiculous!

As for me, I'll take a recreational walk in the park, have a good talk with Jesus, lay my burdens at His feet. He is my source of peace!

Jesus said, *"I am leaving you with a gift—peace of mind and heart. And the peace I give is a gift the world cannot give. So don't be troubled or afraid"* (John 14:27).

MARCH 16

Secret Sins

Tom and his older sister Sharon[4] were excited that they'd be able to spend their summer at their grandpa and grandma's farm. It was so different from the city, with lots of space to run around and have fun. Tom loved to gather eggs and work alongside Grandpa.

Tom learned how to use the slingshot his father had given him. He practised as he shot at things around the farm. Grandpa saw him shoot towards a chicken and warned him not to shoot at living creatures on the farm, as he might hurt them.

One day, forgetting Grandpa's warning, Tom impulsively shot at a lone duck behind the barn. He really didn't want to hurt it, but he hit it in the head. It fluttered around then fell down lifeless. He could hear his heart pounding as he heard Grandpa's warning echo through his mind. He looked around, seeing no one, so he decided he would bury it. No one would know, he thought.

That evening it was Sharon's turn to do the dishes, yet she demanded that Tom wash them for her. When he refused, she told him that she had seen him kill and bury the duck. She would tell Grandpa if he didn't do the dishes. He washed the dishes that day with a sinking feeling in his heart. He couldn't look Grandma or Grandpa in the eye. Tom couldn't get the images of the dead duck out of his mind. His slingshot stayed on its hook on the wall. Tom's fun on the farm turned into drudgery, and his sister got him to do more and more of her work.

One morning as he woke up, he knew what he had to do. He would confess to Grandpa and Grandma what had happened. With his heart in his throat, he sputtered out his confession, expecting to get the worst punishment possible.

Grandma hugged him firmly and with tears in her eyes said, "I saw you kill and bury that duck too. I was waiting for you to tell me. We forgive you. You won't have to do your sister's work anymore." Tom was free! He could look his grandparents in the eye again. The rest of the summer was such a joy on the farm.

Jesus said, *"For everything that is hidden will eventually be brought into the open and every secret will be brought to light" (Mark 4:22).*

"But if we confess our sins to Him, He is faithful and just to forgive our sins and to cleanse us from all wickedness" (1 John 1:9).

---

4 Story true to the best of author's memory. Names changed.

MARCH 17

Assembly Required

We had a wonderful time of fellowship while sharing stories, testimonies, and Scripture verses! We even sang a chorus or two! This brief impromptu meeting just happened as two, then three and four, Christian brothers were supernaturally drawn to each other for Christian fellowship! We couldn't help it!

To illustrate the need for this kind of meeting, the following thoughts come to mind. When I bought a bench to put by our back door, it came in a box not at all resembling the bench I had seen on display. Inside were all the parts, together with an instruction sheet explaining the assembly required. When I followed the instructions and put all the parts together, the bench I had ordered came to reality. Previously, it was only a concept, a bunch of parts scattered around in no particular order, a picture on a box or on the internet. Virtual but not real.

The meeting mentioned above, though not officially planned, was an expression of what the church really is—an assembly. Having gone through 2020–2021 with COVID-19 restrictions, some wonder: Why the big deal? Why do Christians want to get together when we have Zoom, or phone, or texting? The reason is that we're not just a sum of the parts in a box, a picture, an ideological organization, a building, or a virtual reality. We are an actual supernatural body joined together by the Holy Spirit of God! God's Word says, *"And let us not neglect our meeting together, as some people do, but encourage one another, especially now that the day of his return is drawing near" (Hebrews 10:25).* Though we can exist for a time without assembling, we can't be what God meant for us to be without gathering together as an expression of God's children on earth. Nothing else will do!

The assembled bench has been very useful, and I wonder how we did without it! The brief yet powerful meeting of the brothers the other day was invigorating, encouraging, and strengthening. Assembly is essential!

MARCH 18

A Personal Relationship

Recently I was having a discussion with a friend. He mentioned the energy that was between us. He spoke of God as the greatest energy in the universe and how we needed to tune in to all this energy to be properly functional between each other. The energy, he said, was within us and was part of the energy vibrating throughout everything in the whole universe. Positive and negative energy: we have the choice, he said, to choose to tap into the positive energy and spread iteopled, to make everyone happy, or tap into the negative energy to make everyone sad.

As he was speaking, I thought of my grandchildren. They are packed full of energy. They want to try everything new. Sometimes it's a challenge to harness all this energy into positive use! But is that what makes my grandchildren special to me? No, it's their personality that makes them unique, each one very special. If they were only bundles of energy, they'd be nothing more than a vacuum cleaner, a spring storm, or a lightning bolt. But they're people just like all of us, uniquely created in the image of a personal God, created to have a living, personal relationship with Him.

Our problem is that we tend to depersonalize this living relationship into things we do, how we feel, or even into energy fields. This is an offense to God, just as it's an offense for a husband to treat his wife as just an object, or as positive and negative energy, rather than as a person to be loved, cherished, honoured, and respected. God created us in His image so we could have a personal, vibrant, loving relationship with Him, but we have wandered from Him and gone our own way. That's why God calls us all to repent. This means to turn from our own self-made, self-preservation, self-destructive behaviour (sins) and allow Him to have His way in our lives: *"... He commands everyone everywhere to repent of their sins and turn to Him" (Acts 17:30).*

Our Creator God made us. He has a personal interest in each of us and knows the way we should be, how we should behave towards Him and towards others. He has the best in mind for each of us and wants us to personally come to Him so that He can give us an abundant life. Jesus said, *"My purpose is to give them a rich and satisfying life" (John 10:10).*

God sent His one and only Son, Jesus Christ, to give us this life. *"This is the only work God wants from you: Believe in the one He has sent" (John 6:29).*

"How precious to me are your thoughts O God. They cannot be numbered! I can't even count them; they outnumber the grains of sand! And when I wake up, you are still with me" (Psalm 139:17–18).

MARCH 19

Thunderstorms

It sounded like somebody was dragging a heavy chair across the floor. I got up to investigate and realized a thunderstorm was brewing south of us and was working its way north. For the next hour, sitting at our living room window in the wee hours of the morning, I was able to witness a spectacular overhead exhibition of forks of lightning splitting the sky as the earth trembled in response.

Where would the lightning strike next? Our dog was afraid, crouching at the door, seeking a safe place. A number of years ago, lightning hit a tree right next to our neighbour's house. It left a charred scar all the way down the tree and a pile of red rocks at the base.

As the storm disappeared into the north, the rains came to nourish the earth with nitrogen-laden droplets of water. As daylight came, the warm sun peeked through the clouds as it shone through the window.

During the storm, I was reminded of my distant ancestors who, moved by this magnificent power unleashed in creation, through superstition and fear came up with a mythology that included a god who showed himself through thunder and lightning. They worshipped Thor, the "god of the thunder."

I thank God that Christians came to these people with the Word of God and proclaimed the truth of Jesus Christ to them so that many believed in the Creator rather than the creation. Thus, they were set free from the fear and superstition that had gripped them.

Today many superstitions still exist, which cause those who believe in them to respond in false worship and fear. Some believe certain numbers will bring them good or bad luck; others believe that if they point to a rainbow, their hand will shrivel up. Some think black cats are bad luck, and others trust in the horoscope to give them direction for the day or help in times of distress. Yet we have the awesome privilege of personally knowing the Creator of the universe, who loves and cares for us. He's the one who made everything, and He controls the storms of life. Whatever situation we find ourselves in, let's call out to Him. He is our security and strength!

"'LORD help!' they cried in their trouble; and he saved them from their distress. He calmed the storm to a whisper and stilled the waves. What a blessing was that stillness as he brought them safely into the harbour" (Psalm 107:28–30).

"... for God gave us a spirit not of fear but of power and love and self-control" (2 Timothy 1:7, ESV).

MARCH 20

Time

We've all heard the following statements at one time or another: "How much time do we have?" "Can we make it on time?" "What time is that appointment?" "Do you have time for coffee?" "I don't have time for that!" Some say we can save time by doing something more efficiently. But are we really able to save time? Maybe we can only spend it in a different way.

The concept of time is really amazing and even mysterious. Years ago, I watched a movie called *The Time Machine*, in which a man invented a machine that could go back in time as well as forward in time at an accelerated rate. What made the movie intriguing was the ability to control time, but it wasn't in touch with reality, as the passing of time is not in our control. Time is progressing forward day after day. There are 60 minutes in an hour, 1,440 minutes in a day, 525,600 minutes in a year, and if we live to be 70 years old, 36,792,000 minutes in our lifetime.

One important feature of time is that we have choices in how we spend it. Some things we do will only be temporary, while others will last for all eternity.

We might ask how we can do eternal things, how the things we do can really last forever. I believe the answer is that in and of ourselves, we can't, because out of our sinful nature we always have some selfish motive for what we do (James 4:13–16; John 15:5). What God wants of us is for us to totally surrender our lives to Him so that He can live His life through us. If He is the boss of my life, He'll be able to use me to do His work His way, rather than doing it my way or even trying to do His work my way. So the key here is to surrender our lives to Him and let Him have His way with us, then we will be empowered by His Holy Spirit to use our allotted time here on earth to do eternal things for Him (Galatians 2:20, 5:22).

God's Word tells us that there will come a sobering day at the end of our lives, when all of us will have to give an account of how we spent our time here on earth. It will all be revealed, even every word I spoke. Was it for me, or was it for God and for eternity? (Matthew 12:33–37; Hebrews 4:12–13).

"Yes, a person is a fool to store up earthly wealth but not have a rich relationship with God" (Luke 12:21).

Win to Lose

Do you remember Howard Hughes? Some say he was once the richest man on earth and had a lot of power as a result. He excelled as an aerospace engineer, a film producer, and owned billions of dollars. He built the largest aircraft of the time, called the *Spruce Goose*, as it was made out of mostly wood. He broke airspeed records, travelled around the world in record time, and owned an airline. He owned a film studio, produced numerous films, and dated movie stars. He designed and built aircraft, most of which bore his name. He founded the Howard Hughes Medical Institute to discover the what he called "genesis of life itself."

In his later years, even though he had the means to travel and live almost as he pleased, he chose to hide out in penthouse suites of his grand hotels. He would reserve the whole upper floor just for himself and a select few, whom he cautiously trusted, to look after him. Sometimes he would remain in these places locked up for months at a time, watching the same movies over and over again. I remember in the 1970s hearing rumours of him possibly living this way in one of his hotels in Vancouver, BC. It's said he became paranoid about germs, so much so that he wouldn't let anyone cut his hair without wearing surgical gloves. At seventy years of age, he died, emaciated from drug abuse and poor nutrition. He took nothing of his earthly empire along with him, and those who wanted his fortune fought over it for years.

I don't know about you, but this makes me sad. In a biography about him, there was no mention of a faith in, or a pursuit of, God. After pursuing and winning wealth and fame for all those years, he lost it all. It appears Howard Hughes sought to find the "genesis of life" and missed the "Author of Life" (Acts 3:15).

Jesus said: *"If anyone would come after me, let him deny himself and take up his cross and follow me. For whoever would save his life will lose it, but whoever loses his life for my sake and the gospel's will save it. For what does it profit a man to gain the whole world and forfeit his soul? For what can a man give in return for his soul."* (Mark 8:34–37, ESV).

"Better to have little, with fear for the LORD, than to have great treasure and inner turmoil" (Proverbs 15:16).

MARCH 22

Lose to Win

Sundar Singh was born in 1889 to a very religious and wealthy family in India. He hated Christians and persecuted them during his early teen years. He even burned a Bible to show how he hated the Word of God. He was in line to inherit his father's wealth, yet he wasn't content. He became very depressed, and one night in desperation he asked God to show Himself to him or he would commit suicide. That night Jesus appeared to him in a dream, and the sense of God's presence and love for him was so real and overwhelming that he called to his father and woke him up, saying that he had seen Jesus. His father told him that he was going crazy and that he should go back to sleep.

This experience with God changed Sundar's life. He went to Bible school to learn more of this God who loved him so much. This incensed his father, who told Sundar that he was to renounce his faith in Jesus or he would lose his inheritance. His family would not only disown him, but they would consider him as if he had never existed. Sundar chose to follow Jesus and was cast out of his family.

Sundar loved the people of India and was compelled to walk around and tell people about Jesus. They called him Sadhu, meaning he was a holy man who taught spiritual things to them. Many turned to God, but he suffered much persecution. He had no earthly possessions, but God always supplied his needs. A few times he was beaten and left for dead, but with the help of God and other believers, he recovered and continued to tell others of his faith.

Later in his life, his father, seeing the change in Sundar and hearing the message of Jesus' death and resurrection, also became a Christian.

Sundar even travelled to Tibet to tell of God's forgiveness and love. On his fifteenth trip to Tibet, he never returned. No one knows what happened to him, but all knew he was in the hands of God.

Sadhu Sundar Singh, through faith in Christ, lost all his earthly rights and privileges to win a holy and eternal life with God. His greatest love was for Jesus, who loved him and gave him God's love for others.

Jesus said, *"For whoever would save his life will lose it, but whoever loses his life for my sake and the gospel's will save it. For what does it profit a man to gain the whole world and forfeit his soul?" (Mark 8:35–36, ESV).*

MARCH 23

The Mediator

Communication has changed a lot over the years. From the old "party line" crank phone in the 1960s to the modern new smart phones—quite a leap of technological genius.

Yet many things have not changed. We're very limited in where we have cell phone coverage; sometimes I have to move my phone around the room to get a minimal signal to send or receive a text. Many areas along the highway have no coverage. Even if the service is good, we still need to invest in a phone and phone plan to be able to call—that is, if the system is up and running properly. When we do get our call through, we're often met with an impersonal answering machine or a computer that leaves us wondering if we'll ever connect with a real person. Lots of technology, very little real empathy, care, or understanding.

There's a wonderful method of communication that has been around since the beginning of time, which is still available today. It's called prayer. There are no interruptions, impersonal computers, or answering machines on the other end. Actually, there's one who is eager and willing to hear us at any time. It is Jesus, the one who descended from His heavenly throne to live among us for some thirty years, to die a horrible death to pay for our debt of sin. He conquered death by physically rising from the dead and ascended back to His home at the right hand of the Father to intercede and mediate for us so that our earnest prayers will be heard by the only One who truly loves and cares for us.

Since such a wonderful means of communicating with our Maker is so readily available to us, why do we not make it the first and most important thing we do?

"For there is only one God and one Mediator who can reconcile God and humanity—the man Christ Jesus. He gave his life to purchase freedom for everyone" (1 Timothy 2:5–6).

"Thus says the Lord who made the earth, the Lord who formed it to establish it—the Lord is his name: Call to me and I will answer you, and will tell you great and hidden things that you have not known" (Jeremiah 33:2–3, ESV).

"However, those the Father has given me will come to me, and I will never reject them" (John 6:37).

Hell—A Real Place

I'm sure you've heard people use the word "hell" in the course of conversation. Some people say the word quite frequently, though it's often used in the most inappropriate ways. One fellow told me he wanted to go there because that's where all his friends would be. Usually, when questioned further, it seems the people who use the word most frequently believe in it the least.

But is there a place where some will go called hell? If there is such a place, what is it like? How can we be sure to escape this wretched place?

Jesus is very clear that there is a place called hell, and it's not a place that anyone would want to go to (Matthew 5:21–22, 7:13–14, 23:33, 25:31–46; Mark 9:42–50). It's described in God's Word as a place of eternal punishment, of torment, and of burning sulphur (Revelation 20:10–15). Hell is definitely not a place where there will be a big party with all of one's friends.

God's Word is clear that it is our rebellion and sin that separates us from God. If our sins aren't dealt with, then we will be eternally separated from God in hell. God's Word says *"... for all have sinned and fall short of the glory of God" (Romans 3:23, NIV); "For the wages of sin is death ..." (Romans 6:23, NIV)*. This death is not annihilation, as some may think, but as described by Jesus (see verses above), it's an eternity of separation from God in hell.

God is holy and demands complete holiness, a state of complete perfection for anyone who would come into His presence. Anyone who is not perfect will not be able to stand before Him and will be cast from His presence. That's why Jesus came to save us: *"We are made right with God by placing our faith in Jesus Christ. And this is true for everyone who believes, no matter who we are" (Romans 3:22); "... but the free gift of God is eternal life through Jesus Christ our Lord" (Romans 6:23)*. A gift isn't a gift until it's received. When we put our trust in Jesus and receive the gift of forgiveness of our sins, they will no longer be held against us and we are made holy, without even a blemish.

"For God so loved the world that he gave his one and only Son, that whoever believes in him shall not perish but have eternal life" (John 3:16, NIV).

MARCH 25

Heaven—A Real Place

Some friends loaned us a copy of the movie called *Heaven Is for Real*, where Todd Burpo depicts his four-year-old son as having been in heaven. He supposedly saw his grandfather, his sister, angels, and Jesus there.

How do we really know there's a heaven, or even an afterlife for that matter? Do we need to have visions or dreams of heaven to be sure? Do we believe in heaven because we watched the movie or read the book *Heaven is for Real*? Or is it just a hit and miss proposal? Do we only find out if it's real when we get there? Does everyone go to heaven? If everyone does go to heaven, what of Hitler, Stalin, Mao Tse Tung, or Idi Amin? What would it be like living with them for all eternity? If not, who goes to heaven, and how can we be sure we will get there?

We can be sure there's a heaven because God told us in His Word, the Bible, that there's a real place called heaven (Luke 15:7). Jesus, when He taught the disciples to pray, said *"Our Father in heaven, hallowed be your name" (Matthew 6:9, NIV)*. He spoke of going to prepare a place for all those who believed in Him (John 14:1–4) The Bible describes it as a place where there is no more sorrow, no more dying, no more pain. It's a holy, perfect, and eternal place where those who trust in Jesus will spend eternity in the presence of God (Revelation 21:3–4). Heaven is mentioned very often in God's Word.

Jesus made it very clear that there is only one way to get to heaven, and that's through faith in Him. Jesus answered, *"I am the way and the truth and the life. No one comes to the Father except through me" (John 14:6, NIV); "In the same way, I tell you, there is rejoicing in the presence of the angels of God over one sinner who repents" (Luke 15:10, NIV)*.

MARCH 26

Determined

My father was a determined fellow. When we went on a road trip, the destination was the goal; the fewest stops and the shortest, quickest way was always on his mind. Sometimes vehicle problems, or one time even a flood, caused us to be delayed. Yet almost always, we would get to his intended destination. Only when he got older and lost his driver's licence was he unable to go where he wanted. Sometimes Dad's determination was annoying. I am thankful, though, that he consistently encouraged me to have faith in Jesus, no matter how difficult the circumstances.

Jesus was also determined. His resolve came from the heavenly Father and was of divine origin, whereas Dad's may often have come of his human nature.

The Holy Scriptures prophesy the sufferings that Jesus was heading for: *"I offered my back to those who beat me and my cheeks to those who pulled out my beard. I did not hide my face from mockery and spitting."* Isaiah 50:6. His determination was to fulfill all that his Father had planned for him, *"Because the Sovereign Lord helps me, I will not be disgraced. Therefore, I have set my face like a stone, determined to do his will. And I know that I will not be put to shame" (Isaiah 50:6–7).*

Jesus, speaking of Himself, informed His disciples that His destination was to go to Jerusalem, where He would be arrested by the religious leaders and *"They will sentence Him to die and hand Him over to the Romans. They will mock Him, spit on Him, flog Him with a whip, and kill Him, but after three days He will rise again" (Mark 10:33–34).*

Jesus knew that His purpose was to pay the ultimate price—His death on the cross—so all who put their trust in Him would be saved from eternal punishment and instead be given eternal life!

I am thankful that my destination, even after death, is secure because Jesus was determined to fulfill every detail of His mission to save those who are lost!

Have you put your trust in Him?

MARCH 27

The Cure

The whole world was traumatized by the growing pandemic. Even Boris Johnson, the Prime Minister of Great Britain, was in the intensive care fighting for his life. Everyone was hoping for a cure. A number of Big Pharma companies came up with a new type of injection based on a technology called mRNA. It was approved under emergency proclamations of health agencies issued by the UN and most countries of the world. Though it was touted as the only cure, many questioned its effectiveness, as many of the vaccinated still contracted COVID-19. Some say the vaccine has done more harm than good. Time will tell, and the truth will come out!

Some 3,500 years ago, Moses and the children of Israel had a similar tragedy occur while wandering in the wilderness (Numbers 21:4–8). They had grumbled towards God and weren't thankful for His provision for them, thus their camp was inundated with poisonous snakes. The people who were bitten by the snakes died. Everyone was afraid and cried out for Moses to do something. God revealed to Moses that they should make a bronze snake and set it up on a pole. Theeoplee who had been bitten were told to simply look at the snake and they would live! They Were not told to do anything special, to fight the snakes, to beat them to death, or run from them. They were only to look and live!

Jesus refers to this incident when addressing a religious leader of his day: *"Just as Moses lifted up the snake in the wilderness, so the Son of Man must be lifted up, that everyone who believes may have eternal life in him" (John 3 14–15, NIV).* He was speaking of how He was going to die on the cross, how He would take the penalty for our sin so those who realized their sin need only look to Him in faith and they would be forgiven and set free from the eternal death that was awaiting them, and He would give them eternal life instead.

Though physical death is inevitable via COVID-19, cancer, heart attack, or other means, we need not fear spiritual death if we in faith look to Jesus and what He did for us on the cross two thousand years ago! *"For God so loved the world that he gave his one and only Son, that whoever believes in him shall not perish but have eternal life" (John 3:16, NIV).* Look and live!

MARCH 28

A Donkey and a Horse

When Jesus entered the city of Jerusalem one week before He was to be crucified, as prophesied hundreds of years earlier by God through the prophet Zechariah (Zechariah 9:9), He rode a colt of a donkey. He came as a servant to save His people, to set them free from the clutches of the evil one, to take their sin, their burden, their guilt, their shame upon Himself. He did not come to exalt Himself but to serve and to set His people free, to take the punishment of their sin upon Himself by dying in their place on a cruel Roman cross!

The Holy Scriptures prophesy of Jesus coming again, on a white horse, this time to judge the world. As surely as the first prophecy of Jesus came about, so will the second! This will be a very sombre time, as Jesus is coming to judge everyone who ever lived (Revelation 20:15, 21:27).

As this judgement is yet to come, it's most important to repent and receive Jesus as our Lord and Saviour before this dreadful time! Only those who believe and have received Him will escape this terrible judgement.

"The Lord isn't really being slow about his promise, as some people think. No, he is being patient for your sake. He does not want anyone to be destroyed, but wants everyone to repent" (2 Peter 3:9).

Jesus Save Us!

Many had heard Him speak and seen Him heal the sick, the blind, the deaf, and raise the dead. They thought He would somehow liberate them from their earthly captors. They hailed Him with *"Blessings on the King who comes in the name of the Lord! Peace in heaven, and glory in highest heaven!" (Luke 19:38)* as they laid their garments and palm branches on the road before him! Jerusalem was in an uproar! Yet He was riding on a colt of a donkey, not a horse as most conquerors would. He had no earthly sword, no gun, no cannon!

Less than a week later, the crowds turned on Him and had Him crucified to death on a cross. He was dead. The one who had so much promise for them, no longer among them to rescue them, they thought, *but* He had other plans! His Kingdom is not of this world! His Kingdom is eternal; this world is temporary! His Kingdom is of life; this world is of death. His Kingdom is of peace, joy, and love; this world is of war, strife, and hate. His Kingdom is of pure light; this world is of darkness.

Three days later, He rose from the dead and again walked among them. Death could not hold Him because He is the Author of life, the Creator, the Sustainer, and He is the Saviour!

By His death He took the death penalty that we deserved! By His resurrection He proved to us that He truly was the One He said He was! And as He ascended to His rightful place before God the Father, He promised He would send His Holy Spirit to empower all those who would follow Him!

He made the way so we could have a choice to surrender to Him, to follow Him, and enter into His Kingdom, or to continue in this kingdom of eternal death. Which one will you choose?

May your Kingdom come, Lord Jesus. May your will be done! For yours is the kingdom and the power and the glory forever! Amen!

MARCH 30

Must the Stones Cry Out?

It was quite a commotion as Jesus entered the city of Jerusalem. The people were sick and tired of being suppressed by the occupying Roman legions. They were ordered to carry loads for soldiers on demand. They had to pay taxes to Caesar. Everywhere they looked they saw the imposing shadow of the suppressive regime that was ruling over them. They wanted out from under this burden. But how? Some had tried to revolt, but now they were again under the vise-grip of oppression.

They thought that Jesus, the compassionate one who had raised the dead, who had healed the sick, who had spoken with great authority, was now coming into Jerusalem to set them free. He would conquer the Romans and would sit on the throne to rule over them. That was their hope. *"Hosanna, hosanna"* (Save now, save now!), they cried out as they idolized Him, throwing their garments and palm branches down before Him in celebration of the anticipated freedom that would soon be theirs.

The religious leaders of the day were offended as the people venerated Jesus. They protested to Him, telling Him to instruct the people to be quiet. His answer was, *"If they kept quiet, the stones will cry out!" (Luke 19:40, NIV)*.

Little did the Pharisees or the people know that Jesus was their creator—God in human flesh—who was entering the gates of Jerusalem that day! Little did they know that this event had been prophesied many years before. Little did they know that in just a matter of days, some of them would cry out "crucify him" as He would make the ultimate payment of laying down His life so that they could be saved from eternal condemnation in hell and set free from the bondage of sin. Little did they know that, upon His death, the rocks would tremble and split, as an earthquake and darkness would cover the land. Little did they know that He would physically rise back to life in three days, just as He had prophesied would happen.

Today, many of us are oppressed by the circumstances around us. Sin has taken its toll, and the consequences of our rebellion against God are weighing heavy on us. The situation is desperate. Jesus wants to enter into our lives to change our hearts, to give us hope. What will we do with Jesus, the one who made us, the one who sustains us, the one who paid the ultimate price to save us? Are we going to worship Him, praise Him, honour Him, and to cry out for Him to save us—Hosanna! Hosanna!—or will the stones have to cry out?

MARCH 31

Mother Hen

Have you ever observed a mother hen? When brooding over the eggs in the nest, she will fiercely defend them and keep them warm until they hatch. As she ventures out, the chicks follow her around. At the threat of danger or the cold of a storm, they hear her clucking and instinctively come near to her and nestle under the warm protection of her wings. When confronted with danger, she defends them with her life: squawking, scratching, pecking, and beating her wings to drive off the intruder. Jesus used the example of a mother hen to illustrate His love for humanity and His desire for them to trust in Him.

When Jesus was about to enter Jerusalem to be crucified, He said, *"O Jerusalem, Jerusalem, the city that kills the prophets and stones God's messengers! How often I have wanted to gather your children together as a hen protects her chicks beneath her wings, but you wouldn't let me" (Matthew 23:37).* He was referring to the Jews, even the religious ones, whom He had come to save, protect, and empower to live a fulfilled and meaningful life—those who subsequently rejected Him and were about to have Him crucified.

Our Creator Jesus, the only One who can truly protect us, is still calling for us to come to Him (Matthew 11:28). What are we going to do with Him? Will we heed His call? Will we follow Him and run to Him to save us from the wages of our sins (Romans 6:23)? Will we abide under the protection and shelter of His wings to escape the dangers of the world around us (Psalm 91)? Will we turn from the cold hard life to a warm fellowship with Him (Revelation 3:20)? Or will we resist His call and say with the crowd, *"Crucify him" (Mark 15:13, NIV)?*

APRIL 1

He Sweat Blood

When I was still an unbeliever, I thought there were many contradictions and questionable passages in the Bible. One such text is, *"And being in an agony he prayed more earnestly; and his sweat as it were great drops of blood falling down to the ground"* (Luke 22:44, KJV).

Really? Sweating drops of blood? I had never heard of such a thing happening. I thought Luke must have been trying so hard to make a point that he inserted this to make it seem more intense. Maybe it was a figure of speech. But why would this be included? At the time it seemed unbelievable, at best an exaggeration. Then I read an interview in the book *The Case for Christ* that author Lee Strobel had with medical expert Dr. Alexander Metherell. Dr. Metherell clearly explained that sometimes our bodies can, under extreme stress, release chemicals that cause the small blood vessels in the skin to break down, which causes blood to flow and mix into the sweat.

So God's Word was right after all! Jesus really did sweat blood. Here a verse that I had questioned actually became strong evidence for the reliability of the Scriptures. Even more, Jesus' suffering was real. His agony, even before the physical beatings, was almost unbearable. He was already suffering spiritually, emotionally, and psychologically. He knew what was going to happen. He was purposely going to suffer and die, taking on Himself the sins of the world (John 1:29; 1 John 2:2) of all who would believe and receive Him as Lord and Saviour (John 1:12, 3:16–18). The agony of taking on the lies, the guilt, the shame, the deviations, the murders, was almost unbearable for the sinless Son of Man to take. He sweat blood.

Jesus said: *"Yes, it was written long ago that the Messiah would suffer and die and rise from the dead on the third day. It was also written that this message would be proclaimed in the authority of his name to all the nations, beginning in Jerusalem. 'There is forgiveness for sins for all who repent.' You are witnesses of all these things."* (Luke 24:46–48).

APRIL 2

Greatest Battle

In April 2017, Canadians remembered the battle of Vimy Ridge, which had occurred one hundred years earlier during World War I in France. This was an enemy stronghold that had cost over 100,000 previous casualties as others had attempted to conquer it. The Canadians, in a massive four-day assault involving over 15,000 soldiers, took control of this stronghold at the cost of over 3,500 deaths and some 7000 injured. This was a major military victory and turning point in the war and is an event Canadians look back on as a defining moment in World War I and for Canada as a nation.

A much greater battle, a battle for people from every tribe, tongue, and nation, was fought and won some two thousand years ago. Rather than thousands dying in this battle, millions were saved at the cost of one life. The ancient prophets and faithful ones looked forward to the time when God would intervene on behalf of this lost world, and we look back at this most important victory. This is by far the greatest battle that ever happened in history, and it was won singlehandedly by Jesus Christ, the Creator of the universe, the Author of life Himself. He could have called legions of angels to intervene. He could have spoken His enemies out of existence as they scorned, scourged, and swarmed around Him, cruelly whipping Him and nailing Him to the ugly Roman cross, but instead He willingly sacrificed His own life for them. Instead of fighting back, He willingly paid for their sins, declaring, *"Father, forgive them, for they don`t know what they are doing"* *(Luke 23:34).*

At this greatest battle, the central event of all history, the evil forces of darkness were defeated, and the sins of all those who believed in Him were forgiven. This is the reason the Son of God came into the world, to die on behalf of those who would trust Him as Lord and Saviour. Death could not hold Him; He rose from the dead in three days, just as He said He would. Whenever we look back on this event we rejoice because Jesus' death and resurrection have given us life, not only temporarily but for eternity. *"For God chose to save us through our Lord Jesus Christ, not to pour out his anger on us. Christ died for us so that, whether we are dead or alive when he returns, we can live with him forever. So encourage each other and build each other up, just as you are already doing." (1 Thessalonians 5:9–11).*

APRIL 3

Friend of Sinners

I have a friend who loves to pick up hitch-hikers. He told me how he picked up someone he knew who had been on a long drunk, sleeping in the bush and obviously not having an opportunity for a bath for a long time. My friend had just bought a new car and he was not in the least worried about the fellow jumping in and possibly dirtying his new car seats. While on the road, my friend felt led to pray for the fellow, which he did. This brought the fellow new hope, and he hasn't had a drink since.

As we look in the Bible at how Jesus lived, we see that He was a friend of sinners too: *"While Jesus was having dinner at Matthew's house, many tax collectors and sinners came and ate with him and his disciples" (Matthew 9:10, ESV).*

Jesus was criticized by the Pharisees, who were the religious leaders of the day, and Jesus told them, *"I have come to call not those who think they are righteous, but those who know they are sinners" (Matthew 9:13).* Jesus was not repulsed by these people but was attracted to them, because He loved them.

As we reflect on the death and resurrection of Jesus, we see that He was crucified with sinners. Two criminals were also crucified one on each side of Him: *"Those crucified with him also heaped insults on him" (Mark 15:32, NIV).* One of the criminals later changed his mind and cried out, *"'Jesus, remember me when you come into your kingdom.' Jesus answered him, 'Truly I tell you, today you will be with me in paradise'" (Luke 23:42–43, NIV).*

Who did Jesus hang out with? It's quite obvious He was attracted to those who knew they were sinners. Those who thought they were righteous were deceived and thought they didn't need Him (Romans 3:23). As a matter of fact, they were so intimidated by Him that they had Him crucified.

If we find ourselves as sinners needing forgiveness, we have a friend in Jesus. He already knows our sins and loves us so much that He died so that our sins could be forgiven (John 3:16). Like the fellow my friend picked up, or the thief on the cross, Jesus wants us to turn away from our sins. Only He can truly deliver us.

Are we willing to leave our sinful life and follow Him?

Jesus said, *"However, those the Father has given me will come to me, and I will never reject them" (John 6:37, NIV).*

APRIL 4

In My Place

Maybe you saw the news report about the young girl who was playing with her friends when she noticed a runaway SUV coming upon them. This girl may or may not have had time to think of the consequences, but her unselfish love for her friends was obvious. She didn't want to see them hurt, so she pushed them out of the way. They were saved from injury, but she was run over and killed by the vehicle. She could have run out of the way to save herself, but she rather risked her life to save her friends. The Bible tells us, *"Greater love has no one than this: to lay down one's life for one's friends" (John 15:13, NIV).*

This young girl's actions remind me of Jesus, who came to die in the place of all who would put their trust in Him. He came not only to extend our earthly life but to give us eternal life. He could have called thousands of angels to rescue Him, but He willingly laid down His life. His mission was to die as the substitute for sinners (Matthew 16:21). We deserved death; He gave life (Romans 6:23; Revelation 20:15). Without His willing sacrifice, there was no hope for the human race. He came to earth, was born into humanity to be scorned, beaten, and to die on an ugly Roman cross at the hands of the religious and political leaders of the day (Luke 24:45–47). He died in my place! This is good news for repentant sinners, not only at Easter but every day of the year (2 Corinthians 5:18–21; John 1:12, 3:16)! *"You see, at just the right time, when we were still powerless, Christ died for the ungodly. Very rarely will anyone die for a righteous person, though for a good person someone might possibly dare to die. But God demonstrates his own love for us in this: While we were still sinners, Christ died for us." (Romans 5:6–8, NIV).*

APRIL 5

Facing Our Sin

W hy is it that thieves hide when they steal, sneaking around to take something when nobody is looking? Why does criminal activity increase at night? Why do people often hide their faces when they're brought before justice? We're ashamed when we're caught in our sin, and we don't want to take responsibility for it, so we tend to make ourselves look better than we are. We don't want anyone to know how short we really fall, even of our own expectations. Though the Bible clearly states that we're all sinners and fall short of God's requirement (Romans 3:23), still we claim our innocence. We claim we're doing well, put on an air of righteousness and put as great a distance between ourselves and our sin as possible (John 3:19–21). The problem with sin is that I'm right in the middle of it, just as the "i" is in the middle of the word! I am condemned by my own sin, and there is no way of getting away with it, no matter how I try.

Though we tend not to face our sins, Jesus faced them head on. He not only sees our sin, but He even went as far as taking our sins, our guilt, our shame, and the death penalty that we deserved upon Himself. He was whipped until His back was raw. He was spit upon. He was scorned and ridiculed, denied by His followers, even betrayed by one of them (John 18). He was nailed to a cruel Roman cross and crucified, with a crown of thorns placed on his head, naked, an open spectacle for all to see (John 19). Though He could have called thousands of angels to rescue Him, He died there as a criminal for the sins of everyone who would believe in Him and receive Him, so we could be forgiven (Luke 23:34; John 1:12, 3:16). *"For God made Christ, who never sinned, to be the offering for our sin, so that we could be made right with God through Christ" (2 Corinthians 5:21).*

He wants us to repent, to face our sins and take them to Him. He's willing to forgive and restore our relationship with Him. What will we do with Jesus? Will we put our faith in Him as our Lord and Saviour, or will we remain in our sins and remain condemned?

"Whoever believes in the Son has eternal life, but whoever rejects the Son will not see life, for God's wrath remains on him" (John 3:36, NIV).

APRIL 6

Why?

At an early age, children learn the "why" word. Enquiring about the mysteries of life unfolding around them, they ask, "Why, why, why?" Now as we get older, there still remain many "why" questions. Why did God take my loved one? Why this pain? Why this unexpected financial burden? Though we can learn much by questioning our situations, some say it's not wise or it's a sin to ask God "Why?" Though sometimes this may be the case, Jesus, just before He died on the cross, said, *"My God, my God, why have you abandoned me?" (Matthew 27:46).* If Jesus, the perfect, sinless Son of God (Hebrews 4:15), asked God the Father why, then it can't always be wrong.

Jesus had willingly gone to the cross to suffer tremendously, to bleed and die for the sins of all who would put their trust in Him: *"For God made Christ, who never sinned, to be the offering for our sin, so that we could be made right with God through Christ" (2 Corinthians 5:21).* Every kind of our ugly, wretched sins—adultery, lies, hate, murder, every selfish malicious act, word and thought—and our guilt and shame were put on Him. The Holy Father God could not look at the sin; He turned His face away, and Jesus, in His humanity (Philippians 2:6–7) and feeling abandoned, cried out, "Why?" Though He didn't get an immediate answer, a few moments later, just before His last breath, He said, *"Father, I entrust my spirit into your hands!" (Luke 23:46).*

We can learn from Jesus' example. When the why questions come up and the answers aren't there, we can entrust ourselves, our situation, our questions, and all into the hands of Jesus the Son of Almighty God. Jesus said, *"In this world you will have trouble. But take heart! I have overcome the world" (John 16:33, NIV).*

Offence of the Cross

You may have noticed the front-page article in the March 29, 2023 issue of *Houston Today* informing us that Houston council decided to spend over $20,000 to modify some display poles, which supposedly resembled "biblical crosses." In light of this, the following are a few things to think about.

The cross was used by the Romans as a horrific instrument of public execution of criminals. God's Word proclaims of Jesus: *"When he was hung on the cross, he took upon himself the curse for our wrongdoing. For it is written in the Scriptures, 'Cursed is everyone who is hung on a tree'" (Galatians 3:13)*. Yet today some people display, and even wear, a cross as a symbol, as more of a blessing than a curse, because as the Scriptures above state, Jesus *"took upon himself the curse of our wrongdoing"* when He suffered and died on the cross! Thus, the cross has become a symbol of the love, mercy, and grace of God manifested by Jesus taking our place, taking the curse we deserved upon Himself!

Sadly, to some, anything that even resembles a cross becomes an offense and needs to be obliterated. Yet the fact remains that Jesus died on the cross for anyone who puts their trust in Him. The symbol or the cross itself is not sacred, but Jesus' vicarious act of love that occurred on the cross is the only means by which anyone can be saved from the eternal judgement of God. To ignore or take offence to the cross of Jesus has an eternal cost, much more costly than obliterating everything that might remind us of it—such as the power poles we drive past every day!

God's Word is clear: *"There is salvation in no one else! God has given no other name under heaven by which we must be saved" (Acts 4:12)*.

"The message of the cross is foolish to those who are headed for destruction! But we who are being saved know it is the very power of God" (1 Corinthians 1:18).

Ransomed!

The May 2017 cyber attack on thousands of government and big business computer networks around the world has made everyone frightfully aware of the vulnerability of the internet to hackers who would like to cause havoc and destroy internet capabilities.

The latest attack by a ransomware worm called "WannaCry" shut down computer systems in the UK health system, Fed Ex in the US, and many other networks in Russia, China, and around the world. Some estimate hundreds of thousands of computers were affected. The hackers then asked for a ransom of $300 for a fix to unlock the computers again, yet experts say the fix was a sham; the money to fix it was wasted.

We have a much more grievous problem that has infected every human heart. That problem is sin. Sin is universal and shows up in our denial of the true condition of our sinful hearts and ultimately in rebellion against our Creator God. God's Word clearly states: *"For everyone has sinned …" (Romans 3:23).* Sin is inherent in every human heart and brings death not only to our bodies but also to marriages, friendships, interpersonal relationships, and especially to our relationship to God: *"You were dead because of your sins …" (Colossians 2:13).* Just as many people woke up to dead computers because of the WannaCry worm, sin has infected every human heart and brought the sentence of death upon us.

God, because of His great compassion and love, desires a relationship with His people and saw this desperate and hopeless state of death looming over us. We were unable to help ourselves. A ransom had to be paid to forgive us of our sins, to deliver us from the grip of death, and to give us life.

"For you know that it was not with perishable things such as silver or gold that you were redeemed from the empty way of life handed down to you from your ancestors, but with the precious blood of Christ, a lamb without blemish or defect. He was chosen before the creation of the world, but was revealed in these last times for your sake." (1 Peter 1:18–20, NIV).

The one and only true ransom has been paid. Will we in faith receive or reject this precious gift from our loving God?

"For the wages of sin is death but the free gift of God is eternal life through Christ Jesus our Lord" (Romans 6:23).

APRIL 9

How Much?

He always seemed to have something for sale in his front yard. He was a local wheeler dealer looking for a bargain at every opportunity. This time he wanted to buy our young heifer calf. "No use wasting time bargaining," he said. "What's your bottom price?" Is this not how we usually are? It may be something we value, something we think we need, but we don't want to pay more than we have to for it. We want the most for the least price.

Yet the Bible tells us that Jesus willingly paid the ultimate price for all who would believe and trust in Him. He wasn't looking for a bargain; He wasn't waiting for a deal. He was determined to pay for the sins of the world at the price of His own lifeblood. He was rejected, scorned, beaten, brutally whipped, and nailed to a Roman cross for us! Not because we deserved it, not because we earned it, not even because we were good enough, but it was because of His abundant, selfless, overflowing love that He spilled His life blood for us on an old rugged cross some two thousand years ago. Though we were spiritually dead, desperate, hopeless, wretched, and blind, He freely paid the highest price so that we, through faith in Him, could be forgiven of all our sins and come into a living, eternal, relationship with Him!

"Very rarely will anyone die for a righteous person, though for a good person someone might possibly dare to die. But God demonstrates his own love for us in this: While we were still sinners, Christ died for us. Since we have now been justified by his blood, how much more shall we be saved from God's wrath through him! (Romans 5:7–9, NIV).

APRIL 10

Criminals

Sometimes we hear of a rash of break-ins; people have their property broken into and their goods stolen. The whole community is relieved when the thieves are caught and brought to justice. During the time of Roman rule, the sentence for this type of activity was often a cruel death by crucifixion.

When Jesus was unjustly sentenced to be crucified by Pontius Pilate, two criminals were also sentenced to the same fate. God's Word, the Bible, informs us these three were crucified that day, Jesus in the middle and the two criminals, one on each side of Him.

The apostle Matthew informs us that both these criminals scorned Jesus as they hung on their crosses waiting to die a slow and agonizing death (Matthew 27:44). Yet an amazing revelation by Luke speaks of one of the criminals rebuking the other, saying, *"'Don't you fear God,' he said, 'since you are under the same sentence? We are punished justly, for we are getting what our deeds deserve. But this man has done nothing wrong.' Then he said, 'Jesus, remember me when you come into your kingdom'"* (Luke 23:40–42, NIV). Obviously, he had initially scorned Jesus but changed his mind while hanging on the cross next to his Saviour. He recognized his sinful life and the rightful judgement of death he deserved. He saw that Jesus was his only hope for eternal life, and he called out to Him for mercy!

Jesus' forgiving and compassionate answer shows the loving heart of God for sinners, His power to forgive sins and give eternal life to all who believe in Him! *Truly I tell you, today you will be with me in paradise" (Luke 23:43, NIV).*

Just as the criminals on the cross, we have all sinned (Romans 3:23). The Bible clearly teaches *"For the wages of sin is death, but the free gift of God is eternal life through Christ Jesus our Lord"* and *"Everyone who calls on the name of the Lord will be saved" (Romans 6:23, 10:13).*

Have you called out to Him? If you do, He will hear you and save you, as He did the criminal on the cross that day!

Betrayed

Have you ever been betrayed, especially by close friends? I have, and it was deeply painful and caused me to question very seriously whom I can trust. Whether we've been betrayed by a best friend, a corporation, a religious leader, or even the government, the feelings of distrust most definitely will rise up within us. The pain of the feelings surely depends on the closeness of the relationship and the depth of the betrayal.

Though all hope may seem to be lost, could there be any relief from being betrayed? Could anything good come out of this? If a very close and trusted friend lets us down, who can we really trust? The pain of betrayal may drive us to despair, not able to trust anyone anymore, or perhaps we'll be drawn to Jesus, the One who was betrayed by His very own disciples. Judas betrayed Him to death (Luke 22:47,48) and Peter denied he even knew Him (Luke 22:54-62). The Bible clearly states that Jesus, though betrayed by men, put His trust in His heavenly Father. Among His very last words before He died on the cross were *"Father, into your hands I commit my spirit!" (Luke 23:46, ESV)*. Jesus encouraged us to trust God the Father and to trust Him: *"Let not your hearts be troubled. Believe in God; believe also in me" (John 14:1, ESV)*. Though Jesus was betrayed by those close to Him, He stayed true to His Word and went to the cross so we could be forgiven of our sins and have a personal relationship with God!

May we not allow betrayal of people to drive us into the anguish of despair and hopelessness, but let us turn our eyes to Jesus, the only person we can really trust! He said, *"'I will never leave you nor forsake you.' So we can confidently say, 'The Lord is my helper; I will not fear; what can man do to me?'" (Hebrews 13:5–6, ESV)*.

APRIL 12

Happiness & Joy

I wasn't very happy when I cut my finger while changing my tires. Nor was I happy when my back was sore due to the extra strain from lifting the tires, which, by the way, seem to get heavier as I get older! Come to think of it, the pain of a kidney stone didn't bring happiness either. It seems I'm only happy when what happens around me goes my way.

Joy is something completely different. This morning with my sore back and a bandage on my finger, with God's Word in my hand and a prayer on my heart, I consider how amazing our heavenly Father is, that He would send His one and only Son to die for me! He took my sins upon Himself—every gross sin that I ever did, the sins that separated Him from me! The One who created everything became one of us, was whipped and scorned and beaten. Soldiers stripped Him of His clothes, stretched His arms out, and nailed His hands and feet to a cruel Roman cross. While bleeding there for us, He cried out, *"Father, forgive them, for they do not know what they are doing"* (Luke 23:34, NIV). This was definitely not a happy time for Jesus, yet *"For the joy set before him he endured the cross, scorning its shame, and sat down at the right hand of the throne of God"* (Hebrews 12:2, NIV). He had joy because, filled with the Holy Spirit, He knew that His painful obedience would bring many to Himself! Through His suffering, He made it possible for sinful humanity to have a relationship with Him! As we follow and obey Him, we too can have joy, despite what's happening around us!

"But the Holy Spirit produces this kind of fruit in our lives: love, joy, peace, patience, kindness, goodness, faithfulness, gentleness, and self-control" (Galatians 5:22); *"Consider it pure joy, my brothers and sisters, whenever you face trials of many kinds, because you know that the testing of your faith produces perseverance"* (James 1:2–3, NIV).

APRIL 13

Made Right

A city councillor thought he would take his case to the courts. He didn't feel he deserved the charge of speeding or the fine attached to it.

When the judge asked at what speed he was travelling when the police stopped him, he said he was only going three kilometres over the speed limit. The judge immediately interrupted him and told him he was guilty by his own admission. He was guilty even though he somehow thought he wasn't!

Sometimes rather than examining ourselves, we come to the conclusion that we aren't that bad, and we justify our actions. God's Word clearly states that every person has broken the law (Romans 3:23) and that we are all guilty before God. We may think we're doing well by our own estimation, but in the sight of God, who is absolutely holy and without sin, we are all law breakers desperately in need of His mercy and grace: *"Obviously, the law applies to those to whom it was given, for its purpose is to keep people from having excuses, and to show that the entire world is guilty before God"* (Romans 3:19). So what's the solution? How can we be made right with God if we're all proven to be guilty? The Holy Scriptures are clear: *"Therefore, since we have been made right in God's sight by faith, we have peace with God because of what Jesus Christ our Lord has done for us ... And since we have been made right in God's sight by the blood of Christ, he will certainly save us from God's condemnation"* (Romans 5:1, 9).

Who do we have faith in? In ourselves and our own feeble and tainted efforts, or in the forgiveness offered by God through Jesus' death on the cross?

APRIL 14

Can't Help It!

When I purchased my first new car, I could hardly wait to tell my friends! I showed it off to almost everyone I met! I'd always wanted a new car, so I explained the details of it: the motor, the accessories, the tires, the paint job, and how it handled. It seemed I couldn't help but share my new possession with others!

The disciples of Jesus thought they had nothing to celebrate. Jesus had just suffered a cruel and agonizing death on the cross, and their hopes of Him becoming their political leader had vanished. Some of the disciples had witnessed Him saying *"It is Finished"* just before He took His last breath. They saw the Roman soldiers stab their spear into His side as water and blood poured out. They saw His battered and bloody body taken down from the cross and put into a newly crafted tomb. A large rock closed its entrance, and a contingent of Roman soldiers guarded it.

Then on the third day, He rose from the dead. They personally saw the empty tomb, and He physically appeared to them numerous times. Jesus had risen from the dead! Death could not hold the Author of life! They saw Him with their own eyes, spoke with Him, touched Him, and ate with Him. They heard Jesus say He was leaving this earth to intercede for them from the right hand of our Father in heaven. He promised He would send an Advocate, the Holy Spirit, to live in them and to empower them to be His representatives here on earth. So they boldly spoke to everyone they could about the One who had given them life!

The religious leaders were jealous of them and threatened them with severe punishment if they kept on telling others about Jesus! Yet they boldly told them, *"Which is right in God's eyes: to listen to you, or to him? You be the judges! As for us, we cannot help speaking about what we have seen and heard" (Acts 4:19–20, NIV)*. My excitement about the new car was only temporary, yet the new life Jesus has given is eternal. I can't help but share this with others!

APRIL 15

He Is Risen!

It looked like she was sleeping and would wake up at any moment. It was surreal, yet she had died, and not even an earthquake could wake her up. According to the people who knew her, she had faith in Jesus. She had died in peace, knowing that the moment she left her earthly body, she would enter the presence of her Lord Jesus in that wonderful eternal home He had already prepared for her ahead of time. One day, Jesus would resurrect this old body and give her a new one.

Why do we as Christians have this hope? Because Jesus, the Creator of all things, the Author and Finisher of our faith, has the power over sin and death. Some two thousand years ago, He willingly gave His life on a cruel Roman cross so we could be forgiven all our sins. His body was placed in a tomb, and three days later He was raised from the dead. There was a strong earthquake, an angel rolled the stone from the entrance of the tomb, and the guards fainted. The angel proclaimed, *"Don't be afraid ... he is risen from the dead" (Matthew 28:5–6)*. Death couldn't hold the Author of life. All life is from Him—every breath we take and every heartbeat, whether we recognize it or not. He purchased eternal life for all who believe in, trust in, and receive Him. He proved that He had the power to do this by rising from the dead. This is our hope, this is our consolation, even in the face of death.

Just before raising Lazarus from the dead, Jesus consoled Martha with these words*: "I am the resurrection and the life. The one who believes in me will live, even though they die; and whoever lives by believing in me will never die. Do you believe this?" (John 11:25–26, NIV)*.

"Christ died for our sins, just as the scriptures said. He was buried, and was raised from the dead on the third day, just as the scriptures said ... everyone who belongs to Christ will be given new life" (1 Corinthians 15:4, 22).

This is why we proclaim, "He is risen! He is risen indeed!"

APRIL 16

Not a Ghost

After my uncle passed away some years ago, my aunt said she would hear footsteps at the time that he used to come home for lunch, and she could hear the back door open up when he used to come home after work. Then she would look and he wasn't there; the door was still closed. Her mind was so conditioned by his presence for some forty years that she'd expect him at certain times when he was actually no longer there.

After Jesus was crucified and had risen from the dead, He was seen by His disciples as well as hundreds of other people (1 Corinthians 15:5). Some say it was just wishful thinking by minds conditioned to His presence for three years. Others say the disciples purposely make up a story to gain credibility for themselves, or that it was only a spiritual resurrection, and His body didn't really rise from the dead.

Jesus' appearance to His disciples is recorded in God's Word. He said to them, *"Look at my hands. Look at my feet. You can see that it's really me. Touch me and make sure that I am not a ghost, because ghosts do not have bodies as you see that I do"* (Luke 24:39, NIV). The tomb was empty; only the grave clothes were left behind (John 20:1–10). He had risen bodily from the grave. He was dead, and now He is alive! It was not their imagination. He was not a ghost. He had actually physically and spiritually risen from the dead. The grave could not hold Him! Death could not keep its grip on Him!

If Jesus hadn't been able to raise Himself from the dead, He wouldn't have the power to raise anyone else. Had He not risen from the dead, there would be no hope for any person to have eternal life (1 Corinthians 15:12–19). But He, being the very Author of life itself, proved who He was by rising from the dead. Just before raising his friend Lazarus from the dead, Jesus reassured Lazarus' sister Martha with these words: *"I am the resurrection and the life. Whoever believes in me, though he die, yet shall he live, and everyone who lives and believes in me shall never die. Do you believe this?"* (John 11:25–26, NIV).

I am assured, though my uncle is no longer present on this earth, through faith in Jesus, he is present with the Lord.

"Then when our dying bodies have been transformed into bodies that will never die, this Scripture will be fulfilled: 'Death is swallowed up in victory. O death, where is your victory? O death, where is your sting'" (1 Corinthians 15:54–55).

APRIL 17

Encountering the Risen One

She was very devout and performed meticulously all the rituals required by her religion. Ceremonial washings, numerous prayers throughout the day, and reading from her holy book were among the ceremonies she did as an attempt to get through to her deity. However, no matter how dedicated she was in her religious life, she always came up empty. There was a huge palpable void in her life that she couldn't fill.

With the added burden of taking care of her bedridden mother, who was suffering with MS, she decided the best thing would be to end her life. She and her mother made a pact and set a date on which they would both commit suicide. Then everything changed! That day her mother heard the Good News that Jesus, the only Son of God, had come to save her! She, in faith, committed her life to Jesus Christ! Furious, her daughter went to bed, deciding to put off their death pact for another day.

In the morning, she heard someone walking in their apartment. To her astonishment, it was her mother, walking about without any symptoms of MS. Upon thorough medical investigation, the doctors were amazed. There was no sign of MS in her body. Jesus had not only forgiven her mother of her sins and given her eternal life, but He had also physically healed her! She had met the risen Christ! Jesus had rescued her from death and given her life![5]

The apostle Paul speaks of his encounter with Jesus on the road to Damascus, which changed him from a religious Pharisee and hateful persecutor of those who followed Christ to a loving apostle and faithful servant of Jesus. Throughout the ages and to this very day, people, including myself, testify of radically changed lives because of their encounter with the living, risen Christ. No religious activity, no matter how sincere, can fill that void in every human heart. Only Jesus can forgive our sins, only Jesus can fill that empty void, only Jesus can rescue us from death and give us a full and meaningful life for all eternity!

"But because of his great love for us, God, who is rich in mercy, made us alive with Christ even when we were dead in transgressions—it is by grace you have been saved" (Ephesians 2:4–5, NIV); *"We are made right with God by placing our faith in Jesus Christ. And this is true for everyone who believes, no matter who we are"* (Romans 3:22).

---

5 Testimony shared on Voice of the Martyrs "I Am N" series.

APRIL 18

New Life!

When we consider Jesus' resurrection from the dead, the Holy Scriptures remind us that He is the very Author of life (Hebrews 3:15)! He is the Creator who spoke everything into existence (Genesis 1:1–2:1; John 1:1–4), and everything is sustained and held together by Him (Colossians 1:15–17)! Without Him, we can do nothing (John 15:5).

Early on that Sunday morning, as three women went to anoint Jesus' body in the tomb, their immediate concern was *"Who will roll away the stone for us from the entrance to the tomb?" (Mark 16:3)*. This was an impossible task for the women, but as they approached the tomb, they were in for a surprise! Not only was the stone already rolled away, but they were informed by the men standing there, *"Why are you looking among the dead for someone who is alive? He isn't here! He is risen from the dead!" (Luke 24:5–6)*. Jesus had risen from the dead, just as He had promised! Death could not hold the Author of life! Their concern of moving the stone evaporated in the reality that Jesus had conquered death! He was alive!

Sometimes our immediate worries—maybe our health, our finances, our unbelief, or possibly questions of where we will spend eternity—preoccupy our daily lives.

When I see the risen Saviour, all of my worries and stresses vanish in the realization of the eternal life He offers to all who believe in Him! Then we can rejoice with the Apostle Paul, as he encourages the believers in Corinth: *"We know that God, who raised the Lord Jesus, will also raise us with Jesus and present us to himself together with you ... He died for everyone so that those who receive his new life will no longer live for themselves. Instead, they will live for Christ, who died and was raised for them ... This means that anyone who belongs to Christ has become a new person. The old life is gone; a new life has begun!" (2 Corinthians 4:14, 5:15,17)*.

Tell Peter

When Jesus predicted that He was soon going to die on the cross, Peter emphatically resisted Him, saying this would never happen. In response, Jesus severely rebuked him (Matthew 16:22). Later, just before He was arrested, Jesus predicted that Peter would deny Him three times. Peter again forcefully responded that he would never do such a thing (Matthew 26:33–35). Then when Jesus was arrested and was being interrogated by the religious leaders, Peter, when confronted by those observing this, cursed and denied that he ever knew Him, just as Jesus had prophesied would happen. Immediately Peter heard the rooster crow twice, just as Jesus said it would. At this point, Jesus looked Peter in the eye (Luke 22:61), and Peter was broken, deeply grieving for what he had done. Cut to the heart, he went away, weeping bitterly (Matthew 26:69–75).

I can't imagine how long those three days seemed to Peter as he grieved over his indisputable denial of his Lord.

Then the women, having gone to the tomb where Jesus' body had been laid, were confronted by angels, one of which said, *"Now go and tell his disciples, including Peter, that Jesus is going ahead of you to Galilee. You will see him there, just as he told you before he died" (Mark 16:7)*. Peter was specifically mentioned by name! God still had a plan for him!

At Galilee, after having breakfast with the disciples on the beach, Jesus confronted Peter twice, saying, *"Do you love* (in Greek—agape) *me,"* meaning do you love me enough to lay down your life for me? Peter answered *"… you know I love* (in Greek—phileo) *you,"* meaning you know that I love you as a brother or a very special friend. Finally, the third time Jesus asked Peter if he loved (phileo) Him. Peter was hurt by this, knowing his numerous previous bold yet failed defences of Jesus answered that he loved Jesus as a good friend (phileo). Peter had been humbled by his impulsive earlier responses, knowing he didn't have the power within himself to answer, "Yes, Lord, I love (agape) you," as he in himself didn't possess the power to lay down his life for Jesus! (Scriptures from John 21:15–17, comments in brackets mine.)

Yet Jesus commissioned Peter, saying, *"Feed my sheep."* God soon empowered Peter by the Holy Spirit to love Jesus with the deepest love possible—agape—to lay down his life for Jesus!

If there was hope for Peter, there is hope for me! There is hope for you!

APRIL 20

Why Did They Kill Him?

As we read in the Scriptures of the abuse, scorn, beatings, and the excruciating pain and suffering Jesus experienced on a Roman cross some two thousand years ago, one wonders why anyone would do this to Him. What had He done wrong to deserve such treatment? He never killed or hurt anyone. He had healed those plagued with sickness, calmed deadly storms, delivered people from demons, and even raised the dead back to life! What would motivate such hate?

Some time before He was crucified, Jesus, speaking to a religious leader, explained, *"This is the verdict: Light has come into the world, but people loved darkness instead of light because their deeds were evil" (John 3:19, NIV).* Jesus knew He wouldn't be accepted and would be vehemently opposed by many because He, as the light of the world (John 8:12), would expose the truth of each person's sin! The Pharisees were jealous because they were losing their religious grip on the people. Pontius Pilate condemned an innocent man to retain his power; the tax collectors wanted to continue to rip off the people for their own gain, and most of the populace shrunk away as Jesus called out sins such as adultery, lying, cheating, hate, unforgiveness, and rebellion. People chose darkness rather than light—their only choice was to try to snuff out the light, thus they joined in the throng calling out *"Crucify him!"* (John 19:6, 15).

We are confronted today with the same decision. What will we do with Jesus? Will we remain in the darkness of our sinful lives, or will we come into the light and confess our sin and trust in Him?

"But whoever lives by the truth comes into the light, so that it may be seen plainly that what they have done has been done in the sight of God ... Whoever believes in the Son has eternal life, but whoever rejects the Son will not see life, for God's wrath remains on them." (John 3:19, 21, NIV).

Darkness or light, what will we choose?

APRIL 21

Success

Our teacher in grade six told us that to be successful, we had better get an education or we would become "ditch diggers." The idea of becoming wealthy, educated, or having a name in the community was taught as being synonymous with being successful.

When I had a business and landed a big contract I thought, *God is good to me. I'm successful!* In many ways this made my life easier. I could provide for my family. I could buy things I needed and give to those in need. Ah success, sweet success!

I have a friend who has a genetic disorder. She has Down Syndrome. She's a wonderful person. I haven't visited her for some time now, but when I do, I often get a friendly hug from her and a magnificent smile. She loves to watch hockey games with her dad and cheers for both teams! She doesn't have a job but prays a lot, and her mom told me that she prays for me every day! By the definition of success mentioned above, is there any chance that she might have success in life?

One day when Jesus was standing by the temple watching people giving their offerings, He observed some who had great wealth give lots of money. He also observed a widow give a couple of small coins. He said to His disciples *"Truly I tell you, this poor widow has put more into the treasury than all the others. They all gave out of their wealth; but she, out of her poverty, put in everything—all she had to live on"* (Mark 12:43–44, NIV).

Who had success here? Jesus makes it clear that the poor widow was the successful one; by giving her all, she gave more than all the others combined! Amazing!

Sometimes I think we get life all messed up by thinking it's all about us. If I'm doing well, if things are going my way, maybe I can give to God and others from my excess. Yet God knows exactly how much we've really given. I believe my friend could very well be much more successful than me; maybe she's more successful than all of the community combined. It's not so much what we have that counts with God but what we do with what we have that really can make us successful. We can only do this as we completely surrender our lives to God as the widow did.

Success is not having it my way, but God having His way with me!

APRIL 22

Light and Life

Spring is my favourite time of year. The days get longer. The sun begins to thaw the snow, and the bare ground appears, first in small patches then throughout the whole yard. My wife planted some crocus bulbs in the lawn a number of years ago, and every spring they pop up and bloom, sometimes in a place right next to the snow. I look forward to the time when the first leaves appear on the poplar and aspen trees. The trees seem dead, then within a short time they spring to life. The valley becomes green and teeming with life. The light has caused the valley to come to life again! Flowers bloom everywhere, from the small low bush blueberries to the peonies and the Rudolph flowering crab apple tree! I can hardly wait!

Have you ever considered what the world would be like without the sun or without the energy it produces? The Bible tells us Jesus is the creator of this beautiful world: the sun, the moon, the whole universe. *"Through him all things were made; without him nothing was made that has been made"* (*John 1:3, NIV*). It goes on to say that Jesus is *"The true light that gives light to everyone"* (*John 1:9a, NIV*).

Without Jesus there would be nothing but darkness—no universe, no stars, no sun, no earth, no trees, no flowers, nothing. We wouldn't exist. Without Him, there would be no spiritual life either. Jesus (the Word) also came to give us spiritual life: *"In him was life, and the life was the light of men"* (*John 1:4, ESV*). We're not complete unless we have His spiritual life living within us.

Even though the sun shines on us, gives us light, and warms us on the outside, we often forget about the Son who made it all. When we try to live life without Him, life seems so dark. There seems to be no purpose in life, and despair creeps deep into our soul. We become cold on the inside.

God's desire is that we'll turn to Him for life, for purpose, for true meaning. When we do surrender to him, the Bible says, *"From his abundance we have all received one gracious blessing after another"* (*John 1:16*).

Just as the world around us is filled with the beauty of nature, our hearts will be filled with the love, joy, and peace of God. Jesus, the light, will dispel the darkness and warm our hearts.

"The light shines in the darkness, and the darkness has not overcome it" (*John 1:5, ESV*).

APRIL 23

The True Light

The lights were out in Smithers and Telkwa. The power company said it was due to a downed power line. The affected stores had to shut down; it was too dark to do business, and their cash registers and credit card machines didn't work either. Few were prepared with backup generators.

Much of what we absolutely rely on we take for granted, then suddenly everything becomes dark and we're not ready.

Jesus spoke about a time when some people, who took the life they were given for granted, would be thrown into outer darkness, where there will be weeping and gnashing of teeth (Matthew 8:12, 22:13, 25:29–30). This is a serious warning, yet it's a warning with a message of hope for all who will turn to Jesus Christ, the Creator, Sustainer, and Saviour. He holds everything together; without Him nothing in all creation would exist (Colossians 1:15–17). Every breath of every person, even you and me, is from Him (Acts 17:24–26). He is the true light who came to dispel the darkness. He has all authority in His hands. When we call out to Him and put our trust in Him, His light will shine in us no matter how great the darkness around us (John 1:1–5; 2 Corinthians 4:5–7). *"Some sat in darkness and deepest gloom, imprisoned in iron chains of misery. They rebelled against the words of God, scorning the counsel of the Most High. "LORD, help!" they cried in their trouble, and He saved them from their distress. He led them from the darkness and deepest gloom; He snapped their chains. Let them praise the LORD for His great love and for the wonderful things He has done for them." (Psalm 107:10–11, 13–15)*

Let us call out to Him now, while there is still time.

APRIL 24

Who's in Charge?

This morning I look out the window at the beautiful sunrise, the trembling aspen leaves fluttering in the wind, and hear the cheerful chirp of the robin as it greets the dawn. What an amazing sight to see the hand of the Creator through His creation!

Then I ponder the day before me. I have plans. I have ideas. I have an agenda. I want to get these things done. I come before my Maker and ask His help in fulfilling my agenda. Then something inside me says, "Who's in charge here? Is it me, or is it the Almighty God? Have I checked what His agenda might be? Have I surrendered my plans, my ways, my will to Him, or have I assumed that my way is the best?"

This is how so often we go astray. We want control, so we attempt to use the Almighty to help us fulfill our plans. The Holy Scriptures clearly teach that the ways of men are not the ways of God, and the only way we can know God's ways is through His Word (Isaiah 55:10–13; Psalm 119:11; Hebrews 4:12).

We human beings are the only part of the creation made in the image of God (Genesis 1:27). As God's image bearers, we were given the power to choose, while the rest of creation—the sun, the trembling aspen, and the robin, for example, though struggling under the pain of this broken world (Romans 8:18–22)—essentially has no choice but to obey.

Only as we tremble before Him in humble surrender and obedience, by the power of His Holy Spirit, will we produce much good and lasting fruit in our lives (Galatians 5:22). On the contrary, our own way, be it religious or secular, will lead only to heartache and despair. We will actually find ourselves working against Jesus Christ, our Creator (Galatians 5:16–18).

This is the choice, to live in my own corrupted, broken, temporary ways, or in His good, perfect, and eternal will.

"Seek the Lord while He may be found; call upon Him while He is near; let the wicked forsake his way, and the unrighteous man his thoughts; let him return to the Lord, that He may have compassion on him, and to our God, for He will abundantly pardon. For my thoughts are not your thoughts, neither are your ways my ways, declares the Lord. For as the heavens are higher than the earth, so are my ways higher than your ways and my thoughts than your thoughts." (Isaiah 55:6–9, ESV).

Old Dog

Have you ever heard the phrase "You can't teach an old dog new tricks"? I once thought this was true, until experiencing a few lessons from our twelve-year-old dog! Though she has a pleasant demeanour, we were hoping she would keep the deer away from our garden and shrubs, but she didn't seem to get the message and would just look at them and do nothing. So as the deer proliferated in the area, they would gather in our yard, helping themselves to whatever satisfied their taste buds. In an attempt to save our shrubs and plants, I, with the dog at my side, chased them away. Suddenly she realized she could do the same! Now when she sees a deer, she barks and scares them back over the fence, then comes back wagging her tail, seeking an affirmation for what she has accomplished!

Some people think that when we get into our senior years, we too stop learning and stop being useful to God. We think that's just the way we are, and we're just too old to change. But recent research has proven that the human brain remains plastic and able to change until the day we die. We're never too old to change our ways!

The Bible is clear that God created humanity for His glory and that He wants to transform us, young and old, to become more like Him! This happens by allowing God to renew our minds (Romans 12:2)!

It's never too late to surrender our lives and allow God to change us into people who will follow, honour, and glorify Him.

"And in the last days it shall be, God declares, that I will pour out my Spirit on all flesh, and your sons and your daughters shall prophesy, and your young men shall see visions, and your old men shall dream dreams; even on my male servants and female servants in those days I will pour out my Spirit, and they shall prophesy." (Acts 2:17–18, ESV).

APRIL 26

Conspiracy

A healthy fear of the pandemic keeps us physically distancing from others, practising basic rules of hygiene, and following the doctor's orders! We don't want to contract COVID-19. We don't want our loved ones, especially those more vulnerable, to contract the disease. We don't want to be sick; we do not want to suffer; we don't want to hasten our death! Thus, we isolate and do our best to "flatted the curve" to not overload the medical system. A certain amount of fear can be healthy because it keeps us from harm. But if we're honest, many fears pervade our hearts these days that actually do us more harm than good. One of these may be the fear of conspiracies of men. Some say the coronavirus was humanly engineered and purposefully let loose to cause mayhem upon humanity. Others say that it accidentally escaped a lab in Wuhan, China. Others say it's all hyped up and a plot for certain leaders to seize control over the populace. These are only a small sample of ideas circulating the globe these days! Some may be true, yet even if they are, should we allow them to occupy our time and permeate our thoughts?

Conspiracies are nothing new! Some three thousand years ago, the prophet Isaiah penned the following words of scripture for God's people. They are just as pertinent to us now as they were to them then! *The Lord has given me a strong warning not to think like everyone else does. He said, "Don't call everything a conspiracy, like they do, and don't live in dread of what frightens them. Make the Lord of Heaven's Armies holy in your life. He is the one you should fear. He is the one who should make you tremble. He will keep you safe"* (Isaiah 8:11–14).

Fear of God is healthy because He is holy, He is all powerful, He knows the beginning from the end, and He has our good in mind! Let's trust Him, and let's follow Him. He will keep us safe!

APRIL 27

Sudoku

Having never been gifted with numbers, I was a bit disappointed when my wife bought me a Sudoku puzzle book. The temptation was to put it to the side and let it gather dust. I had very little time for trivial things like this, I thought. Yet, somehow drawn into trying something new, I soon learned that each Sudoku puzzle had a solution. It was for me to persist and find it! I also learned that one number out of place messes the whole thing up! Trusting that someone had designed the puzzle with a solution kept me going! Today, I am far from a whizz at Sudoku, but the hesitancy and reluctance are gone. It's an adventure to find the solution.

In a very small way, Sudoku has some similarities to the infinitely greater walk of faith with God. He knows the beginning from the end. He not only knows the solution, but He is the solution! He doesn't ask us to go places that He hasn't already walked. Though the path of life may seem trying at times and we don't see the reasons for the difficulties or the future clearly, He has promised to be with us all the way. He has a finished product in mind, and it's perfect: the right order, the right time, the right place. He's calling us into this marvellous walk of faith in Him!

We are again reminded of how Jesus came just at the right time! He came to suffer and die for us, to pay the price for our sins! Though the way seems impossible at times, will we trust Him and with expectation enter into the great walk of faith? Our eternal destiny depends on it!

"When we were utterly helpless, Christ came at just the right time and died for us sinners" (Romans 5:6).

APRIL 28

How Old?

A friend of mine who lived in Greenland for years shared with us that the Greenlanders had told him the climate there was much warmer five hundred years ago than it is now. This was confirmed by a documentary, which revealed that archeologists excavated ruins of a Viking settlement, which they dated around one thousand years ago. They discovered that the climate was much warmer at that time. They found evidence that the Vikings who lived there raised cattle, turkeys, and chickens. Trees grew where there are presently thick layers of ice. A church and even emblems with crosses were found, indicating some of the people were Christians.

According to the archeologists, the weather became increasingly cold, and the Vikings found it too cold for them to sustain their livelihood, so they moved. The Inuit, who were much more adapted to the cold weather, moved into the area and have lived there ever since.

Then a "scientific" article caught my eye that stated that the present temperature in Baffin Island and Greenland are now warmer than they've been in 120,000 years. They based this on: 1) carbon dating of a piece of moss, which they said was found to be 50,000 years old; 2) core samples of the ice pack, and 3) the assumption that the last ice age was some 120,000 years ago.

I don't claim to be a scientist, but it seems obvious to me that they missed some very important facts unearthed by the archeologists. In my mind, there has to be something very wrong with the conclusions published in the "scientific" article. I don't know about you, but this raises a lot of questions for me.

If, as the archeological dig confirms, the temperatures in the north were so much warmer just a thousand years ago, how did the seals and the polar bears survive? Are they really at risk, as some say, of dying out because of warmer climate trends? Is this present warming trend really from greenhouse gases, or is it just another cycle of nature that happens every so often? Even more important, is the age of the earth really millions and billions of years, or could it be in the thousands of years?

We have an account in the Bible that points towards thousands, not millions, of years (Genesis 1:1–31; Exodus 20:11). Which do you believe? I choose to believe God's Word, the Bible.

"In the beginning, God created the heavens and the earth" (Genesis 1:1, ESV); "By faith we understand that the universe was created by the word of God, so that what is seen was not made out of things that are visible" (Hebrews 11:3, ESV).

119

APRIL 29

Come Alive (Dry Bones)

The voice of a young, very gifted and accomplished song writer/singer often reverberates through the speakers on our old stereo as we sit tapping our foot and letting the words speak to the depths of our soul and heart. Her name is Lauren Daigle. If you haven't yet heard her, you might want to listen on YouTube!

One of the songs, titled "Come Alive (Dry Bones)," is taken from the biblical prophesy of Ezekiel (Chapter 37), where the Spirit of God revealed to the prophet a vision of a valley covered with countless dried out, obviously dead human bones. God told him these bones would come together, and He would breathe new life into them, thus they would become living, breathing people again. As Ezekiel spoke God's prophesy over them, he watched as the dry bones came together and became breathing, living human beings. This prophecy speaks specifically about Israel after having suffered spiritual death through sin, disobedience, and unbelief becoming spiritually alive and returning to their homeland in the future.

Over five hundred years later, God spoke this message of life to all who would have faith and trust in Him: *"As for you, you were dead in your transgressions and sins ... But because of his great love for us, God, who is rich in mercy, made us alive with Christ even when we were dead in transgressions—For it is by grace you have been saved, through faith—and this is not from yourselves, it is the gift of God." (Ephesians 2:1, 4–5, 8, NIV).*

Today God wants each of us to call out, "Oh Lord Jesus, have mercy on me, revive me, rescue me from spiritual death and disobedience! Oh God, breathe on us and give us new life!"

APRIL 30

Our Hope for Today!

As we're faced with a barrage of propaganda regarding pandemics, viruses, vaccines, climate change, etc., the fear of death has a grip on the whole world. We'll go to amazing lengths to escape the inevitable. We will all pass away at some time or another, some sooner and others later, but we don't want to think of such things, so we put thoughts of our mortality somewhere deep in the recesses of our being and do whatever we can to survive another day!

As we seek to find solutions to this dilemma, where do we look? Many people are working on vaccinations, some are spending trillions of dollars to save the planet, and still others are experimenting with medications to counteract the effects of the virus. My prayer is that God will give wisdom to all those involved in these efforts! Yet each of us must face the fact that one day we will die. How can we prepare for this appointment that we can't escape?

Death is the result of sin. When our original parents, Adam and Eve, sinned, death came upon every one of their offspring: *"When Adam sinned, sin entered the world. Adam's sin brought death, so death spread to everyone, for everyone sinned" (Romans 5:12).* Adam and Eve died, their children died, we all die. Yet Jesus clearly stated, *"My purpose is to give them a rich and satisfying life" (John 10:10b).* When Jesus died on the cross, He took upon Himself the sins of everyone who would truly believe in Him: *"For the wages of sin is death, but the free gift of God is eternal life through Christ Jesus our Lord" (Romans 6:23).* Jesus proved who He was by rising from the dead! May His words be an encouragement and be our hope for today! *"I am the resurrection and the life. Anyone who believes in me will live, even after dying." (John 11:25).*

When we put our trust in Jesus, we don't have to live in fear of death by COVID-19, cancer, heart attack, or whatever means, because He has given us eternal life!

MAY 1

Narrow View?

Sometimes I find myself in a bind, a predicament, and wonder how I got there. Recently I was very frustrated over a phone plan I recently bought into. I felt forced into getting something that I had to have but really wished I didn't need. The phone company had forced the move by doing away with an older wireless system, making my old phone obsolete and inoperable.

My focus was on the phone company, the plan, the new phone, and the learning curve ahead. While trying to use this new phone, I grumbled and complained until my wife politely informed me that I should stop, as I was making a fool of myself. And a fool I was, because inadvertently I was acting as if there were no God (Psalm 14:1). My view was narrowed down to myself, my problems, and my solutions. As I realized this, I was embarrassed and asked my wife and God for forgiveness. But what had happened? How did I get to this place?

After bringing this before the Lord, I realized that because of my busyness and being away from home at the time, I had only superficially recognized Him throughout the few days previous. I had spoken to Him of my needs but never recognized His supremacy over every detail of my life. I had unintentionally taken over the command of my life, thus putting myself before Him. So my natural response, with me in charge, was to focus on me, my ambitions, my plans, my hopes, and my abilities. This was a very narrow view indeed. No wonder I felt like I was in a bind. No wonder I was frustrated! I was taking everything on myself.

God knows every detail of my life. As I surrender my all to Him, my view broadens to His capabilities, His plans, and His sovereignty (Ephesians 3:14–21). I can absolutely trust Him in whatever situation I find in this life. When I am unable, He is able. When my plans are surrendered to Him, I realize He has better plans than mine. When it looks hopeless, He gives me hope! When I place all my burdens on Him, the peace that passes all understanding comes over me (Philippians 4:7; 2 Thessalonians 3:16). He is my peace (Ephesians 2:14).

"'God opposes the proud but shows favor to the humble.' Humble yourselves, therefore, under God's mighty hand, that He may lift you up in due time. Cast all your anxiety on Him because He cares for you." (1 Peter 5:5–7, NIV).

MAY 2

Sound Teaching

Having learned some of the local Ft. Babine (Wit'at) First Nations language, I am blessed to have had good teachers. I learned primarily from Mary, an elder among her people who graciously taught me the language and wouldn't let me get away with any mispronounced or inaccurate words. Though it was difficult at times, I am thankful that she insisted on the truth and encouraged me to speak properly! Some others would joke around and try to teach me words that weren't appropriate. I'm thankful I could trust Mary, who is a very fluent and knowledgeable speaker, to insist that I learn this very special language accurately! Having a true and faithful teacher is so important for us to learn well! On the contrary, how can we ever learn if our teachers are not grounded in and insistent on the truth!

This same principle applies to all areas of life, especially in regard to things of God, His Word, and His relationship to us! False teachers will lead us astray (2 Peter 2:1–3), while good teachers will be grounded in the truth of God's Word and will not waver from it!

"But as for you, continue in what you have learned and have become convinced of, because you know those from whom you learned it, and how from infancy you have known the Holy Scriptures, which are able to make you wise for salvation through faith in Christ Jesus." (2 Timothy 3:14–15, NIV).

MAY 3

Control Issues

Since the February 14, 2018 school shooting in Parkland, Florida, many students with tears of grief and deep, painful, heartfelt words are boldly protesting to officials around the United States. The most predominant message coming from them is to do with control—gun control, to be specific.

Anyone in their right mind would admit that something has gone gravely out of control and something needs to happen to bring sanity back to the classroom and society as a whole. It's obvious that we need more control in our society, yet this begs the question: "Who's in control?" Humanly speaking, if we give governments the iron hand of control, we'll have dictatorships. To achieve more control over the traffic and crowds, we'd need more police enforcement. To control the population, we think we need more access to abortions. To rely on guns for our security or to control guns without a fundamental change in individual hearts shifts the violence to other means. To control the mentally and spiritually ill, we would need more prisons. Thus is the horror of human control. What have we come to?

The real problem is that we think we know better than our Creator, and we have, in our arrogance and rebellion, tried to seize control from Him. To our own peril, we have taken God out of our schools, our courts, our governments, and our lives. No wonder we're experiencing problems!

In light of all this, let us consider afresh the life, sacrifice, death, and resurrection of the Lord Jesus. May we surrender our lives to Him and have the same attitude as He had (Philippians 2:5–8). Jesus said, *"... I do nothing on my own but speak just what the Father has taught me." (John 8:28, NIV)*. May we pray as He did when He agonized over the very reason why He came, surrendering in obedience to God the Father and ultimately to die on a terrible Roman cross, to make the payment for the sins of all those who would receive Him: *"... I want your will to be done, not mine." (Matthew 26:39)*.

MAY 4

Justice

It didn't sound right. It didn't look right. It wasn't right! When observing the government's response to the January/February 2022 Freedom Convoy, to me something was obviously wrong. The Prime Minister wouldn't even speak to the issues presented to him and totally refused to engage with the truckers in a peaceful manner. Not even for a minute. Rather, he invoked the *Emergencies Act.*

When watching the video coverage of the protest through the lens of independent, non-government funded media agencies and citizens at the scene, it was quite clear that the mainstream media was not reporting the obvious facts: it was a peaceful protest. The violence started when the police arrived! This corresponds to eyewitness accounts, including personal friends of mine, onsite video coverage, and expert witnesses on the National Citizen's Inquiry. Very little if any of this was reported by the government-funded mainstream media; it seems they took their narrative from the government's official agenda rather than reporting the facts as it happened. Observing the police quash the peaceful protesters with riot sticks, jack boots, and even horses, it looked more like the reaction of Chairman Xi's forces to the protesters in Hong Kong, rather than something that could happen in Canada! The responses of the government, most politicians, judges, and police were way over the top; actually, it was personally disgusting!

On January 23, 2024, Canada's National Observer reported that Judge Richard Mosley of the Federal Court of Canada ruled on the *Emergencies Act* invocation: "I have concluded that the decision to issue the proclamation does not bear the hallmarks of reasonableness—justification, transparency and intelligibility—and was not justified in relation to the relevant factual and legal constraints that were required to be taken into consideration." Thank God for some who are still seeking to stand up for the truth, even in the judiciary! In the end, truth and justice will prevail!

"Whoever speaks the truth gives honest evidence, but a false witness utters deceit" (Proverbs 12:19, ESV); *"When justice is done, it is a joy to the righteous but terror to evildoers"* (Proverbs 21:15, ESV).

MAY 5

Moorings

Prince Rupert is an exceptional, world class port city. It's sheltered from the winds and the waves of the open sea. The waters run deep, so ships can come in without fear of getting grounded on low tide. After being battered by the winds and the waves of the open sea, it provides a safe place for ships to moor, to come in and tie up, to replenish their supplies, and for tourists to safely leave the ship and know it will be there when they come back! Without ports such as Prince Rupert, shipping would be severely restricted, or maybe impossible to take place.

As ships need a sheltered place to moor, so do we. In our daily lives, often full of turmoil, opposition, and urgency, we need a place to rest, to replenish, and to be filled. There's only one place where this can truly happen. This is by spending time in the presence of our Creator, the Almighty God! There our gentle Saviour speaks to us through His Holy Word, the Bible, and He gives us peace and strength to carry on in the difficult journey of life! Without Him we will be as ships floundering at sea without any fuel. Without Him we will be ships drifting onto the rocks on the shoreline, wrecks which will only be a faint resemblance of what we were created to be.

May God help us to long for that time with Him each day. May we find our mooring in Him and Him alone. Nothing, no one else, will do!

"Let me teach you, because I am humble and gentle at heart, and you will find rest for your souls" (Matthew 11:29); "May God give you more and more grace and peace as you grow in your knowledge of God and Jesus our Lord." (2 Peter 1:2).

To Know or to Know About

A friend of mine has studied up on Abe Lincoln and learned a lot about him. His birth, his upbringing, his determination, his faith, his life as President of the United States, famous speeches, important decisions he had to make, his assassination, are all a part of my friend's knowledge of "Honest Abe." Though he knows lots about Abe Lincoln, he does not know him. It's impossible for him to know him because he hasn't spent any actual time with him.

In God's Word, Jesus said *"I am the good shepherd; I know my sheep and my sheep know me ... My sheep listen to my voice; I know them, and they follow me. am the good shepherd, I know my sheep and they know me" (John 10:14, 27, NIV).* What an amazing privilege to personally know our Creator Jesus Christ and to be His follower!

There's a lot of information available about Jesus Christ. We can learn about Him from the Bible, from books, sermons and lectures, or a search in Wikipedia. Just as my friend knew about Abe Lincoln, this is sometimes the extent to which we know about Jesus. Of such people, Jesus said: *"Many will say to me on that day, "Lord, Lord, did we not prophesy in your name and in your name drive out demons and in your name perform many miracles?" Then I will tell them plainly, "I never knew you. Away from me, you evildoers!" (Matthew 7:22–23, NIV).*

These people knew about Jesus, but they didn't know Him, and neither did He know them.

To get to know Jesus we need to spend time with Him in a real, transparent, and honest relationship. He wants to hear from us and wants us to listen to Him as we share our lives with Him. As we get to know Him, we will want to follow and obey Him.

Do you know Jesus or just know about Him? Jesus invites us to a personal relationship with Him: *"Here I am! I stand at the door and knock. If anyone hears my voice and opens the door, I will come in and eat with that person, and they with me." (Revelation 3:20, NIV).*

MAY 7

Best Care!

While walking down the "sunny side" of Main St. in Smithers, BC, I encountered a young couple with two small children walking down the sidewalk. The father was carrying their daughter in his arms, and the mother followed, holding their toddler firmly by the hand. This was such a beautiful sight I couldn't help but compliment them on their wonderful family. Walking together over the next couple of blocks, we shared the wonders of parenthood, and in my case also grandparenthood! The mom shared as the dad, with a smile, nodded his head in approval. She spoke of how their kids needed both Mom and Dad, and that just as they had promised in their wedding vows, they were still absolutely committed to staying together. Separation was not an option. They didn't want their children to be casualties of divorce, as many are today. The message I heard loud and clear was that they knew what was best for both their children and for themselves. They were committed to walk in it, no matter what. As they continued down the street, my heart overflowed with thankfulness that there are still young couples who are determined to live out the plan of parenthood God has laid out for us as part of His wonderful creation.

Though daycare, grandparent care, and foster care are needed at times, nothing replaces the care that Mom and Dad can give their children. Family care is the best care for children and honourable in the sight of God.

God planned for a man and a woman to come together to have a family: *"That is why a man leaves his father and mother and is united to his wife, and they become one flesh" (Genesis 2:24, NIV).* As we celebrate Mother's Day, may we be reminded of this sacred institution that God has blessed us with. My prayer today is for all mothers, that God will empower each one to be all He has called them to be, and that their children will grow up to honour and respect them as they should.

"Children, obey your parents in the Lord, for this is right. 'Honor your father and mother'—which is the first commandment with a promise— 'so that it may go well with you and that you may enjoy long life on the earth'" (Ephesians 6:1–3, NIV).

MAY 8

Heart of Worship

The house was very basic. With only cold tap water, warm water had to be heated by the wood stove. The kitchen was minimal, the cupboards few and very plain. The linoleum on the floor was well worn, with holes in the areas of heavier traffic. No insulation in the walls. No indoor washroom until later years, just an outhouse. Three of us boys shared a tiny upstairs attic bedroom. Mom and Dad's room was of a similar size on the other end of the house. The place was very basic, to say the least.

Yet there was Mom, humming a familiar hymn as she baked bread, cooked supper, or did the laundry in the gas-powered wringer washer! At the time, I didn't realize the significance of that, but Mom's worshipful and contented attitude often permeated our modest abode and brought a sense of peace to our hearts!

How could this be? Peace in such a rustic environment! She could have thought of all the amenities she lacked, that other neighbours had. She could have complained about the plumbing issues. She could have demanded a more updated kitchen. Yet from a heart of worship, we often heard her humming hymns of faith we had sung in the small country church the Sunday before.

Many years before, she had surrendered her life to Jesus, and she had His Holy Spirit in her heart. She couldn't help but worship the God she loved! The song didn't come from her external comfort but from the overflow of the Holy Spirit filling her heart. Her external surroundings weren't the issue, but her indwelling Saviour had given her love, joy, and peace that she could not hold in!

As I reflect on these things, I realize that all of the material things around us—the comforts expected in this day and age—can never truly satisfy us. It surely wasn't her material surroundings that caused her to radiate with a joyful heart of worship. This is a lesson for me in this present materialistic world, where we are inundated with advertisements that promise joy and happiness. These outward possessions can never give me what my mother had. Only the abiding Presence of our Lord Jesus can produce such an inner contented heart of worship, no matter what my outward situation might be!

"May the God of hope fill you with all joy and peace as you trust in Him, so that you may overflow with hope by the power of the Holy Spirit" (Romans 15:13, NIV).

MAY 9

Mom

Mom was a feisty woman. Almost nothing got her down. She was always there when we came home from school. She made some of the best suppers I ever ate, except those my wife makes, of course! Sometimes she was discouraged when we complained about the food or when we disobeyed, but she would always have food on the table, clean clothes for us, a clean house, and a big hug when we needed it. She was the one who encouraged me, even when I didn't do a perfect job mowing the lawn, or when others tried to discourage. Mom not only took very good care of us physically but she also nurtured us spiritually.

Mom loved the Lord and wanted others to know Him too. She went to Bible school to learn to love Him more. When she graduated from Bible school, she wanted to start a Sunday school for her friends who had never heard the Good News of Jesus and His love. She asked the elders of the church if she could start an English-speaking Sunday school, and they told her she could not, as everything they did at the church was in German. So Mom started her own Sunday school, and many of her friends became believers through the message, *"For God so loved the world,"* including them!

I remember as a child going to Kids' Club, craft nights, Vacation Bible Schools, and Sunday school. Mom was instrumental in starting all of these.Mom never gave up on me, even when I rebelled and refused to go to these events anymore. She prayed that I would one day repent and turn my life over to God so that I could also tell others about Jesus and His love for them. I still remember the tears in her eyes when I told her she could pray all she wanted, but that would not happen to me. But she kept praying. Now, with tears in my eyes, I can tell you her prayers were answered! God drew me to Himself, and I became a believer and want others to hear the Good News and turn to Jesus so that they can experience His love too!

I had the privilege of having a Godly mother. Maybe you didn't, but you can become a Godly person if you will let Jesus have His way in your heart and life. My desire for every mother who is reading this is to live, as reflected in the Scriptures, so that *"Her children arise and call her blessed; her husband also, and he praises her: 'Many women do noble things, but you surpass them all'" (Proverbs 31:28–29, NIV).*

A Tribute to Mom

Sometimes we hear people speaking of their in-laws in derogatory or very negative terms, probably because of a strained relationship between them. I can't say this about my mother-in-law. Though she had many difficulties in life, and sometimes we had our differences, we got along very well. The main reason for this, I believe, is that we both have the same faith in Jesus.

Mom was a survivor; she was born as a third sibling of thirteen. She needed to help on the family farm to make ends meet at a very early age. Among many other farm chores, looking after the younger kids and cooking were her main day-to-day duties. Even when having problems with anxiety, and having a nervous breakdown, she persisted in her faith. This was her life before I met her. When I asked her for the hand of her daughter in marriage, she immediately agreed and encouraged us along the way. She shared that at one point in her life, Jesus had become a reality to her, and as I got to know her, it was obvious to me that she had a very personal relationship with Him. Whenever we would get together, the conversation would go towards Jesus and His grace towards us.

My wife remembers her mom singing praises to the Lord as she did her day-to-day work around the house. This down-to-earth faith was passed on to her daughter, and thus, I am so thankful that I have a God-fearing spouse to share life with. In Mom's last days, when she could barely whisper a reply, she would mouth out her favourite songs as we sang at her bedside.

I would not have asked for any other mother-in-law than the one God gave me. She was a blessing to us, and we thank God for the faith she passed on to us. We look forward to seeing her soon at the wedding supper of the lamb (Revelation 21:3–4)!

The apostle Paul encouraged Timothy with these words: *"I am reminded of your sincere faith, which first lived in your grandmother Lois and in your mother Eunice and, I am persuaded, now lives in you also" (2 Timothy 1:5, NIV).*

MAY 11

Spiritual Mother

She and her husband moved to a foreign land looking for a better life. Two boys were born to them. When they grew up, their sons married foreign women. Severe hardship hit. Her husband and her two sons died, leaving her alone in a foreign land with her two daughters-in-law. She was in such loneliness and despair that she called herself Mara, which means "bitter," rather than Naomi, the name her parents had given her, which means "pleasant." Yet she was not alone because her God, the Almighty God, had not left her! Naomi decided to go back to her own land, the land of her people and her God.

One of Naomi's daughters-in-law decided she would go along. She'd seen something in her mother-in-law that powerfully attracted her. Despite all the sorrow and grief they had gone through, Ruth had seen the faith of her mother-in-law, Naomi, and was determined to follow her and her God wherever she went. When confronted by her mother-in-law with the difficulties before her, she still followed in her steps and replied, *"… Where you go I will go, and where you stay I will stay. Your people will be my people and your God my God" (Ruth 1:16, NIV).*

When they settled in Naomi's homeland, Ruth married Boaz, a benevolent relative of Naomi's, and had a son whom they named Obed. He became one of the ancestors of the great King David, who is named in the genealogy of Jesus (Matthew 1:5, 16)!

God had a plan all along. He redeemed Naomi and Ruth and saved them out of misery and hopelessness! There is always hope when we put our trust in the Almighty, who is a redeeming God and has a plan for those who trust in Him!

"For I know the plans I have for you," declares the Lord, "plans to prosper you and not to harm you, plans to give you hope and a future. Then you will call on me and come and pray to me, and I will listen to you. You will seek me and find me when you seek me with all your heart" (Jeremiah 29:11–13, NIV).

MAY 12

Mom's Strength

As I think of my mother, I'm reminded of her amazing strength! Mom was not much over five feet tall, but she was strong!! It showed up in her determination to make it through even the toughest times. She was born to a single mom in what is now known as Russia, just south of Siberia. As a child, she and her mom, my grandmother, emigrated to Canada and were the only two of their people group on the ship that brought them over the Atlantic Ocean. Because of Mom's childhood situation, she endured criticism and outright discrimination from those around her, even those close to her. Yet she persisted in carving out a life that still blesses me today.

She was very industrious in all she did! She would tend the garden, raise chickens, milk the cows, clean the house, do the laundry, prepare meals for us, and make preserves, sometimes all on the same day! She even marketed fruit to friends and relatives in the prairies from our fruit trees. Yet her greatest strength was her faith in the Lord Jesus Christ. She would share what she had to help meet the needs of those around her and would be ready, though not pushy, to share the hope she had in Jesus whenever she could.

When Dad found Mom, he found a gem! Mom's strength was regularly tested by my stubbornness and frequent outright disobedience to her, to Dad, and even to God. Yet she didn't waver! Her Lord always gave her the faith and strength to make it through! I am so thankful she persisted, because through her endurance, I also saw my need for Jesus, salvation in Him, and the meaningful life He offers to all who see their need and turn to Him! Thank you, Mom, for showing me the way!

"A wife of noble character who can find? ... Her children arise and call her blessed; her husband also, and he praises her ..." (Proverbs 31:10, 28, NIV).

MAY 13

Following Jesus

I specifically remember a young man who years ago publicly made a commitment to follow Jesus. I've seen him from time to time since then and have yet to hear a confession from his own lips regarding that commitment, or for that matter see any evidence that he is a follower of Jesus. On the other hand, I witnessed another fellow who resisted Jesus most of his life clearly turn to Jesus and follow Him just before he died.

In light of this, let us consider the question Jesus asked of the leading religious leaders of His day: *"But what do you think about this? A man with two sons told the older boy, "Son, go out and work in the vineyard today. The son answered, "No, I won't go," but later he changed his mind and went anyway. Then the father told the other son, "You go," and he said, "Yes, sir, I will." But he didn't go. Which of the two obeyed his father?" (Matthew 21:28–31).* The answer is obvious, the one who heard the voice of his father and eventually turned from his own way to obey the father was the obedient follower!

Jesus went on to say that the ones who hear, repent of their ways, and turn to God are His true followers. Only Jesus can save (Acts 4:12)! Only as we realize the truth of our sinful ways, even our sinful religious attempts to follow Him, and turn from these ways can we be made right with God. And only then will we be empowered by His Holy Spirit to follow and obey Him (John 15:26)!

Have you decided to follow Jesus? Is there evidence in your life to show it? Are you tired of following your own sinful ways? He is ready to welcome all who will turn to Him and follow Him! Jesus said, "As *it is written in the Scriptures, 'They will all be taught by God.' Everyone who listens to the Father and learns from Him comes to me" (John 6:45).*

Mother's Counsel

The memory of the incident is clear. As very young children, we were coaxed into the barn with the intent of being sexually abused by a fellow considerably older than us. Just before he could get very far into his evil scheme, there was a loud banging on the locked door of the barn. It was my mom asking what was going on and demanding the door be opened! After sending everyone else home, she held me close and gave me pure, plain, pertinent, and Godly counsel that I vividly remember today. She clearly informed me that what had happened in the barn was wrong. She said the fellow who abused us was sexually confused and that I should not allow him to confuse me. She said I was a boy and I would one day become a man. Mom's wise counsel still resonates with me today! I thank God for my mother, who loved me, protected me, and gave me Godly, wise counsel!

Mom didn't have a professional career; she didn't have a degree in education, but she had an intimate walk with Almighty God, who gave her wisdom and love that no one else in the world could give! Though she has since passed on to be with the Lord, I am tremendously thankful for her!

Mothers, be encouraged in your vital role and the high calling of raising your children! You are filling a need in your children's lives that only you can fill!

"Honor your father and your mother, as the Lord your God has commanded you, so that you may live long and that it may go well with you in the land the Lord your God is giving you" (Deuteronomy 5:16, NIV).

MAY 15

Half-Mast

We had the privilege of visiting and touring Ottawa, the capital of our great country of Canada. As we toured Parliament Hill with a good friend and brother in the faith, we contemplated the marvellous heritage we have here in this country. In the evening, as we watched a historical production called "Northern Lights" projected onto the Parliament building, we were again reminded, in the words of the late Prime Minister John Diefenbaker, of the influence of Almighty God in the formation and present function of our government. What an outstanding country we have! We have much to thank God for!

As we observed the flag flying proudly at the top of the Peace Tower, we were reminded, with pride, of the freedoms we enjoy every day. We were reminded of people who have gone before us—of soldiers, parliamentarians, dignitaries, and ordinary people who have contributed their lives to the formation of this magnificent country of Canada. As we honour these, we observe the flag at half-mast.

Contemplating all of this, I thought of the many preborn babies that have passed away over the years, approximately 100,000 per year, 8,333 per month, 1,923 per week, 274 per day, 11 per hour: lives violently taken before they could see the light of day. As I write this, my heart is grieved. Most politicians won't even say a word about this unthinkable evil happening in our land; some political parties call themselves pro-choice when they won't even allow their representatives speak a word on behalf of these little ones, thus actually making them pro-abortion. They won't even allow a debate of when human life begins. I am ashamed.

In my thoughts, I envisioned the flag on the Peace Tower at half-mast in honour of these innocent and helpless ones whose lives are taken before their time. It's not my place or in my power to lower the flag on the Peace Tower. I cannot lower any other flag in Ottawa or Canada, but I can erect a flag pole on my property, and I can fly the flag at half-mast in honour of those innocent preborn human babies whose lives are being taken away as we speak.

In response to this conviction, I am resolved to fly a flag on our property at half-mast until some of our MPs look past their selfish political agendas and gather up genuine courage, morals, and faith to defend the most weak and vulnerable, to pass legislation in Ottawa to protect the lives of these precious little citizens of this exceptional land of ours.

"... but as for me and my house, we will serve the Lord" (Joshua 24:15).

Without Vision

When we toured through the Peace Tower in Ottawa, our good friend, who was very familiar with Parliament Hill, pointed out, way above the main entrance and on each of the two side entrances, inscribed in stone, three scripture verses from God's Word, the Bible. One of these inscriptions quotes *Proverbs 29:18: "Where there is no vision the people perish."* As we look in the Bible, we see that this verse continues, saying, *"but he that keepeth the law, happy is he" (KJV)*. In light of this, we see that this Scripture is obviously not speaking about physical lack of vision or blindness but a spiritual blindness towards the law of God, an unwillingness to obey God's Word, which has been given for our own good.

To illustrate: as we were driving back to the home of our friend, there was much traffic. Yet due to our driver's and other's willingness to submit to the laws of the road, we arrived back at his house safe and sound. If we hadn't stopped at the red lights, turned in the proper lanes, and kept the speed limit, we would have been putting ourselves and others in serious danger. Just as the laws of the road are given for the good of everyone travelling along the highway, the Word of God applies to our everyday lives.

God gave us His Word, the Bible, to show us the way we should live as we travel the path of life He's set out for us. When we as a nation, as people groups, as individuals ignore God's laws and go our own way, we are blindly walking on very dangerous ground and putting ourselves in mortal danger. Though it may not seem like it in the moment, if we take a joy ride through life, following every whim of our own ideas and desires, we are headed for a serious and fatal crash. The consequences of living in spiritual blindness are misery, pain, and ultimately death.

The other option is to repent, ask God to forgive us, ask Him to open our eyes to see, and submit to Him so that He can empower us and give us vision to live a fulfilled and joyful life, so that we can happily arrive at our destination! The choice is ours.

MAY 17

No Cookie Cutter

I once heard a fellow say that God is not a "cookie cutter God." At first glance this seems to be an odd statement, but upon a little more reflection, what he was saying can help one have a meaningful relationship with God.

A cookie cutter is predictable, does the same thing repetitively, mechanistically, with almost identical results. Have you ever noticed that though Jesus healed many people, He never did it in exactly the same way? Though He expected His disciples to follow Him, each one had a different way of expressing this. Though a number of His prayers are recorded, none are the same.

Why? we might ask. I believe this is because He is interested in relationship rather than ritual. Rituals are often done by routine, on a repetitive basis, with little or no thought, emotions, or even care involved. Yet relationships are based on real people, events, times, and places. To have a living relationship, love, care, and heartfelt emotions, among other things, are involved. God created every one of us as an individual with individual needs. Every moment of our lives is unique, as are the events surrounding it.

The way we respond to God is an indicator of how we perceive Him to be. If our relationship is distant and cold, then we will tend to see God as ritualistic and go through the motions, responding to Him in a cookie cutter fashion.

God entered humanity in the person of Jesus Christ. He mingled with people in their everyday lives and met them where they needed Him most. He died so we could be forgiven, and He rose from the dead so we could have a living, personal relationship with Him (John 1:14).

Oh Lord Jesus, cleanse us and change our hearts so we can see your great and mighty love for us! Give us an intimate, living, and vibrant relationship with you!

"... let us go right into the presence of God with sincere hearts fully trusting him. For our guilty consciences have been sprinkled with Christ's blood to make us clean, and our bodies have been washed with pure water" (Hebrews 10:22).

Smoke and Mirrors

The saying "smoke and mirrors" is defined in the Cambridge Dictionary as: "an explanation or description that is not true or not complete and is used to hide the truth about a situation." It's obvious that this reflects an attempt to avoid the truth and to convince others, or possibly ourselves, of a lie.

Yet as we consider the wildfires and resulting smoke that has been so prevalent, even to the darkening of the sun and blocking out of the moon, we could panic, or we could allow some realities to come into focus. Firstly, all that we see around us is temporary and only lasts for a time, even a very short time. Secondly, we have a lot less control over what happens than we care to believe. Thirdly, we need to look past the smoke and look to the Almighty God and His Word to have confidence as we live in this unstable world and to have assurance of the future.

Jesus warned of things to come: *"Heaven and earth will disappear, but my words will never disappear. Watch out! Don't let your hearts be dulled by carousing and drunkenness, and by the worries of this life. Don't let that day catch you unaware, like a trap. For that day will come upon everyone living on the earth. Keep alert at all times. And pray that you might be strong enough to escape these coming horrors and stand before the Son of Man."* (*Luke 21:33–39*).

God's Word is a genuine mirror that reveals His truth to us (James 1:23–25), and as we look at it and desire to obey Him, our confidence and faith in Him will grow, despite our weakness and all that's going on around us in this temporary world!

Oh Lord, may we not be distracted or deceived by the smoke and mirrors around us, but give us faith in You. Give us wisdom, confidence, and strength from Your Word for each new day!

MAY 19

Comfort

To undergo a particular surgery, I had to lose weight—lots of weight. Pounds that had accumulated over the years had to come off somehow. With drastic reduction of food intake on the menu, I found myself in the fridge without thinking of it, sometimes with something already in my mouth! Oh, how I was addicted to food! After considering this for some time, the term "comfort food" came to mind. I realized that I was using food as a form of comfort. (Comfort in the Merriam-Webster dictionary is defined as "to give strength and hope to.") Some food is needed for physical strength, but do I really need so much? *Is food really my hope?* I thought.

The problem with having food or whatever else—material possessions, sex, career, even our reputation, for that matter—as our comfort is that we never seem to have enough. They never completely satisfy! Though these may not be bad in themselves, and may sometimes even be necessary, can we truly find comfort in them?

God's Word, the Bible, clearly indicates that our true source of comfort is God! When the apostle Paul was persecuted to the point of death, he found his comfort in God. In fact, he said the hardships taught him to: *"Praise be to the God and Father of our Lord Jesus Christ, the Father of compassion and the God of all comfort, who comforts us in all our troubles, so that we can comfort those in any trouble with the comfort we ourselves receive from God." (2 Corinthians 1:3–4, NIV).*

When difficulties come our way—and they are inevitable—where will we look for our comfort? Will it be in the temporary and fleeting things of this world, or will it be God, our ultimate source of comfort?

May we all say with the apostle Paul: *"We were crushed and overwhelmed beyond our ability to endure, and we thought we would never live through it. In fact, we expected to die. But as a result, we stopped relying on ourselves and learned to rely only on God, who raises the dead." (2 Corinthians 1:8–9).*

MAY 20

Lesson in Forgiveness

Visiting a former classmate whom I hadn't seen for many decades brought to mind one of our elementary school teachers. Subsequently, I was prompted in my heart to look up that teacher's phone number and give him a call. As we reconnected and reminisced, he soon brought up a mutually painful memory from the past. Due to old age, his recollections of some other occurrences were not completely clear, but this one was distinct to him. He had given me the strap, or corporal punishment, which in those days was accepted practice in schools. He expressed his grief for doing this to me and said he realized it was wrong and he never did it to another student after that. This incident obviously caused him much more pain that it did me! I told him he was forgiven and was immediately convicted, as a particularly difficult student, of my many sins towards him. So I asked his forgiveness of my trespasses. He immediately shared that Jesus had forgiven him so much, so how could he not forgive!

My former teacher had placed his faith in Jesus Christ and was now living for Him! What fellowship we had over the phone! All the past hurts and offences melted away as the love of Jesus filled our hearts! We both expressed the longing to fellowship face-to-face. Rather than having past obscured wounds fester, the offences were confessed, brought into the open, and forgiven. Powerful inner healing took place, and true Christian fellowship ensued!

As the Holy Scriptures say, *"Therefore confess your sins to each other and pray for each other so that you may be healed" (James 5:16, NIV).*

"But if we walk in the light, as He is in the light, we have fellowship with one another, and the blood of Jesus, his Son, purifies us from all sin ... If we confess our sins, He is faithful and just and will forgive us our sins and purify us from all unrighteousness." (1 John 1:7, 9, NIV).

MAY 21

The Root

During this awesome time of year, the plants all around us are springing to life. The lawn is green, and the apple trees are blooming again after a long winter of dormancy. It's so invigorating to take in the magnificence of God's creation and see the fresh, green foliage as a myriad of plants spring to life throughout the valley.

There's a part of the valley that's not so obvious to the eye but that has everything to do with the beauty we see. That's the roots of these magnificent plants. I read that at least as much of the plant that is above the ground is in the root underground. Every plant has a root system that supports it.

We're having some problems with our strawberry plants, and I think the problem is with the roots. The tops aren't healthy looking, and they didn't bear much fruit last year. Maybe it's the soil, not enough nutrition, or maybe pests or a lack of water at times. We'll have to figure it out so we can have some fresh strawberries from the garden again this year. The health of the root has everything to do with the health of the plant.

The Bible also speaks about roots. There is the root of bitterness, where we keep anger, unforgiveness, and resentment in our hearts, and ultimately bitterness results (Hebrews 12:15). Or there is the love of money, which is a root of all kinds of evil. Often the motive behind love for money is a love for power, and power considers only self and not others. Untold misery has manifested itself due to this root of love of money and worldly things (1 Timothy 6:10).

Or we can be rooted in Jesus Christ and the things of God: *"Let your roots grow down into Him, and let your lives be built on Him. Then your faith will grow strong in the truth you were taught, and you will overflow with thankfulness" (Colossians 2:7).*

As we allow God to nurture us through His Word, and as we surrender to His will in our lives, the Holy Spirit will produce a life filled with love, joy, and peace, even in the storms of life (Galatians 5:22).

So where are we getting our nourishment from? Are we rooted in the things of this fallen world, or are we rooted in Jesus, the one who will nurture us and cause us to overflow with a good, wholesome life?

MAY 22

Surprised?

Friends and relatives as far away as Regina called and asked how we were doing, because the smoke from our province has reached across the Prairies. The smoke in Prince George at noontime was so thick it was like midnight, and the headlights of the cars could barely penetrate it.

Thank God the rain has come! We're informed by the BC Wildfire Service that some of the fires are still burning and may not be extinguished until the snow flies. It has been a record year for fires in BC, only surpassing last year's record. Some are looking to climate change as the main cause, and others are blaming the lack of maintenance of the beetle-killed trees. These may be factors, among many others. We all are looking for solutions, as none of us want next year, or the year after, to break another wildfire record!

If we read our Bibles, we shouldn't be surprised about these types of events coming upon us! Jesus predicted: *"Immediately after the tribulation of those days the sun will be darkened, and the moon will not give its light, and the stars will fall from heaven, and the powers of the heavens will be shaken" (Matthew 24:29, ESV).* We're reminded that this earth and our time here is only temporary, and a time is coming when such events will be magnified in intensity, just as in a woman giving birth (Matthew 24:8)! The apostle Peter warns about a time when the heavens and the earth will be burned with fire and pass away, in a time of judgement!

So one might ask: Why has this not happened, as it was predicted so many years ago? *"The Lord isn't really being slow about his promise, as some people think. No, he is being patient for your sake. He does not want anyone to be destroyed, but wants everyone to repent ... Since everything around us is going to be destroyed like this, what holy and godly lives you should live ..." (2 Peter 3:9–11).*

Let us leave our own agendas and turn to God for mercy and grace before it's too late!

MAY 23

Vengeance for Jessica

I remember her mom holding her as a newborn. Jessica grew up to be a very beautiful woman. The last time we saw her, she was on Main Street in Smithers, at the Fall Fair parade. She stopped and we talked a bit. After a little hug, off she went into the crowd, looking for her mother.

Jessica went missing a week later. Everyone was hoping she would show up in a few days. Family, friends, and police began looking for her. A week went by, and she was nowhere to be found. Everyone was seriously concerned, sometimes thinking the worst, but still hoping for the best. After two weeks her body was found, seemingly dumped off a mountain road by someone—God knows who, and so do they.

I can't imagine the pain that her mom, dad, siblings, and family feel right now. We pray for them, trying to help out in small ways, wishing we could do more to help alleviate their pain.

To be honest, when I heard this terrible news, I became so angry that I wanted to take serious vengeance on whoever did this. I am still very angry. Feelings are raw when we hear of such horrendous, wicked, and senseless acts of depraved people. Yet is this really the right thing to do, to perpetuate the violence by hunting the perpetrators down and taking revenge on them?

God's Word, the Bible, clearly says, *"Beloved, never avenge yourselves, but leave it to the wrath of God, for it is written, "Vengeance is mine, I will repay, says the Lord" (Romans 12:19, ESV).*

We pray, "Heavenly Father, please give this family your peace and comfort. May you carry them through this very difficult time. May their faith in you grow, and may they sense your loving Presence as they grieve. You know who did this. May they be brought to justice. We surrender them to you and to your perfect vengeance. In Jesus' name, Amen."

MAY 24

See You Later

His Wet'suwet'en chief name was Wah Tah K'eght. Also known as Henry Alfred. He was a good friend from when we first moved to the Bulkley Valley in 1977. The day we first met is etched into my memory like it was yesterday. It happened at the Highways work yard in Smithers. A grader came in and parked next to me. As I looked up, I saw a big man looking down at me with a huge, friendly smile on his face. He opened the door and asked if I was new here. I explained that it was my first day on the job. He got out of the grader, shook my hand, and warmly welcomed me to the valley. We've had a special heart connection ever since.

Another unexpected encounter was as at Vancouver Airport. There among all the people hurrying to and fro was Henry, with that same friendly, smiling face. He told me he was concerned, as his wife was having major surgery. We sat together, and we prayed together for his wife, for him, for the family, and for the surgeons. Thankfully the operation was a success! We recollected this divine appointment many times after that!

I visited him when he was quite sick in the hospital, yet he greatly encouraged me as we spoke of our common faith in Jesus. We gathered around him and prayed for him. We did not say "goodbye" but "see you later." That was the last time I saw him. This valley will not be the same without him, and I will miss him. Yet I am convinced we will meet again, because Jesus promised:

"Don't let your hearts be troubled. Trust in God, and trust also in me. There is more than enough room in my Father's home. If this were not so, would I have told you that I am going to prepare a place for you? When everything is ready, I will come and get you, so that you will always be with me where I am." (John 14:1–4).

MAY 25

Telling Lies Is Costly

Years ago in Nazi Germany, Joseph Goebbels, the propaganda minister under Adolf Hitler, said, "If you repeat a lie often enough, people will believe it and you will even come to believe it yourself." (azquotes.com) And on the same matter, he said, "A lie told once remains a lie but a lie told a thousand times becomes the truth." (azquotes.com) My first thought was, *This is ludicrous*, because the truth is the truth no matter what anyone says. But after considering the responses of the populace, then and now, to lies, and the effects they have on people, it's evident that repeated lies are interpreted by many as truth.

Goebbels used radio, film, posters, and emotional speeches to get his deceptive message across to the people. Many believed, among other lies, that the Aryan race was superior to other races, that Hitler was the saviour of the world, and that Jews were the enemy and needed to be exterminated. We might think that this could never happen today. On closer examination, we have political parties that won't allow pro-life people to run for their party, yet they call themselves pro-choice. Pro-choice is said to promote women's rights, yet 50 per cent of abortions are preborn women. Then under the guise of dying with dignity, legislation is passed to allow doctors, who have always been mandated to protect life, to euthanize the elderly.

As a result of Goebbels' lies, six million Jews and millions of others were killed. In the end, Goebbels killed his wife, his children, and himself. In our day, just in Canada, the lie of pro-choice has cost the lives of some four million preborn human babies and thousands of elderly and infirm.

Contrary to what Goebbels said, no matter how many times a lie is repeated, the truth will stand. The lie leads to death (2 Thessalonians 2:9–12), and the truth leads to life (John 14:6). Oh Lord God, open our eyes to see what Jesus meant when He said, *"... and you will know the truth, and the truth will set you free" (John 8:32, ESV).*

Need Sleep?

I once thought more waking hours equals more productivity. Yet one cannot go without sleep for even a few days without serious consequences! Even one sleepless night makes me less efficient.

According to extensive research done by the National Sleep Foundation, restful sleep is essential to our emotional, mental, and physical health. On average, a person sleeps about one third of their life.

Interestingly, when I think everything in my sphere of influence is up to me to control, I get the least amount of sleep. This happens either voluntarily, because I stay up late in an attempt to solve pressing issues by my own perceived wisdom, or involuntarily, because of the inability to sleep due to worry and anxiety caused by the stresses of life. In the last few years, by going to bed earlier, I have increased my productivity because my mind is clearer and more alert than when I burn the proverbial candle at both ends!

We were created with a need to sleep. To think we can live with a lack of proper rest is a reflection of our lack of trust in God. In God's Word, King David acknowledged that faith in God and his ability to sleep were in direct correlation: *"In peace I will lie down and sleep, for you alone, O Lord, will keep me safe" (Psalm 4:8).*

What about you and me? Are we losing sleep and anxious because the burden is too great to bear? Jesus said, *"Come to me, all of you who are weary and carry heavy burdens, and I will give you rest. Take my yoke upon you. Let me teach you, because I am humble and gentle at heart, and you will find rest for your souls" (Matthew 11:28–29).*

"For all who have entered into God's rest have rested from their labors, just as God did after creating the world" (Hebrews 4:10).

MAY 27

Marijuana and Speed Limits

As societal values change, we now have the reputation of being the second nation in the world to legalize the sale of marijuana. We can grow it, we can possess it, we can bake it in cookies, we can smoke it, only some can sell it, and the government gets their taxes. In the same vein, some time ago the speed limits on a few BC highways were increased significantly. In both instances, something that was illegal in the past has now become legal. Criminal activity in days past has now become acceptable and sanctioned by the government.

Enough time has passed since speed limits were increased for reports to show a significant rise in motor vehicle accidents. Excessive speed still is dangerous, whether it's deemed legal or not. The same holds true for marijuana use. The dangers of its recreational use remain the same now when it's legal as when it was illegal. Legalizing certain activities does not necessarily remove the dangers associated with them!

Thankfully, as the standards of society change, we can trust in God who *"... never changes or casts a shifting shadow" (James 1:17)*. We human beings were created to function within parameters. The closer we follow the decrees of our Creator, the better off we'll be. On the contrary, the further we get from God and His plan for us, the more danger we'll be in. God has given us His standards in His Word, the Bible, for our good and to keep us from harm. *"Therefore, you kings, be wise; be warned, you rulers of the earth. Serve the Lord with fear and celebrate His rule with trembling. Kiss His son, or He will be angry and your way will lead to your destruction, for His wrath can flare up in a moment. Blessed are all who take refuge in Him." (Psalm 2:10–12, NIV)*.

Share It!

Among the junk mail cluttering our mailbox was one from McDonalds. The bold heading said "Don't share it" above the picture of a McFlurry. Taken aback, the ad got me thinking. This caption speaks to our innate human selfishness. We have something or some information that we want to selfishly hold on to. Take for instance one's favourite huckleberry patch, or that fishing hole where we caught the big one! The temptation is to keep this to ourselves. We take care of "number one" at the expense of those more disadvantaged around us. Too often we clutch to that which God has graciously given us, rather than share the blessing as He intended for us to do (Matthew 10:8).

John the Baptist said, *"Anyone who has two shirts should share with the one who has none, and anyone who has food should do the same" (Luke 3:11, NIV)*. We're reminded of the early church: *"And all the believers met together in one place and shared everything they had" (Acts 2:44)*. Jesus said, *"Give, and you will receive. Your gift will return to you in full—pressed down, shaken together to make room for more, running over, and poured into your lap. The amount you give will determine the amount you get back" (Luke 6:38, NIV)*. Some have used this Scripture as a formula to get more stuff for themselves, thus again being greedy and defeating the very purpose of it!

God is a giving God, and those who follow Him should have giving hearts. As believers, next time we order a McFlurry, let's look around—maybe there's someone we can give it to, buy a meal for, or share an encouraging word with.

If you're not yet a believer, God has the greatest gift ever to offer you: *"For God so loved the world, that He gave His only Son, that whoever believes in Him should not perish but have eternal life" (John 3:16, ESV)*. He will give you a whole new life, and you won't be able to keep it to yourself!

MAY 29

Whose Power?

Have you noticed the power struggles all around us? Google, Apple, Yahoo, and many others want power over the internet. We have to, somehow or other, sign on to all their conditions to use the web. The various countries of the world are vying for power over their region, or even over the whole world! As superpowers, the United States, China, and Russia compete for worldwide control and power. The struggle in the South China Sea, the Crimea, and Middle East serve as a few examples of this. On the streets of the cities of the world, drug dealers and gangs violently fight for their power of influence in certain areas.As individuals, we all have a tendency to want control over what happens to us. We may seek a position of influence over others; we may want the best deal, even at the expense of others, or we may horde wealth to give us a sense of control. To some degree, we all want power over our lives.

God's Word, the Bible, points out that there are two sources of power. One is *"... the work of Satan with counterfeit power and signs and miracles. He will use every kind of evil deception to fool those on their way to destruction, because they refuse to love and accept the truth that would save them" (2 Thessalonians 2:9–10).* Jesus said the work of the devil is *"... to steal and kill and destroy" (John 10:10, ESV).*

On the contrary, the Scriptures clearly declare of Jesus: *"Now He is far above any ruler or authority or power or leader or anything else—not only in this world but also in the world to come" (Ephesians 1:21).* And He has come to give those who believe in Him a *"rich and satisfying life" (John 10:10).*

The choice is ours. Whose power will we live under? Whom will we serve?

Ripple Effects!

This can't keep going as it is. My wife is grumpy, the kids are grumpy, everyone is at each other, everything is falling apart! I want out! These were my thoughts as I lay there in bed early one morning. You could cut the negative atmosphere with a knife. I felt lost as I contemplated the future. What would happen if our marriage fell apart?

In desperation, I called out to God, expressing my feelings to Him and asking Him what I should do. Almost immediately a strong sense of His Presence came over me! I was the problem! I wasn't treating my wife as I ought. I was the one causing the negative and hopeless atmosphere in our family! I didn't have a right attitude towards my wife and the children! I was the one who set the tone in my family. My actions and attitudes needed to change!

As I lay there in bed, the conviction of God was heavy on my heart as I called out to Him to change me so I could be the husband, father, and person He wanted me to be. Something happened that morning, and I got up with a different attitude. That day the Spirit of God completely changed my outlook towards my wife and family. God had tuned me up so I could be a support and joyful leader rather than the cause of strife and conflict. His Holy Spirit overflowed from my innermost being as I allowed Him to have His way with me; the ripple effects of my attitude, in turn, lifted up my wife and children. All of our attitudes changed!

Sometimes this negative, selfish, sinful attitude still comes over me, but as I surrender to the Lord and allow His Holy Spirit to have His way in my heart, He produces His fruit of love, joy, and peace in my life. I thank God for the new life He has given me! This life is available for all who surrender and turn to God in faith!

Jesus said, *"I have come that they may have life, and that they may have it more abundantly" (John 10:10, NKJV).*

MAY 31

Alive and Powerful

Graduation was approaching and celebrations were in order. The father asked his son what he would like as a gift to celebrate his achievements. The impetuous son quickly responded that he wanted a new car. When the time came for the father to present his gift, it came as a neatly wrapped present. Upon opening it, the disappointed young fellow found a Bible. Not appreciating the precious gift before him, he became angry with his father. With disgust, he tossed the Bible on a shelf, not to open it for a long, long time.

Many years later, he realized a vacuum in his life. Desperate to find direction, he was reminded of the Bible on the shelf. He dusted it off and opened it, hoping to possibly find in it some of the wisdom his father had shown in trying times. As he leafed through the pages, to his surprise, a paper fell out. He picked it up to find that it was a generous cheque with a note attached. The note, dated on the day of his grad, was in his father's handwriting, informing him that the money was for his new car as a grad gift. This story serves to illustrate not so much the value of the earthly father's gift but the heavenly Father's treasure contained in His Holy Scriptures.

So often we shun God and His Word to us, thinking we know better than He! We minimize, ignore, or discount the wellspring of wisdom, guidance, and riches hidden in God's holy Word, the Bible. We seek our own desires, our own ideas, our own ways rather than fulfilling the holy path God has set out before us in the pages of His Word. Our Bible might be right before us, gathering dust, while we limp along trying to find meaning in life. Let us look into its pages to find the treasure He has for us while we still have time!

"For the word of God is alive and powerful. It is sharper than the sharpest two-edged sword, cutting between soul and spirit, between joint and marrow. It exposes our innermost thoughts and desires" (Hebrews 4:12); "Your word is a lamp for my feet, a light on my path" (Psalm 119:105, NIV).

JUNE 1

Louder than Words

We have a mining corporation that would like to move into our community. They're making commitments that the mine they are envisioning will have almost no negative effects on the community. The noise, the tailings, the dust etc., they say will be minimal. When speaking with some of their representatives, they said there was speculation that real estate prices would go up in the area! If they're so sure that this is true, then why are they not buying up property as near to the mine as possible, yet one admitted that he had recently moved farther away, to the other side of the valley.

The point here is that our actions speak louder than our words. Our actions show what is really inside our heart. When we really believe and are truly convinced of something, we'll respond according to our beliefs. Yet our selfish nature always looks after our own interests.

So how do we have a true change of heart? How can I become the person God really designed me to be? Jesus gave us the answer when He said, *"Truly, truly, I say to you, unless one is born again he cannot see the kingdom of God" (John 3:3, ESV)*. When we come to faith in Jesus, His Holy Spirit indwells us to empower and change us. When this happens, our heart will change, our thoughts will change, our very being will change, and thus our actions will change. Then the actions as commanded by Jesus will be shown in our lives: *"And you must love the Lord your God with all your heart, all your soul, all your mind, and all your strength.' The second is equally important: 'Love your neighbor as yourself'" (Mark 12:29–31)*.

Are we tired of the self-centred, meaningless old life? Do we desire to change and become the people God wants us to be? Then let us surrender ourselves, our everything, to Him and let Him live His life in us and through us.

"Dear children, let's not merely say that we love each other; let us show the truth by our actions. Our actions will show that we belong to the truth ..." (1 John 3:18).

New Heart

There has been a lot of attention on the news recently about cruelty to animals. One fellow has been sentenced to two years in prison for severely abusing his dog. Another case of cruelty to cows in a dairy is being investigated.

An animal rights activist, in reaction to this animal abuse, is trying to equate our pets to human beings by saying they have personalities just like humans and should be given a bill of rights just like we have. Another person, who had numerous dogs freely roaming wherever they wanted around the house, told me that her dogs are her children.

Animals are not and never will be human beings, yet this doesn't excuse anyone of animal abuse. God's Word clearly teaches that we as humans are to be stewards of His creation, including animals (Genesis 1:28). The answer to animal cruelty is not to raise the status of animals to that of humans but to deal with the root cause—the condition of our heart. The deeper issue here is that all of our attitudes and actions reveal the condition of our heart: *"The righteous care for the needs of their animals, but the kindest acts of the wicked are cruel" (Proverbs 12:10, NIV).*

"The heart is deceitful above all things, and desperately sick; who can understand it?" (Jeremiah 17:9, NIV). Even the words of our mouth reveal what's in our hearts: *"For whatever is in your heart determines what you say" (Matthew 12:34;* see also Matthew 15:19). This universal condition of our human heart has everything to do with whatever we think, say, or do—not only to our animals but also to our spouses, our children, our neighbours, our friends, our enemies, our unborn, and even ourselves.

The only remedy is to surrender our broken selves to God, to call out for forgiveness and mercy to our Creator, the Lord Jesus Christ. He will give us a new heart and empower us by His Holy Spirit, so that we can we live the positive, productive, and meaningful lives He has called us to. The same promise that God gave the people of Israel through the prophet Ezekiel thousands of years ago can be for us today: *"And I will give you a new heart, and I will put a new spirit in you, I will take out your stony, stubborn heart and give you a tender, responsive heart. And I will put my Spirit in you so that you will follow my decrees and be careful to obey my regulations." (Ezekiel 36:26–27).*

JUNE 3

Evidence

Standing beside a logging road in the forest, I was sharing with a fellow worker about God, His presence, His provision, and His love for us. The fellow immediately told me that he was an atheist. He did not believe God existed. To prove his point, he said that God should show He existed by answering his request of bringing down fire upon a large cottonwood tree that was standing there in front of us. If this happened, he said, he would believe. He proceeded to call out, asking God to prove himself by consuming that tree with a ball of fire. Nothing happened. He looked at me and said, "See, there is no God."

Can you imagine what would happen if God had to answer everyone's particular request for evidence that He existed? He would be at the command of every whim of humanity! Furthermore, the Bible is clear that God has already given enough evidence through His creation for people to believe: *"Through everything God has made, they can see his invisible qualities – his eternal power and divine nature. So they have no excuse for not knowing God" (Romans 1:20).*

This fellow was looking for evidence when there was ample evidence right in front of him. There stood the huge, living cottonwood tree with thousands of leaves turning carbon dioxide into oxygen, and its massive roots that were sucking up gallons of water supplying nutrients to feed it. Its ability to produce other cottonwood trees through seeds and roots is marvellous. Cottonwoods can be so large that they're very difficult to move, even with a bulldozer. This tree alone was enough evidence that there is a wonderful Creator God. Then when we looked around, we saw an enormous diverse forest, the river, the animals, us human beings, and so much more. Did he—do we—really need more evidence (Read Isaiah 40:21–31)?

God's Word makes it clear that God our Creator is none other than Jesus Christ (John 1:1–4; Colossians 1:15–17). One day everyone will recognize who He is (Revelation 1:7). It can be now, in awe, willingly in worship, or later, under compulsion in fear, at the judgement. That's the situation we will all face. I choose to worship Him now. *"Therefore God has highly exalted him and bestowed on him the name that is above every name, so that at the name of Jesus every knee should bow, in heaven and on earth and under the earth, and every tongue confess that Jesus Christ is Lord, to the glory of God the Father." (Philippians 2:9–11, ESV).*

JUNE 4

Tank Man

Over thirty years ago, on June 4, 1989, a terrible massacre happened in Tiananmen Square, Beijing, China. After many years of overpowering, brutal, and repressive communist rule, millions of people were hoping for change, for freedom and peace in their country. Many gathered in peaceful protest in Beijing to show their support for a more understanding, open, and democratic rule, hoping to convince the despots of their desire for more freedom and peace. The communist dictators didn't know what to do, as it looked like they were going to lose their power over the people.

They decided to supress the rebellion and brought in their army. They began shooting indiscriminately into the crowds of people, killing hundreds and most likely thousands of their own citizens. The very next day, June 5, as they were moving in some tanks to further suppress the people, a man defiantly stood in front of the tanks and wouldn't let them by, even when they tried to steer around him. He stopped the tanks for a few moments and had words with one of the men in the tank, then some people came and forcibly grabbed him and whisked him away. He was never heard of again. And this massacre has basically been erased from the history books in the People's Republic of China.

Interestingly, Tiananmen means "gate of heavenly peace." But where was the peace? This begs the question: Where do we really find peace? Is it found at the end of a gun? Is the UN really a peacekeeping force? Did the Chinese communists bring peace when they murdered all those people who had a different ideology than theirs?

God's Holy Scriptures are clear that the only real and lasting peace comes as we surrender to our Creator Jesus Christ, the Prince of Peace (Isaiah 9:6–7), who promised His followers, *"I am leaving you with a gift—peace of mind and heart. And the peace I give is a gift the world cannot give. So don't be troubled or afraid" (John 14:27).*

JUNE 5

What I Deserve

He spouted out something like, "You're nothing but a cheat; you're only in this for yourself, you good for nothing #%&+@." Observing his contorted face and smelling alcohol on his breath, I could sense my anger rising. Rather than react in kind, I said, "I don't need to listen to this!" and walked away. In my heart I felt that I deserved better. Though this may hold true on a human-to-human level, the situation is completely different when we face God!

The great prophet Isaiah, when faced with the awesome presence of Almighty God, fell to his face on the ground saying, *"It is all over! I am doomed, for I am a sinful man. I have filthy lips, and I live among a people with filthy lips" (Isaiah 6:5).* Saul, the persecutor of God's people, who later became the apostle Paul, fell to the ground under the intense light of the Presence of Jesus and remained blind for three days (Acts 8:1–19)! When faced with the absolutely pure, Holy Presence of God, no man cries out, "I deserve better!" Rather, my sinful self becomes so obvious, there's nothing I can do that's good enough for Him, and even my best attempts are like a filthy rag covering a festering wound (Isaiah 64:6)! Reality hits, my eyes are opened, and I realize I deserve to be thrown out of His Presence forever, never to see Him again. This is what I really deserve! This is torment; this is hell!

But this is not the end of the story! God Almighty, Creator, eternal, radiant, absolutely pure and Holy, is also rich in mercy (Ephesians 2:4)! Mercy means not getting what we deserve! God's Holy Word is clear: *"The Lord is not slow to fulfill his promise as some count slowness, but is patient toward you, not wishing that any should perish, but that all should reach repentance" (2 Peter 3:9, ESV); "For 'everyone who calls on the name of the Lord will be saved'" (Romans 10:13, ESV);* Jesus said *"... those the Father has given me will come to me, and I will never reject them" (John 6:37).*

Will we repent and call out for mercy, or will we get what we deserve?

JUNE 6

The Battle

On June 6, we commemorated the seventieth anniversary of D-Day, the battle that turned the tide of World War II in Europe. I had a friend who was there. He has since passed away, but he told us younger ones about some of his experiences on the beaches of Normandy. He was a driver for a truck that carried munitions up the beach. His vehicle was briefly under water as he left the ramp of the landing craft that brought him near the shore. The bullets were hitting the water all around him, but he continued up onto the shore, where there were fallen soldiers lying all over the beach and in the water. The water was red in places with the blood of fallen companions, many of whom had spent the previous days with him. He remembers asking God to protect him. Even though he didn't have a personal faith in God at the time, he says he sensed God's presence with him, that God was protecting him as he proceeded up the beach and finally behind the enemy lines to restock the soldiers with more firepower so they could silence the machine guns of the German occupation troops. They proceeded to liberate Europe from the hands of an evil tyrant, who at one time had world domination as his goal.

The end of the Second World War did not put an end to evil. There's another battle raging in every human heart. This battle is spiritual in nature, maybe less obvious at first glance, but it's just as real as the wars that have happened over the centuries. Actually, this spiritual battle is the root cause of all the conflicts and wars that have ever happened. God's Word describes it this way: *"For we are not fighting against flesh and blood enemies but against evil rulers and authorities of the unseen world, against mighty powers in this dark world, and against evil spirits in the heavenly places." (Ephesians 6:12).*

The good news is that Jesus Christ the Son of God and came to fight this battle for us. *"Because God's children are human beings—made of flesh and blood—the Son also became flesh and blood. For only as a human being could he die, and only by dying could he break the power of the devil, who had the power of death. Only in this way could he set free all who have lived their lives as slaves to the fear of dying." (Hebrews 2:14–15).*

"Finally, be strong in the Lord and in his mighty power." (Ephesians 6:10, NIV).

June 7

I Will Never Abandon You!

When speaking to a lady about God's love for her, she told me she had once been a follower of Jesus but had fallen deeply into sin. She said she had sinned too much and now she felt God didn't want anything to do with her. She had gone too far, she thought. "I have sinned too much for God to ever take me back," she said. She was actually believing a lie and didn't understand God's love for her.

I explained to her that she had wandered from God, but God had not abandoned her. God is not in the business of abandoning His children when they wander from Him, are down, or have doubts. When Joshua took over the leadership of the Israelites after Moses died, God promised Joshua, *"I will never fail you. I will never abandon you." (Joshua 1:5).* Over one thousand years later, God spoke to us through the writer of Hebrews: *"I will never fail you, I will never abandon you." (Hebrews 13:5).* It is us who turn away from God; it's our sin that separates us from fellowship with Him. When we come to Him in repentance and faith, He will not cast us away. Jesus came to seek and to save those who are lost (Luke 19:10). He didn't come to condemn but to save (John 3:17).

It's not the severity or the depth of our sin but our unwillingness to come to Him in humility and repentance that keeps us from being set free.

Once she realized that God hated her sin but still loved her, this lady confessed her sin to God, turned from her sin, and surrendered to Christ. She was truly set free to follow Jesus with all the power of the Holy Spirit within her.

Maybe you once followed Jesus Christ and feel you have gone too far, or maybe you've never received Christ as your Lord and Saviour. Your sins are too great for you to carry. I have good news for you! God loves you (John 3:16) and wants you to surrender all your sin, your cares, your burdens to Him. He can set you free!

"Come now, let us reason together, says the Lord: though your sins are like scarlet, they shall be as white as snow; though they are red like crimson, they shall become like wool." (Isaiah 1:18, ESV).

"If we confess our sins, he is faithful and just and will forgive us our sins and purify us from all unrighteousness." (1 John 1:9, NIV).

JUNE 8

Too Late?

I had a coupon for a certain product that I was planning to redeem when I was at the store. Whenever I was there, I realized I had forgotten the coupon, so some time passed before I actually had the item and the coupon. When I did, the cashier read the conditions and said, "You're too late; the coupon has expired." What was worth something a few days ago was now worthless. Other priorities had gotten in the way; I had procrastinated, and now I could no longer receive the benefits of the coupon.

Though the coupon was worth only a little, it reminds me of something of eternal value that can be easily missed if we continually ignore the offer given to us. This is the gift of eternal life, which God is offering to everyone who will receive Him (John 1:12, 3:16). Peter tells us that God *"... is patient with you, not wanting anyone to perish, but everyone to come to repentance" (2 Peter 3:9, NIV).* The apostle Paul expressed he urgency of the situation when he said, *"We speak for Christ when we plead 'Come back to God'" (2 Corinthians 5:20).*

A time is coming when God's gift of forgiveness and grace will no longer be available. If you're sensing the Lord calling you, do not delay. Turn to Him while there is still time, as tomorrow may be too late. We can either turn to Him for mercy and grace, or continue on in our sins and face His judgement and separation from Him forever in eternal punishment (Romans 2:5–8; Revelation 20:11–15).

"So what makes us think that we can escape if we ignore this great salvation that was first announced by the Lord Jesus himself and then delivered to us by those who heard him speak?" (Hebrews 2:3).

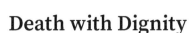

JUNE 9

Death with Dignity

My Uncle Dave was called to be a preacher at the young age of nineteen. He was a gentle pastor who hated gossip and always tried to say something positive, even of the most negative person or situation.

At the age of sixty-three, he was diagnosed with terminal cancer. He suffered enormously with the pain associated with the disease that was slowly eating away at his physical body. As he became weaker, he became more tender to the working of God in his life. He would say to all who came to see him, "I love you." He informed his wife, who faithfully looked after him in his last days, "I have studied much during this earthly life, and now I am going through the university of pain." When he could no longer speak, my aunt heard him whistling softly to the tune of the old hymn, "My Jesus, I love thee, I know Thou art mine. To Thee all the follies of sin I resign ... I'll love Thee in life, I will love Thee in death, and praise Thee as long as Thou lendest me breath; And say when the death dew lies cold on my brow, if ever I loved Thee my Jesus 'tis now."[6]

He realized that pain was not his enemy but a means to draw him closer to God, and death was the time for God to take him from this temporary life here on earth to an eternal life in heaven to be in the presence of the Almighty God forever (Hebrews 9:27; 1 Corinthians 15:22).

He didn't ask a doctor to come with a needle to kill him. He knew he had an appointment with the God who gave him life, and he would rightly leave it up to God to take his life. When the time came, God took him, and he was ushered into the presence of his Lord and Saviour, Jesus Christ. He died with dignity (Psalm 23:4).

"Naked I came from my mother's womb, and naked shall I return. The Lord gave, and the Lord has taken away; blessed be the name of the Lord." (Job 1:21, ESV).

---

6 "My Jesus I Love Thee" by William R. Featherstone 1842–1878. Public domain.

Loving Those We Do Not Agree With!

I met her in town. We paused to speak to each other. I've known her from when she was living the straight lifestyle. She has since proclaimed herself as a lesbian. We had a good chat, catching up a bit on what was happening in our lives. The encounter was brief, but I can say with all honesty that it was good to see her again and to connect. She's a beautiful person created in the image of God.

I am proud to be a heterosexual, a husband, a father, and a grandfather. I am a Christian and do not agree for a moment with her current lifestyle. God created male and female and not the many various forms of sexual orientation people are proclaiming these days (Genesis 1:27). I do not celebrate the many different sexual orientations that people are coming up with and believe this trend has dangerous consequences to the stability of our society. It's fostering confusion even among the very proponents of it. For example, some say LGBTQ could be followed by sixteen more letters behind it, representing so many more orientations that people perceive themselves to be. The preposterous problem of men using women's washrooms has added to the chaos raised by this issue. I don't believe this kind of lifestyle will ever be right, and this is proven out by history, nature, physical anatomy, procreation, God's Word, and ultimately our Creator God. It's obvious that people who choose this lifestyle will also reap the consequences of it.

Yet having said this, I still absolutely respect my friend as a fellow human being, and I believe she respects me too. I don't hate her and neither does God (John 3:16; Romans 5:8, 12:9–10). Actually, God commands me to love her and even to speak the truth to her in love (Ephesians 4:15). We are both human beings, created in His image, and we should love and respect each other as such.

Do we have to agree to get along? Of course not! Yet each of us is responsible for our own decisions and will have to live with the consequences.

"Lord God, open our eyes to see what Your will is and to daily surrender to You in every area of our lives so that we can love those around us as You love them."

"... 'Love your neighbor as yourself.' Love does no wrong to others, so love fulfills the requirements of God's law." (Romans 13:9–10).

JUNE 11

Yun-dummi'

We have a miraculous phenomenon that happens every summer in the Bulkley Valley. Very low, a few centimetres from the ground, unnoticed by most passing by, grow tiny, remarkable plants. After surviving a harsh, cold winter under the snow, their tiny bright green leaves sprout from miniature lifeless-looking stems. In the early summer, hidden under the tiny leaves, petite white and pink frilled blossoms burst forth. These little blossoms are pollinated and begin to grow into tiny green fruit, which ripen to a deep, chalky blue. As the season progresses, the leaves of the plant often turn to a reddish-orange colour.

Some years, such as this year, there's an abundant crop. If one stops to observe closely for a few minutes, one will see a subtle blue hue under the cover of multi-coloured leaves. Upon closer observation, clusters of this almost hidden fruit are observed. Our First Nations people call them Yun-dummi',[7] better known in English as blueberries. We call them low bush blueberries because of their low proximity to the ground. The flavour in one of these tiny two-to-four-millimetre diameter fruits far surpasses that of the ten millimetre fruits of the cultured blueberry!

As I was picking these magnificent little berries, I thought, *Did I plant these? Did I cause them to grow? Did I have anything to do with them blooming, pollinating, or growing fruit?* No, not all! They were put here by the Creator. He created, watered, nourished, and caused them to grow for our nourishment, survival, and enjoyment. Yet I could easily hinder or impede their growth by driving over them, rooting them up, or covering them. I may deter or prevent their growth, but I could never cause them to grow. Only our Creator God could do that! What a wonderful God we have!

In this same way, God wants to produce the fruit of His Holy Spirit in us: *"But the Holy Spirit produces this kind of fruit in our lives: love, joy, peace, patience, kindness, goodness, faithfulness, gentleness, and self-control" (Galatians 5:22–23).* Only He can produce this fruit. If we refuse Him, our lives will be like a barren field without fruit. Only as we believe in and receive Jesus Christ, and allow His Holy Spirit to control us, can He produce His fruit in our lives. Let us not resist Him and hinder the work He wants to do in us.

Just as the Creator causes the Yun-dummi' to produce fruit on the earth, may we have Him do the same in our life. The harvest will be delightful!

---

7 Spelling mine.

163

June 12

Common Problem—Common Bond—and Healing

I'm writing this from Shouldice Hospital near Toronto, situated in a beautiful park-like setting, with walkways meandering through trees, shrubs, and open spaces of lawn. The staff and doctors here are very friendly and accommodating. This hospital specializes only in abdominal hernias, so all the patients here have the same problem—abdominal hernias. I noticed most of the patients are quite open to talk about their hernia, operation, and recovery. I doubt if we'd be talking about it at a supermarket or at the gas station, because others might not understand or want to hear. Recognizing the commonality of our weakness or need has made us more transparent about it. We've all been encouraged to come here for healing. In the same way, we encourage each other on our healing journey.

But how do we tend to deal with our problems or weaknesses in everyday life? Often we don't share them but keep them to ourselves. We may think we're the only ones with this particular problem. We may think there's no cure, or that nobody cares or understands. So we withdraw, and the problem becomes ours to deal with alone. This way we will never find a cure.

As humans, we all have a common problem, called sin (Romans 3:23). When we admit our sins to each other, this can actually bring us closer together. Then we can, in love, pray to our Lord Jesus for each other. We confess our sins to God so that we may be forgiven (1 John 1:9). God's desire is that we would have an open, transparent, and honest relationship with Him. Then He can heal us and set us free.

"Therefore, confess your sins to one another and pray for one another, that you may be healed." (James 5:16, ESV).

JUNE 13

Living Water!

When in the hospital, I was able to question a nurse about her job. Did she enjoy her work? How did she become a nurse? She said she came from another country and studied nursing because she always found it interesting. Now, she said, she loved her job. She didn't come to work because of the pay, and would be a nurse even if the pay was much less. There was no other place she wanted to be; this was the right place for her! It was obvious that she was happy and enjoyed what she did. Her love for her work caused her to be an exceptional nurse, and everyone under her care noticed! With so many who begrudge each day at work, it's like a breath of fresh air, like a sip of cold water to see someone who has found a job they love.

Is life a drag with no purpose, no joy? Do you long for fulfillment in life? How can we find purpose and joy in our lives? Could love and purpose extend even beyond our work into every area of our lives?

God created each of us and has a plan for us. He wants to fulfill that plan by changing our hearts. As we surrender to God and allow Him to have His way in every area of our lives, He will fill us with His love, joy, and peace. This will be evident in and through us wherever we are: at our job, at home, in the hospital, even when we're criticized or are having a rough time. (2 Timothy 1:7). This is all accomplished through the power of the Holy Spirit of Jesus Christ in our lives and can only happen as we receive Him and allow Him to have His way in us. As we open our hearts to Him, we will see and experience His love for us. We'll begin to overflow with love for Him and for those around us. We'll be a spring of love, joy, and peace to those around us (1 Timothy 1:5; 1 John 4:19).

Jesus, speaking of the Holy Spirit who is given to everyone who truly believes in Him, said, *"Anyone who is thirsty may come to me! Anyone who believes in me may come and drink! For the Scriptures declare 'Rivers of living water will flow from his heart'"* (*John 7:37–39*).

JUNE 14

Daddy's Driving!

When I was about five or six years old, I remember travelling to somewhere with my dad and mom in our 1956 Pontiac. We came across an accident, and I got a glimpse of the carnage as we drove by. Disturbed by what I saw, I was afraid that we would have an accident too. I expressed my anxiety to Mom. She held me close and calmly explained to me that Dad was driving. He had never had an accident and was a very careful driver. He knew what he was doing. When he was driving, I didn't have to worry or fear. She assured me that we were in good hands! I soon fell asleep peacefully, resting my head on Mom as she held me close at her side. I remembered Mom's words and was never afraid again when Dad was driving. I didn't have to know where the gas or brake pedals were, or what kind of motor it had. I didn't even have to know what model of car we were driving or if it had seatbelts or not (which, incidentally, had not been invented yet!). All that mattered was that Dad was at the wheel and knew all that needed to be known about driving. I was safe as we motored along!

Sometimes we're distracted by the many disturbing events happening around us. Why deadly viruses? Why wars? Why would God allow misery, pain, and death to happen? When we focus on these things and don't understand why they all happen, fear grips our heart. But when we realize Almighty God is on the throne and focus on Him and His capable care over us, we need not fear!

"God is our refuge and strength, always ready to help in times of trouble. So we will not fear when earthquakes come and the mountains crumble into the sea ... Be still, and know that I am God!" (Psalm 46:1–2, 10).

June 15

God's Family

They were separated by war. Their father had been enlisted as a soldier, and they had lost connection. The war was over, and rumours were that he was injured and in another part of the country. Their mom, still together with their children, was determined to find her husband. She set out on a journey to find him. She didn't want to lose track of any of her children on the journey, so she made bright matching-coloured jackets for each of them. In this way as they travelled, she could recognize her children even at a distance or among a crowd of people. This is how they stayed together as a family as they travelled the war-torn country in search of their father.

Jesus also had a family. God's Word records that his earthly mother was Mary and He had brothers and sisters (Matthew 13:55–56). Yet when Mary and His brothers came looking for Him as He was ministering to crowds of people, He said, *"My mother and my brothers are all those who hear God's word and obey it." (Luke 8:21).* When Jesus called His disciples, He said, *"Follow me."* Each of them, in faith, left their old way of living and followed Him. Essentially each of them had a change of heart and expressed faith in Him by following Him. One of His followers expressed it this way: *"Yet to all who did receive him, to those who believed in his name, he gave the right to become children of God—children born not of natural descent, nor of human decision or a husband's will, but born of God." (John 1:12–13, NIV).*

This is God's family of faith. All those who through faith turn from their ways of sin and shame to follow God and His will for their lives. Just as the war-torn mother mentioned above recognized her children by their distinctive jackets, Jesus recognizes His spiritual family by their obedient faith.

Do I truly believe in God? Do you? This is a question we must all ask ourselves. When we in our desperation call out to Him in faith, He hears us, saves us (Romans 10:13), and makes us His children, children who stand out and are recognizable in the crowd as those who follow Him. Is He speaking to you today? Do you hear His voice calling *"Follow me"*?

JUNE 16

Dad and Mom

When June rolls around, many of us think of our fathers on Father's Day; it was the month of my dad and mom's anniversary as well. We have a picture taken on their wedding day to remind us. They stayed faithful to each other for the duration of their marriage—forty-seven years—until Mom passed away. Part of Dad died that day, and he was never quite the same. *"… a man leaves his father and mother and is joined to his wife, and the two are united into one" (Genesis 2:24).* The two had become one when they vowed "until death do us part" so many years ago! *"So God created human beings in his own image. In the image of God he created them; male and female he created them. Then God blessed them and said, 'Be fruitful and multiply'" (Genesis 1:27–28).* Dad and Mom had four children, and I was the third. They, though not perfect, tried to teach us about God and the importance of receiving Him and following His Word, the Bible. I'm thankful for them and for all they sacrificed for us children. With love and strength from the Lord, through difficult times, they kept their promise to God and to each other. They consistently took care of us in our physical, mental, emotional, and spiritual needs.

Sometimes we attempt to redefine marriage and family. It will never work, because God has created us human beings in His own image to follow His ways. We have all fallen away from Him and His will in one way or another. If we still have breath, it's not too late to repent and turn back to God. Jesus said: *"As for everyone who comes to me and hears my words and puts them into practice, I will show you what they are like. They are like a man building a house, who dug down deep and laid the foundation on rock. When a flood came, the torrent struck that house but could not shake it, because it was well built." (Luke 6:47–48, NIV).*

JUNE 17

Daddy

The senior in the old age home speaking endearing words about his father, the little boy running into his father's arms after a time of separation, the daughter holding on to and hugging her father just before he passes on to his forever dwelling place in heaven—all these experiences exemplify the importance of a father's love in each of our lives. Yet so many people don't have such experiences to remember. Some may have had an abusive, a disconnected, or an absent father. As God created families to have fathers to affirm, love, protect, and provide for them, this can leave a gaping hole in one's life, a longing for a father's love and protection that we never received. We're in a messed-up world where no earthly father is perfect, but we all need the stability and love that only a father can give. As a father, I realize how difficult it is to be the dad I'm called to be. I know that in myself, I'm inadequate for the task.

The Father heart of God is revealed in His holy Word, the Bible: *"Father to the fatherless, defender of widows— this is God, whose dwelling is holy" (Psalm 68:5)*. Jesus, just before He died on the cross, cried out, *"Abba Father"* (Mark 14:36). Paul the Apostle speaks of his relationship with God: *"And because we are his children, God has sent the Spirit of his Son into our hearts, prompting us to call out, 'Abba, Father'" (Galatians 4:6)*. This term "Abba" is an endearing word similar to the word "Daddy," which is used to express an intimate relationship with our fathers.

Do we long to be the fathers God has called us to be? Do we long for that intimate relationship with God? When we call out to Him in childlike faith, when we submit to Him and willingly follow Him, He will give us His Holy Spirit to cause us to be the fathers He intended us to be, as we cry out in praise, *"Abba Father!"*

JUNE 18

Fathers and Sons

The story is told of a young father who had a drinking problem. He would often frequent the local pub instead of spending time with his family. One winter day after supper, as usual, he slipped out of the house to spend time with "the boys." Hearing a sound behind him, he turned to see his young son following him, trying his best to step into his father's footprints in the snow.

"Go back home, son" the father exhorted his determined boy.

His son looked up to the father and said, "No, Daddy, I want to be with you. I want to go where you're going."

The father, convicted in his heart and realizing his corrupt example, picked up his son and carried him home in his arms, never to return to the bar again.

Fathers are extremely important to a family. Their example has a profound effect on their children, especially on their sons. I remember our boys imitating my every move. Now their children are imitating their every move. Thus, the influence of the father carries on from generation to generation.

This should cause each of us fathers to reflect on what kind of an example we are to our children. What do we want our sons to be like? What kind of an example am I? How can I change? I have already blown it; I cannot change the past. These questions and concerns are some that we may have. This may seem too great a task, but the sooner we realize our need and change, the better. While we have breath, there's still hope. Our example will have a profound effect on those we love.

God is our spiritual Father (Matthew 23:9; 1John 3:1;). Fatherhood was His idea in the first place. When we put our trust in Him, He will empower us to be the fathers we should be (John 3:16, 14:1;12–14; Malachi 4:6). He sent his one and only Son to pay for our sins and be our mediator (1 Timothy 2:3–4), and His Holy Spirit to empower us for this task (John 14:15–21, 26). When we surrender to God and His ways, we can be the examples He wants us to be.

"'Come out from them and be separate, says the Lord. Touch no unclean thing, and I will receive you.' And, 'I will be a Father to you, and you will be my sons and daughters, says the Lord Almighty'" (2 Corinthians 6:17–18, NIV).

JUNE 19

Thanks Dad!

As I think of my father, I have much to be thankful for. Though he passed away many years ago, if he was sitting here today, I'd say, "Thank you, Dad, for working at various, sometimes taxing and difficult, occupations so you could provide for Mom and us kids. Thank you for treating Mom with respect, for loving her and keeping your promise to stay with her until the Lord took her to her eternal home. Thank you for teaching us the difference between right and wrong, to speak the truth and live honest lives, even when it would have been easy to do otherwise. Thank you for showing us the pitfalls and dangers of life that are all around us, some harmful and possibly even fatal if we go there. Thank you for disciplining us when we wandered from the good path that was set before us. Thank you for forgiving us when we came to you and confessed our trespasses against you or others. Yes, Dad, the list could go on and on. Certainly you had your own faults, some more glaring and some minor ones, yet I'm thankful that the Lord gave you to me as my father."

Now my dad is gone, yet I still sense his profound influence in my life. Dad's greatest impact on me is that he knew the Lord, and his primary desire was for me to know Him too. One question he would often ask was, "Ken, how are you doing with the Lord?" I remember Dad's excitement when I too became a follower of Jesus! The moment when the Lord opened my eyes and saved me, I was completely changed. Now I have a personal relationship with the heavenly Father, who wants me to call Him "Abba" or "Daddy."

Some of us had caring earthly dads, others had dads who weren't encouraging at all, still others may not have known an earthly father. Yet there is a perfect heavenly Father who is calling for us to put our trust in Him. Then we will be His children and He will be our Daddy forever! *"And because we are his children, God has sent the Spirit of his Son into our hearts, prompting us to call out, 'Abba, Father'"* (Galatians 4:6).

JUNE 20

But He Did!

"You didn't have to, but you did," began the young man as he read hesitatingly from a crumpled-up paper that was shaking in his hand. The words were written in rough handwritten script and went something like this: "You didn't have to take us in, but you did. You didn't have to care for us, but you did. You didn't have to take me fishing, but you did. You didn't have to teach me to work, but you did. You didn't have to love us, but you did. You didn't have to treat us like your own, but you did. You didn't have to, but you did." He concluded with tears in his eyes. "Thank you for loving us even when you didn't have to."

This young man read this tribute at the memorial of his stepfather, who had treated them with love, honour, and respect, raising them and caring for them as his own. I was tempted to ask him for that old crumpled up piece of paper that he had shoved into his pocket, but the moment was too sacred.

Though I don't have the exact recorded words of the young man, we do have recorded in the Bible the words of Jesus when He was being arrested by the people who wanted Him killed: *"Don't you realize that I could ask my Father for thousands of angels to protect us, and he would send them instantly? But if I did, how would the Scriptures be fulfilled that describe what must happen now?" (Matthew 26:53–54).* In another translation, we read, *"twelve legions of angels" (KJV).* The dictionary says one legion of soldiers in Jesus' time was between three thousand and six thousand. That would work out to be many thousands of angels that Jesus could have called on to rescue Him and the disciples. BUT instead He went to the cross to die a cruel death. He willingly became a man to obey His heavenly Father (John 4:34). He came to die in the place of sinners like me, so all those who would call on Him could escape the clutches of sin and eternal death and have eternal life with Him forever (Romans 10:13).

"But God showed his great love for us by sending Christ to die for us while we were still sinners. And since we have been made right in God's sight by the blood of Christ, he will certainly save us from God's condemnation. For since our friendship with God was restored by the death of his Son while we were still his enemies, we will certainly be saved through the life of his Son." (Romans 5:8–10).

God's Children

As Father's Days come and go, we're reminded of the importance the role of a father plays within the family unit. Some have good memories of their father and some not so good. I've heard comments about fathers ranging from "I hate my dad" to "I want to be just like my dad." To have a healthy relationship with our father is important to our human development.

Though I haven't always been the father I would have liked to be, I do have some precious memories. When I would come home from work, sometimes I'd lie down on the floor to rest. My son would come and lie down beside me. If I put my hands behind my head, he'd put his hands behind his head. If I crossed my legs, he'd cross his legs. Whatever I did, he wanted to do. I realized that he wanted to be just like me! I thought, *Wow what a responsibility! What an honour. Do I deserve this? How can I live up to his expectations?*

Some people, for various reasons, haven't had the privilege of knowing their father; others have had fathers that were very poor examples, and none of us had perfect fathers. So how can we have a good father image to follow?

The apostle Paul speaks of an intimate relationship that we can have with our heavenly Father: *"So you have not received a spirit that makes you fearful slaves. Instead you received God's Spirit when He adopted you as his own children. Now we call Him 'Abba, Father'. For His Spirit joins our spirit to affirm that we are God's children." (Romans 8:15–16).*

The gift of having God as our Father and becoming His child is available. All we have to do is to believe and receive, in faith.

JUNE 22

I'm Ok; You're Ok?

I'm sure you've heard the saying, "I'm Ok; you're Ok." When saying this, I think generally people mean, "What you think, say, or do is your business; it really doesn't affect me or matter to me in the least. My version of the truth is just as good as yours. Whatever you believe to be truth is truth for you, and my version is good for me." On the surface this might seem to have some wisdom, but in actuality, nothing could be further from the truth!

First of all, truth is the truth no matter what we think. It's for us to seek the truth and believe it, otherwise we live in a world of make-believe. Jesus said, *"and you will know the truth, and the truth will set you free" (John 8:32, ESV)*. He also said of Himself, *"I am the way, and the truth, and the life." (John 14:6, ESV)*. So the way to find the truth is to seek Him, and He will personally reveal the truth to us through His Word, the Bible, and through the wisdom we receive from His Holy Spirit (Proverbs 2:1–11; Psalm 119:11).

Secondly, in our personal lives, we actually live in a way that cries out, "I'm Ok; you're not Ok." Our sinful human nature wants its own way. We think the universe revolves around me, myself, and I. This is proven out by our reactions when things don't go our way, when someone cuts us off at an intersection, when someone says something we don't agree with, or when a promise is broken. In some way or another, we say, "You are not Ok" at that moment. This is where conflict comes in. I want my way, and they want their way (Romans 2:1–11; James 4:1–12).

If we were honest, we'd say, "I'm not Ok; you're not Ok, but God is Ok" (Romans 3:4). He is the creator of truth in the first place (Genesis 1; John 1:1–5, 7:28). He made us and knows how we should live. Let us seek Him and His way, then we will have healthier relationships. The world would be a better place if we all placed Him first in our lives. *"And we know that the Son of God has come and has given us understanding, so that we may know him who is true; and we are in him who is true, in his Son Jesus Christ. He is the true God and eternal life." (1 John 5:20, ESV)*.

Narcissistic Junco

We have a small bird, a junco, tapping against our window. It's been doing this for at least a month. It goes away for a time but soon returns to flutter and bump against the window. I was wondering why it was so insistent. Did it see the plants inside? Maybe it was looking for a nesting place. It wasn't until looking in from outside that I realized it was only seeing its own reflection. It seems to be enamored with itself. It's an absolute waste of time, and all that's produced from this activity is a dirty window and bird poop on the windowsill.

The ancient Greeks recognized this behaviour, illustrating it by a mythological person called Narcissus. He was so in love with himself that all he could do was look at his own reflection in a pond. Nothing was more important than himself. Everything else passed him by as he gazed upon his image.

Today we have an increasing emphasis on self: You deserve it. If you use this shampoo, when you look in the mirror, you'll look just like the model in the picture. Can you see yourself in that car? You'll be a better person if you own it. These are subliminal messages society is feeding us that appeal our selfish side.

Yet if we only think of ourselves, the rest of the people and events in life will pass us by, and we'll miss the blessings God has intended for us as we relate to others around us. Life is fluttered away, and all that's left, at best, will be a mess! Just like the dirty window left behind by the junco, wasting his time and efforts on himself while beating against our window. And Narcissus was left with only a reflection of himself that was obliterated by the first breeze that came along or pebble thrown into the water.

The Word of God tells us *"... in the last days there will be very difficult times. For people will love only themselves and their money ... But they won't get away with this for long. Someday everyone will recognize what fools they are ..." (2 Timothy 3:1–2, 9).*

"Don't look out only for your own interests, but take an interest in others too" (Philippians 2:4).

Who We Know

I was driving an older car with lots of kilometres on it. This meant more repairs. One time I had a problem with it losing power when accelerating. This was quite dangerous and unnerving at times, especially when in the passing lane!

Though I do some simple mechanical work on it at times, try as I may, I couldn't figure out what was wrong. I took it to a local mechanic, who advised me to take it to the dealership because they'd be able to diagnose and repair it. They had designed and manufactured the vehicle, so they would have the expertise and the equipment to fix it. I followed his advice. They had it fixed in a couple hours. I don't know what they did to make it run so well, but I wished I'd brought it there much sooner.

Often this is the way it is with our lives. We try to manage our own affairs; problems crowd in, and life becomes unmanageable. Something has gone wrong. What can we do? we ask ourselves. We've tried everything to no avail. We can't figure it out; we've run out of power. We've even shared it with friends and the "experts" for advice, but there's still no change. We've have come to the end of ourselves, and we feel like giving up.

There is One we can go to who knows our every need. He's waiting for us to call out to Him. We don't have to understand exactly how He's going to work it out, but we can trust He will, in His time and in His way, because He knows what's best. He is the Almighty God, the One who made us and knows exactly what our problem is. He is the true Expert, and we are the needy ones. He wants us to humble ourselves and surrender to Him and trust Him with our whole lives. The sooner we surrender to Him, the better. It really comes down to Who we know, more than what we know.

"So humble yourselves under the might power of God, and at the right time he will lift you up in honor. Give all your worries and cares to God, for he cares for you." (1 Peter 5:6–7).

JUNE 25

Resistance

In 1956, my father bought a brand-new Pontiac car. He picked it up at the dealership and proudly drove it home. It was two-tone, white and light blue, with lots of chrome—a very fine car indeed. I'm sure heads turned as he drove past his neighbours and friends. But as he pulled it into the driveway, something went wrong. Suddenly it stopped, and the wheels refused to turn. The brakes were locked up, and no movement was possible forward or backwards. The car, with new seats, glossy paint, and chrome, was immobilized and in an absolutely useless state to him or anyone else. It was towed back to where it came from. The mechanics investigated and found that the brakes were installed backwards at the factory and thus tightened up until the wheels wouldn't turn.

This is similar to what happens when we resist the working of God in our lives. He wants us to come to Him so He can deal with those things that immobilize us: our sins, our selfish attitudes, our pride and self-sufficiency. He wants us to be saved and set free to be all He wants us to be. Yet we tend to resist His call and His work, and thus we become immobilized. No matter how good things look, all that we thought was so valuable becomes useless: our possessions, our program, our wealth, or our retirement plan. They will all come to nothing. Everything will become futile in the end unless we turn to Him in repentance and humility, to surrender our lives to Him so He can give us life that lasts forever.

God's Word spoken through Isaiah some 2,700 years ago still applies to us today:

"'Come now, let us reason together,' says the Lord. 'Though your sins are like scarlet, they shall be white as snow; though they are red like crimson, they shall be as wool. If you are willing and obedient, you will eat the best of the land; but if you resist and rebel, you will be devoured by the sword.' For the mouth of the LORD has spoken." (Isaiah 1:18–20, NIV).

JUNE 26

The Means and the End

You've probably heard the statement, "The end justifies the means." What I take this to mean is that we have a goal and we get to that goal in whatever way possible. Some sports celebrities who take steroids to boost their physical capabilities so that they can come in first to win the gold are examples of this. We lie, we cheat, we steal, some have even killed to get to the destination we want for ourselves, our families, or even our country. History teaches that Hitler brought order, industry, and stability to Germany for a time through some very ruthless means. He did whatever he needed to do to get the final outcome he wanted. The final result was exactly opposite to what he thought he was going to accomplish. Only death, war, mayhem, and a broken world were left in the aftermath.

Have you ever sold your own car? Our goal is usually to get the best price possible. How do I get the most I can for it? Do I need to temporarily fix something just to make it look good? Do I cover up the rust holes and rot under the surface? Do I have to tell a little lie, saying that it doesn't use any oil when I had to add two litres between every oil change? All so I can get the price I want.

God's Word clearly says *"Don't be misled—you cannot mock the justice of God. You will always harvest what you plant. Those who live only to satisfy their own sinful nature will harvest decay and death from that sinful nature." (Galatians 6:7–8).*

Most of us want our lives to have meaning. We want to leave a legacy. How will we do this? The conclusion to the above-mentioned verses gives us the answer: *"But those who live to please the Spirit will harvest everlasting life from the Spirit." (Galatians 6:8b).*

God gives His Holy Spirit to all who sincerely ask Him (Luke 11:13). Then, as we surrender to His will and live in the power of His Spirit moment by moment, the end result will be a life filled with fruit that lasts forever.

The means ultimately determines the end.

Say It Now—While You Still Can

We've attended numerous funerals in the last six months, and most of them were close friends. Among some of the last words I spoke with a couple of them were "I love you." As we were standing by the coffin of one friend, remembering this I thought, *I was glad we had those words, but I won't be able to speak with him or visit him here on earth anymore. It would have been nice to have spent more time with my friends and encouraged them more while they were still here. I truly miss them.* Then I looked up and saw all the friends who were standing there, still alive. I could still visit and share my life with them!

Often we take for granted that our friends are with us, but as others pass away, reality hits and we realize we all have a limited time here on earth. God has given each of us a life to live to share with friends, family, and those we meet in everyday life (1 Peter 4:7–9). We need each other, and we need to be compassionate and encourage each other, especially fellow believers. The way that we will truly encourage another person is by allowing God's Spirit to overflow in our hearts. Jesus said, *"I have told you these things so that you would be filled with joy. Yes, your joy will overflow. This is my commandment: love each other in the same way I have loved you."* (*John 15:11–12*, see also 2 Corinthians 8:2; Philippians 1:9; Colossians 2:7, 3:16–17). Let us not delay but do this while we can, while the opportunity is still before us. *"Is there any encouragement from belonging to Christ? Any comfort from his love? Any fellowship together in the Spirit? Are your hearts tender and compassionate? Then make me truly happy by agreeing wholeheartedly with each other, loving one another, and working with one another with one mind and one purpose."* (*Philippians 2:1–2*).

JUNE 28

The Vilest Offender

He saw a man severely beating his own countryman. Overcome with it all, he beat the aggressor to death and then buried him in the sand, hoping nobody noticed. He subsequently spent forty years running from the authorities and from God (Exodus 2:11–15).

Another man followed the dictates of his religion and thus hated Christians. He hunted them down and beat them, imprisoning some. He even stood watching in approval as one was stoned to death right in front of him (Acts 8:1–3, 9:1–2).

A third man was a slave trader. He was vile and had absolutely no compassion in his heart as they caught slaves, cruelly holding them in putrid, dingy ship's holds, bringing them to be sold as chattel in slave markets. He was involved in the death and misery of many slaves.

The first person mentioned here is Moses, the man who later faced God at the burning bush and was called by God to set the people of Israel free from Egyptian bondage (Exodus 3 and 4).

The second person mentioned was the Saul, who changed his name to Paul after his encounter with Jesus on the Damascus Road, when he became a follower of Jesus and an apostle of the Christian Church. God used him to write many of the books of the New Testament in the Bible (Acts 9:3–31).

The third person mentioned above is John Newton, whom God convicted of his terrible lifestyle. He turned his life over to God and became a Christian minister, instrumental in helping the British Empire to abolish slavery. He authored the popular hymn "Amazing Grace."

So is there hope for one who has or is living a gross and vile lifestyle? Can the grace of God reach into the depths of a rotten and sinful life? The above-mentioned people are examples of the extravagant and generous mercy of God to one who truly is sorry for their sin, one who turns from their sin towards God and asks for mercy, desiring to begin a new life that is pleasing to God. *"Come now, let us reason together, says the Lord: though your sins are like scarlet, they shall be as white as snow; though they are red like crimson, they shall become like wool. If you are willing and obedient, you shall eat the good of the land." (Isaiah 1:18–19, ESV). "The Lord is not slow to fulfill his promise as some count slowness, but is patient toward you, not wishing that any should perish, but that all should reach repentance." (2 Peter 2:9, ESV).*

The great songwriter Fanny Crosby had it right when she wrote, "The vilest offender who truly believes, that moment from Jesus a pardon receives."[8]

---

8 From the hymn "To God Be the Glory" by Fanny Crosby.

House or Home?

While riding in a taxi through the streets in Vancouver, I noticed numerous "For Sale" signs on properties, and some said "Home for Sale." I asked the taxi driver how much houses were selling for in the area. He said almost all in that area sold for at least one million dollars. That's a lot of money just for a house! People want a house, but many can't buy one because of the price. But if we bought a house, would it be a home?

Can any amount of money buy a home? What's the difference between a house and a home? A house is the physical structure in which people live, and a home is the place where one is accepted, feels welcome, and knows they belong. It may have very little physical structure to it. It could even be a tent or a lean-to somewhere in the bush. Everyone wants and needs a home. It's a basic foundation of our society. A home is made up of friends, family, and people who love each other. A home can't be bought with money but is built on love, respect, and care for one another, and it's a place where one is always welcome (Isaiah 32:18; Ephesians 5:33).

Many people have very expensive houses but don't really have a home, because those living there don't have a sense of belonging. Sometimes there is discord, strife, isolation, and loneliness. Lack of transparency and communication make a house a difficult place to stay in. They may have shelter but not a home. *"The Lord's curse is on the house of the wicked, but he blesses the home of the righteous." (Proverbs 3:33, NIV).*

The building code tells us how to build a house, but we build a home by having God at the centre of our relationships. Jesus said, *"Anyone who loves me will obey my teaching. My Father will love them, and we will come to them and make our home with them." (John 14:23, NIV).*

JUNE 30

Still Half-Mast

Canada Day was once called Dominion Day, as Canada was at that time called the Dominion of Canada. Dominion Day became a statutory holiday in 1879, and in 1982 the name was changed to Canada Day. We sing "God keep our land glorious and free" as we celebrate freedoms that are based on Christian principles. Evidence of this heritage is engraved on the arches at the front entrance of the Peace Tower, where inscribed are Bible verses, one of which says, *"And he shall have dominion from sea to sea." (Psalm 72:8, KJV)*. It's obvious that this scripture is speaking of the Almighty God exercising His Dominion through the rulers of the land.

Though God ultimately has the dominion over not only Canada but every nation on earth (Psalm 2), we have a serious problem. People want to usurp His Dominion and want to rule by their own ways, with their own desires, rather than His will being paramount. This human display of arrogance in the face of God is manifested in many ways, but one of the most horrendous and grievous in our land today is the wholesale abortion of preborn human babies. One dies every five minutes—100,000 every year. A mother's womb, the place created to be the safest place for the most vulnerable and innocent, has become the most dangerous, mostly for the sake of sexual convenience and a self-crafted lifestyle! God have mercy on us!

As I contemplate this terrible holocaust, my Canadian flag still flies at half-mast, not only on Canada Day but every day of the year, as we grieve the loss and stand up for such innocent ones.

Almighty God, open our eyes. Have mercy on our leaders, our medical personnel, those who have had abortions, and on each of us. Forgive us of this horrendous sin we so blatantly practise on a continual basis before You. Have mercy on us, change our hearts, our attitudes, our ways. May You have Dominion in our hearts, our communities, and our land! In Jesus' name we pray. Amen!

JULY 1

O Canada

I remember singing our national anthem when we were in elementary school: one room, six grades, twenty to twenty-five students. We said the Lord's Prayer and read from the Bible at the start of every school day! Once I entered high school, our homeroom teacher refused to read from the Bible or to pray, even though it was still part of his duties. I didn't think much of the change at the time, because I was intent on following my ways, but now I can see the consequences of wandering from God's Word.

If there's no standard, how can we know what's right or wrong? Is morality just a personal or subjective thing? Does my set of morals have any effect on me, my neighbour, or my nation?

Today we have the Supreme Court changing the Creator's definition of marriage and introducing euthanasia into the health care system. Tomorrow? Who knows what will be next? The standard seems to be set at the whim of the court, the constitution, and the will of men, rather than the will of God, the Creator of it all.

God has a standard that no country, no person, no court, nor any human institution can change without running into very serious problems down the road, even to the downfall of nations. God spoke to His people through the prophet Jeremiah many years ago: *"This is what the Lord says: 'Stand at the crossroads and look; ask for the ancient paths, ask where the good way is, and walk in it, and you will find rest for your souls.' But you said, 'We will not walk in it.' ... 'Hear, you earth: I am bringing disaster on this people, the fruit of their schemes, because they have not listened to my words and have rejected my law.'"* (*Jeremiah 6:16, 19, NIV*).

God's standard is found in His Word, the Bible. As I see us turning our backs on our Creator, my heart cries out, "O Canada, we are at a crossroads. Turn while there is still time. Turn to the LORD God, the Creator of heaven and earth. Follow Him and His ways before it's too late."

Rather than going our own way, we need to humble ourselves before God and pray, seek Him, and turn from our wicked ways. Then He will forgive our sins and heal our land (2 Chronicles 7:14).

July 2

Oh-Oh Canada

A few days after celebrating Canada Day, contemplating this great land of ours and also my own life, I can see comparisons. When I was younger, much younger, trying to make sense out of my life and wanting to live life my way, I came up with some ideas that I thought would be perfect for living life. Thinking about it now, I'm embarrassed to write that I actually had these thoughts, yet it serves as a valuable reminder of a path not to follow! *Too many rules*, I thought. *Let me live my life how I want, with social, moral, and sexual ethics on my terms.* We could have utopia in a society without restraints. Individual freedom, I thought, was based on all I wanted to do. But as I followed this selfish pathway, I suddenly found myself in deep trouble. Very deep trouble. I had come face to face with reality. There was a set of values much higher and greater than I. Had I continued down my self-made pathway, I don't think I would be here today.

Though this was one of the most difficult times in my life, there was beauty shining through the darkness. Mercy, grace, and love shone through as I surrendered to this superior set of values and ultimately to the Source of these eternal precepts. I met the Creator of the universe, the Source of all true morality and ethics! I met Jesus! *"Jesus said to him, 'I am the way, and the truth, and the life. No one comes to the Father except through me.'" (John 14:6, ESV).* I had to let my old ways die and allow Him to have His way with me! He changed me. My perspective changed, and now I realize that His way is the only true way!

I see Canada as a nation going in the same direction as I tried, attempting to find a foundation in other sources than the Almighty God. It will not work; we will run into a wall and self-destruct unless we humbly turn to the only Source, our Creator God: *"... if my people who are called by my name humble themselves, and pray and seek my face and turn from their wicked ways, then I will hear from heaven and will forgive their sin and heal their land." (2 Chronicles 7:14, ESV).*

JULY 3

Social Engineering

In 1994, the BC government tried to manufacture fast ferries, which had not previously been built in Canada. It was an incredible plan to give more work to local people. The hope was that they would build ships for the BC Ferries fleet and even for the worldwide market. Yet after all the effort of hundreds if not thousands of people, it turned into a fiasco. A ballooning budget, design deficiencies, fuel efficiency problems, a larger wake eroding the seashore, and slower than expected speed were among many of the problems that caused the lofty plans to be dashed. The ships were auctioned off at a mere fraction of the costs of building them. Though there had been a noble effort by many, some basic principles of research, engineering, manufacture, and management, among other things, hadn't been adhered to. A great dream was sunk.

If this was a fiasco, a much larger one is looming over us. There are those in our society today who are engaged in a massive social engineering experiment. Many of the God-given values that are foundational to life are being replaced with the ideas of men. The creation ordinance of marriage, the union of a man and a woman, are being redefined. The value of human life from conception to natural death is being eroded. Doctors are given the right, or possibly the obligation, to take lives of our most vulnerable on both ends of the life spectrum, our youngest and oldest. *"There is a way that seems right to a man, but its end is the way to death."* *(Proverbs 14:12, ESV)*. The definition of a family is being reinvented, and sexuality is being morphed into whatever one's imagination might conjure up. The foundations are being eroded, and we're already seeing the effects, such as broken homes and increasing suicide and drug overdose death rates. The fallout from this social engineering experiment will make the fast ferries fiasco miniscule in comparison. *"Hear, O earth; behold, I am bringing disaster upon this people, the fruit of their devices, because they have not paid attention to my words; and as for my law, they have rejected it."* *(Jeremiah 6:19, ESV)*.

Yet there is hope! *"Now therefore, O kings, be wise; be warned, O rulers of the earth. Serve the Lord with fear, and rejoice with trembling. Kiss the Son, Lest he be angry, and you perish in the way, for his wrath is quickly kindled. Blessed are all who take refuge in him."* *(Psalm 2:10–11, ESV)*.

JULY 4

Look up, Canada!

During these times of testing and turmoil, we've heard many bold statements, especially by our world leaders. Our responses to them have often been just as bold. We must remember that every word will ultimately be judged by Almighty God (Matthew 12:36). When President Trump says he's the only perfect one, he is wrong, because God's Word says *"… for all have sinned and fall short of the glory of God." (Romans 3:23, ESV)*. When Prime Minister Trudeau says he is looking after Canada's most vulnerable, he's wrong, because he's paying for and promoting the killing of defenceless preborn human babies who are created in the image of God and truly are the most vulnerable (Psalm 139). And if I say I am better than them, I am wrong, because God's Word says *"You may think you can condemn such people, but you are just as bad, and you have no excuse!" (Romans 2:1)*. These are hard words, but the truth is often hard, and the truth is what sets us free (John 8:32)!

So is there hope for any of us? There was hope for Moses, a murderer who, after turning to God, led God's children out of slavery. There was hope for evil King Manasseh, who turned to God for mercy after God disciplined him for his evil deeds, like sacrificing his own sons in the fire. There was hope for Saul, who vehemently persecuted God's people and encouraged the stoning of Stephen, yet when he encountered the resurrected Jesus, he was transformed and became Paul, a dedicated and powerful apostle of Jesus!

People of Canada, look up! People of the world, look up! Sinners, look up! Jesus, the light of the world, said, *"For the Son of Man came to seek and to save the lost." (Luke 19:10, ESV)*; *"While you have the light, believe in the light, that you may become sons of light." (John 12:36, ESV)*.

Believers, be encouraged, *"Now when these things begin to take place, straighten up and raise your heads, because your redemption is drawing near." (Luke 21:28, ESV)*.

Something Good

As I cleaned out our compost bins, I was again amazed by the beautiful soil that was produced. We had thrown our fruit, vegetable, and food scraps together into the bin. Now over time, a beautiful black soil was produced that we could use to fertilize our garden. The smelly scraps were transformed into nourishing nutrients for the garden. Last year's compost helped to produce a wonderful crop of strawberries and raspberries this year. We even got some cucumbers, peas, and beans. Vegetables grow best in good soil. Rather than throwing out our scraps to pollute the environment, they could be composted to produce something needed and useful.

This reminds me of a verse in God's Word that says, *"And we know that for those who love God all things work together for good, for those who are called according to his purpose." (Romans 8:28, ESV).* Sometimes when difficulties come or wrong decisions are made, everything seems to come to nothing, and all we can see are problems, difficulties, struggles, and hurts—just leftovers from a messed-up life. God is able to transform our messes into something beautiful if we can hand them all over to Him. Just as the food scraps are changed into rich nutrient soil, God can take our broken, wasted lives and transform us into useful, purposeful people. We can then become all God wants us to be.

"Don't copy the behaviour and customs of this world, but let God transform you into a new person by changing the way you think. Then you will learn to know God's will for you, which is good and pleasing and perfect." (Romans 12:2).

JULY 6

One Race

Having just read a story of a young fellow who narrowly escaped with his life while being cruelly persecuted by the Hutus in the 1994 Tutsi genocide in Rwanda, I was reminded of the prevalence of racism in the world today. It raises its ugly head, just like a plague. The conflict mentioned above cost approximately a million human lives. Among many other examples of racism there was the "ethnic cleansing" in Serbia and Bosnia, where many more were killed. More recently, the tensions between the Russians and the Ukrainians have been in the headlines. Closer to home, racism against minority groups is often highlighted in the news.

Yet the Bible reveals that we are all equally human beings, descendants of a couple named Adam and Eve (Genesis 1:26–28; Acts 17:26). They were created in the image of God. He breathed the very breath of life into Adam. At the close of the day, God pronounced their creation with the declaration "very good." This is what gives every human being dignity, worth, and very great value, much more than any of the animals (Matthew 10:29–31).

We should recognize the image of God in every human being we meet, whatever culture or people group they are from. God has made each person in His image and is intimately acquainted with each one. That makes them very special in His sight, so should they be special to us.

Racism is evil and has cost the human race untold horror and grief. If we lived our lives surrendered to God and in light of His Word, the world would be a much better place to live. There is only one race, and that is the human race.

"Owe no one anything, except to love each other, for the one who loves another has fulfilled the law." (Romans 13:8, ESV).

JULY 7

Grace or Karma?

A fellow recently spoke to me about doing good things for people because, he said, it was good karma to do good deeds to others, as these deeds would come back as good in a life at a later time. On the other hand, if we do evil things, then evil will come about in a life somewhere down the road. According to this teaching, what we do determines how our next life will be, good or bad, so we control our own destiny.

I thank God that this is absolutely not the case. If we were left to our own devises. We'd continually spiral down, descending into a bottomless abyss. We only need to watch the news reports for a few minutes to see the terrible deeds that come out of the human heart. Some of the most desperate societies on earth base their beliefs on karma.

God's Word, the Bible, clearly teaches that, *"The human heart is the most deceitful of all things and desperately wicked" (Jeremiah 17:9)*; *"No one does good not a single one" (Romans 3:12)*. Jesus didn't even entrust Himself to men: *"because he knew human nature." (John 2:24)*. Even our righteous acts are as filthy rags (Isaiah 64:6). We cannot save ourselves.

The only reason we can do good is because of the good God has already done for us. He has given us grace, which is favour that we don't deserve. If we want to live a truly meaningful and fulfilled life, we must receive a new heart and a new life from God (Ezekiel 36:26; 2 Corinthians 5:17). Then His Holy Spirit will produce love, joy, and peace in our lives.

God is the only one who can forgive us and save us from ourselves. This is why Jesus, the Son of the Almighty God, came to earth and died to forgive us and give us life. One day each of us will die and face God (Hebrews 9:27). Either we will be forgiven because we believed and received the gift of salvation, or we'll receive the wages of our sins and be eternally separated from God (John 3:16–18; Revelation 20:11–15).

"For by grace you have been saved through faith. And this is not your own doing; it is the gift of God, not a result of works, so that no one may boast. For we are his workmanship, created in Christ Jesus for good works, which God prepared beforehand, that we should walk in them." (Ephesians 2:8–10, ESV),

JULY 8

The Captain

The great city of Jericho stood in the way of the children of Israel occupying the land God had promised them. It was a literal fortress with formidable walls around it. As Joshua approached the city, I'm sure some of his thoughts were: *How will we conquer this city? What military plans should I make? How should I proceed?* Then Joshua saw someone standing in front of him with a drawn sword. When Joshua asked him whose side he was on, he indicated that he was on neither side, but that he was the captain of the LORD's army. Joshua fell at his feet and worshipped God. After this, God informed Joshua how He would conquer the city. God miraculously had the walls fall down as the people shouted, without any intervention of man (Joshua 6:16). Incidentally, the broken-down walls are still there as evidence of the mighty hand of God interceding for His people.

What can we learn from this today? Certainly we can marvel at the amazing power of God, but I think that the greatest lesson we can learn is that God is the Captain. He is the boss; He is the leader, and we are the followers. He has a plan, and only as we fall under His command and sovereignty will we ever have true victory in our lives over the enormous, impossible problems we face.

Do we have an impossible situation in our life? Are there hardships that we can't overcome? Does life seem impossible? God wants us to personally surrender ourselves to Him. When we do, we will find His direction, His guidance, and His power to live this live as He planned for it to be. He doesn't want to just help us out in our situation; He wants us to submit to Him as our Captain. May we learn a lesson from Joshua.

"At this, Joshua fell with his face to the ground in reverence. 'I am at your command,' Joshua said 'What do you want your servant to do?'" (Joshua 5:14).

JULY 9

Faithful Friend

About to address an audience, I was interrupted by a very good friend. He asked me if I had somehow gotten bleach on my shirt, as it was discoloured. It was an awkward moment, but after investigation, we discovered that I had leaned against a chalkboard and some had rubbed off onto my shirt to give it a bleached appearance. We were able to get most of the chalk off the shirt before I got up to speak to the people. Had my friend been too shy or intimidated to address my problem, it would have been a distraction to all who were there. I thank God for faithful friends like this.

When we confront a person in this way, we take a risk that their response may be negative and they will be offended, but a loving friend will do so anyway, for our good, even at the risk of backlash or losing a relationship. In the above-mentioned case, no real harm would have been done, but sometimes life and death could stand in the balance—as in my younger days when, oblivious to me, I had a problem with speeding in my new 1974 Mazda 808. I sped past a semi-truck before stopping at the next town for fuel. The driver of the semi pulled in behind me. He got out of his truck and came directly over to me and told me if I kept driving so carelessly, my little car would become my coffin. He said he had seen it in the past and he could see it happening to me unless I changed my driving habits. At the time, a bit irritated, I wasn't very impressed by this fellow's boldness, but his rebuke rang in my ears, and after that I decided to drive more cautiously. Today, I thank God for that anonymous truck driver, who cared enough to interrupt his busy schedule to correct me. Who knows, he may have saved my life.

"An open rebuke is better than hidden love. Wounds from a sincere friend are better than many kisses from an enemy." (Proverbs 27:5–6).

July 10

Grey Wolf

Renata, BC was a beautiful small community in south central British Columbia that was almost entirely flooded by the reservoir created by the now christened Hugh Keenlyside Dam. Access to this small little piece of earthly paradise was via a very narrow road blasted out of the solid rock of the Selkirk Mountains. The narrowest section of this road was known as Grey Wolf. I'm not sure why it was named this, possibly because of the colour of the rock and the inherent dangers of the road, or that it resembled a grey wolf when viewed from the Lower Arrow Lake, hundreds of feet below.

When driving towards the community on this section of the road, which was only wide enough to accommodate one car at a time, one could hug one side that was bounded by a cliff of solid rock. On the other side was a drop off to the lake, hundreds of feet below. One had to be very careful to stay on the road; any loss of attention, mechanical failure, or careless manoeuvre could leave us careening into the cliff or plunging over the edge into the lake, hundreds of feet below. Though there were other ways into this community, such as helicopter, boat, or the logging road, it is this narrow spot in the road we travelled so often that reminds me of Jesus, who is the only way to eternal life (John 3:16, 14:6; Acts 4:12), true life with meaning and purpose filled with hope, love, joy, and peace, which ultimately leads to heaven, the place of perfect peace and rest for all eternity.

"Enter through the narrow gate. For wide is the gate and broad is the road that leads to destruction, and many enter through it. But small is the gate and narrow the road that leads to life, and only a few find it." (Matthew 7:13–14, NIV); "Jesus said, 'I am the gate; whoever enters through me will be saved. They will come in and go out, and find pasture. The thief comes only to steal and kill and destroy; I have come that they may have life, and have it to the full.'" (John 10:9–10, NIV).

July 11

Crosswalks

Recently we heard of some town councils painting rainbow crosswalks to celebrate certain lifestyles. Some say this is an expression of love for those involved in these lifestyles.

I wholeheartedly agree that we should love one another. We are all human beings created in the image of God. *"So God created mankind in his own image, in the image of God he created them; male and female he created them." (Genesis 2:27, NIV)*. Every human being bears this image of their Creator. There's no room for hatred and persecution of those with whom we disagree. Jesus Christ warns us that anyone who is angry against another person will be severely judged (Matthew 5:21–26), and on the contrary, He told us that we are to love our neighbour as ourselves, and even to love our enemies (Matthew 5:44).

But does loving the person mean that we must agree with, celebrate, or participate in everything they do? Why would we want to celebrate a lifestyle that has many inherent dangers? A case in point, upon a perusal of the U.S. Center for Disease Control website (www.cdc.gov/hiv/group/msm/index.html), we quickly see that those who contract HIV are mostly men who have sex with men (63% in 2010), while they represent only a very small minority of the population (2%). According to the statistics, the incidents of infection are dramatically increasing in this group of men.

We are warned by nature and God that certain lifestyles will reap much grief, pain, and judgement on those involved in them and on society as a whole (Romans 1:24–27). If we truly love others, would we not warn them of these dangers, rather than encourage them by painting a crosswalk in honour of their chosen lifestyle? *"There is a way that seems right to a man, but in the end it leads to death." (Proverbs 14:12, NIV)*.

Furthermore, how are we being inclusive by celebrating a chosen lifestyle of only a few? To be truly inclusive, we'd have to paint every crosswalk for every chosen lifestyle. There are not enough crosswalks to represent every lifestyle.

If town councils want to be inclusive, and they feel they need to express this by painting a crosswalk, would it not be better that they paint it red, yellow, black, brown, and white to represent all of the human race, to the exclusion of none.

"Do not conform to the pattern of this world, but be transformed by the renewing of your mind. Then you will be able to test and approve what God's will is—his good, pleasing and perfect will." (Romans 12:2, NIV).

Love and Hate

He was born to Christian parents. They loved him very much and raised him with Christian values. From an early age it was evident he wanted his own way. As he grew older, his selfishness and rebellion grew more and more evident. He argued with his parents. He got in trouble with the law. His parents loved him but hated what he was doing. He caused them grief and was harmful to those around him, especially, unbeknown to him, to himself. His father cried when he appeared before the judge in court. His mother told him that she was praying for him, that he would be a good person who would encourage others to follow God. His answer to her was, "You can pray all you want, but it will never happen." His mother cried but kept on praying. Even though she hated what he was doing, she loved him.

Some years later, tired of the way of life he was living and seeing the futility in the life of his friends with whom he hung around, he realized the dangerous path he was on. He knew in his heart that even though God hated his sin, God loved him. He got on his knees and confessed his rebellion to God and asked Him for forgiveness. He also asked God to show him the path He had for him, so he could walk in it. God heard his prayer, and at that moment he was given new life from God (2 Corinthians 5:17).

Now, though there are still many struggles in life, especially with himself, he has a purpose for living each day and a hunger for God's Word. He has a personal relationship with Jesus Christ and the Holy Spirit living in him to strengthen in difficult times (2 Corinthians 6:6–10). His mother's prayers have been answered!

Now as he contemplates the past, he is embarrassed at his former way of life and hates the sinful nature that he still struggles with daily. He is able, through the power of God, to love God, his fellow man, and even the new self that God has made him to be!

If there is hope for me, there is hope for you!

"This is real love—not that we loved God, but that he loved us and sent his Son as a sacrifice to take away our sins ... We love each other because he first loved us." (1 John 4:10, 19).

DNA Code

When researching the biological reasons of how cancer works, it struck me that cancer is identified as rebellion against the DNA code. It went on to explain how DNA has a strict built-in code that regulates healthy growth of our cells and how cancer bypasses this and multiplies uncontrollably until it can grow to such an extent that it can kill the host that it lives in. Some researchers call it suicidal for this reason. Every human being has some cancer cells in their body, but the immune system, when healthy, identifies and kills these rogue cells to protect the person. If the cells begin to make headway and a tumour develops, it's essential to remove the cancer before it spreads and grows into an uncontrollable mass that threatens the life of the person. Any doctor who finds such a growth would warn their patient of the dangers and would recommend an operation to remove it. This news is not pleasant for the doctor to reveal, or for the patient to accept at the time. But for the doctor to not inform the patient is an absolute neglect of responsibility and rebellion against the principles of the profession.

As I think on this, it reminds me of sin in our lives, how it often slowly encroaches into our lives, something we think, say, or do against God and His Word, which if allowed to remain, soon grows and becomes hatred, anxiety, or fear, which saps our spiritual life. *"... when sin is allowed to grow, it gives birth to death." (James 1:15).* These sinful attitudes have a way of invading every part of our being: how we see ourselves, how we relate to others, even physically causing health problems and, if allowed to remain, spiritual death.

All of us have sin of some sort or another in our lives (Romans 3:23). Just like cancer, sin needs to be acknowledged and dealt with as soon as it shows up. If we truly love ourselves and those around us, we will identify sin and repent of it before it gets a grip on us and brings death to our soul. Though it isn't pleasant at the time to face our sins and turn away from them, to do anything less would be rebellion against God, ourselves, and those around us.

Jesus said, *"Repent, for the kingdom of heaven is at hand." (Matthew 4:17, ESV).*

Obeying God

History records some horrendous ways that human beings have treated other human beings. One such incident occurred near the beginning of the earthly life of Jesus Christ. The magi, or wise men, were asked to reveal the location of the baby Jesus to the godless King Herod. Being threatened by this child who was born a king, Herod planned to secretly kill Him. The magi, after finding Jesus, recognized who He was and bowed down and worshipped Him. Then, commanded by God, they purposely disobeyed the wicked king by not revealing where Jesus was (Matthew 2:1–12).

The War Crimes Court at Nuremberg, Germany tried some Nazi leaders for horrific crimes against humanity. The court wouldn't accept their defence of having simply obeyed the laws of their country. They said the Nazis should have obeyed a higher law, a higher morality, and disobeyed Hitler. These criminals were convicted on this basis.

Closer to home, the treatment of Afro-American, First Nations, and other people of different ethnic origin has been a constant blight on our more recent history. Dr. Martin Luther King Jr., when standing up for the basic rights of dignity and respect for every human being, regardless of origin, colour, or creed, peacefully yet purposely disobeyed some of the unjust laws made by racist leaders of the day. He drew attention to a higher law that God-fearing people have known since the beginning.

Yes, governments are instituted by God, and we are to submit to them (Romans 13:1–7; 1 Peter 2:13–17). But when governments step out from under their God-given mandate and call us to disobey God by not allowing us to do what God has clearly called us to do, or when they order us to disobey the clear leading of God by doing what we should not, then we must obey God rather than men.

So how will we know when this time has come? How can we know this higher law? We should take a lesson from the magi and bow in worship before Jesus Christ, the King of kings, the Author of life, the Living Word of God (Acts 3:14–15; 1 Timothy 6:11–16) and then obey His will as He reveals it to us in His written Word, the Bible.

The apostles Peter and John, when threatened by the authorities and told to stop speaking of Jesus, answered, *"Do you think God wants us to obey you rather than him? We cannot stop telling about everything we have seen or heard." (Acts 4:19–20).*

Author of Life

My brother invented a mower/brush cutter that mounts on the front of a grader. He patented it and uses it to cut foliage along the side of roads and highways across British Columbia to keep it from crowding in on the road structure. Sometimes these machines break down for one reason or another. When the operator or the mechanic can't figure out what the problem is, they call the inventor, because he knows how to get it going again.

When we think of the physical resurrection of Jesus from the dead, we're amazed as to how this could happen. Usually when someone dies, we make funeral arrangements and put the coffin in the ground. Sometimes the person looks like they're sleeping, but life is gone from their physical bodies, no matter how we plead, or cry, or hope that they come back to life, they still remain dead. No response, no life.

Jesus died a cruel death on the cross of Calvary. He was pierced in his side by the Roman soldier's spear, and blood and water came out, indicating to forensic analysts that He died a very traumatic death. He was buried in a tomb and left to decompose, just as every other person who had died before Him.

Yet on the third day after His death, He miraculously came to life again! How could this be? As we study God's Word, we see clearly that He is the Author of life (John 1:1–14). Everyone who has life—every living creature, human being, plant, or animal—has life because He gave it to them. Now wonder the grave couldn't keep Him down. No wonder death couldn't keep its dark grip on Him (Acts 2:24). Jesus Christ, the Author of life, proved who He was by coming back to life. Not only did He physically come back to life Himself, but He also came to give meaningful life here on earth and eternal life to all who would trust Him.

If we truly want this life, we must come to the Author of life to receive it. He said He would not turn anyone away who would sincerely ask for it.

Jesus said, *"I am the resurrection and the life. Anyone who believes in me will live even after dying. Everyone who lives in me and believes in me will never ever die." (John 11:25–26).*

JULY 16

Balance

When speaking with people, the subject of balance in life often comes up. Many people talk about it, but there's very little balance, peace, and harmony in our busy society today. Mostly, we tend to go with the trend. If everybody is doing it, then we feel we need to get involved. Some examples might be Boxing Day shopping, going to the latest blockbuster movie, buying lotto tickets, or being a workaholic. We follow the crowd and wonder why our lives are such a mess.

On the other end of the spectrum, we want to fight these excesses and adopt a policy of prohibition, which often isolates us from others, especially those who indulge in the excesses mentioned above. Some, in response to this teeter-totter world, try some kind of meditation in an attempt to find balance within ourselves. Eastern forms of this, such as yoga or the concept of yin and yang (balancing good and evil), have infiltrated our society because people are looking for something but can't find it. It's obvious that these methods haven't worked in the East, so why would they now work in the West? Still, there's a sense of unrest deep within. Everyone wants peace and balance within our lives. How can we find it?

God's Word tells us that ever since our original parents, Adam and Eve, rebelled against God, they lost their connection with Him. They tried to find their own way, and their world came toppling down (Genesis 3). Their relationship with Him was severed, a gnawing emptiness remained, and life was unbalanced without Him. For us it still remains so. No matter how we try to regain that balance, we will never find peace without allowing God to rule every area of our lives. This can only be accomplished through faith in Jesus Christ, the Prince of Peace (Isaiah 9:6; Ephesians 2:14).

"Now may the Lord of peace himself give you his peace at all times and in every situation. The Lord be with you all." (2 Thessalonians 2:16).

JULY 17

His Image

They delighted in the splendour of creation. They had intimate communion with their Creator and unhindered affection for each other. They shared in the boundless pleasures that were set before them. When they looked at each other, they could see the very image of their Creator. *"... it was very good!" (Genesis 1:31).*

Then something terrible happened! They listened to the lie of Satan. They thought they could exist outside of the will of their Creator. They disobeyed His explicit command and ate of the forbidden fruit. Their lives shattered like a mirror on the wall hit by a flying missile projected from the pits of hell (Genesis 3:7).

They couldn't recognize themselves or each other for who they really were. All they could see were the shards of their broken lives. At best they could see only an incomplete glimpse of the image of their Creator. They were undone. They were ruined. They couldn't help themselves. With all of their efforts, they couldn't put themselves together again. All hope was gone. In the darkness, they tried in their futility to cope. In the shadows, they hid from their Creator (Genesis 3:8), and out of their brokenness, they blamed each other for their fall from grace and contended with each other to make themselves look good (Genesis 3:12–13). They were cast out of the garden of delights. All of their children were born outside the garden, as broken mirrors not able to see God or recognize His image.

Yet our Creator, our only hope, remembered what we had been, knew what we were, and could see what we could be. Only He could heal us, yet in our blinded brokenness we continue to rebel against Him, still rejecting Him (John 1:10–11). Still, because of His infinite love for us, He came to live among us. He became one of us, was wounded, cut, and bleeding as he walked among the shards of the broken image of humanity (Isaiah 53). The Author of life bled and died, taking our brokenness, our rebellion, our sins upon Himself. Death could not hold Him. He rose from the dead!

When we in our desperate state turned to Him, He healed us, and we could see again (John 1:12–14). We were restored; we could spend intimate time with Him and see His image in each other once again! *"For we are God's masterpiece. He has created us anew in Christ Jesus, so we can do the good things he planned for us long ago." (Ephesians 2:10).*

JULY 18

Taste and See

Grandma was a good cook, and she made healthy food taste particularly delicious. She prepared tasty cabbage rolls, borscht, chicken noodle soup, and an endless list of nourishing culinary delights. She also baked cookies, cinnamon buns, and peach upside-down cake, among numerous other sweet desserts. If left to the eater, the desserts disappeared much more quickly than the meat-and-potatoes-type foods. Grandma would insist that the dessert was eaten after a good meal of the more nutritious food.

On occasions, one grandchild or another would be sitting at the table refusing the main course. Grandma would chuckle and say, "You didn't even taste it yet. Try it; you will like it. It's good for you." Often after a considerable length of time, hunger set in, and with some coaxing, as only Grandma could do, the grandchild would try a little bit, just to find out it actually tasted good! The plate empty, the body nourished, and dessert waiting! Sound familiar?

Sometimes we're so caught up in what we think is good for us, consumed with our own perceived needs, that we miss or even resist the Lord and His will for us. We want our way, which seems right to our senses at the moment, rather than the Lord, who will meet our every need. Sometimes we must have all these stripped away before we realize our absolute need for Him.

David was in such a situation. He was desperately running from King Saul and looking for what he thought would be a refuge among the enemy forces (1 Samuel 21:10–15) when he realized God was the only one who could ultimately protect him. Then he declared, *"Taste and see that the LORD is good. O the joys of those who take refuge in him! Fear the LORD, you his godly people, for those who fear him will have all they need." (Psalm 34:8–9).*

God is waiting for us to look to Him, to trust Him, no matter what the immediate apparent want or need is. Only as we finally surrender to His will and come to His table to commune and feast with Him will we find He is good and He is all we really need.

Blessings in Adversity 101

Have you ever thought of pain as a waste of time, and hardship as something to evade at all costs? I have, but experiencing a number of health issues has caused me to reflect on this and change my mind. I've come to the conclusion that pain, hardship, and adversity actually have some very important benefits.

In years gone by, especially the teen years, the feeling of being almost invincible permeated much of my life. This caused me to live in a very reckless way, not reflecting very seriously on God and the important issues of life. Life was more about me and the pleasure I could enjoy. Pain and hardship were to be avoided at all cost.

When going through a very painful incident with kidney stones, I realized how fragile we really are. Now, every day is seen more as a privilege than a right. Life is a treasure to be enjoyed and shared with others while I still have breath. The small things—the robin singing outside our window in the morning, the smile of a little child, the very breath we are given—all have become more meaningful. It's through hardships and pain that thankfulness towards God and His care and grace towards us is magnified. By allowing pain in our life, God is causing us to change our attitude from selfishness to thankfulness. Though we never look for or enjoy painful experiences, when pain and hardship come our way, may we be trained by them. Thank you, Lord, for these painful but life changing lessons!

"But God's discipline is always good for us, so that we might share in his holiness. No discipline is enjoyable while it is happening—it's painful! But afterward there will be a peaceful harvest of right living for those who have been trained by it." (Hebrews 12:10–13).

JULY 20

Blessings in Adversity 102

Toronto Raptors basketball star Landry Fields shares in his testimony of how he was sidelined due to a dysfunction of his hand. He wasn't able to shoot the ball, so his whole world came unglued at the seams. All he had lived for up to that point became naught. The identity he built himself around—his basketball career—came to a screeching halt. After some desperate, futile attempts to regain the life he had built for himself, he finally turned to God. God didn't heal his hand, but He healed his heart. His relationship with God grew, and his identity became rooted in Jesus rather than in himself. Even his struggling marriage was strengthened.

By taking away his ability to play basketball, God had dethroned the idol of stardom from Landry's life. What at first seemed to be an awful curse became a beautiful blessing. Previously his esteem was built on his ability to perform on the basketball court; now his esteem is based on the performance of his Creator and sustainer, Jesus Christ. Now he has a growing, living, eternal relationship with the King of kings and Lord of lords!

Adversity has a way of humbling us and causing us to look to God in faith instead of ourselves. God knows what we really need. When He takes away something of great value to us, we can trust that He will give us something much better. So when hardship comes our way and leaves us weak and needy, may we look to God and trust that He knows what's best and has something good in store for us.

Sometimes we resist when God is trying to humble us and we become bitter. The choice before us is to either become bitter or in faith allow God to make us better when adversity comes our way.

"Humble yourselves before the Lord, and he will lift you up." (James 4:10, NIV).

Blessings in Adversity 103

We often hear phrases like "the most powerful man on earth" or "the great one" when referring to the President of the United States or certain sports figures. But are they really any greater than you or me? Have they achieved their status and success by sheer willpower and self-effort? Reflecting on the life of the great King Nebuchadnezzar should give us some insights regarding who really is great and powerful.

In his time some 2,600 years ago, he was one of the most powerful rulers among men. God's Word, the Bible, speaks quite extensively about this king and his victories, even over God's chosen people, the Israelites. Nebuchadnezzar boasted that it was by his own might and power that he accomplished these great feats. Yet in the book of Daniel, it says *"The Lord gave him victory over King Jehoiakim of Judah and permitted him to take some of the sacred objects from the temple of God." (Daniel 1:2)*.

Though Nebuchadnezzar was quite insistent that he had accomplished these things in his own power (Daniel 4:30), God had some serious lessons in adversity for Nebuchadnezzar, through which He humbled him and opened his eyes to show him who really was in charge. Through the prophet Daniel and various dreams and visions, God showed Nebuchadnezzar that it was He who had given him this power to discipline God's own people for their sin against Him. Finally, through an extensive experience with insanity, Nebuchadnezzar finally realized that God was the One who held all power and authority. We read how Nebuchadnezzar, through all this adversity, was blessed to have a faith in the Almighty God that completely changed his attitude towards God.

The subsequent confession from the mouth of Nebuchadnezzar should be the confession of every one of us, including presidents, prime ministers, and sports heroes.

"His rule is everlasting, and His kingdom is eternal. All the people of the earth are nothing compared to Him. He does as He pleases among the angels of heaven and among the people of the earth. No one can stop Him or say to Him, 'What do you mean by doing these things?' ... Now I, Nebuchadnezzar, praise and glorify and honor the King of heaven. All His acts are just and true, and He is able to humble the proud.." (Daniel 4:34–35, 37).

July 22

Blessings in Adversity 104

Speaking with a good friend of mine who has since passed on about pride and conceit, he gave me the following example from his life. Being a very effective itinerate minister, he spoke at many different churches in his area. Visiting these churches, he became aware of some of the inner struggles that went on in some of them. Having the opportunity to speak at one of these churches, he thought he would set them straight. He had all the words figured out, and from his prideful self was going to give them a blast to correct them.

The time came for him to preach, and as he walked towards the pulpit, he tripped on a cord that was crossing his path, falling flat on his face right in front of all the people. Extremely embarrassed as he lay face down on the floor, he was confronted head-on with his pride. He knew at that moment God had allowed this to humble him, to break him. He said his attitude immediately changed, and he was able to speak the truth in God's love rather than out of his own arrogance.

The apostle Paul had something similar happen to him. Some kind of infirmity came upon him: *"Therefore, in order to keep me from becoming conceited, I was given a thorn in my flesh, a messenger of Satan, to torment me ... to keep him from becoming proud."* (2 *Corinthians 12:7, NIV)*. Even though Paul requested three times for God to take it away, God allowed it to remain, to keep him in check.

When hardships inevitably come, in whatever form, let us be encouraged. God is still God; He has not changed, and He knows what is happening to us. Often God allows adversity to keep us from going our own way and becoming proud and conceited, so that He can have His good and perfect way with us. Rather than fleeing from adversity or becoming bitter, may we draw close to God and let Him teach us through it, to trust in Him rather than ourselves.

My prayer is that we can say with the apostle Paul: *"So now I am glad to boast about my weaknesses, so that the power of Christ can work through me. That is why I take pleasure in my weaknesses, and in insults, hardships, persecutions, and troubles that I suffer for Christ. For when I am weak, then I am strong."* (2 Corinthians 12:9–10).

Blessings in Adversity 105

Did you ever get a spanking at home or at school for doing something wrong? It seems spankings are looked down on these days, but as I look back in time, I'm glad for most of the spankings I got, because the lessons I learned prevented me from getting deeper into trouble than I already was in.

We had a number of fruit trees and a garden on our property, which were an important part of the income my parents needed to pay the bills throughout the year. We were told of the value of the fruit and warned not to throw it at each other, because it was a waste to do so and also would stain our hard-earned clothes.

One time, as I remember it, my brother and I were supposed to be picking cherries, and we thought it would be more fun to throw the ripe cherries at each other instead of harvesting them. Dad caught us and gave us a spanking, a good stinger that gave us second thoughts the next time we were tempted to hurl this juicy fruit at each other. Through my parents' warnings and subsequent discipline, I stopped this wasteful entertainment and learned to value the produce from the orchard and garden. So when some other kids from the community wanted me to go with them to raid other people's gardens, I remembered the instruction and discipline I got at home and didn't go along. On one occasion, they got caught and ran into trouble with the police.

Though the spankings were painful at the time, I'm thankful that my parents loved me enough to discipline me for my ultimate good. God used our parents to discipline us when we were young and now continues to discipline us by various means throughout our lives. Hopefully we will be trained by it to help us escape greater loss.

"My son, do not reject the LORD's discipline and do not be upset when he corrects you. For the LORD corrects those he loves, just as a father corrects a child in whom he delights." *(Proverbs 3:11–12).*

JULY 24

Blessings in Adversity 106

Quite some time ago, I was attacked by someone. This was not a physical attack but an attack of words and accusations. It was very distressing to hear these accusations through friends, who were told these things behind my back. The most painful part was that the person doing this was someone I considered a friend. At first, I defended myself and made plans to keep a record of these false accusations, to prove this person wrong and to take revenge. This became an obsession for me. I tremble with fear when I think what might have happened had I continued down my path of vengeance. Then, through reading God's Word, my attitude began to change. Some of the verses I read were: *"They dig a deep pit to trap others, then they fall into it themselves" (Psalm 7:15)*; *"Love ... keeps no record of wrongs." (1 Corinthians 13:5, NIV)*; Jesus said, *"But I say to you, Love your enemies and pray for those who persecute you, so that you may be sons of your Father who is in heaven." (Matthew 5:44–45, ESV)*.

After a very difficult struggle deep within my heart and the conviction and strength of God's Holy Spirit, I was able to let go of my vengeful obsession, to forgive and give it over to God. When I did this, I found an unexplainable peace come over me. Instead of being vengeful, I was free to bless!

We have much to learn in this area of discipline from Joseph, whose own jealous brothers wanted to kill him. At the suggestion of a more merciful brother, they instead sold him to travelling slave traders, who in turn sold him in Egypt to an influential person named Potiphar (Genesis 37:18–36). As a slave in Potiphar's home, he was falsely accused by this man's wife of sexual abuse and put into prison (Genesis 39). But the Word of God tells us *"... the Lord was with him. And whatever he did, the Lord made it succeed." (Genesis 39:23, ESV)*. In all this adversity, *"The LORD tested Joseph's character." (Psalm 105:19)* to prepare him to become the man in charge of Egypt, second only to Pharaoh, the King of Egypt. Later, when Joseph had the chance to take revenge on his brothers, he rather blessed them and consoled them with the words: *"Don't be afraid. Am I in the place of God? You intended to harm me, but God intended it for good to accomplish what is now being done, the saving of many lives. So then, don't be afraid. I will provide for you and your children." And he reassured them and spoke kindly to them." (Genesis 50:19–21, NIV)*.

Oh heavenly Father, give us the strength to love, bless, and forgive, even when falsely accused!

JULY 25

Ritual or Relationship

I can remember when I was much younger, my mother and father taught me how to say my prayers. Most of them were quite short, and others a bit longer. The shortest one, as I remember, was "Thank you God for food and drink, Amen." A longer one was the Lord's Prayer. The one we often said before going to bed at night was, "Now I lay me down to sleep; I pray the Lord my soul to keep." Sometimes we'd say our short-memorized prayer within a few seconds before a meal or at bedtime without even a thought of what we were actually saying. It was a ritual that really meant very little to us. Though we spoke words of thanksgiving, we were not necessarily thankful at all. We didn't recognize that it was only by God's grace that we even had any food, let alone the very next breath.

Sometimes even today, though I seldom pray prayers by rote anymore, I find myself speaking words without really thinking much about what I'm saying or to Whom I'm speaking. When I catch myself doing this, I realize that I'm taking my relationship with God for granted and have substituted a ritual for the living, personal, intimate relationship God desires us to have with Him (Isaiah 29:13; Jeremiah 12:2; Matthew 6:5–8). Then I need to bare my heart, soul, mind, and will before Him to let Him tune me up to the realization that I am absolutely desperate and lost without Him, to ask Him to humble me because I don't have the ability even to humble myself. Then through the power of His Holy Spirit, He humbles me, opens my eyes to see more clearly, and gives me a thankful heart. Not only words of thanksgiving, but a truly thankful heart (Romans 8:15–16)! Every day becomes Thanksgiving Day! Thank you, Jesus, for loving me (John 3:16)!

What do we want, rote prayers with little or no meaning, or an overflowing heart of thanksgiving that words often cannot express? I'll take the relationship over the ritual anytime!

"Enter his gates with thanksgiving and his courts with praise; give thanks to him and praise his name. For the Lord is good and his love endures forever; his faithfulness continues through all generations." (Psalm 100:4–5, NIV); "You are worthy, our Lord and God, to receive glory and honor and power, for you created all things, and by your will they were created and have their being." (Revelation 4:11, NIV).

JULY 26

He's My Brother!

Waiting at a stop sign to get onto the highway on my way to an appointment in town, I noticed a good friend heading in the same direction. We have a special connection, so memories of past experiences came to mind: the times we had spent in prayer together, Bible studies, men's group meetings, as well as more difficult times of mutual sickness and seeking a sense of God's presence when nothing seemed to make sense. I pulled onto the highway a couple of cars behind him and, out of a heart of concern and brotherly love, felt compelled to pray for him as we drove along. Arriving at the appointment, who should also be there but my friend! We arranged to have breakfast together after our appointments were done. We had an incredible time of sharing, fellowship, and prayer over breakfast. We were encouraged by each other, feeding not only on physical food but spiritual food, and we were both drawn closer to God.

Why was this time so special? Because he's my brother! Not a biological but a Christian brother. We were both born into the family of God when we received Jesus Christ as our Lord and Saviour. When we received Jesus, we also received His Holy Spirit to live within us and bind us together as no other bond could. Now having Jesus in common, we have, among other things, His Holy Spirit in common. We have His Word, the Bible, in common. We have our faith in common. We have our eternity in common. We have the love of God in common. This is why we have this special relationship! Each time as we come together for breakfast, work, fellowship, prayer, sharing, and even in our pain and suffering, we are brought closer to each other and to God.

It makes my heart rise with joy as I look around and see many other brothers and sisters who also belong to this great family of God! May we not be too busy to come together to share fellowship and encourage each other in our common Christian love. *"We proclaim to you what we have seen and heard, so that you also may have fellowship with us. And our fellowship is with the Father and with his Son, Jesus Christ. We write this to make our joy complete." (1 John 1:3–4, NIV).*

Do you hunger and thirst for this kind of fellowship? *"But if we walk in the light, as he is in the light, we have fellowship with one another, and the blood of Jesus, his Son, purifies us from all sin." (1 John 1:7, NIV).*

JULY 27

Two Ears—One Mouth

Have you ever been annoyed by someone who dominates a discussion, not allowing you say what you'd like? I have, and it's frustrating! Yet I've noticed that sometimes the person dominating the discussion is me! After meeting with someone in this way, I feel empty and realize I didn't learn anything about them. I was arrogantly speaking of myself, even giving answers to questions that I hadn't really heard. What a shame!

On the other hand, it's quite a learning experience to listen to and even encourage others to speak. An example of this is with a fellow I had seen frequently but spoken with very little. When we met, I listened to his story and found a very unique individual of many exceptional talents. I also heard the voice of a very lonely and hurting person, one who needed a friend. A friend who would listen! Through listening, I learned to know this special person better. Had I dominated the discussion, I would have learned very little, if anything. What a gift to be able to listen!

God gave us two ears and only one mouth for a reason. God's Word has good advice on this: *"You must be quick to listen and slow to speak ..." (James 1:19)*; *"Spouting off before listening to the facts is both shameful and foolish." (Proverbs 18:13)*; *"Fools think their own way is right but the wise listen to others." (Proverbs 12:15)*.

This same principle holds true when approaching God. When we come to Him with all our requests without listening to His Word, we learn nothing from Him. Jesus said, *"My sheep listen to my voice; I know them, and they follow me." (John 10:27, NIV)*; *"So pay attention to how you hear. To those who listen to my teaching, more understanding will be given. But for those who are not listening, even what they think they understand will be taken away from them." (Luke 8:18)*.

Oh Lord, please cause me not to be so full of myself that I'm not able to listen to you or to others. Teach me to be wise, to listen and to learn to speak with wisdom only when you would want me to.

True Riches

Have you ever thought of all the things you could do if you had lots of money? Sometimes when the subject of riches comes up, especially in light of large lottery jackpot, people say how they will pay off the mortgage, buy a new car, go on a holiday to some exotic place, or even help others in need. The attraction to spend money on the lottery or the casino is very evident as we see people gather around to check the numbers on the lottery display, or as we observe the number of cars in the casino parking lot.

I think one of the reasons we'd like to win such large amounts of money is because we want to be in control. We want to do what we want, whenever we feel like it. The love of money is rooted in the false love of self. We think lots of money will improve our situation, yet statistics show that most jackpot winners don't end up better off. Many go broke within a few years, and others suffer divorce, alienation, addictions, or even suicide.

As we look into what God says about this in His Word, the Bible, we see some serious warnings: *"For the love of money is a root of all kinds of evil. Some people, eager for money, have wandered from the faith and pierced themselves with many griefs ... Command those who are rich in this present world not to be arrogant nor to put their hope in wealth, which is so uncertain, but to put their hope in God, who richly provides us with everything for our enjoyment." (1 Timothy 6:10, 17, NIV)*.

So next time we walk past the lottery terminal, where will we put our trust? Whom will we serve? Self, money, and the riches of this world, or will we put our trust in God and the eternal riches He has in store for those who trust Him? One is only temporary and fleeting, while the other is lasting and eternal. The choice is ours.

Jesus said, *"No one can serve two masters. Either you will hate the one and love the other, or you will be devoted to the one and despise the other. You cannot serve both God and money." (Matthew 6:24, NIV)*.

I for one choose to look away from the temptation of deceptive, temporary riches and look up to our great and Almighty God for our needs!

July 29

True History

Having had the opportunity to see a number of court proceedings, it's been interesting to hear the testimony of witnesses on the stand. All have sworn an oath to tell the truth, but often their testimony is clearly contradictory. Maybe one is telling the truth, or both are lying, but usually the truth is uncovered and the true version of the past revealed. The credibility of the witness is shown through their true or false rendition of the historical past.

When we look at the truth of God's Word presented to us in the Bible, we see an amazing historical account of past events. Some of these events have been questioned by those who might try to disprove the Bible or even the existence of God Himself, yet on all accounts, the Bible stands true.

Take for instance the account of the ancient city of Jericho. Some say Joshua is a mythical person and Jericho never existed. Yet the ruins of Jericho have been discovered, fallen walls and all. They found that the city was burned; the goods were left in place when the place was sacked. All this shows in meticulous detail the authenticity of the biblical account (Joshua 2 and 6). One amazing detail is the rescue of the prostitute Rahab. Her house was built into the wall, yet she wasn't touched when the walls came down. Archeologists have found that part of the wall didn't come down, and to this day the archeological record confirms God's merciful protection of this wonderful woman as she surrendered in faith to the Almighty God (Hebrews 11:31).

"Even if everyone else is a liar, God is true. As the Scriptures say about him, 'You will be proved right in what you say, and you will win your case in court.'" (Romans 3:4).

"The grass withers and the flowers fall, but the word of our God endures forever." (Isaiah 40:8, NIV).

Out of Bounds

Too often we hear reports of skiers, snowboarders, and hikers wandering outside of the safe boundaries set by ski hill and recreation area directors. Even after repeated warnings and clearly marked boundaries, some seek adventure or excitement by crossing over into the out-of-bounds area, even though it's a very dangerous place indeed. Inevitably, when they are lost and in trouble, we hear of their dilemma. Thankfully the Search and Rescue usually find and come to the aid of these people, though sadly some do not make it out alive. I don't have much patience for people who blatantly disobey the rules; however, it is obvious that the compassionate thing to do is to look for them and find them, even if they purposely went out of bounds.

As I think about this, I'm amazed at the patience, mercy, and grace that Jesus our maker has for us. God's Word clearly declares that all of us, from our political and religious leaders to the common people on the street, all including you and I, have wandered out of the will of God: *"All of us, like sheep, have strayed away." (Isaiah 53:6, NLT)*; *"... like sheep without a shepherd." (Matthew 8:36)*.

God has set clearly marked boundaries in His Word, the Bible, for us to live within, yet every one of us finds ourselves outside of these boundaries. Many times we ignore God and step out of bounds and the safety of His will, as expressed in His Word and commandments. Sometimes we pretend they don't exist because we think we can enjoy life more fully outside the safety plan God has set in place for us. Consequently, we find ourselves in a very dangerous and helpless position, unable to find our own way out, in danger of eternal death.

But we have much hope, as Jesus is intent on patiently seeking to rescue each of His wandering ones: *"For the Son of Man came to seek and to save the lost." (Luke 19:10, ESV)*; *"Instead he is patient with you, not wanting anyone to perish, but everyone to come to repentance." (2 Peter 3:9, NIV)*.

Investments

In my younger days, I had the opportunity to invest in a new technology. If I remember right, the inventor's name was Gladue, and he'd come up with a way of cleaning up pulp mill smokestack emissions. This toxic smoke polluted the surrounding area with not only an unpleasant smell but also a corrosive vapour. My dad claimed that this contaminated mist prematurely rusted his 1956 Pontiac, as it settled on the car while he worked at the mill. A smokestack scrubber, which would eliminate most of this pollution from the environment, seemed to be the invention of the day.

I invested a substantial amount of money into this innovation, with a promise that it would multiply many times. By getting in on the ground floor, I'd become rich, I thought. It was exciting to think of all I could have and do with the profits. Yet I never saw a penny and even lost the original sum. Though it was disappointing at the time, I'm thankful that through this loss, there was a lesson to be learned. Earthly, human ventures have only temporary rewards at best.

So what can we put our trust in? What really will last? People? Retirement plans? A backwoods home that would make us self-sufficient?

God's Word plainly says that the only One we can really trust is our Creator God. His Word is sure. His ways are eternal. He has us and our future in His capable hands. *"Teach those who are rich in this world not to be proud and not to trust in their money, which is so unreliable. Their trust should be in God, who richly gives us all we need for our enjoyment."* (1 Timothy 6:17). Jesus said, *"Do not lay up for yourselves treasures on earth, where moth and rust destroy and where thieves break in and steal, but lay up for yourselves treasures in heaven, where neither moth nor rust destroys and where thieves do not break in and steal."* (Matthew 6:19–20, ESV).

AUGUST 1

Others

When observing the political scene, it's obvious that certain people are grasping for power. Power is incessantly pursued: power to lead the country, power to change the world, power to impose one's ideas on others, power to call the shots. Though this tendency to dominate is possibly more apparent among political leaders, if we're completely honest, we see that it's fundamentally prevalent in every human endeavour. It runs deep within my own sinful nature. I want to find the shortest checkout at the store, and I want to keep my place! I want to win the game and will be frustrated if I don't. Even if I do something good, I want some kind of recognition. If I don't get the credit, I'm disappointed! I could go on and on because this pre-occupation with self runs so deep.

When the mother of two of Jesus' disciples asked for her sons to have the most important place in His Kingdom, He answered, *"It shall not be so among you. But whoever would be great among you must be your servant, and whoever would be first among you must be your slave." (Matthew 20:26–27, ESV)*.

When our own inherently selfish nature loves to be served, how can we become true servants? How can we become people who truly look out for the interests of others before our own, to serve rather than be served? This seems an impossible task because this pre-occupation with self tends to be so strong. The answer rests in the Holy Scriptures: *"For even the Son of Man came not to be served but to serve others and to give his life as a ransom for many." (Matthew 20:28)*. We are to follow Jesus, our Maker, to give Him precedence in our hearts (Philippians 2:6–8). The power to live this life of servanthood is fulfilled when we consider ourselves dead to the old selfish way of life and surrender to Jesus, who has the power to live His life in and through us! The apostle Paul expressed it this way: *"My old self has been crucified with Christ. It is no longer I who live, but Christ lives in me. So I live in this earthly body by trusting in the Son of God, who loved me and gave himself for me." (Galatians 2:20)*.

Wouldn't this world be a much better place if we lived this life of servanthood to which Jesus has called each of His redeemed followers?

AUGUST 2

HUSH

Recently we saw an article in the newspaper regarding a cow moose that had been killed and left beside the road, the hind quarters taken, but the rest left to rot. Being a cow moose, this is even more concerning, because of all of the offspring she would bear over the years. The conservation officers (COs) are looking for information on those who did this. As the truth comes out, the COs will have the evidence to convict and stop this obvious wanton disregard for wildlife and breaking of the law. Obviously, the perpetrators are hoping the information will not get out.

Now what would happen if the COs were also supressing the information about the incident? What if they weren't protecting the moose? What if the government was passing laws that actually allowed and encouraged the killing of pregnant cow moose? We would certainly be in a desperate state, would we not?

Yet according to a documentary film titled *HUSH*, which I watched recently, this is the case concerning human abortions and their effects on the woman's health. Punam Kumar Gill, who believes women should have the right to have abortions, heard about possible health risks of having abortions. These risks include a link to breast cancer, future premature births, and negative psychological effects. She researched various studies that showed these were indeed a concern. Yet women are typically not told about these possible side effects when they go for an abortion. When Ms. Gill confronted the various health agencies and abortion proponents with these questions, she was either confronted with silence or given pat answers. Why would they respond in this way? Do they have something to hide? If there's nothing to hide, there would be no secrets, and open dialogue on the harms towards women would be paramount.

If this cover-up is true, we're in a desperate state indeed, more desperate by far than the death of a cow moose and her baby. Are women actually being liberated, or are they being used? We have precious women who are being deceived by the lack of information given them, and many are having serious complications due to their abortions.

I believe everyone, especially young women, should see this unbiased documentary and decide for themselves where the truth lies in this matter. A trailer can be seen and a copy can be purchased at www.hushfilm.com.

"And you will know the truth, and the truth will set you free." (John 8:32, ESV).

AUGUST 3

Advertising Works

Having just acquired high speed internet, I'm amazed at how companies advertise. Pop ups appear out of nowhere. At first, I wondered where these ads came from. Then I realized the sneaky way they use technology to intrude into our privacy. Just dragging the cursor over an ad triggers it to consume the whole screen. I understand they even put "cookies" into our computer so that these ads pop up automatically. What an intrusion! What an annoyance! Why do they go to such extreme limits to get their stuff into our face? I believe it's because advertising works. The more they can show their product, the more sales, and the more sales, the more profit! What we see affects how we think, and how we think affects what we do. Advertising draws our attention, it triggers our desires, it causes us to think we need this, so we take action and buy it.

Ever wonder why we have so much violence and sexual assault on the streets? Could it possibly have something to do with what people are watching? Extremely violent movies are accessible at the stroke of a computer key. Sexually explicit pornography is available to anyone who knows how to use Google. When enquiring of a man regarding his nasty thoughts, depression, lack of motivation, and fatigue, he indicated he was up until 2:00 or 3:00 a.m. watching images from the pits of hell. No wonder he's depressed, disturbed, and dishevelled. If this is what he is feeding his mind, what will it produce next?

We are warned in God's Word, the Bible: *"For the world offers only a craving for physical pleasure, a craving for everything we see ... These are not from the Father, but are from this world" (1 John 2:16).* We are told of those who follow this path: *"They commit adultery with their eyes, and their desire for sin is never satisfied." (2 Peter 2:14).*

On the other hand, we're encouraged as we read, *"Don't copy the behavior and customs of this world, but let God transform you into a new person by changing the way you think. Then you will learn to know God's will for you, which is good and pleasing and perfect." (Romans 12:2).* We can have this abundant life as we look to Jesus Christ (Hebrews 12:2; Philippians 2:5–8). May our prayer this day be that of the ancient psalmist: *"Turn my eyes from worthless things, and give me life through your word." (Psalm 119:37).*

The Cart and the Horse

Have you ever heard the expression, "You have the cart before the horse"? When one stops to think about it, this describes a difficult situation. When the horse is behind the cart, the cart has a tendency to jack-knife, and movement becomes impossible. Yet when the cart is pulled by the horse, much can be accomplished. Both the cart and the horse are important ingredients, but of course the order has to be right—the horse has to be in front of the cart!

Though this illustration might at first glance seem elementary, it might explain why life can become so difficult. Often it's because we have our priorities out of order. This can also be true in our walk with God. Let me illustrate.

Somehow in my search for a true spiritual life, I felt I needed to do something to get right with God. By my actions, I would somehow try to please Him by attempting to do the right things: obey the commandments, do good to others, be honest, and read my Bible more. These were among the countless efforts I made. It was frustrating to say the least. Actually, I found it impossible to live this life. It was like trying to push a cart in front of a horse!

Coming to the end of myself, I desperately called out to God. Then it became clear. I could not produce faith by doing things (Titus 3:5). I would only be able to live this life through faith in Jesus Christ, then He would empower me to do the things He has asked me to do. He gave me a new life in which obedience is a natural product of exercising the faith He had given me. Faith in Jesus first, then out of faith came the new life, which produced those actions that pleased God!

God's Word says it this way: *"For by grace you have been saved through faith. And this is not your own doing; it is the gift of God, not a result of works, so that no one may boast. For we are his workmanship, created in Christ Jesus for good works, which God prepared beforehand, that we should walk in them." (Ephesians 2:8–10, ESV).*

Are you frustrated with a religious life? Tired of trying hard to be what God wants you to be? In faith turn to Jesus for forgiveness, and trust Him for the new life He has to offer. Then the works of God will supernaturally follow!

The Truth Hurts

Having just bought a 1950 Chevrolet Fastback from my older brother, I was itching to take it for a spin. Dad, realizing my inexperience in driving, reluctantly let me go, with a stern warning for me to be careful. With a cocky attitude, I told him that I knew how to drive. *Who does he think he is, warning me in this way?* I thought. I left the house and jumped confidently behind the wheel.

Just a few miles down the road, gazing at something in the distance, I suddenly heard a loud bang. The front of the car jolted into the air, narrowly missing a tree in the path of the vehicle. Quickly coming to a stop, I realized that the front tire had hit a stump just off the edge of the road, which had bounced the car back onto the road, miraculously causing it to just miss the tree. I had a bent rim and a flat tire with no spare. What was I to do? Reluctantly, I realized I had to go back to my father and tell him the truth. My pride said no, but everything else said I had to confess.

Though my pride was hurt, Dad was amazingly gracious and helped find a spare and get the car home again. As I remember, he never criticized me or my driving skills even once. I think he was just relieved that I hadn't hit the tree, which would have caused considerably more dire consequences!

We all have a tendency to turn away from God's good path that He has set before us: *"There is a way that appears to be right, but in the end, it leads to death." (Proverbs 14:12, NIV)*; *"... for all have sinned and fall short of the glory of God" (Romans 3:23, NIV)*. Yet our heavenly Father is gracious to us when we come to Him, truthfully admitting that we have drifted from His tender, watchful care. It may hurt our pride to admit that we've sinned and wandered from following His perfect decrees, but it's much more hurtful, even dangerous, to follow our own ways, which in the end lead to death.

"If we confess our sins, he is faithful and just and will forgive us our sins and purify us from all unrighteousness." (1 John 1:9, NIV).

The choice is ours to follow our own arrogant way and eventually crash, or to swallow our pride and face the truth, confess our rebellion against God, and ask Him to lead us in following His good and perfect way.

AUGUST 6

The Truth Heals

When taking a First Aid course, we were informed that some people, especially men, who when having symptoms of a heart attack are reluctant to admit their pain and go for help. Sometimes this reluctance to face the truth causes them to suffer severe medical distress and even death. If they would go for help sooner, they could be spared untold grief.

Emotional pain in our hearts can cause just as much heartache and loss if we keep it pent up inside of us. Often this pain in our hearts produces bitterness, stress, anxiety, and anger, which can lead to physical problems such as high blood pressure, heart disease, and cancer.

Healing can come when we face the truth and share our pain with a trusted friend or counsellor, and especially as we ultimately surrender it to the Lord. This is often difficult to do because we don't want others to think we are weak, or we don't want to be judged. Yet it's imperative that we share our burdens with someone else: *"Carry each other's burdens, and in this way you will fulfill the law of Christ."* (Galatians 6:2, ESV).

A trusted Christian friend, pastor, or counsellor can share our pain by listening, empathizing, and praying with us to encourage us to take the pain to Jesus, who is our ultimate burden bearer and healer: *"Cast your burden on the Lord, and he will sustain you; he will never permit the righteous to be moved."* (Psalm 55:22, ESV); *"He heals the brokenhearted and binds up their wounds."* (Psalm 147:3, ESV).

Even when some sin that we've committed is burdening us, we can find forgiveness and healing by speaking the truth about it with others and Jesus (1 John 1:9). *"Therefore confess your sins to each other and pray for each other so that you may be healed. The prayer of a righteous person is powerful and effective."* (James 5:16, NIV).

AUGUST 7

The Truth Sets Free

She had an affair and as a result became pregnant. Ashamed, she didn't want anyone to know. So she chose to quietly have an abortion. She immediately felt the pain of "the procedure," as they called it at the clinic, but the emotional pain was even greater and grew daily. She was in a daze as she methodically went through each day, trying to forget what she had done. There was no relief. Feelings of hopelessness and despair became more intense as time went on. The people she shared her secret with spoke to those she had tried to keep it from. Now the word was out. She was absolutely devastated and decided she would end her life to escape the pain of it all.

Then a friend prayed for her. The next morning, she felt hope again, and the desire to commit suicide left her. She knew Jesus had touched her, and a personal relationship with Him became an increasing priority. Jesus began to heal her. With the help of trusted Christian friends, she was able to say goodbye to her baby and to leave it with Jesus, until the day they would meet again in heaven. She forgave all those involved: the man she had an affair with, those who spoke badly of her, those who actually did the abortion, and she forgave herself. Then she was able to speak openly with others about her experience, the pain of abortion, and the wonderful forgiveness and healing of Jesus.

Now she counsels and powerfully ministers freedom to many women (and men) who are hurting from the terrible consequences of abortion. She's a living witness to the forgiveness, freedom, and healing that's revealed in Jesus when we become truthful with Him about our desperate state. There was hope for her; there is hope for you and me. There is hope for everyone who turns to Jesus, no matter what we have done.

We met this beautiful lady. Her story can be read in her book *Will I Cry Tomorrow?* She faced the truth, and the truth has set her free!

"Jesus said, 'Then you will know the truth, and the truth will set you free.'" (John 8:32, NIV).

AUGUST 8

Out of the Shadows

I noticed an image of someone outside, creeping around in the yard among the trees in the dark shadows. *Who's in my yard and what is he up to? Why would he be hiding in the darkness? He must be up to no good!* These were my thoughts as I watched him move when I moved. Could he see me looking out the window at him? Then I realized it was me! I was looking at my own reflection in the window! I had been the intruder, the thief, the stalker in the shadows of my own back yard!

Subsequently, my thoughts brought up an image of Jesus going to the cross and not one person standing up in his defence—not one! Those whom He had miraculously healed lurked in the fringes. The disciples dispersed, with no voice to defend Him against the horrendous acts of darkness being done to their leader. I could see both thieves scorning Him as they hung on crosses to His right and to His left. Suddenly, there I was among them, scorning Him, demanding a miracle, arrogantly using His holy name in vain. Instead of the focus on the others who abused, mocked, whipped, and cruci-fied Him, the focus was on me! I was no different than the rest: the rebel, the thief, the mocker, the arrogant Pharisee, the foreigner nailing the Author of life to an old wooden cross! Realizing I was one of those lurking in the shadows, my obvious need of forgive-ness overwhelms me, and I cry out, "Remember me, Lord Jesus, forgive me, have mercy on my soul!"

Then I'm reminded of the Holy Scriptures: *"But he was pierced for our rebellion, crushed for our sins. He was beaten so we could be whole. He was whipped so we could be healed. All of us, like sheep, have strayed away. We have left God's paths to follow our own. Yet the LORD laid on him the sins of us all."* (*Isaiah 53:5–6*); *"anyone who belongs to Christ has become a new person. The old life is gone; a new life has begun!"* (*2 Corinthians 5:17*).

Thank you, Lord Jesus, for forgiving me, taking my punishment, and giving me new life!

AUGUST 9

Driving Out Evil

With the news of the horrific bombing of twenty-two people, including young children, in Manchester Arena on May 22, 2017, we're again reminded of the horrendous capabilities of sinful humanity. How depraved and wicked can human beings become?

Only hours before the bombing, the US President Donald Trump challenged the Muslims of the Middle East to "drive out" this evil from their communities, their places of worship, from the earth.

The question arises: How do we drive out evil? We may attempt to drive out the evil from our midst through sanctions, counter attacks, missiles, and military means, yet evil originates deep inside the human heart. Human effort may subdue and force compliance on unwilling people but will never be able to drive evil out and will never bring real peace.

Yet God's Word, the Bible, is clear that there is only One who can truly bring peace into this evil war-torn world. The prophet Isaiah prophesied some seven hundred years before Jesus was born that He would be called the *"Prince of Peace"* (Isaiah 9:6). When Jesus was born into the world, a host of angels from heaven declared, *"Glory to God in the highest heaven, and on earth peace to those on whom his favor rests." (Luke 2:14, NIV).* Then Jesus promised to those who believed in Him the gift of his Holy Spirit: *"Peace I leave with you; my peace I give you. I do not give to you as the world gives. Do not let your hearts be troubled and do not be afraid." (John 14:27, NIV).* Jesus Christ is the only One who can bring true peace in our hearts, and thus we can extend His peace to our families, to our communities, to our nation, to those in other nations, and to all the earth.

The real issue here is if we will truly trust Jesus Christ, the One who made us. Will we surrender to Him and allow Him to have His way with us, deep in our hearts? Then He will drive out the evil, and His peace will prevail in us and through us. *"Do not be anxious about anything, but in every situation, by prayer and petition, with thanksgiving, present your requests to God. And the peace of God, which transcends all understanding, will guard your hearts and your minds in Christ Jesus." (Philippians 4:6–7, NIV).*

AUGUST 10

Y2K

I ran across a glossy little booklet put out by the federal government some years ago that brought back memories of the forthcoming danger facing all computers and networks at the turn of the century. The experts said computers weren't programmed to deal with the transition from the numbers 1999 from the past century to the new century, represented by the numbers 2000. A major crash was imminent.

Many people around the world were in panic mode. The word was out that every computer and network were going to crash: power failures, nuclear plant meltdowns, even possible spontaneous missile launches were feared. The United Nations, Western governments, and corporations spent hundreds of billions on preparing for this coming disaster in year 2000! Closer to home, some people bought generators, stored up water and food, and others bought camping supplies. Yet when New Year's Day came on Y2K, nothing happened. All the panic was for nothing, and those who had done nothing or very little to prepare for this disaster were just as well off as those who had spent billions. People who promoted the Y2K panic were disgraced and quickly turned their blushing faces away to other things!

What can we learn from all of this? If humanity can't even understand or manage the works of their own hands, how can we understand or control those things over which we have absolutely no power, like sun spots, earthquakes, the weather, how we take our next breath, or even when we'll take our last breath?

Though we like to think we are masters of our own fate, in truth, we control very little, if anything. This should cause us to long to know and trust Jesus, the One who knows it all, the One who holds it all together (Colossians 1:17). Rather than put our trust in human wisdom, would it not be better to trust in our Creator, who has supremacy over everything from the beginning to the end? When we completely trust Him, there is no need to panic, no need to fear, no need to be embarrassed, no matter what the future might have in store for us.

"Christ is the power of God and the wisdom of God. This foolish plan of God is wiser than the wisest of human plans, and God's weakness is stronger than the greatest of human strength" (1 Corinthians 1:24–25); "For the Scripture says, 'Everyone who believes in him will not be put to shame.'" (Romans 10:11, ESV).

AUGUST 11

Real Food

After a hot day in the sun, it seemed so refreshing to guzzle down a couple of sodas to quench my thirst. During the day, a chocolate bar and some other sweets gave the quick energy I needed at the moment. Chips, pop, and ice cream were favourites at the time too. Little did I know that I was poisoning my body with all this junk food. After a time of illness and subsequent research into nutrition and the importance of eating the right foods, health is returning to my body. We need to eat wholesome food to live a healthy life.

Just as we need to eat and digest good food for our bodies, we also need to take in spiritual food for our spiritual growth, but not just any spiritual food will do. There are many books written by people that are no better than junk food for our spiritual health. At best they may give a temporary high; however, in the end they bring spiritual malnutrition and even death. Yet God has given us His Word, the Bible, for true spiritual sustenance. God's Word is inspired by God (2 Timothy 3:16–17). As we read it, meditate on it, and digest it, our mind, our spirit, and our soul will be fed and nourished so that we can be the spiritually healthy people God intended us to be: *"Jesus answered, 'It is written: "Man shall not live on bread alone, but on every word that comes from the mouth of God."'" (Matthew 4:4, NIV).*

As the scriptures speak to us, they will reveal and point us to our Creator, our Sustainer, and our Saviour, Jesus Christ. As we surrender to Him and allow Him to feed us, we will experience a satisfying, intimate spiritual life in Him! We will become more like Him and will become an encouragement and a light to those around us who are seeking to fill that gnawing spiritual hunger that only He can satisfy. Jesus declared, *"I am the bread of life. Whoever comes to me will never go hungry, and whoever believes in me will never be thirsty." (John 6:35, NIV).*

God is offering us real food for our spiritual journey. Why would we settle for anything else?

AUGUST 12

Number One

We attended a retirement celebration for some friends recently. Having worked together with them some fifteen years ago, time had gone by just like a breath. Now they were about to retire. Amazing how the end of our life draws near so quickly! As we spoke with many people afterwards, especially among us more graying folk, conversations often led to the reality of aging and the meaning of life.

As we age, we realize that our earthly life quickly slips behind us. With a decreasing amount of time here on earth ahead of us, we tend to see more of our weaknesses, our bodies are not as strong as they used to be, and our memory might fail us more often. The hills seem steeper, our breath is shorter, aches and pains show up more frequently. Many priorities we thought so important in the past fade and become a vanishing mist before us. Sometimes we see the legacy we had hoped to leave dwindle before our eyes. Wealth, health, careers, investments, retirement, looking out for number one, did not work out as well as we'd hoped. It hauntingly becomes more evident—if "me" is the sole focus of my life, it will be me standing alone at the end of life. So one might ask, "How can I live a meaningful life? What is most important?"

God's Word, the Bible, is clear that I am not number one but that God alone takes that spot! This is evident from God's words to the great King Nebuchadnezzar: *"that everyone may know that the Most High rules over the kingdoms of the world." (Daniel 4:17).* Jesus also proclaims, *"Love your enemies! Do good to them. Lend to them without expecting to be repaid. Then your reward from heaven will be very great, and you will truly be acting as children of the Most High ..." (Luke 6:35).*

It was obvious from the heartfelt testimonies of all those who were touched by our "retiring" friends that their desire is to serve Jesus by making Him first. They have certainly done a lasting work for God as they surrender to Him daily.

As we contemplate what is most important in our lives, let us bow our knee before the Almighty and let Him have Hhis way in us today, so that we can live a useful, lasting, and purposeful life for Him every day of our lives.

August 13

Crazy Daisies

We bought a package of wildflower seeds at the recommendation of some friends. The package had various types of flower seeds that it promised would produce a beautiful array of wildflower blossoms to brighten up our place. Sure enough, when we planted the seeds, they sprouted and soon produced the much-anticipated garden of spectacular wild wildflower blossoms!

Yet among them were daisy plants. Soon this flowering plant proliferated and began to take over the flower garden. When we observed this, we were able to eradicate it from the immediate flower garden, but without us noticing, the seeds had spread outside of the garden and around the property. Wherever the flower had been transported, by wheelbarrow, on our clothes, snagged by a bicycle, or many other means, daisies began to grow. Before we knew it, the yard was infested with crazy wildflower daisies! Now we're having a battle with this weed. It's tenacious and threatens to take over the whole yard. What we thought would be a wonderful addition to the beauty of our place has actually become a curse.

This reminds me of the wise words of the apostle Paul in God's Word, the Bible: *"Do not be deceived: God is not mocked, for whatever one sows, that will he also reap. For the one who sows to his own flesh will from the flesh reap corruption, but the one who sows to the Spirit will from the Spirit reap eternal life." (Galatians 6:7–8, ESV).*

This principle of harvesting what we plant is not only true of our physical gardens but also of our spiritual lives. When we think that we can do our own thing, follow our own selfish desires and the attractions of the world around us, it will always produce seeds of discord, dissention, greed, and other undesirable weeds in our lives. If we are honest, we don't have to look very far to see these weeds of the crazy, selfish life growing in and around us!

Yet on the other hand, if we submit to God and allow His Spirit to lead us and guide us, we are promised: *"But the fruit of the Spirit is love, joy, peace, patience, kindness, goodness, faithfulness, gentleness, self-control; against such things there is no law." (Galatians 5:22–23, ESV).*

Which would we rather have? The choice is before us. My prayer is that we will choose to allow God to have His way in our hearts and lives so that He can produce the beautiful garden He has planned for us all along!

AUGUST 14

Monetary Misgivings

Why do people spend money on lotteries? It might be to pay off debt, get that dream home or luxury car, just to make ends meet, or even to help family or friends. To win the jackpot is a long shot, a very long shot! To win the 6/49, the odds are about 1:14,000,000. Some say one is more likely to be hit by lightning, get flesh eating disease, or be killed by a terrorist while travelling than to win the big one. People I have asked said they would be happier if they won. Yet many find themselves with all that cash in their hands in very unhappy situations that they never expected. One winner told me he gets calls day and night from friends and strangers asking for money. Some think the car, the house, the boat will make them happy, but in reality, the happiness quickly diminishes after picking up the winnings. If you don't believe this, speak to someone who has won, or google "lottery consequences." Promises of happiness through money or material things are nothing short of a fading mist.

We shouldn't be surprised at this, as God's Word, the Bible, clearly warns us, *"For the love of money is a root of all kinds of evils. It is through this craving that some have wandered away from the faith and pierced themselves with many pangs." (1 Timothy 6:10, ESV).* When we seek money as the solution to our problems or needs, when we think money and things will make us happy, we are fooling ourselves, because the only way we can find true happiness and joy is to allow God to change our heart. God promises not only happiness but true joy when we put our trust in Him. The ancient scriptures as recorded by King David still ring true today: *"But let all who take refuge in you be glad; let them ever sing for joy. Spread your protection over them, that those who love your name may rejoice in you." (Psalm 5:11, NIV).*

True joy is found not in our possessions but in a personal relationship with our God, Creator, and Saviour, Jesus Christ. When we follow Him and let Him have His way in our lives, His sure promise of joy wells up in our heart. Jesus said, *"I have told you this so that my joy may be in you and that your joy may be complete." (John 15:11, NIV).*

AUGUST 15

Proof

Her car stopped. She needed help. Not being a mechanic, I couldn't diagnose the problem. She called a friend of hers who claimed to be a mechanic, and he came over and said it wouldn't be a problem; he knew what was wrong and could fix it quite easily. The part was purchased, and I watched as he nimbly removed the broken part and replaced it with the new one. When he asked her to start vehicle, everything was working again. The man who claimed that he could fix the car proved that he could by getting it going again! I am still amazed how quickly and smoothly he worked!

When Jesus walked on this earth, He often said to people, *"Your sins are forgiven."* The religious leaders of the day became very angry with Him because they knew that only God could forgive people of their sins. What bothered them was that by Jesus saying this, He made Himself out to be God. These were also miracles that only God could do. One time in front of the religious leaders, Jesus spoke to a paralyzed man and said *"... your sins are forgiven." (Matthew 9:2, NIV)*. Knowing the accusations of the religious leaders, Jesus said *"'But I want you to know that the Son of Man has authority on earth to forgive sins.' So he said to the paralyzed man, 'Get up, take your mat and go home.'" (Matthew 9:6, NIV)*. The man was instantly healed, got up, and went home! Jesus healed those born blind, cleansed lepers, cast out demons, and raised people from the dead. By doing these miraculous works that only God could do, He showed that being God, He also had the power to forgive one's sins! The Pharisees were so angry about this that they eventually got Him crucified.

The question for them then and for each of us today is: What will we do with Jesus? He proved who He was. Will we believe who He is and come to Him to forgive our sins and be saved from judgement, or will we respond like the religious Pharisees of Jesus' day?

"Salvation is found in no one else, for there is no other name under heaven given to mankind by which we must be saved." (Acts 4:12, NIV).

AUGUST 16

Time to Pray

As wildfires blaze in summer of 2017, we're all concerned for our fellow British Columbians in the southern interior who either have been evacuated or are on evacuation alert. Tens of thousands of hectares of land has been burned, some privately owned. Livestock and animals left behind are endangered. Numerous homes have been burned, and thousands of people are staying in emergency shelters in surrounding towns or cities, hundreds of miles away from home. The situation is desperate, yet thankfully, to date, no lives have been lost. The fire fighters and emergency crews are exemplary, many risking their own lives to save lives and property. The government and relief organizations have stepped in. Ordinary citizens have rallied in compassion and reached out to those in crisis with food, supplies, shelter, money, and whatever is needed. The compassion of many is amazing, and we must be thankful.

Though there is little, if any, mention in the news about calling out to the Almighty in prayer and asking Him to intercede in this desperate time. This is definitely a time to pray.We can be thankful to God for those who are laying their lives on the line to help others. We can thank Him that no lives have been lost so far. We can pray for the safety of all those who are in danger of the flames. We can pray that the rescue efforts would go smoothly. We can pray that many will turn to God through this tragic time. We can pray that God would change the weather and send rain.

When the disciples were caught in a mean storm on the Sea of Galilee and were concerned that their boat would sink and they would drown, they called out to Jesus, who had been sleeping in the boat. He subsequently got up and rebuked the storm: *"And he said to them, 'Why are you afraid, O you of little faith?' Then he rose and rebuked the winds and the sea, and there was a great calm. And the men marveled, saying, 'What sort of man is this, that even winds and sea obey him?'" (Matthew 8:26–27, ESV).*

Jesus, the Creator, Sustainer, and Saviour, knows what we are going through and desires to hear from us in good times and in bad. Let us call out to Him, as He is the One who is the Author of life and giver of every good thing, even every breath that we take (Acts 17:24–31).

Jesus desires a personal relationship with us. Sometimes desperate times come before we even think of praying. Yet God desires us to be in an attitude of prayer continually (Luke 18:1; 1 Thessalonians 5:17; Romans 12:12).

This is a time to pray!

AUGUST 17

Weakest Link

When working on the farm, we often used a combination of chains to lift a heavy load. Sometimes we would unwisely join a couple of chains together with a makeshift link to make it long enough. Though it might hold for a time, inevitably under load, the chain would break at the homemade link because it was the weakest link. Thus comes the old saying, "A chain is only as good as its weakest link."

This weak link could illustrate a spiritual principle on righteousness taught in the Scriptures. God's Word, the Bible, clearly indicates God's requirement: *"But now you must be holy in everything you do, just as God who chose you is holy. For the scriptures say 'You must be holy for I am holy.'" (1 Peter 1:15–16).* Again it says, *"... for those who are not holy will not see the Lord." (Hebrews 12:14).* For us to be right with God, we need to be totally holy and righteous. We can have no sin between us and God.

Our natural human response is to try to be righteous through our own effort; this is called self-righteousness and is represented by the weak homemade link in the chain mentioned above. To try to be holy in our own effort is like the farmer trying to use some haywire to fashion a link in a chain to lift a heavy load. The Scriptures say, *"... for all have sinned and fall short of the glory of God." (Romans 3:23, ESV); "For whoever keeps the whole law but fails in one point has become guilty of all of it." (James 2:10, ESV).* It's clear that we all stand absolutely guilty before God and totally helpless in rescuing ourselves.

The only remedy is to cry out to God: *"God, be merciful to me, a sinner!" (Luke 18:13, ESV),* for God is a merciful God. *"And to the one who does not work but believes in him who justifies the ungodly, his faith is counted as righteousness." (Romans 4:5, ESV).* This was accomplished through Jesus' death on the cross some two thousand years ago, for all those who would trust in Him. He promised He would save all those who call out to Him in faith! (Romans 10:13; Acts 2:21).

AUGUST 18

Design or Delusion?

We had the very special privilege of seeing our newest grandson just hours after his birth. So amazing! So wonderful, marvelous, miraculous—words can't express how awesome it is to see and hold a newborn baby, especially when he is your own family! Everyone sees the resemblance to Mom or Dad, even to Nana or Bapa. The DNA from ancestors in the distant past is expressed in this little bundle of joy! Yet he is absolutely unique. There is only one of him!

The doctor came to check him out and did a thorough examination to determine if everything was in order. Digestive system, hips, urinary and respiratory systems were checked. Thankfully he came through the examination with flying colours! Yet much more than the complexity of physical forces is involved here. Emotions, love, joy, and thankfulness are flowing from parents to child. The child needs to be held, nurtured, and loved. The more I think of it, the more I'm amazed! *"Such knowledge is too wonderful for me; it is high, I cannot attain unto it." (Psalm 139:6, KJV)*.

I have a choice. Am I going to recognize how our Creator designed us and acknowledge with King David, *"I will praise You, for I am fearfully and wonderfully made; Marvelous are Your works, And that my soul knows very well." (Psalm 139:14, NKJV)*? Will I recognize the image of God in my grandson that every human being bears (Genesis 1:26)? Am I going to give thanks to our Maker and bow down and worship Him?

The alternative is ludicrous. For me to do anything else, such as believe that this all happened by chance, that we are the product of trillions of random chance happenings over billions of years, would be absolutely delusional. To know we are so wonderfully created yet not be thankful to our Creator would be brazenly disrespectful, insolent, and rude.

With my little grandchild in my arms, I can't help but give God the glory for all He is and has done, to surrender to Him and worship Him. How could I do anything less?

"Thou art worthy, O Lord, to receive glory and honour and power: for thou hast created all things, and for thy pleasure they are and were created." (Revelation 4:11, KJV).

Who Am I?

I can remember back when I was younger and wondering what life had in store. One teacher said we should get an education or we'd end up being a manual labourer. This was clearly not something one wanted to be, according to him! Was I going to be a labourer, a dentist, a chiropractor, a contractor, or something else? I tried to find my identity in my own mind, in human ideology. Our destiny was in our own hands was the message we often heard. As time unfolded, I realized nothing could be further from the truth. Life was full of variables that I couldn't control. I didn't even know what was in store tomorrow let alone years down the road. *"A man's steps are of the Lord; How then can a man understand his own way?" (Proverbs 24:20, NKJV).*

In grade eight, a teacher died as a result of an automobile accident; in grade ten, two of my classmates met the same destiny. After graduation, two others took their own lives. It became increasingly obvious that I desperately needed to put all my trust in the One who knows the beginning from the end—the Creator who has a plan for me. Though I had many ideas and tried many different ways, ultimately I could entrust all of life, from the beginning to the end, into His hands and follow Him. *"The heart of man plans his way, but the Lord establishes his steps." (Proverbs 16:9, ESV).*

Now my identity, not of my own doing but only by the grace of God, is not in my occupation, social status, or imagination but in Him! Among other things, I am a child of God (John 1:12), a friend of Christ (John 15:15), bought with a price, not my own (1 Corinthians 6:19–20), a new creation (2 Corinthians 5:17), joint heir with Christ (Romans 8:17), forgiven and made righteous (Romans 5:1), free from condemnation forever (Romans 8:1), have His Spirit living in me (1 Corinthians 2:12), I no longer live but Christ lives in me (Galatians 2:20), predestined to be a child of God (Ephesians 1:5), a citizen of Christ in heaven (Ephesians 2:6). This identity is for all who believe and trust in Him!

"Trust in the LORD with all your heart; do not depend on your own understanding. Seek his will in all you do, and he will show you which path to take." (Proverbs 3:5–6).

AUGUST 20

Knowledge and Wisdom

We are experiencing senseless violence in cities around the world. August 17, 2017, a van ran over numerous people, killing thirteen in Barcelona, Spain. A few days before, on August 12, a person ran over protestors in Charlottesville, Virginia with his car, killing one. Meanwhile, world leaders threaten to use nuclear weapons to annihilate other countries. Obviously, something is terribly wrong.

We're in an age when knowledge is increasing at such an astounding rate that no one can keep up. Lost or missing people can be found through GPS technology, while this same technology can precisely guide a cruise missile to extinguish an entire city. Doctors can almost miraculously save the life of a tiny preborn baby, or they can kill the same little baby by abortion if the baby isn't wanted.

Knowledge is important. We have universities, colleges, and schools that have helped to raise the standard of living and given people the tools to better their lives by cutting through the darkness of ignorance and superstition. Yet what has happened? Why are educated people using their knowledge to do such horrendous acts to fellow human beings?

Knowledge without wisdom can be extremely dangerous, because through knowledge we have access, as mentioned above, to more powerful means to hurt or destroy others. God's Word, the Bible, clearly says we have a desperate need for wisdom, as deep inside every human heart lurks the ability to do evil: *"Claiming to be wise, they instead became utter fools ..." (Romans 1:22)*; *"The human heart is the most deceitful of all things, and desperately wicked. Who really knows how bad it is?" (Jeremiah 17:9)*. The Holy Scriptures are clear about the condition of the God-less, fallen, human heart: *"Only fools say in their hearts, 'There is no God.' They are corrupt, and their actions are evil; not one of them does good!" (Psalm 14:1)*.

Because of the deceptiveness of our natural human condition, the solution does not lie primarily in education or in left-wing or right-wing ideologies but in being born again of the Spirit of God and receiving true wisdom from our Creator God. Until we come to God and ask Him to change us and give us His wisdom to guide us, we won't have the best interests of ourselves or others in mind.

"If you need wisdom, ask our generous God, and he will give it to you. He will not rebuke you for asking. But when you ask him, be sure that your faith is in God alone." (James 1:5–6).

AUGUST 21

In the Present

It's been refreshing to get together with family and friends during the summer months! We recently had a wonderful time with a friend from Ontario, whom we have known for many years. This brought back so many special memories of times past, some very special and some more difficult, but we had a precious time reminiscing and reflecting on the former days and how God has worked everything out for good (Romans 8:28)! Yet we found that our current life experiences were even more exciting, as they bear witness to the fact of God's faithfulness in the now—what the Lord is doing in our lives in the present. The past is great, and it's good and encouraging to remember God's goodness to us then, but we're living in the present—today. God is working in our lives right now! Yesterday is gone, and we can't bring it back or change it. Tomorrow may never come for us, but we have the here and now. What is God doing in our life today?

We are reminded in God's Word, the Bible, of His present love and care over us (Psalm 46:1). May we rejoice today as we consider the unwavering love of God in Christ Jesus (Hebrews 13:5–6, 8) and as we meditate on the following ancient words of Holy Scripture: *"Oh give thanks to the Lord, for he is good; for his steadfast love endures forever! ... This is the day that the Lord has made; let us rejoice and be glad in it." (Psalm 118:1, 24, ESV).*

AUGUST 22

Open Dialogue

Maybe you read a recent newspaper article written by a fellow welcoming open dialogue about Islamophobia and hatred against Muslims? I totally agree that this dialogue should happen, yet the dialogue wouldn't be complete without a deep look into each of our own hearts. Every Christian, Muslim, Buddhist, atheist, agnostic needs to examine their own heart and take responsibility for any hatred or prejudice lurking there.

Speaking to a newfound Pakistani friend and discussing the status of Christians in his home country, he said Christians are being persecuted and killed just because of their faith. Somewhat hesitant, repeatedly looking over his shoulder as he spoke, he said there is no open dialogue there, but he was glad we had it here! Christians in his homeland are not free to openly speak out about their faith or question anything about Islam or Muhammed. I have heard of the same type of persecution in Iran, Iraq, Saudi Arabia, Libya, Somalia, Sudan, Palestine, Lebanon, etc. Why is this taking place? Why the hatred and killing of Muslims in the crusades by supposed Christians at that time? Why the hatred of White supremacists to those of colour other than their own? Why?

These all arise from the evil that comes from the fallen human heart (Jeremiah 17:9).

No religious or political legislation, even the best plans and schemes of man, can deal with the issues of the heart. Only God can do that (Jeremiah 3:22).

Jesus said, *"You have heard that it was said, 'You shall love your neighbor and hate your enemy.' But I say to you, Love your enemies and pray for those who persecute you, so that you may be sons of your Father who is in heaven." (Matthew 5:43–45, ESV)*. Only through a supernatural work of God in our hearts can we do this!

Only as we allow our Creator, Jesus Christ, the Prince of Peace, to have rule over us will we have peace in our hearts. Only then will we have love and peace for those who persecute us. Only then will we hate the sin that causes such hatred. *"And the peace of God, which surpasses all understanding, will guard your hearts and your minds in Christ Jesus." (Philippians 4:7, ESV)*.

"For to us a child is born, to us a son is given; and the government shall be upon his shoulder, and his name shall be called Wonderful Counselor, Mighty God, Everlasting Father, Prince of Peace. Of the increase of his government and of peace there will be no end." (Isaiah 9:6–7, ESV).

AUGUST 23

Hate Evil—Love People

He was falsely accused for "crimes against the state" and relegated to a life sentence of solitary hard labour under the brutal rule of North Korean dictator Kim Jong Un. He dug holes in the hard dirt to plant trees; at other times he broke up coal. In summer, he endured under extreme heat, and in winter, his feet were freezing. He was under constant surveillance and wasn't able to speak to his family or church for the full duration of his time there. Having served over two- and one-half years, he was miraculously released.

Pastor Hyeon Soo Lim's response to his detainment and treatment was amazing! In an interview with CBC's Rosemary Barton, he said he wasn't angry at those who did this to him. In fact, he said that he forgives them and that he loves them! This is not the response one would expect from having been abused in this way, especially when all he was trying to do was help the orphans, the poor, and the needy. Where does this kind of response come from? Jesus exhorts us in the Holy Scriptures: *"But I say, do not resist an evil person! If someone slaps you on the right cheek, offer the other cheek also." (Matthew 5:39)*; *"But I say, love your enemies! Pray for those who persecute you!" (Matthew 5:44)*; *"'You must love the LORD your God with all your heart, all your soul, and all your mind.' This is the first and greatest commandment. A second is equally important: 'Love your neighbor as yourself'" (Matthew 22:37–39).*

Pastor Lim is a follower of Jesus. Jesus said He would empower His followers with His Holy Spirit, and one of the fruits of the Holy Spirit is love (Galatians 5:22). Rather than hate his enemies, Pastor Lim recognized this extremely difficult trial as discipline from God to help him to, in his own words, "serve God more sincerely." This is true Christian faith in action! Would the world not be a much better place if we all practised our faith in this way?

Yes, we should hate the evil that people do to others, the evil that resides within every human heart. We should hate the wars, the murders, the killing, the gossip, the racism, the abuse, the selfishness, the greed, yet we are to love people, even our enemies, who are all created in the image of God!

"Three things will last forever—faith, hope, and love—and the greatest of these is love." (1 Corinthians 13:13).

AUGUST 24

Nabeel

Nabeel Qureshi has been a monumental encouragement to many. His testimony can be found in his book *Seeking Allah, Finding Jesus*. He became a Christian through honestly pursuing the truth. He was a devout practicing Muslim at one time, until he found Jesus and surrendered his life to Him. Nabeel wrote at least a couple of other books: *Answering Jihad: A Better Way Forward* and *No God but One: Allah or Jesus*, in which he explains very clearly his reasons for becoming a Jesus lover! Though never having met Nabeel face to face, he encouraged me immensely through his writings and YouTube postings.

Not long ago, he was diagnosed with stage four stomach cancer. Though he asked the Lord to heal him, he passed away at the age of thirty-four on September 16, 2017, leaving behind a beautiful wife and young child. We might ask why did God not heal his earthly body. Why would He take him so early in life? Why could he not live on to write more books? These are all questions we may never know the answer to, but there are some things that we do know.

God did heal Nabeel! He stands complete and whole in the Presence of his Maker, Jesus, the one who he put his trust in! *"He will wipe away every tear from their eyes, and death shall be no more, neither shall there be mourning, nor crying, nor pain anymore, for the former things have passed away." (Revelation 21:4, ESV)*. Nabeel now has a new eternal and glorious home, the heavenly place made for every person who trusts in Jesus as their Lord and Saviour! *"For we know that when this earthly tent we live in is taken down (that is, when we die and leave this earthly body), we will have a house in heaven, an eternal body made for us by God himself and not by human hands." (2 Corinthians 5:1)*.

As the songwriter Jim Hill so aptly wrote, "What a Day That Will Be!"

This eternal life is available to all who call to Jesus for forgiveness and mercy (John 1:12, 3:16)! Certainly it will be a wonderful day for God's children when He calls us Home!

AUGUST 25

Is My Name Written There?

When on a trip a few months ago, I had a filling fall out of one of my front teeth. It left a very sharp edge and was quite uncomfortable, so I sought out a dentist in the city near where we were staying. At the office, they took my personal information and proceeded to replace my filling. Before I left, I paid with my credit card. They stapled my receipts together, and I left with a numb face! A couple of months later, I needed additional information and called their office. The secretary looked and said my name was not on the record. I spelled out my name again and she double checked. I was not recorded there. When checking the receipts they had originally given me, I realized that the credit card receipt was stapled over the name on the other receipt. The name recorded was not mine. Even the address had mistakes! Calling them back, I proceeded to point out the error and had it corrected. Now my name is recorded in their books! This was all very perplexing at the time, and it's a good reminder that it's important to keep the records straight.

There's a much more important book mentioned in the Bible, in which it is most imperative to have our name recorded. Our eternal destiny depends on it! It's called the Book of Life. It's essential to have one's name recorded in this book to enter into eternal life in heaven: *"Nothing impure will ever enter it, nor will anyone who does what is shameful or deceitful, but only those whose names are written in the Lamb's book of life." (Revelation 21:27, NIV).* We can't write our own names into this book, nor can we earn our way into having it written there. *"Many will say to me on that day, "Lord, Lord, did we not prophesy in your name and in your name drive out demons and in your name perform many miracles?" Then I will tell them plainly, "I never knew you. Away from me, you evildoers!" (Matthew 7:22–24, NIV).*

The price has already been paid by Jesus dying on the cross two thousand years ago! All who believe and receive this precious gift will have their names written in the Book of Life (John 1:12, 3:16)!

"For the wages of sin is death, but the gift of God is eternal life in Christ Jesus our Lord." (Romans 6:23, NIV).

AUGUST 26

Sidewalk to Nowhere

While going for a walk with my grandsons in the town of Smithers, BC, near where we live, we had the opportunity of walking back and forth a few times on the infamous "sidewalk to nowhere." This very short piece of sidewalk was built because the town had certain rules on the books that required businesses that were upgrading their buildings to also upgrade the sidewalk in front of their business. Town council decided they had to enforce the law and insist the business build a sidewalk. Since no sidewalk existed in front of this business, or for that matter anywhere in the vicinity, a redundant, costly edifice sticks out like a sore thumb paralleling Highway 16, for every observant passerby—a "sidewalk to nowhere."

This sidewalk serves as a reminder to me of so many times I have relied on my own wisdom rather than trusting in Almighty God and seeking His wisdom. My own human wisdom seeks my own solutions, my own desires, and always comes up wanting, becoming ultimately a path to nowhere.

One of the most blatant blunders in human-generated wisdom is in trying to save ourselves and attempting to live life in our own way, without God. God's Word, the Bible, says of such efforts, *"Claiming to be wise, they instead became utter fools." (Romans 1:22).* This type of wisdom may seem profound at the moment but in the end leads to nowhere or, even worse, to death!

God's wisdom is available to us because Jesus Christ has made the way for us to have an intimate and personal relationship with God (1 Timothy 2:5–6). When we in faith call out to Him to save us, recognizing our absolute need for Him, His direction, and His wisdom to rule our lives, He will give it and not hold back: *"If you need wisdom, ask our generous God, and he will give it to you. He will not rebuke you for asking. But when you ask him, be sure that your faith is in God alone." (James 1:5–6).*

Jesus said: *"I will show you what it's like when someone comes to me, listens to my teaching, and then follows it. It is like a person building a house who digs deep and lays the foundation on solid rock. When the floodwaters rise and break against that house, it stands firm because it is well built." (Luke 6:47–48).*

Dear Lord Jesus, cause us not to rely on ourselves and our wisdom that leads to nowhere but to call out to you for your eternal wisdom, each and every day!

Who Made You?

A First Nations friend related to me an incident that he witnessed many years ago regarding his grandfather, who was a strong man of faith. It happened something like this.

They were in a restaurant. After receiving their food, as always, his grandfather bowed his head and blessed the food and gave thanks. Another man sitting near him asked him what he was doing. The elderly man replied that he was thanking God for his gracious provision of food. At this, the other fellow replied that there was no God, so why talk to him. The elder reached into his jacket and pulled out his pocket watch. He asked the doubter who he thought might have made the watch. The fellow acknowledged it was made by a watch manufacturing company. Pointing to the heavens and the creation outside, the elder asked who might have made the stars, the moon, the sun, and the rest of creation, and he asked "Who made you?" The unbeliever didn't know what to say and left without saying a word.

Since Adam and Eve, the whole of humanity has turned to our own way and rejected our Creator by making Him out to be what we want Him to be, or by even denying His existence. God's Word, the Bible, is very clear: *"For although they knew God, they neither glorified him as God nor gave thanks to him, but their thinking became futile and their foolish hearts were darkened. Although they claimed to be wise, they became fools." (Romans 1:21–22 NIV).*

Why is it that we easily recognize that the simple things around us have been made, yet we often refuse to believe that the infinitely more complex world around us was created by Someone far more superior than us? Could it possibly be that we don't want to admit that we have a Creator because then we would have to come under His authority and worship Him?

Again, the Holy Scriptures are very clear that everyone will one day face Him and bow our knee before Him, and every person will ultimately confess that Jesus Christ is Lord (Philippians 2:10–11). Will this be now, in thankfulness and worship, as our First Nations elder did, or will it be when it is too late for mercy but in fear and trembling, when every person will stand before Him and give account for every thought, word, and deed in the final judgement?

"Seek the Lord while he may be found; call on him while he is near." (Isaiah 55:6, NIV).

AUGUST 28

Transparency

During a time of group prayer, an opportunity arose for each person to voice a personal prayer request. After an uncomfortable period of silence, one person spoke up. With tears in her eyes, she shared a very personal weakness with the group, asking for prayer in this delicate area of her life. Touched in our hearts, tears formed in the eyes of many others in the room. Then, one by one, most of us present in the room, in a mutual time of vulnerable transparency, shared very personal areas of our own experience and also asked for prayer. Needless to say, the prayer time was powerful as these honest requests were expressed to our almighty, compassionate, and healing God.

Though God already knows every one of our sins, inadequacies, failings, hurts, and the ensuing guilt and shame, He wants a transparent heart, an open relationship with Him, so as we are exposed to His light of truth, we may be healed.

As an illustration, when a transparency is exposed to the bright light of an overhead projector, the light is able to dispel the darkness and expose what is on it. That which needs to be changed or erased can easily be seen and dealt with until the pure, clean image that is meant to be there is projected onto the screen. In a similar way, the more transparent we are with God and trusted friends, the more truthful we are, the more His healing light can shine in and through us so that we can become more like the person He created us to be. On the contrary, if we put a closed book onto the overhead projector, the light can't shine through, as nothing is exposed to the light. If we remain closed, the sin remains in the dark recesses of our soul. Though God knows every detail and need in our lives before we expose them, we need to be honest and allow His truth and light to shine on every area of our lives to be healed and become the true person He has created us to be.

"But if we are living in the light, as God is in the light, then we have fellowship with each other, and the blood of Jesus, his Son, cleanses us from all sin." (1 John 1:7).

AUGUST 29

Jesus Everywhere

Years ago, I was asked to pray at the naming of a young First Nations Chief. Afterwards, three older women Elders approached with tears in their eyes and said, "Thank you for coming to pray. We need Jesus here; we need Jesus everywhere." One of those ladies is presently in the hospital palliative care room with only hours left to live. If she should live for four more days, she would reach her ninetieth birthday. I was asked by the family to pray for her yesterday, just before her imminent departure to her eternal home with her Lord Jesus.

Over the years of getting to know her, it was obvious that she didn't have an easy life. Whenever I would meet her, she'd speak of her faith in Jesus and share concerns that she was praying about and encourage me in my faith. She's a very special lady who wasn't afraid of sharing her faith in Jesus. I consider it an honour to have had the privilege of knowing her.

Though she had little formal education, her perception of "needing Jesus everywhere" is profound. Her wise words bring to mind the following Scripture verses: *"Seek the LORD while you can find him. Call on him now while he is near." (Isaiah 55:6)*; *"His purpose was for the nations to seek after God and perhaps feel their way toward him and find him … now he commands everyone everywhere to repent of their sins and turn to him." (Act 17:27, 30)*.

It was clear that this wonderful lady had a personal relationship with Jesus. She would be the first to admit that she was far from perfect, yet she understood that the payment was made for her sins through the death of her Saviour Jesus Christ. She recognized her daily dependence on Him for everything. She was concerned for others, especially for her family and their faith in the Lord. As a result, some of her children, grandchildren, and great grandchildren also trust in the Lord.

Now at the end of her earthly journey, she is soon to hear her Creator say, *"Well done, my good and faithful servant. You have been faithful in handling this small amount, so now I will give you many more responsibilities. Let's celebrate together!" (Matthew 25:23)*.

Born That Way

I have a friend who, at a medical checkup, was diagnosed with a hole in her heart. The doctor told her she was born that way. A subsequent surgery was successful, and now she's perfectly well. A similar diagnosis happened to me when I was having back problems. The X-rays showed that one of my vertebrae had not formed completely while I was formed in my mother's womb. This wasn't so easily mended, but with some stretching exercises and restraint with heavy lifting, I can take safeguards to mitigate the effects.

God's Word, the Bible, says we all have something much more seriously wrong with us from birth. We are born with a sinful nature. This nature was inherited from our ancestors Adam and Eve and is inherently rebellious towards God (Psalm 51:5; Jeremiah 17:9; Romans 3:23).

The first couple, Adam and Eve, were created pure by God to live in a perfect place, the Garden of Eden, in perfect harmony with Him. They sinned against God, and something died in them, and their intimate spiritual relationship with God was severed. Because of their sin, they were thrown out of this paradise. All their offspring, that is the whole human race, including us, were born outside that garden with a sinful, rebellious nature towards God (Genesis 3). This has affected every part of our humanity: our spirits, our bodies, our emotions, even our sexuality.

When my friend and I found out about our physically inherited biological defects, we desired to have our bodies restored to the way God created them to be in the first place. Yet the spiritual condition we are all born with is a condition no fallen human being can correct. However, God Himself, because of His infinite love and care for us, came to forgive us of our rebellion, to give us a new nature and restore our relationship with Him! Jesus said, *"My purpose is to give them a rich and satisfying life" (John 10:10)*; *"This means that anyone who belongs to Christ has become a new person. The old life is gone; a new life has begun!" (2 Corinthians 5:17).*

Each of us now has a decision to make. Will we remain in our rebellious condition, or will we receive the amazing gift of forgiveness and new life offered to all those who trust in Him (John 1:12, 3:16)?

"And I will give you a new heart, and I will put a new spirit in you. I will take out your stony, stubborn heart and give you a tender, responsive heart." (Ezekiel 26:26).

AUGUST 31

Hands Off!

If you've been watching the news recently, you've most certainly heard about all the celebrities who are being accused of sexual harassment. From politicians to comedians, the accusations keep coming.

What a disgrace! Such things should never happen! No woman, even in the most vulnerable of circumstances, should ever be exploited, abused, or taken advantage of. Any real man would protect a woman, just as he should his own daughter. Yet these things are happening on a regular basis, not only among the celebrities but throughout our society.

Why would men entrap, abuse, take advantage of, and molest women? God's Word, the Bible, says that all people are sinners and have a selfish, sinful nature. This sinful nature produces all kinds of wicked things, including sexual immorality and selfish ambition (Galatians 5:19 21). Though some of the men admit to impropriety, others categorically deny anything has happened. Just the fact that these men often go to great lengths to deny doing such things shows that they see such actions are wrong.

Granted, some of the accusations may be false (see Genesis 39). Yet I believe these revelations of abuse are only scratching the surface, as most abused women have been so severely hurt that they don't want to expose themselves to more hurt and victimization from the men who would vehemently defend themselves if exposed. But God knows every incident; He knows exactly what happened. He knows even the thoughts and motives of every person, whether sinful or righteous. One day every one of us will stand before God to give an answer for even the most secretive deeds we have done (Matthew 5:22; 1 Timothy 5:24; John 16:8–11).

In the meantime, God's desire is for all people to transparently come to Him and confess our sinful ways so that He can forgive us and change us into people who will honour Him and those around us. He wants us to surrender to Him so we can receive His Holy Spirit and the new life that only He can give. Then we can be the men and women He planned for us to be! Then men will keep their hearts, eyes, and hands from this abusive behaviour. Men will rise up to be the protectors we were created to be! Women will be protected and honoured. Men, women, and children will be safe, and love will prevail!

"But the fruit of the Spirit is love, joy, peace, longsuffering, kindness, goodness, faithfulness, gentleness, self-control. Against such there is no law." (Galatians 5:22–23, NKJV).

SEPTEMBER 1

Time with Our Maker

Every anniversary, new year, or birthday that comes along reminds us of the passing of time. Some say time passes slowly, and others, especially as we get older, remark how quickly the years have passed! Yet we all have been given twenty-four hours in a day; there is no exception. Sometimes we find ourselves running around with not enough time in a day to get all the things done that we had planned. Other times, hopefully, we might be able to relax and have no particular plans for the day. Our busyness, or lack of it, comes from how much "business" we have planned for the time we've been given! This underscores the importance for us to spend the time we have on the most important things before us.

What could be more important than spending time with our Maker, the One who made us, the Almighty God? He says in His Word, the Bible, *"If you look for me whole-heartedly, you will find me." (Jeremiah 29:13)*; *"This is what the Lord says—your Redeemer, the Holy One of Israel: 'I am the Lord your God, who teaches you what is good for you and leads you along the paths you should follow.'" (Isaiah 48:17)*.

As we seek Him and spend time with Him in His Word, we will get to know Him and will learn His will for our lives! This is my desire: to know Him better, to seek Him and His guidance for every day He has given!

Jesus said, *"Let me teach you, because I am humble and gentle at heart, and you will find rest for your souls." (Matthew 11:29)*.

September 2

Identity

There are many studies and theories about how and when our First Nations people came to North America. In a recent news article, the diversity of opinions was quite obvious. What caught my attention was the statement by one person that the assertion of more recent dates for their arrival was an attack on their identity. It was quite clear that this person felt her identity was linked to their ownership of and length of time they had been occupying the land. It seems this belief has been the case for most every people group over the years, and if I'm totally honest, I find it in myself. Even as individuals, we often put our identity in our longevity, our land, and our possessions. The more land and stuff I have, the longer I've been here, the richer I am, the more significant I am. This is the underlying principle.

If my identity comes from how long I've been in a place, or the value of my possessions, it's tentative at best. The fact is that nations, people groups, and individuals come and go on a regular basis. Our lives and status on this earth are very brief indeed. And when we depart from here, we leave every earthly thing behind, even our mortal bodies. As God's Word, the Bible, states, *"Why, you do not even know what will happen tomorrow. What is your life? You are a mist that appears for a little while and then vanishes." (James 4:14, NIV)*. What a great disappointment when we have to leave it all behind!

Our true identity comes from personally knowing Jesus Christ, our Creator God, and following Him to fulfill the true purpose we were made for. Jesus once encouraged a very rich man, *"If you want to be perfect, go, sell your possessions and give to the poor, and you will have treasure in heaven. Then come, follow me." (Matthew 19:21, NIV)*.

Life

I can remember sitting in on a pro-life meeting many years ago when some people were warning that taking the lives of the innocent, preborn babies was a precursor to euthanasia. How right they were! Now doctors, who have historically been instruments of healing and defenders of life, can potentially become purveyors of death of both the young and the old. Some three hundred years before Jesus walked on earth, Hippocrates recognized the inherent truth of respect for human life, as he wrote: "I will give no deadly medicine to any one if asked, nor suggest any such counsel; and in like manner I will not give to a woman a pessary to produce abortion With purity and with holiness I will pass my life and practice my Art." (Britannica.com)

One of the fundamental foundations of a free society is the protection of life for all, especially the most vulnerable. Without this basic freedom, the life of some will be contingent on the will of others more powerful than they. As Mother Theresa of Calcutta so aptly said, "And if we can accept that a mother can kill her own child, how can we tell other people not to kill one another?" (azquotes.com)

How could we have fallen so far? Where is this going to lead us? We have forgotten the basic truth of God that every human being is created in His image (Genesis 1:27). We have usurped from God the prerogative of taking of human life and taken it into our own hands (Exodus 20:13).

Oh Lord Jesus, have mercy on us, forgive us our sins and restore us to faith in You and your holy Word. Do not let us fall into the hands of the devil, who desires to take our life from us. May we trust in You, the source of all truth and giver of life (John 14:6).

Jesus said, *"The thief's purpose is to steal and kill and destroy. My purpose is to give them a rich and satisfying life." (John 10:10).*

SEPTEMBER 4

Pot Heads

In my younger days, we used to call those who used marijuana "pot heads." The effects of the drug seemed obvious, as those who used it were less attentive and seemed spaced out. As one user said, he was "taking a trip without leaving the farm." One of these users was my math teacher, who spent a considerable amount of time "teaching" us about his experiences with marijuana use. He said it enhanced his mental perception, that he had never really appreciated music as much as when he was high on the drug. When confronted by a student of the possibility of marijuana being a gateway drug to more lethal drugs, he responded that this was absolutely not the case, insisting that the drug was the great mind-expanding wonder drug of the day! According to a student in his class, six years later, this same teacher was extolling the use of the much more potent LSD as a wonderful mind-expanding drug!

You might be shocked and surprised that this actually happened in a public school! Yet much to our dismay today, our governments are rushing to legalize the use of marijuana with little or no warnings as to its serious negative side effects. We hear much about medical marijuana, and I have yet to see clear warnings from the government of the serious negative side effects of this drug.

According to www.drugfreeworld.org, some of these include, among other things, memory and co-ordination problems, decreased IQ, poor school performance, increased potential for starting opiate abuse, sexual problems, paranoia, strange behaviour, panic, hallucinations, increased risk of heart attack and stroke. Sounds like a life gone sadly wrong!

I would rather find my fulfilment in a living relationship with our Creator, Jesus Christ. He is the only one who can truly fulfill all our desires and needs. As the Scriptures so clearly declare: *"And may you have the power to understand, as all God's people should, how wide, how long, how high, and how deep his love is. May you experience the love of Christ, though it is too great to understand fully. Then you will be made complete with all the fullness of life and power that comes from God." (Ephesians 3:18–19).*

SEPTEMBER 5

Anticipating the Test

Definition of anticipate 1: to give advance thought, discussion, or treatment to 2: to meet (an obligation) before a due date 3: to foresee and deal with in advance (merriam-webster.com)

With an upcoming medical procedure designed to determine if I am still cancer free, I have some apprehension as to the outcome. Having been disappointed with the results of past tests, which exposed the cancer in the first place, I have hopefully learned to put my trust in God no matter what the outcome. Though I do not know what the future holds, I do anticipate that it will be somehow Okay.

In the past, having experienced some substantial disappointments as the outcome I had anticipated was not what actually happened - I am determined to keep my eyes on the Lord and trust that He has me in His capable hands! Whatever the outcome I will still trust Him! My anticipation is not so much in the outcome of the test but in what the Lord has in store for me! Since He knows all things and loves me, what should I be afraid of? After all He is my Maker and the ruler of the universe! He determines our time here on earth and our eternity with Him!

Our experience in this broken world can either lead us to a closer walk with God or to drive us away from Him. I am determined that whatever the outcome, I will trust Him and give glory to His Holy Name!

"And I am convinced that nothing can ever separate us from God's love. Neither death nor life, neither angels nor demons, neither our fears for today nor our worries about tomorrow—not even the powers of hell can separate us from God's love. No power in the sky above or in the earth below—indeed, nothing in all creation will ever be able to separate us from the love of God that is revealed in Christ Jesus our Lord." Romans 8:38-39

SEPTEMBER 6

Paradise

When you think of paradise, what comes to mind? To some it might bring images of sunny beaches, perfect temperatures, and a peaceful perfect life with no worries or fears. A fellow I spoke to recently commented that the most peaceful time he had ever experienced was to walk alone with his dog through the forest right here in BC! We all have glimpses of what paradise might be like. But is there really such a place, or is it just in our imagination? Can our best experiences here on earth even come close to what true paradise is like?

The apostle Paul speaks of an experience he had: *"And I know how such a man—whether in the body or apart from the body I do not know, God knows— was caught up into Paradise and heard inexpressible words, which a man is not permitted to speak." (2 Corinthians 12:3–4, NASB).* Jesus said to the dying criminal who called out to Him, *"Truly I say to you, today you will be with Me in Paradise." (Luke 23:43, NASB).* He also spoke of a place with many rooms that He was preparing for those who trusted in Him (John 14:1–4). We are promised: *"Behold, the tabernacle of God is among the people, and He will dwell among them, and they shall be His people, and God Himself will be among them, and He will wipe away every tear from their eyes; and there will no longer be any death; there will no longer be any mourning, or crying, or pain; the first things have passed away." (Revelation 21:3–4, NASB).*

Paradise is a real place, an eternal place, a place where God lives, a place Jesus is preparing for those who believe in Him! If we think of our best experience ever on this earth and multiply it a million times, we might be touching on what He has in store for His children!

"It is finished! I am the Alpha and the Omega—the Beginning and the End. To all who are thirsty I will give freely from the springs of the water of life. All who are victorious will inherit all these blessings, and I will be their God, and they will be my children." (Revelation 21:6–7).

SEPTEMBER 7

One Bean

Our First Nations people have a remarkable way of explaining age old truths. This was very evident when listening to a Hereditary Chief from Fort Babine (Wit'at) Nation describe to me the importance of meaningful prayer, taught to him by his grandfather. As I remember it, he said his grandfather, a devout Catholic Christian, faithfully prayed morning, noon, and evening and any time prayer was required during the day. This seemed excessive at the time to my friend, so he asked his grandfather why he prayed so much. What was the use? His grandfather explained how important it was to pray to God, who desires us to call out to Him, but he also told him that it was important to pray in a meaningful way. To illustrate this, his grandfather told him the following story.

There was a fellow who prayed a lot, and he was proud of it. So proud that every time he said a prayer, he would take a bean and put it in a bag. After some time, he thought the bag must be full, as he had prayed a lot. He wanted to see how many times he had prayed, so he went to count the beans in the bag. When he emptied the bag, only one bean rolled out! My friend asked his grandfather why there was only one bean when he had prayed so much. He explained that the one bean represented the only prayer that was truly sincere! All the prayers of rote meant nothing, as they were just empty recited words without real meaning.

Jesus taught this same important truth: *"When you pray, don't babble on and on as the Gentiles do. They think their prayers are answered merely by repeating their words again and again. Don't be like them, for your Father knows exactly what you need even before you ask him!" (Matthew 6:7–8).*

Oh Lord Jesus, please teach us to be honest and sincere, and help us pray meaningful and heartfelt prayers!

King of the Woods

Have you ever heard the expression "We're not out of the woods yet"? Sometimes when in a difficult or seemingly impossible situation, we get the feeling of being lost, of the immediate troubles crowding in on us. Not knowing the outcome or the direction, a fear comes in and tries to overtake us, giving us a sense of being lost on this trail of life. I felt this way when I was confronted with cancer. The word itself has power because it shows my mortality, the fact that one day I will die, that I control very little in my life. All my plans are put on hold. I don't know which direction I should turn. For example, should I take the path the medical system has laid out for me? Should I take the natural cure? If so, which one? A sense of fear and paralysis overtakes me.

Then I look to the Author and Finisher of our faith, the Creator of everything. He made the sun and the stars as well as every cell in each one of us—even our DNA! He is our Maker, Sustainer, Saviour, and Friend, Jesus Christ! He has it all in His hands! He has me in His hands! Whatever happens, He will be with me! I have nothing to fear! He knows every tree, every leaf, every molecule of not only the woods but also of me! The woods, the trail, the way belongs to Him, and I trust Him! After all, He knew this would happen before the beginning of time (see Psalm 139)! As I pick up my Bible and read the inspired Word of God, all fear is gone! Jesus has come near to my heart; He ministers His eternal words to me and gives me peace! Though I am not out of the woods yet, I will trust the King of the woods!

"Search me, O God, and know my heart; test me and know my anxious thoughts. Point out anything in me that offends you, and lead me along the path of everlasting life." (Psalm 139:23–24).

SEPTEMBER 9

Lost in Lies

The bodies of Kam McLeod and Bryer Schmegelsky, the lost boys suspected of murdering three people in northern BC during the summer of 2019, have been found near the Nelson River in northern Manitoba! The RCMP are to be commended for their determined persistence in searching for these fellows. The nation can take a breath of relief, as the danger of being confronted with these boys has come to an end.

Yet this nation still has much to fear, as these young men did not become what they were without deceptive input from the society surrounding them. These deceptions may not influence everyone in the same way, but all who are touched by them are affected in one way or another. Though we may never know the exact reasons why these men did what they did, I'd like to address one dangerous, damaging deception that detrimentally affects our society today.

I believe that the false ideology that we are objects of chance has an enormously destructive effect on how we see ourselves and others. If we are objects of random chance, our reason for existence is just as random as the evolution that created us. If there is no creator, no design, no standard, then anything goes. Who are we to say what is right or wrong if there is no absolute standard? Who says it's wrong to kill, to steal, or to destroy? It becomes the survival of the fittest. And the fittest can be brutal!

When we believe God's Holy Scriptures—that we are made in the image of God with design and purpose—we can have respect for our lives and the lives of others. Only then can we know the true purpose of life. Only then can we have a true standard that we can point to for the fulfillment of our lives!

"Have you never heard? Have you never understood? The Lord is the everlasting God, the Creator of all the earth. He never grows weak or weary. No one can measure the depths of his understanding." (Isaiah 40:28).

SEPTEMBER 10

We're Not Animals

A friend once stated that her dogs were her children and she treated them as such! Though we are to take care of our animals, they are not humans. Though sadly, at times people act like vicious animals or even worse. (What animal creates a bomb to blow up others of its kind?) We're not animals. Nothing could be farther from the truth!

God's Word, the Bible, clearly states that animals were spoken into existence just as the rest of creation, humanity! Man was uniquely formed from the ground. God breathed His own breath of life into him and created him in His own image (Genesis 1 and 2)! This life is expressed by the amazing superior abilities of humankind to create, to plan, to reason, to read, to write, to add, to subtract, to speak, to love, and so on.

The belief that we are no different from the animals around us denies the very Creator who created us for His special purposes! Taken to its full conclusion, this lie manifests itself in horrendous ways, such as murders, wars, holocausts, ethnic cleansing, racism, abortion, rape, and the like. If we're nothing more than an animal, why not act like one?

But we are inherently special because we are created in the image of God! To settle for anything less is to believe a lie and suffer the consequences! Are we going to believe God, take Him at His Word, and respect all human life? Or will we believe a lie and spiral into the path of behaving like beasts? That is the question!

"From one man he made all the nations, that they should inhabit the whole earth; and he marked out their appointed times in history and the boundaries of their lands. God did this so that they would seek him and perhaps reach out for him and find him, though he is not far from any one of us. 'For in him we live and move and have our being.' As some of your own poets have said, 'We are his offspring.'" (Acts 17:26–28, NIV).

SEPTEMBER 11

Magnificent Mess

After an intensive manhunt across Canada, the RCMP found the once handsome two young men who caused the whole of Canada to hold their breath in fear after murdering three people in northern BC in the summer of 2019. Everyone could breathe easier. Autopsies showed they had died by suicide. Recordings left by them revealed them admitting to the killings but demonstrating no remorse. What happened? Why would these young men with so much potential do such a thing? If we're not animals but are specially created in the image of the Almighty God, why would such a tragedy like this happen? Why do people purposely harm others?

The Holy Scriptures clearly inform us, *"When Adam sinned, sin entered the world. Adam's sin brought death, so death spread to everyone, for everyone sinned." (Romans 5:12).* The magnificent creation has come under the curse of sin and death. Humanity, created in God's image, chose to go our own way and has fallen from a vibrant, living relationship with God, with each other, and with the rest of creation, reaping death instead of life—death of the body, spiritual death, death to relationships, death to marriage, and death to the living relationship with God! Though the image of God in man is still abundantly evident, it is stained by sin in every aspect (Isaiah 64:6). So today we see the magnificence of God in every human being, but we also see a mess with the stench of death all around us—all as a result of our rebellion against our Creator God!

We could be overcome and tempted to give up when focusing on these evil deeds, but there is still hope for all of us who are still alive! We can become children of God controlled by His Holy Spirit to produce good fruit, rather than our sinful nature (Galatians 5:19–23)! *"As for you, you were dead in your transgressions and sins, in which you used to live when you followed the ways of this world and of the ruler of the kingdom of the air, the spirit who is now at work in those who are disobedient. All of us also lived among them at one time, gratifying the cravings of our flesh and following its desires and thoughts. Like the rest, we were by nature deserving of wrath. But because of his great love for us, God, who is rich in mercy, made us alive with Christ even when we were dead in transgressions—it is by grace you have been saved." (Ephesians 2:1–5, NIV).*

SEPTEMBER 12

Will to Fight

Is there ever a time to fight? I know that since my diagnosis of cancer, I'm going to fight for my health more than I ever have! I'll use whatever reasonable means to fight the hideous disease! Though I believe everyone who has saving faith in Jesus will ultimately be healed, either in this body or in the perfect body He has promised after death, there is a time to fight while we're still here! We should always submit to the will of God in every situation, but we should not necessarily submit to every situation.

Though the battle with disease in this world is very real, especially as we get older, there's a much more dreadful and intense spiritual battle going on in this world since our ancestors Adam and Eve rebelled against our Creator God. It begins in the minds and philosophies of every human being, even you and me! It's from our thoughts that we speak and act. Our thoughts are based on our beliefs, and if our beliefs are warped, so will our speech and actions be warped! As we look around us today, we see this battle happening while at the same time make ourselves look better than we really are! We hide the truth about a lie we may have said or lived. We think our ways are better than God's ways. We question if we were truly created. We question God's sovereignty over us, His creation. We question our sexuality. We even question if there is a God! This is a battle with dark forces that are masquerading as light and vying to deceive every human soul. Only the truth can set us free! *"For though we live in the world, we do not wage war as the world does. The weapons we fight with are not the weapons of the world. On the contrary, they have divine power to demolish strongholds. We demolish arguments and every pretension that sets itself up against the knowledge of God, and we take captive every thought to make it obedient to Christ." (2 Corinthians 10:3–5, NIV).*

SEPTEMBER 13

Truth Personified

Sometimes certain people who look like Elvis try to emulate him. Some even try to seek success by having "Elvis concerts," impersonating him all around the country! Yet ultimately their true nature shines through. We come to the reality that there was only one Elvis, and though only a man, there will never be another like him!

God is a God of truth. The truths of honest science reveal His truth in nature all around us. His truth is also revealed to us in His Word, the Bible (John 17:17–19). When He made promises to His people, He said, *"... in my holiness I cannot lie." (Psalm 89:35).*

About two thousand years ago, the most amazing event in all of history happened! The very truth of God became flesh and lived among us! Jesus Christ, the Son of the living God, became God in human form! *"For God in all his fullness was pleased to live in Christ." (Colossians 1:19); "the Word was God ... So the Word became human and made his home among us. He was full of unfailing love and faithfulness. And we have seen his glory, the glory of the Father's one and only Son." (John 1:1, 14).* Jesus is God personified! That's why He could say with authority, *"I am the way, the truth, and the life. No one can come to the Father except through me. If you had really known me, you would know who my Father is. From now on, you do know him and have seen him!" (John 14:6–7).* That's why He said to Pilate just before He went to the cross to suffer and die to take the penalty for all who would put their trust in Him, *"... I was born and came into the world to testify to the truth. All who love the truth recognize that what I say is true." (John 18:37).*

In this world of ruse and deception, if we want to know the truth, if we want to live the truth, we must put our trust in and surrender to Jesus Christ, who is the only true and perfect personification of truth!

Living in the Truth

When the controversy over political interference by our Prime Minister with the then Minister of Justice was being exposed, the Minister of Justice said she was going to give "her truth" before the committee enquiring of her what really had happened. Could there really be more than one truth here? Is not the truth the truth no matter what?

So often we put our personal spin on our view of events and facts that we come up with our own version of truth, which is not the truth at all! Take for instance the truth of creation. Somehow in our effort to get rid of our Creator, we've come up with an absurd theory that says everything just happened by sheer chance over millions of years! We've come to believe that we came from animal-like creatures, thus we are no different than animals! We say we decide what sex we are, when it's obvious God has created us as male and female. We deny the Creator and His Word to us and boldly announce the discovery of a so called "god particle." As God's Word proclaims, *"They exchanged the truth about God for a lie ..." (Romans 1:25, NIV).*

Sometimes the truth hurts, especially when I get honest about myself and my own sins and lies that I have succumbed to!

The only way we can live in the truth is to surrender to God our Creator, the One who is the truth, Jesus Christ (John 14:6). When we put our trust in Him and receive Him into our lives, He gives us His Holy Spirit, the Spirit of truth, who bears witness to the truth in every area of life. His Word, the Bible, will become precious to us. We will only find purpose and peace when we accept the truth of who He is!

"For the Spirit teaches you everything you need to know, and what he teaches is true—it is not a lie. So just as he has taught you, remain in fellowship with Christ." (1 John 2:27).

Darkness to Light

The vision in one eye was gradually becoming dimmer. Objects in front of me were fuzzy and distorted. Bumping into and stumbling over unrecognizable objects was becoming more prevalent. I couldn't see things the way they really were. The specialist ordered laser surgery on my eye. A bit hesitant at first, the desire to see overcame the fears, and I allowed him to do his work! Literally as the laser cut away the obstruction, the light coming into my eye became brighter! Thankfully I can see clearly again! Thank God for physical eyesight, but how is our spiritual sight?

Why do we as human beings do such terrible things as killing one another in war, murder, and abortion? Why do we tear one another down with hateful words? Why do we take advantage of another person when trying to get the best price for our goods? Why is it so difficult to do to others what we expect from them? Why do we judge others according to their culture or creed? Why do we not to see other people as we see ourselves? God's Word clearly says, *"people loved the darkness more than the light, for their actions were evil." (John 3:19).*

Is there any hope for sin-sick humanity? Is there a cure? The Scriptures are clear! The prophets of old prophesied, *"The people who walk in darkness will see a great light. For those who live in a land of deep darkness, a light will shine." (Isaiah 9:2).* The apostle John proclaimed, *"The one who is the true light, who gives light to everyone, was coming into the world." (John 1:9).* Jesus Himself boldly declared, *"I am the light of the world. If you follow me, you won't have to walk in darkness, because you will have the light that leads to life." (John 8:12).*

The cure is available for our spiritual blindness, our stumbling in the darkness! Will we put our trust in Him?

In the Valley

What a privilege to live in the beautiful Bulkley Valley of British Columbia! The mountains are so majestic, especially this time of year, with the fresh snow on the peaks! During the summer, there's nothing like hiking over the summits where vegetation is only millimetres high, where moss and lichens grow, while taking in the tranquil green, blue, and multi-coloured landscapes of the valleys below!

Yet when we come down from the mountaintops, we enter back into the bustle of life in the valley! Sirens, noise of vehicles, and dangers of traffic become a reality again. Though we hesitate as we enter back into life in the valley with all its difficulties, we realize life has its mountaintop experiences that we can enjoy for the moment, but life there is not practical or sustainable. It's in the valley that we live. It's in the valley that we grow!

Though God is God of the mountaintops, He is also God of the valleys! Jesus experienced both and has overcome! *"I have told you these things, so that in me you may have peace. In this world you will have trouble. But take heart! I have overcome the world."* (*John 16:33*).

As we experience the inevitable adversities of life, we can either try to dismiss them and wish we were on the mountaintop, or we can learn from these hardships, to overcome them through faith in God and grow stronger. *"Who is it that overcomes the world? Only the one who believes that Jesus is the Son of God."* (*1 John 5:5*). The choice is ours!

"Endure hardship as discipline; God is treating you as his children. For what children are not disciplined by their father?" (*Hebrews 12:7, NIV*).

Thank Who?

I looked out the window and there was a precious Christian friend throwing off a load of firewood! Then my grandsons showed up and helped split and pile the wood in our woodshed! What a blessing! This scenario has repeated itself over and over again in different ways through various people, especially as I've had some physical issues lately and was limited in what I could do. How can I thank them enough? Though I know this was not done for the thank yous but out of a heart of love, I still struggle with how I can properly express my thanksgiving to all those who are such a blessing to us!

One friend told me not to thank him but to thank God! Although I remain so very thankful to each and every one of our friends and for their various expressions of love towards us, I know what he said struck to the very heart of thanksgiving! The following Scripture verse sums it all up! *"Every good and perfect gift is from above, coming down from the Father of the heavenly lights, who does not change like shifting shadows." (James 1:17, NIV).* Our heavenly Father, the Creator of the universe, the sun, the moon, the earth, and all that is in it, and especially every precious human being, is ultimately the One to whom we are to be thankful!

May each of us, on Thanksgiving Day and every day, in every circumstance, be thankful to Almighty God, the giver of all good things!

"Enter into his gates with thanksgiving, and into his courts with praise: be thankful unto him, and bless his name." (Psalm 100:4, KJV).

SEPTEMBER 18

Breaking Bones

Apparently as a veiled threat to protestors in Hong Kong, Chairman Xi, communist leader of the People's Republic of China, warned, "Anyone who attempts to split any region from China will perish, with their bodies smashed and bones ground to powder."[9] As witnessed by a constant stream of reports of suppression of their people, China has proven to be a regime that rules by fear, intimidation, manipulation, and brute force. The Tiananmen Square massacre in June 1989, and the more recent violence in Hong Kong, stand as stark reminders of this.

At first glance, some of us might think only despots, politicians, and tyrants act this way, until we are personally antagonized in some way and honestly analyze our own reaction! Some of the most bitter and acrimonious battles happen between spouses, in families, and in close relationships. One only has to watch the proceedings in a divorce court to witness how we defend our "rights" to realize how pervasive these attitudes are among us. When such reactions unfold before our very eyes, we wonder if there's any hope for us in this fallen, broken world.

The same day that I read the above quote by Chairman Xi, I read a proverb from the Bible: *"Patience can persuade a prince, and soft speech can break bones." (Proverbs 25:15).* What kind of bones could be broken by patience and soft speech? Could one of these bones be the bone of contention? Can the strife caused by my hard heart and my stubborn ways be broken?

The first response mentioned above is natural; the second one is supernatural and available to all who submit to and follow Jesus Christ! Then His Holy Spirit will produce His fruit in us and empower us to break the bones of contention with His patience and gentleness (Galatians 5:16–23)!

"Always be humble and gentle. Be patient with each other, making allowance for each other's faults because of your love." (Ephesians 4:2).

---

9 As quoted by BBC on Oct 14, 2019.

Global Warning

Climate change protestors, from school children to the elderly, were out in large numbers. Main stream media (NBC, CBC, etc) reported that Greta Thunberg addressed the UN Climate Change Summit on September 23, 2019, with an emotional and impassioned speech, saying, "How dare you, you have stolen my dreams and my childhood ... I should be back in school ..."

If we exclusively watch the mainstream media, it seems the verdict is in: we are doomed because of the increase of carbon dioxide gas. Yet when we listen to many expert scientists, the evidence is not so clear. Dr. William Happer, Freeman Dyson, Dr. William Soon, Dr. Patrick Michael, James Taylor, Tom Harris, Dr. Richard Keen, Dr. Terry Gannon, Dr. Jay Lehr, Stanley Goldenberg, Dr. John Clauser, and Dr. Patrick Moore are just a few among possibly thousands of scientists who seriously question the premise that carbon dioxide emissions cause catastrophic global warming. Most of the above-mentioned scientists point to actual statistics that show the computer-generated predictions of the climate change alarmists are already seriously failing in their own cataclysmic predictions!

Though Greta should probably go back to school and learn what the above scientists have to say about the climate change she so fears, what is starkly evident is the palpable silence on either side of the debate concerning God, the Creator and Sustainer, Who by the power of His Word spoke everything into existence (Genesis 1; Hebrews 11:3), and who by His power holds everything together (Acts 17:22–31; Colossians 1:15–20). Nor do we hear of a coming judgement that no one will escape! *"They deliberately forget that God made the heavens long ago by the word of his command ... He does not want anyone to be destroyed, but wants everyone to repent. But the day of the Lord will come as unexpectedly as a thief. Then the heavens will pass away with a terrible noise, and the very elements themselves will disappear in fire, and the earth and everything on it will be found to deserve judgment."* *(2 Peter 3:5, 9–10).*

Judgement is coming! Will we fearfully face the Almighty God as our judge, or will we humbly bow down and worship Him as our Lord and Saviour?

SEPTEMBER 20

Sing It Out!

One of my earliest memories is my mother humming her favourite choruses while doing her work in the kitchen of our simple country home. This had a soothing influence on all of us children as we witnessed her express heartfelt worship of the Almighty God from deep within her soul. As we gathered with others to worship in our old country church, Mom would often lead the singing with her favourite evangelical hymns penned by Fanny Crosby, Horatio Spafford, John Newton, and others. Sometimes on special occasions, such as Father's Day, Mother's Day, Christmas, or Easter, she'd have all of us children in front of the church singing at the top of our lungs! Though often reluctant to sing it out at the time, my mother's example had a profound effect on my view of life and my worship of my Saviour and God even to this day!

Sometimes due to the many difficulties life brings, I lose focus on the reality of God's wonderful love and grace towards me. In these times, I tend to look at the clouds of adversity rather than realize the tender care of our ever-loving God for all who seek Him! Though the clouds of doubt and pain may be manifestly evident, the marvelous, endless, and unwavering love of God is greater and is constantly shining upon us (Lamentations 3:22–23)! As someone so aptly said, "The sun is always shining above the clouds!"

So when I am desperate, caught in the storms of life, which is often these days, I ask the Lord for a song of worship to Him. If I still my heart and wait on Him, He gives praise to my lips and lifts me out of the pit of despair with songs of worship and praise! *"I will sing unto the Lord as long as I live: I will sing praise to my God while I have my being. My meditation of him shall be sweet: I will be glad in the Lord... Bless thou the Lord, O my soul. Praise ye the Lord." (Psalm 104:33–34, 35b, KJV).*

Evidence-Based Faith

Many scientists, politicians, and media are loudly proclaiming that they are basing their attack on the coronavirus on evidence-based science. So they inform us that we should rest assured that we are in good hands as they tell us how to respond to this deadly epidemic! Yet on the other hand, there's almost no mention of prayer or God in the whole process. Somehow faith in God is relegated to the back burner and even seen as contrary to real evidence.

Yet one of the great pieces of evidence everyone witnesses every day is creation itself! As we look around, we can't help but see amazing and intricate design! We see the flowers, the trees, wildlife, and fellow humans able to exist and replicate their own kind! The evidence is so strong that God Himself has told us in His Word, the Bible: *"For since the creation of the world God's invisible qualities—his eternal power and divine nature—have been clearly seen, being understood from what has been made, so that people are without excuse." (Romans 1:20, NIV).*

Rather than turn to our Maker and give Him the glory and ask Him for wisdom, we in our sinful nature tend to invent ways to relegate Him off the scene! We formulate supposedly wise yet ridiculous and absurd ideas that all this design somehow happened by chance and buy into one of the greatest lies ever told! Deceived, we think that God is now out of the picture, and we can come up with our own solutions, our own way, and continue to ignore Him. But He is the very One who gives us every breath, every heartbeat, even while we proclaim that He doesn't exist! The evidence is overwhelming. What are we going to do with it?

"Seek the Lord while he may be found; call upon him while he is near." (Isaiah 55:6, ESV).

SEPTEMBER 22

More Evidence-Based Faith

"If only I would have known" we often say. Many investors wish they knew what the stock market was going to do before it dramatically changed—up or down! Farmers and city dwellers alike would like to know what the weather will be over the next weeks to make plans for the future. We'd all like to know the future, but not one of us, including the weatherman, can know for sure what will happen in the next hour, let alone the weeks, months, and years ahead!

Yet we have a book, and a good portion of it foretells the future. Events involving leaders, nations, and the world were often prophesied well in advance, before they ever happened! For instance, King Cyrus of Medo-Persia (Isaiah 45:1) and Alexander the Great of Greece (Daniel 8) were prophesied many decades before their time. The re-establishment of the nation of Israel in 1948 was prophesied thousands of years before it happened.

This begs the question: Who knows the future but God? The prophecies of the Bible are sure evidence of its divine origins—that God is intimately involved with His creation! Not only does this book describe future events, but it also explains our origins and even the workings of the inner thoughts and motivations of every human heart!

Many try to ignore God's Holy Word; others have tried to disprove the Bible, but it still stands as the inspired Word of God!

When was the last time you have read from this precious book given to us by the inspiration of God? If we read it and heed it, it will profoundly change our life!

"Above all, you must realize that no prophecy in Scripture ever came from the prophet's own understanding, or from human initiative. No, those prophets were moved by the Holy Spirit, and they spoke from God." (2 Peter 1:20–21).

In His Image

The images of George Floyd's last moments are horrific. Such brutality and disregard for human life should never happen in any civilized society. I must admit, watching the video, as the minutes ticked by, I felt like kicking officer Dereck Chauvin in the head to get him off of Mr. Floyd.

There's a great moral outcry among most people in the USA. Yet we also see looting in the streets of major cities. People have been beaten to death, molested, and robbed in their own homes. Some of the protesters are doing the very thing they supposedly want to change. Fear has gripped the nation; people are crying out for change. It's obvious that human beings should not act this way and there needs to be a transformation, but how? There are many voices, but what does God's Word say?

The very first chapter of the Bible says, *"So God created man in his own image, in the image of God he created him; male and female he created them." (Genesis 1:27, ESV)*. We are created—all of us! We didn't come to exist by some random process, as taught in most of our educational institutions. Random evolution is supposedly based on "survival of the fittest." Living like animals, devouring, killing, and demeaning each other shouldn't be a surprise to the evolutionist! God's Word declares we are fearfully and wonderfully made (Psalm 139:14). Not only were we created, but each of us are created in the image of God. This gives every human being inherent worth, purpose, and great value! God gave us a nature like His to love, choose, be creative, gracious, kind, and to belong. We were created to respect each other and to worship our Creator God!

We have lost our way; God's image in us has been marred by sin, and we have turned against our God. Racism, disrespect, and injustice have become systemic in every sinful human heart! What is the answer? *"... now he commands everyone everywhere to repent of their sins and turn to him." (Acts 17:30)*.

SEPTEMBER 24

Why Police?

When I was in my early teens, my parents housed and cooked for a couple dozen men who were working to clear the reservoir for what is now known as the Hugh Keenleyside Dam on the Arrow Lakes in southern BC. These men came from, it seemed, every walk of life, every people group and background. It was a good lesson in humanity and the reason for law and order. Some of these men were friendly and polite; others were arrogant and demanding.

Every week or two, a policeman would come by and visit the camp, checking who was there, mixing with us and the men, making sure all was peaceful and in order. Once in a while he would take one of the fellows away, usually because he had previous run-ins with the law. One fellow even kept a pistol under his pillow!

Sometimes men would bring liquor to the camp and would get plastered drunk. Fights would occasionally break out at this time. Yet the overshadowing possibility of the presence of the RCMP had a way of keeping these men in check! The peace officer was our friend and their friend because he kept the peace, and his presence kept the rebellious from getting out of hand!

Whether we want to admit it or not, we all have a tendency to rebel in one way or another to authority. God's Word, the Bible, clearly states that we all have a sinful, rebellious nature *(Romans 3:17–18)*. This rebellious nature needs to be kept in check either through the presence of authority outside of us (police) or by submitting to God's authority within our hearts. If each of us would surrender our hearts completely to God, we wouldn't need the police to keep the peace! *"If any of you wants to be my follower, you must give up your own way, take up your cross daily, and follow me." (Luke 9:23)*; *"For God is not a God of disorder but of peace …" (1 Corinthians 14:33).*

SEPTEMBER 25

Everything Is His!

I don't know who came up with the term "possession is nine tenths of the law," but it appears to ring true, especially among the nations. China is acting this way in the South China Sea. Russia has annexed the Crimea. Closer to home, the early colonists took over the very land that we call Canada today. But who really owns the land—the animals, the vast oceans, and the people, including you and me? God's Word, the Bible, is very clear: *"The earth is the Lord's, and everything in it, the world, and all who live in it."* *(Psalm 24:1, NIV)*.

So why is it in such a mess? Nations are rising up against each other; rioting is in the streets. Murder, rape, and stealing are on the news every day. What's wrong? Again, the Scriptures are clear: *"They exchanged the truth about God for a lie, and worshiped and served created things rather than the Creator ... Furthermore, just as they did not think it worthwhile to retain the knowledge of God, so God gave them over to a depraved mind, so that they do what ought not to be done."* *(Romans 1:25, 28, NIV)*.

Yet there is hope, because God is a redeeming God. *"He was in the world, and though the world was made through Him, the world did not recognize Him. He came to that which was His own, but his own did not receive him. Yet to all who did receive Him, to those who believed in His name, He gave the right to become children of God— children born not of natural descent, nor of human decision or a husband's will, but born of God."* *(John 1:10–13, NIV)*.

God chose to create us with the ability to chose! He intervened into the human race through the person of Jesus Christ. Jesus came to buy back, through His death on the cross, all the rebels who would turn to Him!

What will we do with the free gift of eternal redemption that He has offered? Will we trust Him and be saved or continue in our misery and rebellion for all eternity?

September 26

Descent Into Tyranny

As many of us have our eyes on Ottawa these days, we are faced with tyranny in action! The measures that are being taken by our governing leaders are unprecedented, especially against peaceful, ordinary hard-working people who have been forced to come to parliament to "parley" because they have been shut out of any other way of making their concerns known! Our Prime Minister has chosen to shut them out. Statesmen dialog, dictators use force!

There is a pattern here that we concerned citizens need to open our eyes to. That is the role of propaganda in the descent into tyranny! When Hitler took control of Germany, he controlled the media. The same happened in the Soviet Union, the media was filled with lies - one of the main propagators of these lies was a newspaper falsely called Pravda. (translated "truth"). Today is no different. Our state sponsored mainstream media has not honestly reported the events in Ottawa or anything leading up to this. They echo our Prime Ministers' lies calling the truckers among other things, "people who wave swastikas," and "people who wave the Confederate flag…", while nothing could be further from the truth. I have numerous friends that regularly go to Ottawa to observe what is actually happening. Their observation, which has also been reported by independent journalism, is that what we hear on CBC and the mainstream media actually has no resemblance of what is in fact happening on the ground. Don't believe what you hear from our state sponsored propaganda machine!

I would call each concerned God fearing Canadian to turn off the mainstream media propaganda machine, get on our knees to ask God to have mercy on Canada and bring a revival of truth to our land!

Jesus said, *"Those who speak for themselves want glory only for themselves, but a person who seeks to honor the one who sent him speaks truth, not lies." John 7:18.*

"But God shows his anger from heaven against all sinful, wicked people who suppress the truth by their wickedness." Romans 1:18.

Self and the Saviour

Surely you've heard the statement, "You can do anything if you put your mind to it." In other words, we are to think positive, use our imagination, and then take action to make our dream come true. At first glance there seems to be some truth here. Decades ago, a certain preacher spoke boldly of this very idea. He even asked people to donate money to his dream of a magnificent cathedral. If they donated a certain amount, they could even get their name engraved somewhere on the building. The cathedral materialized, and the self esteem sermons proliferated. Then the ministry went broke, and the cathedral was sold. The dream had crumbled.

I've had similar experiences in my life, wanting to buy property, start recovery homes, etc. When the vision became the focus, my eyes were not on Jesus the Saviour! It became obvious that I, in and of myself, could not produce anything truly good or lasting. As Jesus said, *"For apart from me you can do nothing." (John 15:5, ESV).* When self is ruling in my heart, selfishness and pride prevails. *"Pride goes before destruction, and a haughty spirit before a fall." (Proverbs 16:18, ESV).* Self and Jesus cannot both rule in our heart at the same time! The problem is that our sinful self has been corrupted by sin, and the only way we can be who God created us to be is by absolute surrender to Him! When Jesus rules in our heart, the Holy Spirit of Almighty God produces His fruit in our life (Galatians 5:22–25)!

The Apostle Paul recognized this fact in his own life when he said, *"I have been crucified with Christ. It is no longer I who live, but Christ who lives in me. And the life I now live in the flesh I live by faith in the Son of God, who loved me and gave himself for me." (Galatians 2:20, ESV).*

"Humble yourselves, therefore, under the mighty hand of God so that at the proper time he may exalt you." (1 Peter 5:6, ESV).

Idols

Sometimes we only think of idols as some physical entity we have formed or carved out that we bow down or sacrifice to. I vividly remember a news item depicting some South American tribal people worshipping carved images that they sprayed with chicken blood as part of their religious ritual to appease spirits that had come to haunt them. Certainly these are idols, but do we in our culture have idols too?

Dr. Doug Weiss in a teaching on recovery from addictions defines an idol in this way: "When you are in pain, you go to your idol. When you are in need, you go to your idol. When you are hurt, you go to your idol. When you want to celebrate you go to your idol."[10]

Some examples of this might be: When I go to the fridge for food rather than to God for my comfort, food has become my idol. When I trust myself rather than God, self becomes an idol. When my finances are more important than God, money becomes an idol. If booze or illicit drugs are my coping mechanism, then they have become my idol. If pornography is a way of seeking pleasure, then it has become my idol. If any outward religious formality takes the place of true heart worship of God, my religion has become an idol. I become addicted to my idol, which then controls me.

We have the privilege of worshipping the one true God. To worship anything else is an offence to Him and a detriment to us (Exodus 20:3–4; 1 Corinthians 10:14; Galatians 5:20; Colossians 3:5–8).

The only cure is to honestly turn to God in repentance, admitting our idolatry and surrendering to Him daily and allowing Him to set us free from our vices. Only then can we truly be the people God has created us to be! Jesus came to set us free from the idols that bind us! *"So if the Son sets you free, you will be free indeed." (John 8:36, ESV).*

---

10 Conquer Series DVD 2.

Brave Men

Two men met in a Saskatchewan courthouse. One was Jaskirat Singh Sidhu, who on April 6, 2018, drove a transport truck through a stop sign into the Humboldt Bronco's team bus, killing sixteen young men from the Humboldt Broncos hockey team. The other was Scott Thomas, the father of Evan Thomas, one of the team members killed in that crash.

The charges were sixteen counts of dangerous driving causing death and thirteen counts of dangerous driving causing bodily injury. The suspense in the courtroom was broken by the words from Mr. Sidhu's own mouth: "I plead guilty, Your Honour." Mr. Sidhu's lawyer said his client was devastated and expressed remorse for his actions. He wanted to plead guilty to all charges, no plea bargains, no trial, because he wanted to spare the families of the victims any additional grief. He was a brave man who took full responsibility for his actions.

The words of Mr. Thomas were equally remarkable. Visibly shaken, the pain in his voice palpable, it was obvious the guilty plea by Mr. Sidhu had a profound impact on him. Though he could have lashed out with hate, for revenge and punishment, this was obviously not the case with Mr. Thomas. He expressed relief by the plea and had gained some respect for Mr. Sidhu. He indicated his willingness to meet with Mr. Sidhu and said the door to forgiveness was still open. If the world had more men of this calibre, it would certainly be a better place!

My prayer is that these men will encounter (if they have not already) Jesus, the One who made healing, forgiveness, and reconciliation possible by dying on a cruel Roman cross two thousand years ago. *"He was despised and rejected by men, a man of sorrows and acquainted with grief; and as one from whom men hide their faces he was despised, and we esteemed him not. Surely he has borne our griefs and carried our sorrows; yet we esteemed him stricken, smitten by God, and afflicted. But he was pierced for our transgressions; he was crushed for our iniquities; upon him was the chastisement that brought us peace, and with his wounds we are healed." (Isaiah 53:3–5, ESV).*

Broken beyond Repair

I had a dream about trying to fix something. The more I tried to fix it, the more problems arose! In the end, it was just a bunch of junk, a mess with no working parts. I couldn't fix it; it was broken beyond repair! It reminded me of my old life and how I tried so hard to fix myself! When I awoke, these words from God's Holy Scriptures stood out to me: *"They rejected my advice and paid no attention when I corrected them. Therefore, they must eat the bitter fruit of living their own way, choking on their own schemes ... But all who listen to me will live in peace, untroubled by fear of harm." (Proverbs 1:30–31, 33).*

Jesus, when approached by a religious leader named Nicodemus, said *"Humans can reproduce only human life, but the Holy Spirit gives birth to spiritual life. So don't be surprised when I say, 'You must be born again.'" (John 3:6–7).* The sinful nature we're born with is broken and bent on disobeying God and doing things our way. It's no use trying to fix it, because it's broken beyond hope. Only God by His Holy Spirit can make us into a totally new person, a new creation! Only then can we truly live the life God created for us! This is not a patch up job or a temporary fix of men. It's a transformational work of the Almighty God!

Have we surrendered to God and allowed Him transform us into a new creation, or are we content with trying to fix ourselves? Ultimately our response to this question will determine our eternal destiny!

I am thankful, by the grace and mercy of God, that I can wholeheartedly say I have been born again to a new life through the Holy Spirit of God and no longer need to choke on my own schemes!

"... anyone who belongs to Christ has become a new person. The old life is gone; a new life has begun!" (2 Corinthians 5:17).

OCTOBER 1

Direction

Vancouver is a big city, especially to us country folk! To be honest, I find it somewhat intimidating to make our way around there, so we purchased a GPS device to give direction in the seemingly never-ending maze of cars, streets, avenues, and highways.

We were driving from one location in Vancouver to another with our trusty GPS to guide us along. Some of the directions it displayed seemed confusing. We didn't fully trust the GPS and the route it was taking us; we thought we knew better and instead decided to go the way we thought was right. Before long, we were lost on a cul-de-sac somewhere in North Vancouver! Then we turned on the GPS and followed the directions to the place we were going. We should have followed its instructions in the first place!

Have you ever wondered where you were going in life? Have you ended up completely directionless, at a dead end? I have, and it's scary and dangerous. The comfort is to know that there is One who knows the beginning from the end. He is the Almighty God, the only One we can trust. He has left us with His instruction manual for life, which is His Word, the Bible! When we follow God's Word, though we may wonder at times where He's leading us, we can trust that He knows the way better than any human being or any humanly-crafted scheme ever will!

Have you put your trust in Him? Do you obey His Word? May the words that the psalmist wrote almost three thousand years ago be our encouragement throughout your life!

"I pondered the direction of my life, and I turned to follow your laws. I will hurry, without delay, to obey your commands ... I used to wander off until you disciplined me; but now I closely follow your word ... Your commandments give me understanding; no wonder I hate every false way of life. Your word is a lamp to guide my feet and a light for my path." (Psalm 119:59–60, 67, 104–105).

OCTOBER 2

The Writing on the Wall!

Have you ever heard the saying "The writing is on the wall."? It originates from a historical event recorded in God's Holy Scriptures (Daniel 5), which happened some 2,600 years ago.

King Belshazzar, a descendant of the great Nebuchadnezzar, King of ancient Babylon, was having a wild drinking party with his family and dignitaries. As the party progressed, in an act of scorn, pride, and defiance towards God, he drank from the gold and silver cups that had been taken from the temple of God when Jerusalem was captured by Nebuchadnezzar. Just then, a hand appeared and wrote on the wall, *"Mene, Mene, Tekel, and Parsin." (Daniel 5:25, ESV)*. Daniel interpreted this for the king: *"This is the interpretation of the matter: Mene, God has numbered the days of your kingdom and brought it to an end; Tekel, you have been weighed in the balances and found wanting; Peres, your kingdom is divided and given to the Medes and Persians," (Daniel 5:26–28, ESV)*. That very night, the message from God written on the wall was fulfilled. Belshazzar was killed and his kingdom taken over by the Medes and the Persians.

The message is still the same today. We can either continue in our sins and suffer God's judgement, or we can humbly turn to God to forgive our sins and ask Him to give us the strength to live a life that is honouring to Him. Jesus said, *"And you will perish, too, unless you repent of your sins and turn to God." (Luke 13:3)*. He also said, *"... I tell you, there is joy before the angels of God over one sinner who repents." (Luke 15:10, ESV)*.

The writing is on the wall. What will be our response?

October 3

Culling

As I was harvesting our garlic, I noticed a few bulbs that were yellowish in colour, some had a worm, and others were just plain rotten. A few, a little off colour, looked almost the same as the healthy bulbs yet had a bitter taste and were unusable. So I culled all these out and threw them out to be burned. I also noticed that the culling of these diseased ones caused less of the malady to be present in the next years crop. Planting healthy bulbs grows a healthier crop. The plants now can grow and be useful, as they were created to be!

Sin is a lot like these diseased garlics. When allowed to grow in us, it tends to spread until it becomes predominant in our lives and makes us virulent, even harmful, to ourselves and others. Take for instance bitterness, hatred, and revenge towards someone. If we dwell on it and let it grow, it will take over our mind, our emotions, and our lives until we are consumed by it. But if we take our sin, these evil thoughts, to God (2 Corinthians 10:5) and let Him fill our minds with pure and uplifting thoughts, we will have useful and productive lives, encouraging ourselves and those around us.

Jesus died on the cross to forgive the sins of all who would come to Him in faith! He gave to everyone who believes in Him His Holy Spirit to empower us, so that we could be all that God created us to be! Let us surrender our sinful thoughts and lives to Jesus and let Him cleanse us so we can grow and be strong for Him (1 John 1:5–7)!

"... whatever is true, whatever is honorable, whatever is just, whatever is pure, whatever is lovely, whatever is commendable, if there is any excellence, if there is anything worthy of praise, think about these things." (Philippians 4:8–9, ESV).

OCTOBER 4

Telemachus

Theodoret, Bishop of Cyrrhius, recorded a very significant event in history about a Christian monk named Telemachus, who lived in the early fifth century AD.

The story is told that Telemachus was strongly impressed by the Lord to go to Rome. He wasn't sure why, but because of the intense call of God, he obeyed and went. When he arrived, he was caught up in a crowd of people who were going to the Coliseum. In the Coliseum, gladiators were battling it out to the death, which was a common sight in those times. Telemachus was appalled at the cruelty and bloodshed being displayed as the crowds cheered. Again, compelled by the Lord, Telemachus cried out repeatedly and insistently, "In the name of Jesus, stop! In the name of Jesus, stop!" The crowds were upset by this and in a frenzy stoned him to death. Honarius, the emperor at the time, a Christian, was deeply upset by the actions of the crowds and the brutal killing of Telemachus, thus he ordered that there would be no more gladiator sports in the Coliseum again. The murder of Telemachus marked the end of the barbaric practice of killing before the crowds in Rome.

This story has been told by various people in the past with some differing details, but nonetheless, there are some things we can learn from Telemachus. We don't need to understand all the details of the battle; we just need to listen to and obey the One in charge, our general, the Lord Jesus Christ. Telemachus was obviously tuned in to God, thus he was convinced God was calling him to Rome. He didn't know the details of how this would all work out, but he obeyed and went.

When Telemachus was confronted with something that was obviously against the teaching of the Bible and the heart of God, his heart was stirred and he didn't hesitate to speak up. It cost him his earthly life, but the lives of many others were saved, and this brutal display of heartless cruelty was stopped, because unbeknown to Telemachus, God was also speaking to the emperor.

What are God's plans for us? Are we in touch with our Creator? Are we willing to obey Him at all cost? Is there anything in our heart that would stop us from obeying Him? The simplest act of obedience can have profound and eternal consequences.

"Trust in the LORD with all your heart; do not depend on your own understanding. Seek his will in all you do, and he will show you which path to take." (Proverbs 3:5–6).

OCTOBER 5

Hope for the Desperate!

Over thirty years ago, I was at an evening church service and the phone in the office rang. I answered it, and there was a desperate man on the other end. He said he had a drinking problem, his wife had kicked him out, he'd lost his job and his car motor had blown up on his way to town. He didn't know what to do, so he was seeking out God. Maybe God could help.

We met at the front door and then sat on the church steps, because he said he wasn't worthy to step inside the church. He knew he was a sinner who needed help. As we spoke about things of God, he relaxed and came in. That night he surrendered his life completely to the LORD.

The next day I met up with him, and he expressed concern over his relationship with his wife. He was anxious about his job and wondered about transportation. We prayed together and gave it all to the LORD. That evening I drove him to his home town. Anxiously, he waited as his wife came to the door. She seemed surprised to see him, but she didn't hesitate to give him a hug and welcome him back. She was glad to see him! They invited me in, and she began to tell him that his boss had phoned and wanted him back on the job. There was also a used vehicle available for his use. As we sat there, we realized that all he had been so anxious about, all his prayer requests, had been answered. God was gracious and good!

I connected this fellow with some Christian friends in his hometown and he eagerly learned more about the LORD and grew in his Christian life. He was born again of the Spirit of God. His life of desperation was changed to a life of faith.

Maybe you can relate to some of this fellow's story. Maybe you've lost your way. Maybe you're desperate and everything is falling apart, and you need a new life. Maybe you're sick of your sinful way of life. You are not alone! We're all in a desperate state without God in our lives, whether we recognize it or not. There is hope!

Jesus said, *"Those who are well have no need of a physician, but those who are sick. Go and learn what this means: 'I desire mercy, and not sacrifice.' For I came not to call the righteous, but sinners."* (Matthew 9:12–13, ESV). He also said, *"I am the door. If anyone enters by me, he will be saved and will go in and out and find pasture. The thief comes only to steal and kill and destroy. I came that they may have life and have it abundantly."* (John 10:10, ESV).

OCTOBER 6

Today Is the Day

Isn't it wonderful to see the vast fields of grass that have grown up, green and ready for harvest? This year we were blessed with lots of rain at the beginning of the year and now plenty of sunshine. I think most farmers have a good crop of hay, by the looks of it. As long as they make hay while the sun shines! It's urgent to get the harvesting done before the harvest time is over!

I noticed this is true for most things in life. There is only a window of time for arriving to work on time, phoning to greet someone on their birthday, returning a library book before the deadline, or pulling out and passing safely on the highway.

There's another critical decision with eternal consequences that we all must make before it's too late, and that is to call out to God for mercy while there is still time. The Bible tells us, *"For the wages of sin is death, but the free gift of God is eternal life in Christ Jesus our Lord"* *(Romans 6:23, ESV)* and *"Today, if you hear his voice, do not harden your hearts"* *(Hebrews 4:7, ESV).*

I had a friend who for years would have nothing to do with the LORD, then he got sick and, on his deathbed, asked for someone who could tell him how he could get right with his Creator. Someone came and introduced him to Jesus Christ, and he surrendered his life to God. He died two weeks later, his eternal destiny secure.

Should we all wait, like my friend, almost to the very end before receiving mercy and grace from the LORD? If we did, it would be like the farmer who, on a sunny day, ideal for harvest, says "There's lots of time. I'll wait until next week or the week after." The problem is, we don't know what's going to happen next week, or tomorrow, or the next moment, for that matter.

"For God says, 'At just the right time I heard you. On the day of salvation I helped you.' Indeed the 'right time' is now. Today is the day of salvation." (2 Corinthians 6:2).

OCTOBER 7

Thankful Heart!

As I'm thinking of Thanksgiving Day, my memory of a wonderful lady comes to the forefront of my mind. She had fought with cancer for years. After experiencing numerous serious debilitating surgeries and therapies, she was informed that she needed another operation that would cause her much pain. As I visited her in the hospital, I was amazed at her attitude! All she could do was thank God for every detail of her life: her husband, her family, her doctors, her previous surgeries, even for the surgery awaiting her and for the home in heaven Jesus had promised was waiting for all those who trust in Him after they pass from this world to the next. All she asked for was that the post-surgery pain not be too great for her to bear. As I thought about her amazing attitude, I realized she could only do this because her heart was full of thankfulness. Her eyes were on Jesus, her Creator, Saviour, and friend, not on her temporary, desperate situation! Her faith and confidence in the Almighty were obvious to all who spoke to her!

What situation do you or I find ourselves in? Does it seem impossible? Do we find ourselves with nothing to be thankful for? May you and I turn our eyes to Jesus. May we find our hope in Him! May He fill our hearts with thanksgiving! He didn't promise that life would be without suffering here on earth, but He promised He would always be with those who trust in Him (John 16:33; Hebrews 13:5)!

"Therefore, as you received Christ Jesus the Lord, so walk in him, rooted and built up in him and established in the faith, just as you were taught, abounding in thanksgiving." *(Colossians 2:6–7, ESV).*

True Thankfulness

We have a friend who's a physiotherapist and has spent much of her life working among lepers. Those with leprosy can, as the disease progresses, be stricken with blindness and deformed limbs. Until fairly recently, leprosy was a disease so greatly feared that lepers were shunned by the community and had to live in colonies totally separate from others. When approached by others, they were to cry out, "Unclean, unclean!" to notify them that they were there, so not to spread the dreaded disease. At that time there was no cure, but today leprosy has a cure and is not so much of a dreaded disease as it once was. Our friend and the mission she worked with are attempting to rid the world of this debilitating illness and the stigma that goes with it.

A little piece of history is recorded in the Bible when Jesus visited a village where ten men with leprosy cried out to Him, *"Jesus, Master, have mercy on us!" (Luke 17:13 ESV).* Jesus heard them and responded by healing all ten of them. Can you imagine how happy they were when they looked at themselves and realized that they were healed? They ran to show themselves to the priest to prove they were healed. Only one turned back to Jesus and actually thanked Him.

Jesus questioned why only one came back and thanked Him. I'm sure the others were thankful that they were free to go back to their families and their life of freedom. Yet Jesus took special note of the one who came back to personally thank Him. This begs the question: Can we be truly thankful if we're just excited in our hearts about what happened to us? Is it just a feeling or is it more? Should not our blessing be translated into thankfulness to the One who has blessed us?

Thanksgiving Day is a special day set apart for us to remember the many blessings we often take for granted. How can we truly be thankful without personally thanking God for His provision, the life he has given us, the beautiful creation we are a part of, and especially for the sacrifice He made in the death of His Son to save us from the penalty of our sins?

"Don't worry about anything; instead pray about everything. Tell God what you need and thank him for all he has done." (Philippians 4:6).

OCTOBER 9

Be Thankful—Always

What a blessing to have a National Day of Thanksgiving set apart for the whole nation to be thankful to God for all His benefits and blessings towards us, including food, shelter, health, and peace in the land. This day of thanksgiving should be a corporate expression of our heartfelt individual daily thanksgiving to God throughout the year.

But what if we don't have good health? What if we're having trouble making ends meet? What if we're from a country where there is no peace? What if we're going through some almost unbearable pain? How can we be thankful then?

Having gone through some excruciating pain myself, I must say that it's impossible for me, in myself, to be thankful when I'm in the middle of it, when the pain is at its worst. I could not be thankful for the pain or the situation I was in at the time.

One thing I did realize, though, is that God is still God. He doesn't change, no matter what I am going through or how I'm feeling (Malachi 3:6; Hebrews 6:17). I also know He has promised never to leave me or forsake me. In the moment, He may seem quite distant and the pain very present, yet God's promises still stand. He knows the pain we're going through. His Holy Spirit lives in every one who believes and doesn't leave us just because we're going through a hard time (Hebrews 13:5; Isaiah 43:13).

When we have a personal relationship with God through faith in Jesus Christ, who suffered immensely and gave His life for us (John 3:16; Luke 24:45–49), we are His children. We belong to Him, and He has a purpose for everything. We don't have to understand it all. Maybe we will understand by and by, or maybe not, but one thing we know is that He is our God, He is good, and we are in His hands. This is the witness of His Holy Spirit with our spirit (Romans 8:16), who can give us an attitude of thanksgiving and joy deep in our heart, even when we, in ourselves, find it difficult to be thankful (James 1:2; Galatians 5:22). Let us keep our eyes on Jesus and be thankful for Him and all that He is (Hebrews 12:2).

"... give thanks in all circumstances; for this is the will of God in Christ Jesus for you." (1 Thessalonians 5:18, ESV).

OCTOBER 10

Refuting Satan

US President Donald Trump called the October 1, 2017 massacre at a Las Vegas music festival "pure evil." Others have said it was "absolute hate," "a nightmare," and "horrific." One fellow said "It just all went to hell." An eleven-minute shooting spree into a crowd of concert goers caused the death of 59 people with at least 527 injured. It's quite clear to many that this work was, at its roots, the work of Satan, the evil one. Jesus called him a thief and said that the work of the devil is to *"... steal and kill and destroy." (John 10:10, ESV)*. Sometimes it takes horrendous acts such as what happened in Las Vegas, for us to recognize Satan's work, but his evil work starts undercover, in deception and lies.

In the Holy Scriptures, Jesus clearly defined the work of the devil: *"He was a murderer from the beginning, and does not stand in the truth, because there is no truth in him. When he lies, he speaks out of his own character, for he is a liar and the father of lies." (John 8:44, ESV)*. Every lie that is on our tongue, every time we don't represent the truth, is ultimately the work of Satan. We sometimes call this deception a white lie or an innocent lie. There is no such thing. A lie is a lie, and it falls under the realm of Satan's heinous work. Obviously, the man who did this evil act started to believe and follow a lie somewhere in his life. Had Stephen Paddock pursued the truth earlier in his life, this horrible tragedy would have never happened.

We can find freedom only in the truth. The truth reveals the lie. If we follow the truth, we will recognize the lies. The schemes of Satan will be exposed and refuted. As we pursue the truth, we will find that Jesus is the Author of life and truth, that the only way to a meaningful life here on earth and an eternal relationship with God is through faith and trust in Him (John 14:6). Jesus said, *"I came that they may have life and have it abundantly." (John 10:10, ESV)*; *" ... and you will know the truth, and the truth will set you free." (John 8:32, ESV)*.

Every day of the year, and especially during this Thanksgiving season, let us be thankful to God for the truth that sets us free!

OCTOBER 11

True Identity

Have you ever had your identity stolen? What is our identity? How is our identity determined? Some voices proclaim that we determine our own identity, whether it be our social status, our reputation, our financial situation, or even our sexuality. If we attempt to determine, in our own imagination, who we identify as, we come up with a plethora of conflicting ideas. Most likely we'd come up with as many identities as there are people in this world, each person having their own definition of who they are!

Then who am i? one might ask. How can I know my true identity? Are we just products of random chance, left here on our own to figure out who we really are?

We humans share a common identity given to us by our Creator. He reveals this to us in His Word, the Bible. It would be wise of us to pay attention to what He has to say rather than trust in our own limited, self-conceived ideas!

"So God created mankind in his own image, in the image of God he created them." No human being is a product of random chance but, through God's amazing plan, bears the image of God! In the same verse, God continues to proclaim our sexual identity: *"male and female he created them." (Genesis 1:27, NIV).* By faith in Him, we can mature in appreciation of our identity as His children! *"Yet to all who did receive him, to those who believed in his name, he gave the right to become children of God." (John 1:12, NIV).* Unless we find our true God-given identity, we will forever grasp at straws and fall short of our true and eternal purpose in life.

"I praise you because I am fearfully and wonderfully made; your works are wonderful; I know that full well ... Search me, God, and know my heart; test me and know my anxious thoughts. See if there is any offensive way in me, and lead me in the way everlasting." (Psalm 139:14, 23–24, NIV).

OCTOBER 12

Sin and the Saviour

She was caught red-handed! She had nowhere to turn! The penalty under the law for her sin was death by stoning. Her accusers dragged her away, leaving behind the man who had been caught in adultery with her. What were they going to do with her? Where were they taking her? She wasn't able to cover her sin! Nowhere to go, heart pounding, afraid, ashamed, hopeless, helpless, condemned—she found herself dragged before her Creator! The man who was with her did not defend her. The men who had caught her accused her, but Jesus did not! He faced her accusers and they left, one at a time, from the oldest to the youngest! She was left standing alone with Him. *"Jesus straightened up and asked her, 'Woman, where are they? Has no one condemned you?' 'No one, sir,' she said. 'Then neither do I condemn you,' Jesus declared. 'Go now and leave your life of sin.'"* (John 8:10–11, NIV),

What did she do to deserve such forgiveness? What did she do to deserve love like this? There was nothing she could do—nothing! Jesus did it all! If she had run from and denied her sin, she would have stood condemned, but she did not. She believed that Jesus had not come to condemn her but to save her!

Have you or I been caught in our sin? Will we receive the free gift of salvation that Jesus has to offer?

"For God so loved the world that he gave his one and only Son, that whoever believes in him shall not perish but have eternal life. For God did not send his Son into the world to condemn the world, but to save the world through him. Whoever believes in him is not condemned, but whoever does not believe stands condemned already because they have not believed in the name of God's one and only Son." (John 3:16–18, NIV).

OCTOBER 13

Sincerity and the Saviour

When I was younger, we used to write letters to friends and family with pen and ink! We would send them through the mail, as some still do, though most communication today is through social media. In those days it was very common to end the letter with the words "Sincerely yours" followed by our name. I have noticed that this is a very rare occurrence these days. Though this was considered to be a proper and traditional way of closing a letter, did we actually know what it meant to be sincere? Noah Websters 1828 Dictionary defines sincere as: "Being in reality what it appears to be; not feigned; not simulated; not assumed or said for the sake of appearance; real; not hypocritical or pretended."

This is the attitude God wants us to have before Him: a sincere, true, honest confession from the heart as to our condition before Him. If we are truly honest with ourselves and with God, we will realize that we are far short of God's holy standard! Rather than coming to Him with a pretentious, self-righteous attitude of having everything together, He wants us to come to Him in honesty, agreeing with Him that we are sinful and broken, in absolute need of Him! Thus, an adulterous woman who was involved in a deeply sinful life—with an honest and contrite confession—is in a position to be forgiven, while the one who falsely comes to God with a self-righteous attitude remains unforgiven (see John 8:1–11).

Do you sense your sinfulness before God and man? Do you feel unworthy of God's love and forgiveness? Do you have the sense of having gone too far, not good enough to pray to Him? Join the crowd, as not one of us is worthy (Romans 3:23)! Be encouraged. There is hope! He wants to hear from you! Sincerely!

"If we confess our sins, he is faithful and just to forgive us our sins and to cleanse us from all unrighteousness." (1 John 1:9, ESV).

OCTOBER 14

Oil of the Spirit

I had a car that had well over half a million kilometres on it. To keep it going, I needed to have fuel in the tank and check the oil from time to time. Without fuel, the car would stop beside the road. Even more serious, if I let it run out of oil, major damage would happen to the motor!

As I think of the obvious situation mentioned above, I'm reminded of the absolute need for me to be reading and meditating on God's Word, the Bible. A daily diet of His Word is absolutely essential to properly function as a Jesus follower! Just as essential is the work of the Holy Spirit in my life—to have His Word appropriately applied to my heart.

Lately I've had some difficulties with my body reacting to cancer therapy. As a result, I missed reading God's Word for a day or two. And when I read it, I didn't wait on the Spirit of the Lord to apply it to my heart. I became very frustrated and difficult because I was both running low on fuel and oil! I was like a car trying to get somewhere with the tank on empty and the oil below the dipstick!

As the oil is hidden in the motor, and the fuel is hidden in the tank on our vehicles, they may seem insignificant until we're sitting beside the road lacking either or both! Sometimes we miss the obvious when we're not feeding on God's Word and allowing the Holy Spirit of God to apply it in the proper places of our life! I can honestly say that when I regularly read God's Word and wait on the Holy Spirit to speak to me through His Word, I am able to travel this road of life in a positive and meaningful way, no matter the condition of the road!

Jesus said, *"It is the Spirit who gives life; the flesh is no help at all. The words that I have spoken to you are spirit and life." (John 6:63, ESV).*

Plumb Line

When I installed the four-hundred-pound stove, I thought it was there to stay, never to move. Yet after a time, I noticed that the stovepipe was out of plumb; the stove had crept backwards slightly. Over more time, it had moved significantly, and I needed to move it back into place; if I had not, it would have crept too close to the wall to be firesafe! How did this happen? Whenever I had a large piece of wood that had to be pushed into the firebox, the stove would move an imperceptible amount. This added up significantly over time, which ultimately had to be corrected!

I have noticed that my personal moral standard is much the same. For instance, when I'm out and about and hearing certain words that are offensive to me at first, over time the words become less offensive, and eventually those very words might be coming out of my mouth! This could also happen in many areas of my life, such as what I allow my eyes to see, where I allow myself to go, or how I conduct my business! When this permeates our society, our nation becomes corrupt and, ultimately, we can't trust those in our own family, or even ourselves!

When God created this world, He made it according to certain standards, and these standards are recorded in His Holy Word, the Bible. When we read and meditate on His Word, we realize how far off we really are! *"For the word of God is living and active, sharper than any two-edged sword, piercing to the division of soul and of spirit, of joints and of marrow, and discerning the thoughts and intentions of the heart." (Hebrews 4:12, ESV).* We realize that in and of ourselves, we are hopeless and helpless! What are we to do? The Scriptures are clear: *"Believe in the Lord Jesus, and you will be saved ..." (Acts 16:31, ESV).* It is through faith in Jesus Christ that we are forgiven and given a new life, empowering us by His Holy Spirit to love and obey Him!

"Your word is a lamp to my feet and a light to my path." (Psalm 119:105, ESV).

OCTOBER 16

Words Have Power

Have you ever spoken words you've regretted? I have, and after realizing the consequences, I wished I could take those words back! In haste or self defence, and out of the dark side of my sinful nature, I have at times verbally hurt even my wife, the one person on earth that I should love the most!

We don't have to look very far to hear degrading words spoken about others, even in the highest places of government, business, and education. From our members of parliament, corporate executives, and university professors, we often hear demeaning words describing especially those with whom we disagree! How can this happen in a civilized society? How can this happen to me?

God's Word says: *"And among all the parts of the body, the tongue is a flame of fire. It is a whole world of wickedness, corrupting your entire body. It can set your whole life on fire, for it is set on fire by hell itself. People can tame all kinds of animals, birds, reptiles, and fish, but no one can tame the tongue."* (James 3:6–8).

So if I in my sinful self can't control my tongue, is there any hope? Yes! Our hope comes through surrender to our Creator God! By allowing His Holy Spirit to control our lives, instead of having our selfish sinful nature spew out defensive, hurtful, and demeaning words, we will in His power speak uplifting words of wisdom, respect, and encouragement.

God didn't create us to tear one another down but to encourage each other with words of gentleness and respect (Proverbs 15:1; 1 Peter 3:15; Galatians 5:22–23)! May God Almighty have His way in me and in you, so that we can be part of the solution rather than the problem!

"May these words of my mouth and this meditation of my heart be pleasing in your sight, Lord, my Rock and my Redeemer." (Psalm 19:14, NIV).

Righteous Anger

The box somehow broke open and the steaming, freshly cooked chicken fell onto the dirty pavement. I became angry—at myself for being so clumsy, at the people who invented the flimsy box, and at those who had not given me a bag to carry it in. I mumbled, not too quietly, a few words that I'm embarrassed to repeat as I threw the chicken into the nearby garbage can! I felt terrible. I had lost it. Where had my self control gone? Oh Lord, please forgive me!

Should we ever become angry? How about when a husband beats his wife, or someone of another people group is slurred with racist comments, or a clerk is mistreated by a client for an honest mistake, or when a marginalized person is wrongfully convicted by the courts of the land? What about when God is demeaned and made fun of in your presence, or when those in privileged positions abuse those they have power over, as is often demonstrated through political, religious, or corporate autocrats? How should one respond in these circumstances? God's Holy Scriptures say, *"Be angry and do not sin; do not let the sun go down on your anger, and give no opportunity to the devil."* (Ephesians 4:26–27, ESV); *"Let all bitterness and wrath and anger and clamor and slander be put away from you, along with all malice. Be kind to one another, tender-hearted, forgiving one another, as God in Christ forgave you." (Ephesians 4:31–32, ESV).*

When unrighteousness presents itself in any form, whether in others or in ourselves, we should recognize it and stand up for what is right by speaking up or doing something about it! Yet we must discern between sinful human-motivated anger and God's righteous anger (James 1:20), for *"Beloved, never avenge yourselves, but leave it to the wrath of God, for it is written, "Vengeance is mine, I will repay, says the Lord." (Romans 12:19, ESV).*

OCTOBER 18

The Power of Love

Anthony Ray Hinton spent thirty years in an Alabama prison, most of which were on death row, for murders he didn't commit. Ray festered in anger and hate for three of those years, refusing to speak to or care about almost anyone, except for his mother and friend who visited him on a regular basis. Then he heard a fellow inmate in a solitary cell nearby him weeping bitterly. Though he didn't know the man, Ray, out of a new felt compassion, asked him what was wrong. The fellow inmate informed him that his mother had died. This incident ignited a love in Ray that his mother had instilled in him and that he had learned in church throughout his growing up years. Then and there he decided that love was more powerful than hate, and he would love his fellow inmates no matter what they had or had not done.

Ray's exuberant love for all touched everyone on death row: the guards, the prison administration, and even some in the justice system. Ray, a Black man, through the love of God, lead a KKK member in a cell next to him to faith and forgiveness in Jesus before his execution. Ray was released in 2015 and is now a free man. His testimony, recorded in his book *The Sun Does Shine*, is well worth reading for anyone willing to have their heart touched by the love of God that is more powerful than any circumstance or situation we might find ourselves in!

"Love is patient and kind; love does not envy or boast; it is not arrogant or rude. It does not insist on its own way; it is not irritable or resentful; it does not rejoice at wrongdoing, but rejoices with the truth. Love bears all things, believes all things, hopes all things, endures all things ... So now faith, hope, and love abide, these three; but the greatest of these is love." (1 Corinthians 13:4–7, 13, ESV).

A Little While

I was so excited, I said "Hallelujah!" The doctor checked and said he could see no signs cancer! After much prayer, surgeries, and immunotherapy, I was ecstatic!

The past year and a half had been, among other things, a lesson in the brevity of life. Though we know we are all going to die some day, the cancer was a sort of reminder that made me appreciate each day to a greater extent! Now the "death sentence" of cancer was removed, and even though I still don't know how long I will live, there was an enormous relief when the good news came! I was excited because I had the sense that God wanted me to be around at least for a little while longer!

God's Word says, *"How do you know what your life will be like tomorrow? Your life is like the morning fog—it's here a little while, then it's gone." (James 4:14)*. Given this brevity of life, I should look at every day as a gift from God and rejoice in it, no matter what it brings or how long I live!

"Lord, give me the desire to be all that You want me to be each and every day of my life, through the storms, the rain, and the sunshine! I want to be thankful for every day I have while here on this earth, for Your Presence with me in every victory and every struggle, for the eternal life You have promised to all those who put their trust in You!"

As I meditate on God and His promises, I can't help but praise Him together with the psalmist: *"This is the day that the Lord has made; let us rejoice and be glad in it ... You are my God, and I will give thanks to you; you are my God; I will extol you. Oh give thanks to the Lord, for he is good; for his steadfast love endures forever!" (Psalm 118:24, 28–29, ESV)*.

OCTOBER 20

Deliverance from the Penalty!

How did I get into this predicament? Against many warnings by my parents about situations such as this, hiking up a mountain I wandered off the trail and tried to take a shortcut up a steep rock cliff. Halfway up the cliff—glancing at the boulders far below—I froze! How could I have been so stupid? How could I make it down? There was no one to help; my head started to spin. I could picture myself falling to my death, battered on the rocks below! Then I thought to pray. "Lord God Almighty, please help me!" With new hope, my senses came back to me, and I miraculously found my way back down to safety.

In my disobedience and arrogance, I found myself in this deadly situation, and it was no one's fault but my own. But I know God rescued me from death that day!

In the same way, God's Word says we have all wandered in sin from God's holy standard (Romans 3:23), and the wages of this sin is death (Romans 6:23). We find ourselves on a precipice as it were, with eternal death looming over us! The only solution is to turn to God in repentance and ask Him for mercy! The Bible is clear that *"everyone who calls on the name of the Lord will be saved." (Romans 10:13, ESV)*. When we sincerely call out to Him, He will have mercy and save us from the death penalty of our sin!

Do you find yourself in a predicament in which you can see no way out? If you still have breath, it's not too late to call out to God for mercy and forgiveness! No matter how far we've wandered, He will hear and forgive!

"... let the wicked forsake his way, and the unrighteous man his thoughts; let him return to the Lord, that he may have compassion on him, and to our God, for he will abundantly pardon." (Isaiah 55:7, ESV).

Deliverance from the Power of Sin

With the threat of a massive outbreak of the coronavirus in every part of the world, it's encouraging to see some desire by political and cultural adversaries to work together, at least in some aspects, as they recognize that we all have a common enemy in this pandemic. Yet as these attempts are made, the divisions within humanity become more obvious every day!

There's a much more pervasive enemy often overlooked, which is common to every country, culture, people group, and person. It causes division, greed, and destruction among us. It is sin within each of our hearts. When we sin, we rebel against our Creator either in thought, word, or deed. Sin comes between us and God, who made us to serve Him and to live an abundant life as we obey Him. As God's Word clearly says, *"The human heart is the most deceitful of all things, and desperately wicked. Who really knows how bad it is?" (Jeremiah 17:9).* Sin causes unrest in our own hearts and thus causes division between us as human beings; this is why there is so much turmoil in the world today.

The apostle Paul clearly articulates this struggle in his own heart: *"Oh, what a miserable person I am! Who will free me from this life that is dominated by sin and death? Thank God! The answer is in Jesus Christ our Lord." (Romans 7:24–25).*

Can peace ever come to earth? Can love, peace, and joy ever dwell within our own hearts? The answer is a resounding yes, as we surrender in faith to our Lord Jesus Christ!

"But now you are free from the power of sin and have become slaves of God. Now you do those things that lead to holiness and result in eternal life. For the wages of sin is death, but the free gift of God is eternal life through Christ Jesus our Lord." (Romans 3:22–23).

OCTOBER 22

Consensual Sin

As we witness the increasing disregard for God's Word and the subsequent breakdown of marriage relationships; the shattered trust, the pain and ensuing brokenness is real - even palpable - visibly evident throughout our human driven society today. Those who have gone through such a breakup, have usually been scarred for life. Inevitably, the children are even more severely and permanently damaged than their parents. As the frequency of these breakups become more common, the disintegration of the foundations of our society are so clearly obvious. Those who have experienced such a breakup and are truly honest with themselves know the depth of this despair!

The sexual revolution, in the guise of "sexual freedom", has belittled God's pure and holy standard of true intimate practice of sex between one man and one woman - a husband and wife, and traded it for deep seated pain, distrust, and ultimate destruction of full and meaningful relationships.

The contemporary adopted standard is that sex is ok as long as the two are in agreement. This prevalent deception of consensual sex between just any two human beings is in reality consensual sin, a lie from the pits of hell. It is driven by the unrestrained desires of our sinful nature! As we go back to the foundational teachings of God's word we read; *"That is why a man leaves his father and mother and is united to his wife, and they become one flesh." Genesis 2:24 NIV*. Jesus, referring to this essential and foundational ordinance warned, *"Since they are no longer two but one, let no one split apart what God has joined together." Matthew 19:6.*

If we continue to spurn God and His commands, choosing our own way, the very fabric of our society will be torn apart. We are left with a warning that our actions today will inevitably produce consequences for the future, either for good or for bad. It's up to us, which will we choose?

"Do not be deceived: God cannot be mocked. A man reaps what he sows."
Galatians 6:7 NIV

Not Ashamed!

As a young teenager beginning to claim my own independence, I remember at times not wanting to be seen or identify with my parents because some of my peers expressed this as a weak, sissy, or "apron strings" type of behaviour. I was blinded by what others said and didn't see the love, protection, and wisdom that my parents offered, so I distanced myself from them. As I think back on this, I'm ashamed of myself and realize how foolish I was and how this must have hurt them.

Honestly, sometimes I think of God in this way. As a human being created in His image and forgiven by the precious work of Jesus on the cross, at times I know I should speak up for Him and I don't—even though He's the One who gives me every good thing, my life, and every breath I take—all because I'm concerned about what others might will think, say, or do. I don't mention Him because I'm ashamed.

Have you ever felt this way? Maybe you've been a believer for many years, or maybe you're considering becoming a believer. Is shame keeping you from being all God wants you to be?

The apostle Paul, knowing the reality of experiencing shame, exhorted his spiritual son Timothy: *"Therefore do not be ashamed of the testimony about our Lord, nor of me his prisoner, but share in suffering for the gospel by the power of God ... But I am not ashamed, for I know whom I have believed, and I am convinced that he is able to guard until that day what has been entrusted to me." (2 Timothy 1:8, 12, ESV).*

Lord Jesus, may we realize who you are and what you have done. May we not miss the blessing you have for us by being ashamed of you. Cause us to unashamedly express our faith in You in all we think, say and do!

Above the Clouds

Looking out the window this morning, we are greeted by heavy snowfall. I see shoveling to be done, cumbersome winter clothes, slippery roads, and long winter nights ahead. After a long, cool, wet summer, winter seems early this year, and I am not looking forward to it! In addition to this, I think of the mess the world is in and how the nations rage against God, wondering what the future will hold (Psalm 2).

I think of the old phrase, "The sun is shining above the clouds." I know this is true. Then I'm reminded of the truth that there is a God who is present far beyond the clouds and even the sun! He is the only true God, the Creator, Sustainer, and Saviour of the world! As a matter of fact, He loves me so much that He came to earth to become part of the rebellious people whom He created in His image, to save them from their own demise! That's me! He came to save me and to have a personal relationship with me! I know He is totally aware of my situation and loves me much more than I can ever imagine. He knows what it's like to live here on this earth, to experience the storms of life and the wrath of evil men.

A scripture song comes to mind, based on *Revelation 4:11: " Thou art worthy, O Lord, to receive glory and honour and power: for thou hast created all things, and for thy pleasure they are and were created." KJV*

The weather, raging nations, or whatever else that seemed so daunting fades away as I am lost in worship of the God of the universe, who is enthroned far above the clouds and who lives in my heart!

OCTOBER 25

Hear My Cry!

Sometimes my heart is heavy. It may be because of some distressing event or disappointment that might have happened, or I feel inadequate for the task before me. At times I feel a lack of direction, lost in the commotion of life. Today is one of those days. Concern for the state of our freedoms in our land due to wanton disregard for God and the ensuing chaos that is developing as a result are on the forefront of my mind. It's like a storm is brewing and only getting worse!

My prayers don't seem to be getting through, and the heaviness persists. Then a song comes to my heart, an old one translated from the ancient Hebrew Scriptures to English in 1611. It was given by God to King David, who put it to music to be sung by the people of God. The original tune has been lost, but the words remain the same. I begin to sing the ancient words to a present-day tune: *"Hear my cry, O God; attend unto my prayer. From the end of the earth will I cry unto thee, when my heart is overwhelmed: lead me to the rock that is higher than I. For thou hast been a shelter for me, and a strong tower from the enemy." (Psalm 61:1–3, KJV)*.

My heart is lifted up as I sing praise to my God, the only true God, the Creator and ruler of all. He is still on His throne on high and knows every detail of what is happening in the hearts of every person in every nation on earth—even our thoughts, motives, and intentions! He is my only hope! I know He hears my prayers, and I am safely in His hand! I cry out with the apostle Paul, *"For from him and through him and to him are all things. To him be glory forever. Amen" (Romans 11:36, ESV)*.

OCTOBER 26

Near the Cross

We don't desire pain, and we don't want our loved ones to suffer hurt! The grossness of suffering and pain usually causes us to want to look away, wishing it was somehow not happening. As I think of this, I'm reminded of the cross of Jesus, not the one on the wall or hanging around someone's neck, but the historic cross where Jesus, the dearest and best, the Creator who took on human form, hung and bled and died. Few of His followers were there as He suffered and died to take the penalty and curse of death for all who would call out to Him! But those who were near, for the love of Jesus—though deeply disturbed by the sight and smell of the blood, the cries of agony and pain, the curses of those nailing him there, and the accusations of the religious power brokers of the day—had a blessing associated with His sorrow, pain, and death. Some heard Him say, *"Father, forgive them, for they don't know what they are doing." (Luke 23:34)* as they nailed Him to the cross. Hanging there beside him another heard, *"I assure you, today you will be with me in paradise." (Luke 23:43)*.

What does the cross mean to you today? Is it a distant, empty religious symbol, or is it near to your heart? May it be to you and me a constant reminder of Jesus' costly sacrifice for us, as it was to Fanny Crosby as she wrote, "Jesus, keep me near the cross, there a precious fountain, Free to all, a healing stream, flows from Calvary's mountain. Near the cross, O Lamb of God, Bring its scenes before me; Help me walk from day to day, With its shadows o'er me."[11]

"May I never boast except in the cross of our Lord Jesus Christ, through which the world has been crucified to me, and I to the world." (Galatian 6:14, NIV).

---

11 Fanny Crosby, 1869 "Near the Cross," public domain.

OCTOBER 27

Flowing Freely

With the recent cold weather, somehow our waterline into the house froze, and we are without running water. Presently, we're using water filled from the well and carried into the house. Though we're thankful that we still have access to water, it's more laborious and difficult to haul containers than to have free-flowing water through the pipes, to say the least. We have become very accustomed to running water, and I realize we've been taking it for granted!

I know this is sometimes the case with my relationship with God. At times He seems distant and not intimately involved in my life. My prayers don't seem to be heard, and it seems He isn't present. The fellowship with Him has somehow been blocked. Though I realize in my mind that He blesses me beyond anything I deserve, my emotions don't connect with the reality! Then as I deliberately thank and praise Him, despite my feelings, I hear Him speak to my heart again! My heart begins to be thankful, not so much for the benefits, but just for Him! I realize it wasn't He who left me but I who wandered from Him! I recognize that He gives me every breath and holds all of creation together! Then I am lifted up above my circumstances, and my eyes are focused afresh on Him. His Holy Spirit gives me living water to nourish my parched soul. I no longer need to struggle to fill my thirsty heart, but He fills it to overflowing. He has thawed out my frozen heart so that the living water of His Holy Spirit can freely flow again!

Jesus said, *"Let anyone who is thirsty come to me and drink. Whoever believes in me, as Scripture has said, rivers of living water will flow from within them." (John 7:37–38, NIV).*

OCTOBER 28

Assessment

As the annual property assessment notices appear in the mail, we're reminded of the value of land in the eyes of the BC Assessment Authority. Soon property tax notices will come out based on the assessment. The tax bill indicates when the taxes are due and penalties for late payments, etc. Upon further examination, we find that if the taxes aren't paid by a certain time, the property will be sold for the taxes owing! As I contemplate this, I realize the temporary nature of land "ownership." In effect, land owners are practically temporary renters of the property that they occupy!

God's holy Scriptures remind us who the real owner is! *"The earth is the Lord's, and everything in it, the world, and all who live in it." (Psalm 24:1, NIV)*. He created everything for His good pleasure (Revelation 4:11)! Yet when we get our land assessment, or we occupy the land for a time, we act as if it were ours. Wars are fought over land. Often, we not only claim ownership but we put more value on the land than on God Himself! The Bible says, *"They exchanged the truth about God for a lie, and worshiped and served created things rather than the Creator—who is forever praised. Amen." (Romans 1:25, NIV)*. Jesus said, *"What good is it for someone to gain the whole world, yet forfeit their soul? Or what can anyone give in exchange for their soul?" (Mark 8:36–37, NIV)*.

When we stand before God one day, will land and earthly things really matter? May we put our faith and trust in God and worship Him rather than earthly temporary things! May we be encouraged by the words of the songwriter Helen H. Lemmel: "Turn your eyes upon Jesus, Look full in His wonderful face, And the things of earth will grow strangely dim, In the light of His glory and grace."[12]

---

12 Heather H. Lemmel, 1922, "Turn Your Eyes upon Jesus," public domain.

OCTOBER 29

Checkup

We are encouraged to arrange annual medical and dental checkups to diagnose any lurking health complications that might be arising in our bodies. Many symptoms may remain hidden without a determined and thorough examination. High blood pressure or diabetes may be present, a cavity started, a mole may be precancerous. Doctors are trained to catch some of these symptoms before they become unmanageable. Something amiss may be diagnosed and dealt with before it becomes a full-blown danger to our physical being and possibly our life!

This is true in our spiritual lives as well! Something may be amiss between God and I. Sin may have crept in, and I may be headed in a direction that is detrimental to a healthy relationship with God, others, and myself. This may manifest itself in, among other things, fear, anxiety, anger, frustration, self-centredness, hostility, addictions, shame, and perhaps physical sickness. I may not be aware of it, but God knows exactly what's going on (Psalm 51 and 139)! God may use others to point out my impudence, to expose my unhealthy attitude before I'm aware of it myself! To heal, I need to be open to their observations and criticisms of me! Sometimes God uses His Word, the Bible, to expose hidden, corrupt attitudes and sin in my life. Other times I am abruptly confronted with direct consequences of my disobedience to God!

In any case, I need to surrender myself to God and confess my sins and unhealthy sinful behaviour and character traits as soon as I am made aware of them—before they take a grievous toll on my walk with God! To examine ourselves on a daily, moment-by-moment basis, and to let God have His way in our lives will keep us from the lethal effects of living an unproductive life, contrary to the good life God has planned for us!

"Search me, God, and know my heart; test me and know my anxious thoughts." (Psalm 139:23, NIV); *"Examine yourselves to see whether you are in the faith; test yourselves."* (2 Corinthians 13:5, NIV).

OCTOBER 30

Most Humble Royal Visit

Royal visits have been taking place in Canada since 1786. These events are meticulously planned well in advance and are usually very pompous and ceremonial in nature. The royal family are treated with special admiration and respect. The airwaves are abuzz with the comings and goings of the sovereigns. To be recognized by the Queen, even in passing, would be a lifetime memorable event for most people! I once spoke to a person who was in a crowd as the Queen passed by only feet away from them. This event took place many years ago but was still vivid in the memory of this person! While a royal visit has great importance to some, others couldn't care less, possibly too busy with events of their own life to pay any attention!

The earth witnessed a marvellous royal visit some two thousand years ago when the Sovereign Creator of the universe entered the human race in an amazingly humble and unassuming way! He didn't come with a great human entourage. He came as a little baby, born to a humble couple in a barn. His birth was not announced to the human dignitaries who lived in palaces but to the ordinary shepherds who slept in the fields watching their flocks. Most missed this monumental event.

May we not be distracted and miss the fact of His visitation! Every day, may we in humility recognize, worship, and bow down to the King of kings and the Lord of lords, as the shepherds did so many years ago!

"Though he was God, he did not think of equality with God as something to cling to. Instead, he gave up his divine privileges; he took the humble position of a slave and was born as a human being ... that at the name of Jesus every knee should bow, in heaven and on earth and under the earth, and every tongue declare that Jesus Christ is Lord, to the glory of God the Father." (Philippians 2:5–7, 10–11).

OCTOBER 31

Bless or Curse?

"Trick or treat!" We hear this on Halloween night as the little people come around disguised in their costumes. Many of them wear scary masks, even masks of skeletons and costumes of the dead. Some shriek and make gestures to scare others. *Let them have fun*, some may think, *no harm is done*. Yet do we really want tricks done to us? Do we not have enough scary things in this world that we and our children have to deal with? Why would we want to instill fear in each other anyway? I can remember when we would wake up on the morning after Halloween, and some very nasty tricks had happened through the night. Outhouses were moved into the middle of the road; windows were covered with wax, and things left out were sometimes hidden or taken away so the owner couldn't find them. Some people even had firecrackers thrown into their house. But even more sinister "tricks" happen deep in the heart and emotions as we get involved in this supposedly "innocent" activity.

Is this really an innocent activity? Is it something we want to encourage for our children? Does Halloween really promote any goodwill in our society? Why the preoccupation with fear and death? If we focus on the hocus pocus, let us not be surprised when we and our children are captivated with fear and anxiety. Rather than being fixated on fear, death and demons, let us turn our life over to God and focus on Him and the good life He has for all who believe and trust in Him.

God's Word, the Bible, is clear on this: *"Do not be overcome by evil, but overcome evil with good." (Romans 12:21, ESV)*. Jesus said, *"bless those who curse you, pray for those who abuse you." (Luke 6:28, ESV)*. The apostle John said, *"... perfect love casts out fear." (1 John 4:18, ESV)*. And again, the apostle Paul said, *"Finally, brothers, whatever is true, whatever is honorable, whatever is just, whatever is pure, whatever is lovely, whatever is commendable, if there is any excellence, if there is anything worthy of praise, think about these things." (Philippians 4:8, ESV)*.

NOVEMBER 1

Glorious Ruin

Cars that drive themselves, spacecraft on Mars, buildings that reach to the sky, and submarines that can deliver guided missiles carrying atomic bombs that could annihilate it all in seconds. Closer to home, the desire for intimacy in marriage and the ability to break up this holy union in a moment of selfishness, anger, or unfaithfulness. Amazing power for good, bent towards evil. Why do these contradictions exist?

The Scriptures in Genesis declare that the father and mother of us all, by choosing to disobey God and follow their own desires, fell from fellowship with their Creator, the Almighty God! The moment they disobeyed, they died spiritually, intellectually, emotionally—every area of their being was corrupted. We, their offspring, inherited this sinful nature! The glorious image of God, still evident in every human, has been ruined by the effects of rebellion against God (Genesis 6:5–6). Rather than acknowledge that we've been created in the image of God, we attempt to create God in our own image. We chose to worship ourselves, creation, and man-made idols rather than God. Thus, we even deny the existence of the One who created us and holds all things together! On our own we don't even seek God; our hearts and minds are in constant rebellion against Him! In our attempts to be good, we fall short, unable to be what He created us to be (Romans 3:23). Rather than being God-centred, we've become self-centred and have become gods unto ourselves. Francis Schaeffer refers to this condition as a "glorious ruin."

Our only hope is turning in faith to God!

"He sent his own Son in a body like the bodies we sinners have. And in that body God declared an end to sin's control over us by giving his Son as a sacrifice for our sins. He did this so that the just requirement of the law would be fully satisfied for us, who no longer follow our sinful nature but instead follow the Spirit." (Romans 8:3–4).

NOVEMBER 2

Unconditional Surrender

Every Remembrance Day we are corporately reminded of those who gave their lives in defending our country through numerous battles and wars. Most veterans express that they never want to see such conflict again. Some find it difficult, or even impossible, to speak of their horrendous experiences as combatants in conflict. The sight of the unconditional surrender of the adversary brought a sense of relief, not only to the individuals on the front but also to everyone at home.

Though we enjoy many freedoms today, the foe has by no means been completely vanquished. As God's Word clearly states, a spiritual battle against the devil rages for every person. This battle can only be won by the power of our Creator, Jesus Christ. *"For we do not wrestle against flesh and blood, but against the rulers, against the authorities, against the cosmic powers over this present darkness, against the spiritual forces of evil in the heavenly places." (Ephesians 6:12, ESV).* We can't win this battle on our own. It was won by Jesus when He went to the cross of Calvary and paid the price for the rebellion of all who would surrender in faith to Him (John 3:16; Acts 14:38–39, 16:31). He empowers each of those who surrender in faith to Him with His Holy Spirit, to be overcomers in this battle that rages within and around us (Ephesians 1:13–14, 6:10–18).

The day is coming when every human being will unconditionally surrender and bow the knee to the Lord Jesus Christ (Philippians 2:9–11). Will we bow willingly now while He extends His forgiveness, mercy, and grace? Or will it be later, when He comes to judge every unrepentant sinner?

"Seek the Lord while you can find him. Call on him now while he is near. Let the wicked change their ways and banish the very thought of doing wrong. Let them turn to the Lord that he may have mercy on them. Yes, turn to our God, for he will forgive generously." (Isaiah 55:6–7).

The Manual

I am not a mechanic but often do work on our own vehicles. Usually I buy a service manual to help to figure out how to maintain or repair the vehicle. I read about and diagnose the problem before even beginning the repair. As the work progresses, often a reference back to the manual is helpful. Sometimes friends give some verbal advice, which may be of help or sometimes a hindrance. Ultimately the manual is the most reliable source of information. The manufacturer knows best because they designed the vehicle in the first place!

What about our life? How should we live? Where can we find answers to direct us in the everyday decisions we have to make? Are we just left to grapple with life on our own? We all have a need to understand the nature of God, His ways, His desires, and His instructions to guide us towards Him and through the toils and snares of life. We can find lots of information on the internet, on the news, or on other media these days. Some of this information might, at first glance, seem quite wise and spiritual. Other times we may get advice from others that might be OK or sometimes outright deceptive. How can we know what is true and good or what is untrue and evil?

Thankfully, God didn't leave us in limbo, grappling with our own broken ideas. He gave us His Word, the Bible, as our life manual, so we could learn what His will is for us, to encourage us and explain to us how we should live. It's imperative that we follow the will of our Creator to save us untold misery and grief! The Bible, inspired by the Creator Himself, is the only truly reliable manual for life.

"All Scripture is God-breathed and is useful for teaching, rebuking, correcting and training in righteousness, so that the servant of God may be thoroughly equipped for every good work." (2 Timothy 3:16–17, NIV),

Discipline

Speaking to a semi-retired trucker one day about how we were raised as children, he shared with me how his parents kept him in line. As an example, he said when he was caught smoking in grade two, he got the strap at school, and after that his dad gave him a spanking at home. It was painful. He got disciplined twice for one offence, yet he didn't hold this against his dad, because he deserved it, he said. Though it wasn't pleasant at the time, he said he knew that his dad gave him that spanking because he loved him. He said that now, many years later, he is still thankful that he got disciplined, because in the long term it made him a better person. All through the conversation he spoke very highly of his dad and his mom.

This reminded me that the Bible tells us *"For the Lord disciplines the one he loves, and chastises every son whom he receives" (Hebrews 12:6, ESV).* God's discipline may come in various forms. Sometimes it comes when we suffer the consequences of our rebellion and sins, such as crashing a car when driving recklessly, or by facing a judge for having broken the law in some way or another.

Other times God disciplines us not because of a particular sin but just to make us stronger people of God, just like the army or police force, who put their recruits through strict discipline to make them into better people, good soldiers, and responsible police officers.

In fact, God tells us in the Bible that we are to *"... endure hardship as discipline." (Hebrews 12:7, NIV).* So when something difficult or painful happens to us, we should realize that God is in control and we can either allow this to make us bitter or better.

Because God loves us, His discipline is always to make us better and more useful to Him, if we will allow ourselves to be trained by it.

"For our earthly fathers disciplined us for a few years, doing the best they knew how. But God's discipline is always good for us, so that we might share in His holiness. No discipline is enjoyable when it is happening—it's painful! But afterward there will be a peaceful harvest of right living for those who are trained in this way." (Hebrews 12:10–11).

NOVEMBER 5

Transaction

When we bought our first house, it was a learning experience. I remember securing a mortgage, making a down payment, and going to the lawyer to sign the papers. It wasn't until this transaction was made that we could really call the home ours. We had to take ownership of it by agreeing to the terms of the transaction. Before this, we imagined what we would do to make the place our home. Landscaping, furniture, finishing the basement, and painting the rooms were plans we made before we even had possession of it. Once we took ownership, we moved in, and it was now our home.

Before I received Jesus Christ as my Saviour, I thought about what it would be like to be a Christian. I observed others who were Christians. I went to church and even read the Bible to learn more about Jesus and what it meant to be a follower of Him. To be totally honest, sometimes I pretended to be a Christian when I knew I was not.

I remember back in Slocan, BC, on January 13, 1973, when I took ownership of what Jesus had done for me. I realized I was a hopeless sinner and only He could save me from my sins. God convicted me. He was my only hope, and I could resist no more. There was nothing I could do but surrender to Him. I got down on my knees, repented of my sins, and cried out to Him for mercy. True to His Word, He heard me and saved me: *"For everyone who calls on the name of the Lord will be saved." (Romans 10:13, ESV)*. A transaction was made that day, and Jesus made me part of His family. That was over fifty years ago, and every day I praise God for His mercy and grace and the new life He has given.

Jesus said, *"And I, when I am lifted up from the earth, will draw all people to myself." (John 12:32, ESV)*. God's Word also says, *"The Lord is not slow to fulfill his promise as some count slowness, but is patient toward you, not wishing that any should perish, but that all should reach repentance." (2 Peter 3:9, ESV)*.

Have you received Him? Is He your Lord and Saviour? He has a new life waiting for all who will come to Him. *"But to all who did receive him, who believed in his name, he gave the right to become children of God." (John 1:12, ESV)*.

NOVEMBER 6

Humans, Not Animals

With the question of euthanasia being front and centre these days, there are many reasons people put forward to justify it. I heard someone say, "We put our animals out of their misery, why would we not do the same with our loved ones?" I couldn't help say, "But we're not animals. We're human beings. Human life is sacred." The reply was, "I think we're animals." To this I replied, "If we're animals, what makes it wrong for one human to eat another? We do this with turkeys, cattle and sheep." If we're animals, anything goes. Then there's no longer any right and wrong, no standard by which we should live our lives. Then we can, and will, act like beasts, because there is no higher morality, no higher law, no higher One than what we perceive in our own minds.

The "ethnic cleansing" we've witnessed from times past to modern times is based on such deception, on man's ideas and not God's standard. People who didn't meet man's standard were eliminated. Murder of other human beings became the law in many countries caught in the grip of such deceptive humanistic ideology. When God is forgotten, man becomes a law unto himself, and everyone does what is right in his own eyes (Judges 17:6, 21:25). Animals act like animals by instinct, but human beings are accountable to a higher standard.

The fact remains, we are humans. Humans, among other things, are creative, have the ability to decide and plan for the future, to love, and to have faith in God. Even the ability to read and write shows the unique and amazing God-given gifts possessed by the human being. Animals cannot do any such things; there is a very wide gap between humans and animals.

The Bible clearly teaches that we have been fearfully and wonderfully made (Psalm 139:14). We are created as human beings in the image of God our Creator (Genesis 1:27). We are responsible for our actions, and we will answer to our Creator for our every thought, word, or deed (Hebrews 10:26–27, Revelation 21:8). Human life is sacred and must be respected. No doctor should ever be asked to euthanize another person, no matter what the situation.

"Now choose life, so that you and your children may live and that you may love the LORD your God, listen to His voice, and hold fast to Him." (Deuteronomy 30:19–20, NIV).

The Bond

Plywood is an amazing invention. A number of thin, fragile layers of wood glued together to make one strong, cohesive sheet. It has amazing strength because the layers are glued together. The glue is the bond that gives it strength.

One time I was riding with a fellow who was carrying a sheet of plywood over the top of the cab of his pickup. A gust of wind caught it and broke it in half. The glue gave way, the wood shattered, rendering it a mess, mostly useless.

This reminds me of marriage. God instituted marriage between one man and one woman at creation, two united in marriage for a lifetime. When a man and woman are married, the Bible teaches, God is the One who bonds them together as one: *"This explains why a man leaves his father and mother and is joined to his wife, and the two are united into one." (Genesis 2:24)*.

My wife and I recently celebrated our forty-eighth anniversary. What a privilege to be one with her for all these years. Is it because we worked at our marriage, or somehow had the right chemistry, or loved each other a lot, that we made it for forty-eight years? I believe all of these have a part, but the ultimate and overriding power in sustained wholesome marriage is God. He is the One who gave us life in the first place. He is the One who had the wonderful idea of making us male and female. *"So God created mankind in his own image, in the image of God he created them; male and female he created them." (Genesis 1:27, NIV)*. Marriage and family were His idea from the beginning. He is the One who empowers us, as we trust in Him, by giving us His Holy Spirit to live out marriage in a way that would honour Him.

This is not a time for us to boast in ourselves. But we boast in our Creator God. With thanksgiving we worship and praise Him, giving Him all the honour and glory. We look to Him who is the bond that keeps us together, in plenty and in need, in joy and in sorrow, in sickness and in health, for better or for worse, as long as we both shall live.

Let us proclaim with Jesus, *"So they are no longer two, but one flesh. Therefore what God has joined together, let no one separate." (Matthew 19:6, NIV)*.

Boxes

While waiting at a railway crossing, it's interesting to see hundreds of stacked container boxes pass by. The container box was invented to mitigate theft, prevent damage, and increase efficiency for cargo on the way to its destination. With the products sealed inside, they provide safe and orderly transit of goods from one place to another.

Sometimes, to help us understand God better, we put our understanding of Him in mental or theological boxes. These boxes can show up on lists or statements describing God, what He is like, how we relate to Him, or how He relates to us. These boxes of understanding, if based on God's Word, can help us to cope with the immensity of Almighty God. They are needful to keep us on the rails, as it were, and for us to begin, in a very limited way, to comprehend the eternal, all knowing, all powerful, awe-inspiring God. A problem arises when we limit Him to the confines of our boxes, thus limiting Him to our own understanding. Then our faith in Him is also restricted to the size of our box. Though the box may accurately represent Him to an extent, He is so much larger than any box we confine Him to. *"Not even the highest heavens can contain him." (2 Chronicles 2:6).*

Just as the boxes on the railcar aren't designed to permanently confine the goods inside them, neither are our God boxes intended to fully describe God. He is the truth. How vast is the truth? Is there any end to it? He is eternal, no beginning, no end, and we cannot begin to comprehend eternity. He is all powerful, and nothing, absolutely nothing, can stop Him. He is all knowing. Nothing escapes His notice, not even a hair falling from our head (Matthew 10:30). When confronted with Him, we are compelled to bow down and worship Him. Thank God for the boxes through which He has chosen to reveal Himself to us, but may we never limit Him to our little boxes.

We can be thankful that God chose to become part of the human race to reveal Himself to us in the person of Jesus Christ. When we know Jesus, we know God and can have a personal relationship with the awesome, eternal, all-powerful, all-knowing God. Some day we will see Him not only through our boxes but face to face.

"For now we see only a reflection as in a mirror; then we shall see face to face. Now I know in part; then I shall know fully, even as I am fully known." (1 Corinthians 13:12, NIV).

NOVEMBER 9

Foolishness

God, through the prophet Isaiah, predicted the virgin birth of Jesus hundreds of years before it happened (Isaiah 7:14). When I asked a group of people what they would think if I said a virgin was going to give birth, one fellow answered, "Ridiculous, that's impossible." I agreed that it is humanly impossible, but God was the one who told the prophet to speak these words (2 Peter 1:20–21). The words were proven true by the virgin birth of our Lord Jesus Christ.

I went on to share that the little baby in the manger was God in human flesh. The Son of God existing from eternity past was the creator of everything that is. He spoke everything into existence in six days (Genesis 1; John 1:1–4; Colossians 1:15–17). Then the same fellow piped up and said, "Evolution, evolution," and went on to say that God had not created anything but evolution had caused it all. The fellow didn't stay long enough for us to have a thorough discussion on this subject, but there are obvious contradictions in his reasoning.

Evolution, in this context, says the first people showed up through many chance happenings and mutations over millions of years. The sun, the moon, the stars, and the planets all just came about out of nowhere, without any intervention of anyone. Thus, babies are conceived and born without God, we take every breath on our own, our thoughts and reasoning power, the creativity of man is just a product of chance, all out of nowhere, just by chance. On one hand this fellow is saying this whole universe came into existence all on its own without the help of anyone, and on the other hand he's saying that it's impossible for a virgin to give birth. Seems obvious to me that it's much easier for a virgin to give birth than for the whole universe to come into being all by itself! Yet both are absolutely impossible without God!

When God is left out of the picture, nothing makes sense. It's absolutely foolish to believe that all of this wonderful, intricate creation, including humanity, just came into being without a Creator. It's one of the most absurd ideas humanity has ever come up with. God's Word, the Bible, says, *"The fool says in his heart, 'There is no God.'"* (Psalm 14:1, ESV).

"By faith we understand that the universe was created by the word of God ..." (Hebrews 11:3, ESV).

"The Son is the image of the invisible God, the firstborn over all creation. For in him all things were created: things in heaven and on earth, visible and invisible, whether thrones or powers or rulers or authorities; all things have been created through him and for him." (Colossians 1:15–16, NIV).

Surrender

On November 11, 1918, World War I ended as an armistice was signed between Germany and the Allies. Annually on this date, many people in the free world gather to remember the horrendous casualties and sacrifices of those who fought in not only World War I but numerous subsequent wars. US President Woodrow Wilson declared World War I as "the war to end all wars," but even as we write this, there are several battles raging in various places around the world. Closer to home, we see a battle raging on our streets; the carnage of the drug overdose crisis is claiming hundreds of our people. The temporary sense of euphoria that the drugs bring actually becomes the very thing that claims one's life. If we're honest and look a little deeper, we'll realize that there's a battle raging in every human heart, in your heart and mine. Our human attempts to calm this unrest in our heart, be it through meditation, materialism, comfort food, or prescription drugs provide only a temporary fix when reality hits. A hope for peace, even a sense of peace, isn't really peace at all. How can we have real peace among the nations, on our streets, with our fellow man, in our heart?

The only way we can have true, lasting peace within ourselves is as we surrender to our Creator God. We were created to have an intimate personal peace with Him and within our hearts. Until we recognize Him as the sovereign of the universe and of us, until we completely surrender to Him, we will only at best have a fleeting, temporary sense of peace that really isn't peace at all.

When a nation surrenders, they realize that the one they're fighting is stronger than they. There is One infinitely stronger than any nation, person, or problem. He is our Creator God. May we daily, moment by moment, humble ourselves and bow our knees in surrender to Him, that we may receive the true peace only He can give.

Jesus said, *"Peace I leave with you; my peace I give you. I do not give to you as the world gives. Do not let your hearts be troubled and do not be afraid" (John 14:27, NIV); "Do not be anxious about anything, but in every situation, by prayer and petition, with thanksgiving, present your requests to God. And the peace of God, which transcends all understanding, will guard your hearts and your minds in Christ Jesus." (Philippians 4:6–7, NIV).*

November 11

Sacrifice

Every year on November 11, we remember the many thousands of young men and women who sacrificed their lives for our country. World War I was supposed to be the war that ends all wars. Since then, there have been many more wars: World War II, the Korean War, the Vietnam War, to name a few, while war is presently going on in Ukraine and the Middle East. Though we are thankful for those who died for our freedom, will there ever be a war that ends all wars? It seems these wars have, at best, given a reprieve for a time. But will there ever be peace on earth?

There is One who sacrificed His life so we could have peace. He is the Son of God, the One who created everything by the word of His mouth, Jesus Christ. Jesus willingly suffered and died at the hands of evil people, sacrificing His life to pay the penalty for our sins and to purchase for us peace between God and man. We can have peace with God today as we, through faith, put our trust in the finished work of Jesus.

Since humanity is so persistent in trying to live life our own way, without Jesus, we aren't experiencing much true peace with God, among the nations, between people groups, in our families, or even in our own lives (Psalm 2; Romans 3:17–18). Until we submit to Jesus, the Prince of Peace, there will not be true national or personal peace.

There is a time when Jesus will return to this earth and bring an end to all wars. He will bring peace on earth that will last forever. I look forward to that day when all the nations of the world live in peace and harmony with each other.

In the meantime, let us with thanksgiving in our hearts submit our lives to Jesus today so we can experience peace with God, with ourselves, with our families, and with those around us. *"For Christ himself has brought us peace." (Ephesians 2:14).* He has promised to give peace to us if we only trust in Him and, through faith, let Him be the Lord of our lives. *"Therefore, since we have been justified through faith, we have peace with God through our Lord Jesus Christ." (Romans 5:1, NIV).* Jesus said to His disciples, *"I have told you these things, so that in me you may have peace. In this world you will have trouble. But take heart! I have overcome the world." (John 16:33, NIV).*

Ultimate Sacrifice

Did you wear a poppy on Remembrance Day? I wore one to help me to remember the freedom we have and the sacrifice that so many young men and women made so that we could enjoy life as we do today. These people gave their lives, they shed their blood, so we could have freedom. This is something we should take time to remember at least once a year, and hope and pray that we will never see this happen again.

There are poppies in Flanders Fields, but there are also crosses, thousands of them, each symbolizing at least one precious life lost. One whose mother or family would not see come home again. Why crosses? Why not some other symbol, like a tombstone, a stake, or a plaque of some sort? The crosses point towards another cross, a Roman cross on which the Creator of the universe cruelly suffered, bled, and died some two thousand years ago. The men who died in all the wars died for a temporary, at best tentative, peace. Jesus died for peace with God and man forever (Ephesians 2:14; Philippians 4:7). The men who died in the battles of the world hoped they would make it home alive, but Jesus was born to die; He knew this was His life purpose. Though He could have easily saved Himself, He willingly went to the cross and died for the sins of all who would believe (Matthew 26:53). The bodies of men are still in the ground; Jesus bodily rose from the dead after three days in the grave, proving He was the Author of life (Luke 24:39; Acts 2:32).

So the poppy reminds me not only of those who died in these horrible, senseless conflicts of men, but it also reminds me of the One who willingly died for us to pay the debt of our sin, so that we can have life for all eternity. I will put it on my car sun visor as a daily reminder of Jesus, the dearest and best, who paid the ultimate sacrifice.

"Greater love has no one than this, that someone lay down His life for His friends." (John 15:13, ESV); "By this we know love, that He laid down His life for us ..." (1 John 3:16, ESV).

NOVEMBER 13

The Forgiven Forgive!

It's amazing how some people can forgive others for the atrocities that have been done to them and their loved ones. Corrie Ten Boom forgave the Gestapo, who killed her father and her sister in the Nazi death camps. Sokreaksa Himm forgave those who killed most of his family and left him for dead in the killing fields of Cambodia. He sought these killers out and forgave them face to face and prayed for them in their presence. Another man, Christopher LaPel, who narrowly escaped the Khmer Rouge with his life, now visits a man in prison who was convicted of killing and torturing some fourteen thousand people, including his cousin, during the Pol Pot regime of terror.[13]

How is this possible? This doesn't come naturally to us. We want revenge. Hatred and a desire to settle the score fill our hearts as we remember the offenses done against us. Possibly you can think of someone that you think of in this way.

The only way we can truly forgive someone from the heart is to have a change of heart: *"... it is a change of heart, produced by God's Spirit." (Romans 2:29;* see also Psalm 51:10*).* When we realize what it cost Jesus to forgive us, we have no alternative but to forgive others who have sinned against us. *"For if you forgive other people when they sin against you, your heavenly Father will also forgive you. But if you do not forgive others their sins, your Father will not forgive your sins." (Matthew 6:14–15, NIV).* We obtain a new heart and attitude when we surrender our lives to God (Ezekiel 36:26–27; Galatians 5:16–17). As we turn our sins and our sinful selves over to Him, He forgives us, changes us, and empowers us with His Holy Spirit to live as Jesus lived (Romans 8:1–17). Then we will have the power to forgive. This is the heart of God, to forgive (Numbers 14:18; Psalm 86:5; Isaiah 55:6–7; Matthew 11:29)!

"Bear with each other and forgive one another if any of you has a grievance against someone. Forgive as the Lord forgave you." (Colossians 3:13, NIV).

---

13 You can read these stories in *Tramp for the Lord* by Corrie Ten Boom and *After the Heavy Rain* by by Sokreaksa S. Himm. Christopher LaPel's story can be read in Lee Strobel's book *The Case for Grace.*

Contraband

When we see containers going past on railway cars, we don't know what's inside them. They're each marked with various brand names, but the shippers have the contents of each container marked on a shipping statement or manifest. Sometimes what the shipping manifest indicates and the actual contents don't match. The paperwork may say it contains automobiles, but when opened for inspection, it actually contains hidden illegal drugs, stolen goods, or personal items. Somewhere along the line, someone intercepted the intended use of the system for their own selfish gain. These illegal substances are sometimes called "contraband."

God has chosen to reveal Himself to us through His Word, the Bible. We can conclude certain things about Him from His revelation to us based on the truth of His Holy Scriptures, the Bible (Psalm 119:160; John 17:17). Even though we have God's infallible Word, sometimes we try to make up our own explanation of what God is saying to us, or what He's like. At first glance it looks good and seems correct, yet when we carefully look at God's Word, we see that it is contrary to the truth.

An example of this might be that some say we can work our way to heaven. The thinking may go something like this: "If I'm good enough, then my good will outweigh the bad. God will look on the good I have done and will be pleased and let me into heaven because of my sincere efforts and good works." At first glance, this could seem to make sense, but when we check God's Word, we realize this is completely contrary to the truth, which says, *"When we display our righteous deeds, they are nothing but filthy rags"* (Isaiah 64:6) and *"For by grace you have been saved through faith. And this is not your own doing; it is the gift of God, not a result of works, so that no one may boast." (Ephesians 2:8–9, ESV).* It's clear that we can be saved only through faith in Jesus Christ (John 3:16; Acts 4:12).

We must carefully study God's Word (2 Timothy 2:15), guided by His Holy Spirit (John 14:26), then we will be able to discern the difference between what is false and the truth (John 14:17). Jesus said, *"... and you will know the truth, and the truth will set you free." (John 8:32, ESV).*

NOVEMBER 15

Encrypted?

D o you remember some years ago when a young teenager hacked into the private schedule of Buckingham Palace? He knew all the information on meetings and official plans of the Queen. He had decoded encrypted messages to gain access to their secret plans. The people in charge quickly added another layer of encryption in an attempt to keep the information secret.

Sometimes we try to hide our plans, thoughts, words, or deeds that we don't want anyone else to know about. Maybe it's something we plan to do, or something we've done in private. We think nobody knows, as it's safely encrypted in the recesses of our mind. Yet there is One who knows every detail, no matter how many layers of protection we attempt to cover it up with. We may hide it from people for a time, but no amount of encryption can hide anything from God, even for a moment.

God's Word, the Bible, reveals that there are no secrets before God. He is the all-knowing One. No matter how hard we try, we can keep no secrets from Him: *"For he knows the secrets of the heart." (Psalm 44:21, ESV)*; *"He alone examines the motives of our hearts." (1 Thessalonians 2:4).*

Jesus said, *"For everything that is hidden will eventually be brought into the open, and every secret will be brought to light" (Mark 4:22).* His Word goes on to say, *"This will take place on the day when God judges people's secrets through Jesus Christ, as my gospel declares." (Romans 2:16, NIV).*

Initially, this makes me very uncomfortable. It's sobering to think that He knows every thought, that all will be brought into the open, and that He will judge even my motives. My first reaction is to cover it up, to hide and add a layer of encryption, as the people at Buckingham Palace did. Yet there is a better way. God wants us to come into the open, to transparently come clean and confess everything to Him. Only then will He forgive us, heal us, and set us free!

"If we claim to be without sin, we deceive ourselves and the truth is not in us. If we confess our sins, he is faithful and just and will forgive us our sins and purify us from all unrighteousness." (1 John 1:8–9 NIV).

Choose Life

I've never been to Holland, but I understand it's a beautiful country. Much of it has been reclaimed from the sea with dykes. It's a fertile land that gives life to many plants and provides food for the people living there. Holland is known for its flowers, especially the tulip. Vast, spectacular fields of multi-coloured tulips are often seen on pictures of this wonderful land.

Yet something terrible is happening there. A culture of death has permeated the land. Medical personnel travel the streets to end the life of the next person who wants to die. Doctors who were educated to preserve life now administer death to certain people who are no longer needed. Euthanasia, the killing of another person, was seriously discussed in the Netherlands in 1973. At first it was for those who were terminally ill and suffering terribly, but after a while it was for those who wanted to die for whatever reason. Now some older people are afraid of going to their doctor or the hospital because so many elderly people have been euthanized. Not only has a person been given the legal right to kill themselves, but in a giant leap into the abyss of human depravity, someone else has been given the right to take the life of another person. The very institution that is there to preserve life has been given the mandate to take life. Rather than lovingly giving comfort and proper palliative care, a person takes the life of another. There are reports that some are even killed without their consent! A subtle ideology of death has slowly crept in and has a grip on this beautiful nation. Though seen by some as progressive and enlightening, this is nothing short of legislated murder.

Now our government in Canada has opened the doors to this very same thing, calling it merciful, compassionate, and dying with dignity—medical assistance in dying (MAID). Can we not learn from history and the example of other nations? Can we not hear the Word of God (Romans 13:9–10; Revelation 21:6–8)?

God's Word, through Moses to Israel, still rings true for us today: *"This day I call the heavens and the earth as witnesses against you that I have set before you life and death, blessings and curses. Now choose life, so that you and your children may live and that you may love the Lord your God, listen to his voice, and hold fast to him." (Deuteronomy 30:19–20, NIV)*.

The Zookeepers Were Right!

You've probably heard the news of the tragic death of a gorilla named Harambe in the Cincinnati Zoo. It's sad to hear that this endangered species of gorilla had to be put down.

Apparently a four-year-old boy somehow squeezed through a safety enclosure and entered the area in which the gorillas were kept. Harambe, the male gorilla, roughly dragged the boy around, forcing the zoo personnel to shoot the gorilla to save the life of the boy. Some people are lashing out at the mother for letting the child get out of her sight, while others are blaming the zookeepers.

We raised three children, and I know how impossible it is to keep constant watch on children of that age. I am sure that the last thing the mother wanted was for her son to be hurt and, for that matter, for the gorilla to die. Together with her, let us be thankful to God that the life of her son was spared. For those who don't see it this way, think: If this was your son in the same predicament, would you not want the boy to be saved at all costs? The answer from any loving parent would be, "Yes, please save my child. Do whatever it takes, but please save my child." Many parents would be ready to give their own lives for the sake of their child.

The zookeepers should be commended for their prompt response in saving the boy's life. As difficult as it was, they were absolutely right in the decision they made. They had no other choice. One little human child is worth infinitely more than thousands of gorillas, no matter how endangered their species. The reason? Humans are created in the image of God; gorillas are not. As His image bearers we have great value to God (Matthew 10:28–31; Mark 10:13–16), much greater value than any animals.

As I ponder how much God truly values us, I'm reminded of the love He has shown to us in the person of the Lord Jesus Christ. Though we wandered from Him into the clutches of sin and death, He did not come to condemn, but He voluntarily sacrificed Himself to save and rescue all those who would put their trust in Him (John 10:11, 14:6; Hebrews 12:2–3).

"Jesus gave his life for our sins, just as God our Father planned, in order to rescue us from this evil world in which we live. All glory to God forever and ever! Amen." (Galatians 1:4–5).

Saved!

A good friend recently shared with me his harrowing experience with death. He was riding on a horse beside a raging river. As he looked at the swirling current and treacherous murky waters just below him, the thought came into his mind, *I'm glad I'm not in there. I would never make it in that swift and deadly current.* Just as this thought entered his mind, the bank he and the horse were on gave way, as it had been under-mined by the torrential river. Before he knew it, he and the horse were in the swollen, angry river. The thought of possibly jumping off the horse briefly flashed into his mind, but he knew he could never survive in the boiling waters on every side. Then he noticed that the horse could swim and keep afloat, even with him on its back! So he held firmly to the horn of the saddle and stayed with the horse. Before long the horse found a foothold and climbed back to safety on the shore of the river. He knew beyond a doubt that it was God who had met him there and spared his life. God used this experience to show him his desperate state spiritually, and he surrendered his life to God and became a follower of Jesus Christ.

Sometimes we think we're doing quite well on our own, but through the convicting work of God through the Holy Spirit, we become acutely aware of our own sin and the currents of sin and corruption around us. All seems hopeless, and our very life is threat-ened. The prophet Isaiah found himself in this situation and desperately confessed to God, *"Woe is me! For I am lost; for I am a man of unclean lips, and I dwell in the midst of a people of unclean lips; for my eyes have seen the King, the Lord of hosts." (Isaiah 6:5, ESV).* Yet upon hearing Isaiah's despairing cry, God forgave him and gave him the message, *"... your guilt is taken away, and your sin atoned for." (Isaiah 6:7, ESV).*

God is still willing to save all who will trust in Jesus Christ, the only one who can save us (John 14:6; Acts 4:12).

"For with the heart one believes and is justified, and with the mouth one confesses and is saved" (Romans 10:10, ESV); "If we confess our sins, he is faithful and just to forgive us our sins and to cleanse us from all unrighteousness." (1 John 1:9, ESV).

NOVEMBER 19

Terminal or Eternal?

I had heard he was not well but had not spoken to him since hearing the news of his sickness. Then there he was, standing at the checkout. As I approached him, we began to talk. Though he looked well, he related to me that he was on pain killers and was actually very sick. He told me, in earshot of all those standing around the checkout, that the doctors told him he was terminal. As we continued to share together, we both agreed that all our lives here on earth are terminal; we will all die sooner or later. Then he said he was looking forward to his ultimate healing, having a new body in heaven, when his time came to be with the Lord. He expressed absolutely no fear of death but actually had a sense of anticipation in his attitude as he shared.

I was very encouraged by this brother's faith in the Lord. After having heard the news that he'd probably not be around here on earth for very much longer, he with great hope and assurance spoke in faith of the place that was prepared for him by his Lord and Saviour Jesus Christ.

How can this be? Is this not the most dreaded news one could hear, that one has a terminal disease? That one will soon die? Why was he not afraid? How could he have this positive attitude? It's obvious his confidence comes from a living relationship with Jesus Christ, the Author of life, the eternal One who has all things in His hands. His trust is in his Maker, the Creator of the universe (John 1:3–4; Colossians 1:15–17; Acts 3:15), the One who promised that He has a place prepared for all those who trust in Him (John 14:1–4)! Yes, our life here is definitely terminal, but our life in Christ Jesus is eternal (John 6:68). If we confess our sins, He is faithful and just to forgive us our sins and to cleanse us from all unrighteousness.! My friend knows nothing will separate him from the love of Christ (Romans 8:31–39).

This confident life of faith is available to all who will turn to the Lord (Hebrews 7:25). We, in faith, can have the confidence that God Almighty knows all things, and we can trust Him, even in death (Psalm 23:4).

"Yet I am not ashamed, because I know whom I have believed, and am convinced that He is able to guard what I have entrusted to Him for that day." (2 Timothy 1:12, NIV).

Three Sides

I'm sure you've heard someone complain about mistreatment or injustice at the hands of another person. Their perspective sounds so convincing that we come to the conclusion that they must be right. We empathize with them and are tempted to take their side. Sometimes we even mistakenly take their side of the story as the total truth before checking with the other person to find out their side of the story. Then when we hear the other side of the story, it sounds totally different—sometimes so different that we wonder if they're talking about the same situation.

This is the cause of many quarrels, hostilities, and even wars. The two parties don't consider each other's outlook or feelings, and others come into the picture, taking one or the other's side, and before we know the truth, we have a battle on our hands! Countries do it, people groups do it, couples do it, individuals do it, and I do it; we all do it at some time or another. We have these self-protective strategies that kick into high gear when we're offended.

Often we forget that there's another side to the story—God's side, which always represents the truth. If both of the original people had allowed God to have His way in their life, the original disagreement would have never happened, and if the people who got involved in taking sides really sought God, their view of the situation would have been totally different too. There may be many sides, but God's side always prevails.

The Bible tells us we are to be humble, like Jesus was, and to consider others as better than ourselves (Philippians 2:3). Only as we let God have His way in our lives will we have true humility. When we find our identity in Him, we're not so preoccupied with protecting ourselves or making an identity of our own. It's much more difficult to become offended when we find our security in our relationship with Jesus Christ.

"Let no one seek his own good, but the good of his neighbor." (1 Corinthians 10:24, ESV); *"But I say to you, Love your enemies and pray for those who persecute you, so that you may be sons of your Father who is in heaven. For He makes His sun rise on the evil and on the good, and sends rain on the just and on the unjust." (Matthew 5:44–45, ESV).*

Church Gathering

When speaking to the late Jim Davidson, then Mayor of Smithers, he indicated that when a town was established, the first priority was to build a church. Most of the people knew their help came from the Lord. They got together to worship Him weekly. They had special times of worship at Christmas, Easter, Thanksgiving and other important events such as weddings, baptisms, christenings and funerals. Some would gather to pray or have Bible study during the week. They would pray for rain when there was a drought, or for peace in times of war. One fellow told me that his mother would hitch up the horse and buggy and head for church in the morning and would return in the evening singing hymns all the way back and throughout the week!

The building was important as a gathering place but their faith in the Lord, the God of heaven and earth, was paramount. The church was the people, the community of faith. It is the same today! The church still exists and gathers regularly throughout Canada and the free world! Most towns have numerous churches. Some gather in large buildings others in homes, yet the people meet together to worship!

In totalitarian countries the church is usually suppressed, yet despite this they meet anyways - often in homes or secret places to escape the persecution of the state. A Chinese believer once commented that a major difference between the church in the free world and China was that their church had no money budgeted for building programs but the church in the west had billions set apart for their building programs! So many differences but one essential – to know and worship God together with other believers!

Do you trust Jesus as your personal Lord and Savior? If you have faith in Him, then you are part of the church! Hope to see you in church!

"And let us not neglect our meeting together, as some people do, but encourage one another, especially now that the day of his return is drawing near." Hebrews 10:25.

Education in Eternal Things

He was a faller most of his life. He is acclaimed by others in the industry as one of the best who ever practised the art of hand falling trees. He fell many trees six to eight feet in diameter, with the largest being thirteen-and-a-half feet in diameter. He fell trees in the opposite direction of their lean by using jacks to jack them away from fish bearing streams. He learned the trade in the School of Hard Knocks and had a keen eye and a sixth sense when it came to sizing up each tree as he knocked them down in a pattern that made the job of the skidder man a lot easier. This man is a legend in the logging industry. He had very little formal education, but I believe he should have been awarded a Doctorate in Hand Falling.

Though schools, colleges, and universities definitely have their place in society, we often ignore the fact that we're all learning through everyday events in our life. Much of our education is acquired outside of the formal learning institutions. We can even learn from the creation around us (Job 12:7). God is speaking to us through all He has created and through His Word, the Bible. All the worldly knowledge we pick up, either formally or through day-to-day experience, will never replace that of getting to know and having an intimate relationship with the Almighty God. The most important education is to learn to know the Lord and to follow in His path (Jeremiah 9:23–24).

My friend, the hand faller, committed his life to the Lord and learned what it means to be a follower of Jesus. His expert knowledge in the logging industry was of temporary importance, but his faith and learning of things of God is eternal. He has since gone to his eternal home with Jesus!

Wisdom says, *"Incline your ear, and hear the words of the wise, and apply your heart to my knowledge, for it will be pleasant if you keep them within you, if all of them are ready on your lips ... That your trust may be in the Lord, I have made them known to you today, even to you."* (Proverbs 22:17, 19, ESV).

Jesus said, *"Let me teach you, because I am humble and gentle at heart, and you will find rest for your souls."* (Matthew 11:29).

Without God, Anything Goes

He said he was an atheist. We had numerous conversations about God. He would always defend his position of the nonexistence of God.

One day he mentioned that Adolf Hitler was a terrible person. Though I agreed with him, I played the devil's advocate and asked him, "What was so wrong with Hitler? What makes what he did so wrong? He thought he was right, so what's the big deal? It's his word against yours. Who's to say he was wrong? If there's no God, then there's no ultimate truth. What basis do you stand on to say that you are right and he was wrong? If someone were an adulterer, murderer, thief, or whatever he felt was right, who are you to say he is wrong?"

He became very quiet, and the next morning, the very first thing he said to me was, "Hitler was OK." This is exactly what happens when we try to live our lives without God. Without God, anything goes.

Some say that it's the opinion of the majority, not God, that dictates what is right or wrong. I believe the same applies to the majority as to the individual. The farther we wander from God, the farther we fall into the abyss of moral, ethical, and practical depravity. Again, Nazi Germany was a good example of this. The majority went along with Hitler. Did that make what he did right?

We've heard of a notable radio announcer who says beating women is OK. We have accusations of politicians sexually assaulting other politicians on Parliament Hill. They're discussing euthanasia in the halls of our government. We shouldn't be surprised at this; when we invent our own moral agenda, all hell breaks loose. Who says what is right or wrong?

We have a Maker who didn't leave us in a moral vacuum; He knows exactly how we should live. We will only find our way as we seek Him. He gave us His Word, the Bible, for our good, to show us how we should live. He instructed in the Ten Commandments not to have any other god but Him, not to murder, not to commit adultery, not to steal, not to testify falsely, and not to covet (see Exodus 20:1–17). Jesus said, *"love your neighbor as yourself." (Mark 12:33, NIV)*; *"Do to others as you would have them do to you." (Luke 6:31, NIV)*.

"I am the Lord your God, who teaches you what is best for you, who directs you in the way you should go." (Isaiah 48:17, NIV).

One of Us

As the response to the COVID-19 pandemic progresses, it's becoming clearer that God is not being considered in the picture by most involved! Vaccines, health, government, social distancing, masks, and mandates have distracted us from the most important one! Any distraction from God and His Holy Word becomes the downfall of a society.

Among all the distractions, we are ultimately faced with the real meaning of life! Jesus our Creator, Sustainer, and Saviour came to be one of us so that we could become one of His! When we think of this, it's absolutely astounding that our Maker, the One who spoke everything into existence, came down to actually become one of us, whom He created in His image. What makes it even more profound is that He knew that those He came to rescue would reject Him and eventually kill Him in one of the cruelest methods of death known to man. Furthermore, He knew that His death was essential to the salvation of His rebellious creation! This is all summed up in God's Holy Word!

"Have this mind among yourselves, which is yours in Christ Jesus, who, though He was in the form of God, did not count equality with God a thing to be grasped, but emptied Himself, by taking the form of a servant, being born in the likeness of men. And being found in human form, He humbled Himself by becoming obedient to the point of death, even death on a cross. Therefore God has highly exalted Him and bestowed on Him the name that is above every name, so that at the name of Jesus every knee should bow, in heaven and on earth and under the earth, and every tongue confess that Jesus Christ is Lord, to the glory of God the Father." (Philippians 2:6–11, ESV).

What are we to do with this man who claimed to be God? Who came to forgive us our sins? Will we bow our knee to Him and be saved, or will we continue to reject Him?

That is the most important question we face in our lifetime!

Power to Change

He found himself on the streets in the downtown east side of Vancouver. His addictions had sapped him of all meaningful purpose in life. His earthly possessions were in a shopping cart that he pushed around with him. He tried any drug he could get his hands on to get a new high, to numb himself to the reality of this seemingly hopeless situation. His arms were red, infected, and inflamed from the countless times he sought relief at the point of a needle. He slept wherever he could find a bit of warmth, somewhat sheltered from the threat of the elements. He wanted to beat the habit, but it seemed hopeless after nine attempts at various treatment centres. Then his parents arranged for him to go to a Christian recovery centre, hoping "religion" might help him.

After sitting under the teaching of the Word of God, he met and surrendered to his Maker and Healer, the Lord Jesus Christ. He hasn't been the same since! He continued to study and read the Bible together with other believers as he grew in his faith. He was miraculously healed spiritually, emotionally, and even physically, set free to be the person God wanted Him to be. The message and power of God's Word, the Bible, had become reality in the life of this precious brother. *"But these are written that you may believe that Jesus is the Messiah, the Son of God, and that by believing you may have life in his name."* *(John 20:31, NIV).*

God's Word has the power to change anyone who reads and heeds its message. C.S. Lewis, Malcomb Muggeridge, Stuart Hamblin, Lee Stroebel, and Nabeel Qureshi are among millions, including myself, who attest to the power to change that the Bible has wrought in our lives.

My prayer is that many more people, including you, will proclaim with the apostle Peter in saying, *"For you have been born again, but not to a life that will quickly end. Your new life will last forever because it comes from the eternal, living word of God."* (1 Peter 1:23).

Meeting Our Maker

A childhood friend of mine was naturally a very friendly and encouraging fellow. I'm still impressed by his restrained response when I accidently hit him in the nose with my hockey stick when eagerly trying to get the ball between the goal posts as we played "dirt hockey" on our improvised hockey rink! He didn't curse or threaten me but reminded me that high sticking was against the rules. Fortunately, he didn't get a nose bleed! Though I have fond memories of him, I never heard him mention God or Jesus in those early years. But when he was on his deathbed, he asked for someone to tell him how he could be made right with his Maker. Thankfully, someone who knew Jesus introduced him to his Creator, and he was saved only days before he died!

As we contemplate Christmas and the physical visitation of our Creator the Lord Jesus Christ to us here on earth, how will our meeting with Him be? Will we in faith seek for Him as the shepherds did? Will we bow down and worship Him as the wise men did? Will we be intimidated by Him and want to be rid of Him as King Herod did? Or will we, as many do, just ignore Him and pretend He doesn't exist? Our response to Him will have eternal consequences for each one of us.

God's Holy Scriptures clearly state: *"Therefore God has highly exalted Him and bestowed on Him the name that is above every name, so that at the name of Jesus every knee should bow, in heaven and on earth and under the earth, and every tongue confess that Jesus Christ is Lord, to the glory of God the Father." (Philippians 2:9–11, ESV).*

Ultimately everyone will bow before Him. Some now willingly bow in sincere worship, while others will bow out of fear and dread of their coming judgement. What will you do with Jesus?

"Indeed, the 'right time' is now. Today is the day of salvation." (2 Corinthians 6:2).

NOVEMBER 27

Gift of Peace

I'm sure you've experienced the pressure that builds up around this time of year. Pressure to find the right gift for the ones we love. Pressure to get the decorations up. Pressure to have all the fixings for the Christmas meal. Pressure on the pocketbook! If we're honest, we'll have to admit that these pressures exist within our hearts and lives at any time of year!

Jesus was born into a world of tension and pressure. Pressure to find a safe place for Him to be born. Pressure from evil actors such as King Herod. Pressure to make ends meet! Yet He was able to sleep in the manger among the animals (Luke 2:7). As a young boy, He wasn't concerned about His return home when He sought the wisdom of the elders in the temple (Luke 2:41–52). Another time, He slept in the boat when the waves threatened to capsize it (Mark 4:38). The Source of His peace and rest was evident as He vocalized His last words as He hung dying on the cross: *"Father, into your hands I commit my spirit." (Luke 23:46, NIV).*

Stress, anxiety, and hypertension are very prevalent today. They're often caused by the constant tensions of life. Holy Scripture encourages us to *"Cast all your anxiety on Him because He cares for you." (1 Peter 5:7, NIV).*

Have the pressures of life affected your spiritual and physical health? God has a special gift for each one who calls out to Him and desires to follow Him. May we receive this special gift that Jesus promised: *"I am leaving you with a gift—peace of mind and heart. And the peace I give is a gift the world cannot give. So don't be troubled or afraid." (John 14:27).*

The Light

Waking up in the middle of the night, I noticed something was different. It was completely dark—no yard light, no night light, not even any moonlight, as dark clouds had covered the night sky. The power was out. I got up, bumping into the furniture and other objects in the room as I looked for a flashlight. After wandering for some time, to my relief I eventually found it and turned it on. The path before me was illuminated, and I could find my way around again.

As we look at what's happening in the world, in our communities, and even in our own lives, we can see a lot of stumbling in spiritual darkness. The nations talk of peace, yet war abounds. The politicians try to stop the drug problem, yet record numbers of people continue to die of overdoses. Discord in homes spills out onto the front page of the newspapers. Some in personal despair take their own life. Where is the light? Is there some light to give us direction?

God clearly expresses to us in His Word, the Bible, that we have lost our connection with our Maker and are trying to stumble along on our own dark path without His guiding light (John 3:19–20; Psalm 119:176). *"The way of the wicked is like deep darkness; they do not know over what they stumble." (Proverbs 4:19, ESV).*

Yet He has given us clear direction as to how we should live: *" Your word is a lamp to my feet and a light to my path." (Psalm 119:105, ESV).* And He promises to empower us to live in the light as we surrender to Him. Jesus said, *"I am the light of the world. Whoever follows me will not walk in darkness, but will have the light of life." (John 8:12, ESV).*

Will we choose to surrender to Him and walk in the light of His Word, or will we continue to stumble around in darkness?

NOVEMBER 29

Immaculate Conception

As Christmas approaches and businesses gear up for increased sales, we are easily side-tracked by Santas, reindeer, gifts, and Christmas trees all around us, whether it be walking down the street or on the internet. Though there are many distractions, Christmas should be a time when we consider the virgin birth of Jesus Christ into the human race desperately in need of a Saviour.

The Bible reveals the sinless conception of Jesus, by the Holy Spirit, through the virgin Mary, coming into the world to redeem sinful mankind. But somehow the immaculate conception of Mary evolved over the centuries and was officially proclaimed by the Roman Catholic church in 1554, when Pope Pius declared that it was Mary who had been conceived and born sinless. In this way, they say, Mary, the mother of God, could bear the sinless Christ into the world. This has become part of the faith of many in the Roman Catholic church. Some even consider Mary, among other things, a co-redemptrix, a dispenser of God's grace, a sinless person, as she virtually takes the place of Jesus, the only true Saviour of humanity.

No matter how many "biblical gymnastics" are used, the Bible clearly does not teach such things about Mary. In fact, she recognized her own need of a Saviour when she said, *"My soul magnifies the Lord, and my spirit rejoices in God my Savior." (Luke 1:46–47, ESV).* The only true immaculate conception is when Jesus Christ, conceived of the Holy Spirit and born of the virgin Mary, took on human form and came into the world to save sinful humanity, including Mary herself.

Any religious beliefs or Christmas trappings that distract us from Jesus Christ and His conception, life, death, and resurrection are a serious affront to His finished work on the cross.

"This is good, and it is pleasing in the sight of God our Savior, who desires all people to be saved and to come to the knowledge of the truth. For there is one God, and there is one mediator between God and men, the man Christ Jesus." (1 Timothy 2:3–5, ESV).

He Became Poor

The Motilone-Bari people knew they had wandered from their Creator but couldn't find their way back to Him. As a young man of nineteen years old, Bruce Olsen left the comforts of his home in the US to live among the militant Motilone-Bari. At first, he suffered rejection from them and others, but through an obedient walk with God, he was able to love those who persecuted him and to be an example to them of a true believer. In time, many Motilone-Bari people, as well as others, even communist guerillas, came to faith in the Lord Jesus Christ. Their lives were changed forever. They were transformed to be the people their Creator intended them to be. This would be done as someone, in this case Bruchko (the name the Motilone-Bari people called him), fully surrendered and gave up his earthly comforts so he could bring God's message of hope to the Motilone-Bari people in their own cultural setting. Why would he do such a thing? Bruchko was compelled to bring the Good News to the Motilone-Bari people by following in the steps of his Lord.

Some two thousand years ago, Jesus the Creator, eternally existing as God from eternity past, left His high place in heaven to become a human baby. Conceived through the power of the Holy Spirit and through birth by the virgin Mary, He became part of the human race. Born in a manger, He became one of us so that He could show us our desperate situation and suffer the ultimate price of death on a cruel cross to pay for the sins of those who would believe in Him. God's Word, speaking of Jesus, says: *"Though he was God, he did not think of equality with God as something to cling to. Instead, he gave up his divine privileges; he took the humble position of a slave and was born as a human being. When he appeared in human form, he humbled himself in obedience to God and died a criminal's death on a cross." (Philippians 2:6–8).*

Despite all the distractions of the season before us—lights, celebrations, gifts, and even delicious turkey dinners—may we remember that Christmas is really about Jesus and what He has done for us. *"For you know the grace of our Lord Jesus Christ, that though he was rich, yet for your sake he became poor, so that you by his poverty might become rich." (2 Corinthians 8:9, ESV).*

May we put our complete trust in our Creator, Jesus Christ. Just as with the Motilone-Bari people, our eternal destiny rests in Him.

DECEMBER 1

Majesty in the Mundane

Growing up on a small mixed farm there were many chores to do. Feed and milk the cows, clean the barn, get in the hay, water the garden and fruit trees, cut the lawn, get in the fire wood were some of the chores expected of us. These chores, day after day, became very mundane, routine, and uneventful. So I can imagine the shepherds some two thousand years ago, in the fields watching over their flocks at night, just another night waiting for the sun to rise to another day. Then the most unexpected happened! Heaven opened, the glory of God shone around them, and an angel appeared among them announcing: *"Fear not, for behold, I bring you good news of great joy that will be for all the people. For unto you is born this day in the city of David a Savior, who is Christ the Lord. And this will be a sign for you: you will find a baby wrapped in swaddling cloths and lying in a manger." And suddenly there was with the angel a multitude of the heavenly host praising God and saying, "Glory to God in the highest, and on earth peace among those with whom He is pleased!" (Luke 2:10–14, ESV).*

At first the shepherds were terrified, but after seeing the baby Jesus, they were amazed. They told all the people around them all they had seen! *"And the shepherds returned, glorifying and praising God for all they had heard and seen, as it had been told them." (Luke 2:28, ESV).* I am sure their lives were forever changed!

Is life routine and boring? Do you feel lost, without purpose? What's the use? we might think when faced with the day-to-day routines of life. Yet when we put our trust in and receive Jesus the only Saviour, we too are changed, and even the mundane is given purpose! He came so those who trust in Him will never be the same (Luke 19:10; John 10:10)!

"But these are written that you may believe that Jesus is the Messiah, the Son of God, and that by believing you may have life in his name." (John 20:31, NIV).

DECEMBER 2

Default Destiny

Picture a highway with a volcano at its end. It's crowded with people busy listening to their radios, texting and thinking they have a safe destination ahead, while others don't care where they're going, as they're just enjoying the ride. Still others know they are lost and are looking for a way off this six-lane maze! Everyone has been on this highway at some time or another. All who remain on this highway are destined to drive into the volcano. It has become their default destiny—unless they take the only alternate route, which leads away from this inferno to a life of peace and rest! Signs along the way warn of the imminent danger: *"There is a way that appears to be right, but in the end it leads to death." (Proverbs 14:12, NIV)* and *"I tell you, no! But unless you repent, you too will all perish." (Luke 13:3, NIV)*. Some, who have found the off ramp, are pointing to the signs, hoping others will take the only way to safety. Yet most ignore the signs and continue along the highway, oblivious to their end.

This is an illustration of the walk of life. Jesus warned, *"Enter through the narrow gate. For wide is the gate and broad is the road that leads to destruction, and many enter through it. But small is the gate and narrow the road that leads to life, and only a few find it." (Matthew 7:13–14, NIV)*; *"I am the gate; whoever enters through me will be saved. They will come in and go out, and find pasture." (John 10:9, NIV)*.

This is the real meaning of Christmas! Jesus our Creator, Sustainer, and Saviour saw our desperate state and came to seek and to save those who are lost (Luke 19:10). He is our only hope (John 14:6)! Will we heed His words and turn to Him for mercy and grace while there is still time? Or will we merrily continue on the highway to hell?

DECEMBER 3

For the Love

As we honestly contemplate the real reason to celebrate at Christmas, we can't help but think of God's love as expressed in His Word, the Bible: *"For this is how God loved the world: He gave his one and only Son, so that everyone who believes in him will not perish but have eternal life." (John 3:16).* God's love expressed to us is something we should look at in more detail.

In our English language, we mention love in a very broad and general manner, but God's Word, written in the original Greek, is much more specific. For example, today some might say people are making love when they're having sex. This was expressed by the Greek word *eros*, which was a commonly used word in the Greek of biblical times. This is where the English word "erotic" comes from. Another word translated as love in English is *phileo* in Greek, which means friendship or family type of love. BUT the word in the scripture verses mentioned here is *agape*, which is the deep love of God towards the people He created: *"There is no greater love than to lay down one's life for one's friends." (John 15:13, NLT).*

We, out of our sinful nature, can't make this love; we of ourselves can't work up or express this love even to our most loved ones on this earth. Agape love comes from God! This is why Jesus came to earth! He was born to die for us! For the love of humanity, He came to pay the penalty for the sins of all who would believe and receive Him (John 1:12). Jesus the Creator and Sustainer expressing agape love, came to save us, His rebellious people, created in His image! *"This is real love—not that we loved God, but that he loved us and sent his Son as a sacrifice to take away our sins." (1 John 4:10).* This is the real meaning of Christmas; this is true love! This is good news today, tomorrow, next year, and forever!

The Truth Matters

One of the ads in the local newspaper caught my attention.[14] In large letters it read, "Dressing it up does not make it true." Farther down it states that "truth matters." I couldn't agree more!

As we enter the Christmas season, we are inundated with Frosty the Snowman, Santa Claus, bright flashing lights, Christmas trees, tinsel, and glitter. Children are told before they first begin to walk that Santa is coming from the North Pole with his reindeer, Rudolf in the lead, to land on the roof of the house. Santa will slide down the chimney to deliver presents under the Christmas tree! This has become the substance of Christmas for many! All the while many ignore Jesus, the substance of not only Christmas but our very existence.

A journalist by the name of Lee Stroebel lived his life as if Jesus didn't exist, until his wife became a serious believer in Jesus. Because of his strong opposition to faith in the Almighty, he set out to prove that Jesus was a farce. The more he studied the evidence, the more he realized that Jesus had lived, was who He claimed to be, and the record of his life as recorded in the Bible was true. Stroebel honestly sifted through his preconceived notions and the hype of the world around him to become a devoted believer in Jesus as his Creator and Saviour. His fascinating journey to faith is recorded in two of his many books, *The Case for Christ* and *The Case for a Creator*.

Truth does matter, especially when our eternal destiny is at stake! An honest investigation into the claims of Jesus as recorded in the Holy Scriptures will bring eternal rewards and freedom to any honest seeker of the truth!

Jesus said, *"I was born and came into the world to testify to the truth. All who love the truth recognize that what I say is true"* (John 18:37); *"And you will know the truth, and the truth will set you free"* (John 8:32); *"I am the way, the truth, and the life. No one can come to the Father except through me."* (John 14:6).

---

14 Ad by Advertising Standards Council.

DECEMBER 5

Clouds

It was with interest that I read an article featuring Nobel prize winner Dr. John Clauser sharing of the influence of clouds on the climate. He declared that climate change alarmists are ignoring the enormous effects of clouds and falsely demonizing carbon dioxide (plant food) regarding climate change.

As I read this, I thought of the numerous times from the creation account in Genesis through the Psalms and New Testament that clouds are mentioned in God's Word. They're even commanded to praise God together with all creation: *"Praise the Lord from the earth, you great sea creatures and all ocean depths, lightning and hail, snow and clouds, stormy winds that do his bidding." (Psalm 148:7–8, NIV).* We don't have to fear climate change, as God has command of every detail of what happens, whether it be turmoil among the nations, evil plans of men to destroy the earth, or changes in the weather. We have absolutely nothing to fear when we put our trust in Almighty God! He came to earth to become one of us, to die in our place. He rose from the dead and ascended to the right hand of the heavenly Father. He promised He would return!

This is a day that everyone should take very seriously—the day when Jesus the Creator and Sustainer will physically return on the clouds to judge every human being: *"Then will appear the sign of the Son of Man in heaven. And then all the peoples of the earth will mourn when they see the Son of Man coming on the clouds of heaven, with power and great glory." (Matthew 24:30, NIV).*

Just as surely as God's Word is true, this day is coming! Will it be a day we look forward to with joy and anticipation, or will it be a day of dread and fear? My prayer is that many will turn to Him and trust in Him to receive His free gift of salvation!

"At that time they will see the Son of Man coming in a cloud with power and great glory. When these things begin to take place, stand up and lift up your heads, because your redemption is drawing near." (Luke 21:27–28, NIV).

DECEMBER 6

Marginalized

A young, unmarried woman expecting a child while only engaged; lowly shepherds, probably not educated, smelly from the nature of their work, not welcome in the homes of the elite; domestic animals, sheep, and a feeding trough—these are all images described in God's Holy Word as the setting the Creator chose to make His dwelling among men. It was not to the religious leaders in their places of worship. It was not to the governing authorities in their palaces and seats of human power. It was not to the rich in their immaculate houses. It was to those on the outer fringes of society that the Creator chose to make His physical entrance into His rebellious creation.

Not only did He appear among the marginalized, not only did He reach out to outcasts and sinners (Matthew 9:10–14), but He became one of the marginalized! *"Though he was God, he did not think of equality with God as something to cling to. Instead, he gave up his divine privileges; he took the humble position of a slave and was born as a human being. When he appeared in human form, he humbled himself in obedience to God and died a criminal's death on a cross." (Philippians 2:2–8).*

His human genealogy includes women who were marginalized due to their former sinful lifestyles (Matthew 1:1–16). This is not what we would expect. Usually when one wants to make a grand entry, one would give his best resume, a perfect report, but Jesus did not—even though He was sinless and His credentials were impeccable! Why would He choose such a humble estate? The answer again lies in the Holy Scriptures. Jesus said, *"Healthy people don't need a doctor—sick people do."* Then he added, *"Now go and learn the meaning of this Scripture: 'I want you to show mercy, not offer sacrifices.' For I have come to call not those who think they are righteous, but those who know they are sinners." (Matthew 9:12–13).*

Are you feeling marginalized, maybe too sinful to mix with those who seem so rich, religious, or righteous? Do you desire to be forgiven and made right with God? Does your heart yearn for a personal relationship with the Almighty God? Then Jesus came for you. He came for me! This is the true good news that we can celebrate at Christmas! With His arms wide open, He is ready to welcome into His kingdom anyone who in faith will call out to Him (Romans 10:11–13)!

DECEMBER 7

Miraculous Visitation

An avowed atheist boldly proclaimed to me that he had come to believe there was no God before he believed there was no Santa Claus. Beliefs like this often begin at childhood, as people teach their children that Santa is real while in the same breath telling them that there is no God. When we think this way, we've brought in the magical but have missed the miraculous!

Two thousand years ago, an amazing miraculous event happened when the Creator of all things made His visitation to earth in the person of Jesus Christ! As prophesied by the prophets of God, hundreds and even thousands of years ago, God entered the human race by causing Mary, a virgin, to conceive by the power of His Holy Spirit! The Creator of everything humbled Himself, took on human form—human DNA—and was born in an animal shelter! This event was announced by angels. He was given gifts and worshipped by wise men of the day. Though He was hunted by jealous kings and both admired and scorned by religious leaders, He grew up and lived a humble, sinless life. He withstood the temptations of Satan, spoke with authority, and demonstrated His power over nature, disease, demons, and death itself!

Though we don't know the exact day of His birth, it is celebrated by many of His followers on Christmas Day. Though some have made the day and the gifts more important than the person, others are distracted by dead saints, snowmen, and reindeer. Still others claim to be atheists, but the fact of His miraculous visitation still remains! The question at Christmas, or any day of the year for that matter, is "What will we do with this man Jesus who came to rescue us?"

The answer for us today is the same as it was many years ago for a trembling, desperate Philippian jailer: *"Believe in the Lord Jesus, and you will be saved ..." (Acts 16:31, NIV).*

DECEMBER 8

Play the Odds or Trust God?

Many years ago, before ultrasound imaging was in use, a friend of mine predicted that his wife, who was already pregnant at the time, was going to have a baby boy. The odds were 50-50 that this would happen, but it didn't, and they had a wonderful healthy baby girl! The part of this story that was not so wonderful is that he had said God had told him it would be a boy. It was obvious he had not heard from God, because God does not lie (Psalm 89:35; Titus 1:2).

One of the factors that sets God's Word, the Bible, far apart from any other book is that much of the Bible was written as prophetic predictions made through and recorded by God's prophets. Many of these prophecies were recorded hundreds, even thousands of years before they were fulfilled (2 Peter 1:20–21; Daniel 12:9).

As we approach the Christmas season, we're reminded of many prophecies that predicted the coming of Jesus Christ the Redeemer, the One who would be God incarnate in a man, the One who would buy us back from sin and judgement. Just one of these numerous prophecies is found in the Old Testament book of Isaiah: *"Therefore the Lord himself will give you a sign. Behold, the virgin shall conceive and bear a son, and shall call his name Immanuel." (Isaiah 7:14, ESV)*.

What are the odds of this happening? "Come on," you might say, "a virgin giving birth? The odds are impossible." Yet it happened some seven hundred years later.

"And Mary said to the angel, "How will this be, since I am a virgin?" And the angel answered her, "The Holy Spirit will come upon you, and the power of the Most High will overshadow you; therefore the child to be born will be called holy—the Son of God." (Luke 1:34–35).

Later when the angels appeared to the shepherds, it's recorded, *"And the angel said to them, 'Fear not, for behold, I bring you good news of great joy that will be for all the people. For unto you is born this day in the city of David a Savior, who is Christ the Lord.'" (Luke 2:10–11, ESV)*.

What will we do? Will we play the odds and continue to trust in our own limited and inaccurate understanding, or will we turn our eyes upon Jesus and trust in our Creator God, who knows the beginning from the end?

He has given us His Word; may we with the angels proclaim, *"For nothing will be impossible with God." (Luke 1:37, ESV)*.

DECEMBER 9

Glitz or Grief?

If you were given a choice of a million dollars in the bank or a million dollars of debt, which would you choose? How about an old worn-out Kia or a shiny new hybrid Cadillac? Or would you rather have a brand-new home bought and paid for or and old dilapidated barn? Most of us would choose the more valuable option. Yet Jesus chose to take the position of sorrow and grief over the glitz of the world. He could have demanded the respect and worship of His rebellious creation, yet He took the path of a humble servant, ready to take on Himself the sins of those who sinned against Him! The Creator of the universe becoming a fragile baby, willing to humble Himself before the very ones who hate Him, goes contrary to every part of the fallen human psyche. What a stark difference in His attitude from that of us self-oriented human beings!

The prophecy of His coming, His work, and His attitude as recorded in the Holy Scriptures hundreds of years before His arrival expresses it so well!

"He was despised and rejected by men, a man of sorrows and acquainted with grief; and as one from whom men hide their faces He was despised, and we esteemed Him not. Surely He has borne our griefs and carried our sorrows; yet we esteemed Him stricken, smitten by God, and afflicted. But He was pierced for our transgressions; He was crushed for our iniquities; upon Him was the chastisement that brought us peace, and with His wounds we are healed. All we like sheep have gone astray; we have turned—every one—to his own way; and the Lord has laid on Him the iniquity of us all." (Isaiah 53:3–6, ESV).

We would be wise to take heed and humble ourselves in surrender to Him, to receive His mercy and grace before it's too late when He comes to judge every human heart.

DECEMBER 10

A Sword

As we consider the birth of Jesus and the prophecy that the elderly Simeon spoke over Mary, the mother of Jesus, we hear *"... and a sword will pierce through your own soul also ..." (Luke 2:35, ESV)*. We ponder what this sword might be. Looking back on it, we can see it as a prediction of the pain in her heart as the soldiers beat her firstborn, nailed Him to the cross, and ultimately pierced His side with a spear to ensure that the ultimate goal of their evil deed was achieved. The pain of seeing Him who did no wrong be so cruelly put to death. The pain of seeing the rejection and persecution of the One who claimed to be God in human flesh! How could this be? Why had they not recognized Him as the only One who could save them from their sins? Why? Oh, the pain!

Today the followers of Jesus know that His death has brought us forgiveness of sins, a purposeful life, power to endure, and a promise of eternal life in the future! Yet the painful assault against the truth still goes on, as the Holy Scriptures clearly say, *"Indeed, all who desire to live a godly life in Christ Jesus will be persecuted." (2 Timothy 3:12, ESV)*.

The wonderful part of all this is that this pain of the heart, this persecution, this assault on truth is only short-lived! Jesus did not remain in the tomb; He rose from the dead and ascended to intercede for us at the right hand of Father God!

If we're going through a particularly painful time, we can be assured that Jesus is aware and is ruling from on high! And we can be sure that soon He will take us to be with Him for all eternity, where the pain of the sword will be put away forever! *"He will wipe away every tear from their eyes, and death shall be no more, neither shall there be mourning, nor crying, nor pain anymore, for the former things have passed away." (Revelation 21:4, ESV)*.

DECEMBER 11

Safest Place

This Christmas, hopefully we will cut through the obvious distractions and seriously consider the historical account of the incarnation of Jesus Christ, the very Word of God, into the human race. As we consider this, we're confronted with an amazing truth: *"He was in the world, and the world was made through Him, yet the world did not know Him. He came to his own, and his own people did not receive Him" (John 1:10–11, ESV).* The rejection of His creation was almost immediate! The jealous, power-hungry King Herod was determined to annihilate anyone who might threaten his perceived position of power! Thus, he hunted down the infant Jesus and caused a wholesale killing of young children in his pursuit of Him. Joseph was warned in a dream to flee to Egypt for a time to escape this horrendous slaughter of the innocents.

When Jesus began His ministry, after He read the prophecy of His mission on earth from God's Holy Word, those who heard Him attempted to throw Him off a cliff (Luke 4:14–30)! Numerous times throughout His ministry, His very life was threatened by those who rejected Him (John 5:18, 8:59; 10:31, 11:53, to name a few). Yet Jesus escaped these many threats until the time had come for Him to die on a cruel Roman cross to make the payment for the sins of each and every one of those who would repent and put their trust in Him!

How could Jesus have escaped all these threats? One reason is that Jesus was always in the very centre of His Sovereign Father's will! This is demonstrated by His words just before He went to the cross: *"… yet not my will, but yours be done." (Luke 22:42b, NIV).*

How should this affect our lives in our walk with God? Our desire when we follow Him should always be "Your will, Oh God, be done, not mine." The safest place is always the very centre of God's will! Thus, no matter what should come against us, we are still safely in the care of our heavenly Father!

DECEMBER 12

Best Gift Ever

With most people in the West celebrating Christmas in one way or another, wondering what's in the wrapped gift under the tree, Canadians Michael Spavor and Michael Kovrig have little such hope. Having been detained in 2018 on what appear to be very spurious charges, their incarceration in crude prison cells in Communist China could continue for years to come. It goes without saying that news of their release would be more important to them and their families than any gift awaiting them under the Christmas tree here at home!

As we approach the Christmas season, so easily preoccupied by gifts, trees, wrappings, and feasts, are we aware of the greatest gift that could ever have been given to humanity? The Creator of everything, including you and me, became a part of broken humanity. In humility He arrived as a baby, born in a stable, with a mission to die thirty-three years later to sacrificially take the death penalty for us rebellious and sinful people. This is the greatest gift we could ever receive! Forgiveness and reconciliation with God Almighty at no cost to us and all the cost to Him! Eternal life with Him forever, no condemnation, and an open and living relationship with the King of kings! The greatest One became the least so that we, the least, could become children of the Most-High God! He proved He had authority over life and death by rising from the dead! Death could not keep Him! This the greatest gift of all, everlasting life, is there for all who will receive. Or will we leave it unopened for all eternity? *"It was recorded for our benefit, too, assuring us that God will also count us as righteous if we believe in Him, the one who raised Jesus our Lord from the dead. He was handed over to die because of our sins, and He was raised to life to make us right with God." (Romans 4:23–24).*

Note: The two Michaels have since been released and now can celebrate Christmas with their families!

DECEMBER 13

Immanuel

A fellow related to me an experience that convinced him of the existence of God. He said he was hitchhiking on a very cold winter night. Someone had given him a ride to a remote intersection on Hwy 16. Standing there late at night, in the extreme cold and wind, he realized he needed to catch a ride soon. But no cars came by as he felt the cold penetrate his clothes and numbness begin to set in. He wished someone would come by—anyone—but none did, as the cold kept incessantly attacking his shivering body. He decided to hide from the wind in a low spot on the snowbank.

As he lay there, he felt totally alone and thought this would be his demise—freezing to death beside the highway. Though not a believer in God, he thought of calling out to Him as he recognized his desperate situation. He called out, asking God for mercy and pleading for Him to spare his life. Instantly he felt a warmth come over him and penetrate to his innermost being! God answered him! God was near! God knew his dilemma and spared his life! Basking in the warmth, peace, and presence of God, he fell asleep and later awoke to a car stopping to pick him up!

One of the names for Jesus is Immanuel, which means "God with us." King David realized God was with him throughout his life, even before his birth or when he was trying to hide from Him (read about it in Psalm 139)! Not only is He always present in Spirit, but He showed His love for humankind by becoming one of us! This is what we celebrate at Christmas! God sent His only begotten Son to save us from our own demise! *"Look! The virgin will conceive a child! She will give birth to a son, and they will call Him Immanuel, which means 'God is with us.'" (Matthew 1:23).*

Will we call out to Him to save us?

DECEMBER 14

No Ordinary Baby

When the angel Gabriel came to the virgin Mary and said, *"The Holy Spirit will come upon you, and the power of the Most High will overshadow you. So the baby to be born will be holy, and He will be called the Son of God." (Luke 1:35)*, Mary knew she would give birth to the Son of God!

When the angel came to Joseph in a dream and told him that Mary, though expecting a child, was a virgin and would give birth to a son conceived by the Holy Spirit, and that His name was to be Jesus, both the angel and Joseph knew He was superior to any other baby!

When the shepherds heard the announcement that Jesus was born and went to see Him in the manger, they knew this baby was very special!

When the wise men came from distant lands to give gifts to the baby Jesus and to worship Him, they knew He was born to be a King.

When some thirty-three years later in Jerusalem, as they watched Him die a criminal's death on the cross for the sins of all who would trust Him, the soldiers proclaimed, *"This man was truly the Son of God!" (Matthew 27:54)*.

Now as we are given these eyewitness accounts of this little baby as recorded in God's Holy Scriptures, what will we do with Him? Will we leave Him in the manger scene in a store window? Will we allow the distractions of the world to drown out the call of His Holy Spirit for us to trust and worship Him above all else? Or will we receive Him as our only Saviour and hope in this messed up world?

"For a child is born to us, a son is given to us. The government will rest on his shoulders. And he will be called: Wonderful Counselor, Mighty God, Everlasting Father, Prince of Peace. His government and its peace will never end." (Isaiah 9:6–7).

The Spirit of Christ

"Wishing you the blessings of the season."

"Have a wonderful holiday season."

"May the spirit of Christmas be with you throughout the holiday season."

"Merry Christmas and a Happy New Year!"

"Wishing you a wonderful holiday season and a world of peace and beauty."

These are all Christmas sayings and comments we've heard or spoken. I have noticed that many people are more positive and outgoing during this time of the year. Why is this? Maybe it's the beautiful presents that are coming, or maybe it's the music of peace and love. There's a definite general change in attitude this time of year. But what about the rest of the year? How will we feel when the bills come in at the end of January?

The apostle Paul wrote: "*So if there is any encouragement in Christ, any comfort from love, any participation in the Spirit, any affection and sympathy, complete my joy by being of the same mind, having the same love, being in full accord and of one mind. Do nothing from selfish ambition or conceit, but in humility count others more significant than yourselves. Let each of you look not only to his own interests, but also to the interests of others. Have this mind among yourselves, which is yours in Christ Jesus, who, though he was in the form of God, did not count equality with God a thing to be grasped, but emptied himself, by taking the form of a servant, being born in the likeness of men. And being found in human form, he humbled himself by becoming obedient to the point of death, even death on a cross ... for it is God who works in you, both to will and to work for his good pleasure.*" (Philippians 2:1–8, 13, ESV).

The "spirit of Christmas" may only last for a few days or weeks, but the Holy Spirit, the Spirit of Christ that lives in every true Christian, is with us throughout every day of the year.

My prayer is that our hearts will be filled with faith in Jesus Christ, that the Spirit of Christ will lead us into a life filled with love, joy, and peace throughout the coming year and for all eternity.

"*No eye has seen, no ear has heard, and no mind has imagined what God has prepared for those who love him.*" (1 Corinthians 2:9).

DECEMBER 16

Jesus, Santa, and Satan

Shifting around a few letters in a word can sometimes change the meaning significantly! This happened with the folks at the *Comox Valley Record* newspaper when they were advertising the Comox Valley Christmas Parade and a special time when folks could get their pictures taken with Satan! Placing the "n" at the end rather than in the middle got a few Santa lovers' feathers ruffled.

Some remarked that the religious folks would certainly be offended by this. But why would Jesus lovers be offended? What is the actual offense? The utmost offence is against Jesus Christ, whose arrival on earth is often shunned and forgotten on the knee of Santa at the bidding of Satan, who will use any distraction to get our eyes off of the truth.

Some two thousand years ago, the Creator of the universe humbled Himself to become one of His creation. He was born as a little baby in a manger in Bethlehem to live a sinless life among those who had rebelled against Him. He came to die on a cruel Roman cross to make the ultimate payment for the sins of all rebels who would call on Him and confess His name! Yet He is shunned and not even mentioned by many when we gather to celebrate His birthday! This Christmas, may we not be distracted and robbed of the truth by Satan's shifty lies, but let us focus on the One who has come to save us from our sins and give us a purposeful and meaningful life!

Jesus said: *"Yes, I am the gate. Those who come in through me will be saved. They will come and go freely and will find good pastures. The thief's purpose is to steal and kill and destroy. My purpose is to give them a rich and satisfying life." (John 10:10).*

DECEMBER 17

Don't Be Afraid!

He had pulled me over; I had definitely been speeding, and now I had to answer. My hands shook as I looked through the glove compartment for the car registration. I could hear my heart pounding in my ears as he asked, "Do you know how fast you were going?" A few minutes before that, I had been cruising along in my own little the world, yet suddenly, out of nowhere, reality hit. I was confronted with my transgressions, fear, and a greater authority than myself.

Can you imagine the shepherds in their fields, sitting around their campfires after a hard day's work? Suddenly heaven opened up. It became brighter than daylight as the radiance of God's glory shone upon them. Their daily routine was interrupted by the authority of heaven. They were confronted with their frailty, their helplessness, their sins; the awesomeness of the Almighty God had come through to them, piercing the darkness around them. What could they do? Where could they go? Astonished, they looked in amazement and fear. But the angel had a message from God for them. *"Don't be afraid."* This same message was given only a few months previously to the priest Zechariah (Luke 1:13), to Joseph (Matthew 1:28), and to Mary (Luke 1:30) as they were also visited by an angel bringing good news from the very throne of God.

Has reality hit us in some way today? What fears do we face? Do we fear not measuring up? Do we fear some impossible events that are facing us today? Do we fear persecution, punishment, or judgement? Do we fear sickness, poverty, pain, or death? The message that was given to those long ago is the same message God has for us today: *"Fear not, for behold, I bring you good news of great joy that will be for all the people. For unto you is born this day in the city of David a Savior, who is Christ the Lord." (Luke 2:10–11, ESV).*

In Jesus' own words: *The Spirit of the Lord is upon me, because he has anointed me to proclaim good news to the poor. He has sent me to proclaim liberty to the captives and recovering of sight to the blind, to set at liberty those who are oppressed, to proclaim the year of the Lord's favor." (Luke 4:18–19, ESV).*

If we put our trust in Him today, do we have any reason to fear?

DECEMBER 18

Neglected Baby

I t's so grievous when we hear about a baby found in a dumpster or in a washroom, left there neglected, with little hope for the future. The traumatized mother not able to care for the infant, lost, not knowing what to do—not being able to help the beautiful little one she has birthed to grow up to be the person he or she was meant to be, whether a father, a mother, a skilled labourer, or a doctor!

As we think back two thousand years or so, we're reminded of baby Jesus, loved by His parents but neglected by many. The innkeeper sent Mary to the stable to give Him birth. Herod hunted Him down. Some called Him an imposter, and ultimately, He was crucified by the very ones whom He'd created. No one defended Him. He was left to die on a cruel Roman cross, alone. He did this all so there would be the hope of salvation for all who would believe Him, receive Him, and follow Him!

This is the real message of Christmas, the most important message of all history! This baby Jesus had a purpose. He was on a mission. Though neglected by humankind, He was sent by Father God to redeem those who were lost and floundering without hope, dying, unable to save themselves!

Lord Jesus, Son of Almighty God, may we not neglect you, our only hope! Have your way with us. We bow down and worship You!

"So we must listen very carefully to the truth we have heard ... So what makes us think we can escape if we ignore this great salvation? ... the Son also became flesh and blood ... and only by dying could he break the power of the devil, who had the power of death. Only in this way could he set free all who have lived their lives as slaves to the fear of dying." (Hebrews 2:1, 3, 14–15).

DECEMBER 19

The Alternative

Joseph and Mary needed a place to stay. She was almost due and in need of a place to give birth to her firstborn son. They knocked on the door of the inn, but the innkeeper turned them away and sent them to the stable, where she bore Jesus into the very creation He had made.

Just think of what a blessing the innkeeper missed in sending this obviously needy couple away. Was there not a more suitable place in the whole town of Bethlehem to give birth to a child? Could he not have put them up in his own place? Rather than surrender some of his own turf, he decided to take control and send them away.

Little did he know that the King of kings was about to be born. He had the opportunity to either let Him be born inside or to send Him out with the animals. Maybe he didn't even know Mary was pregnant, but it is obvious he made a decision to leave Joseph and Mary outside. He was too busy managing the inn to notice the heavenly plan of God that was unfolding before him.

When considering this, the lack of compassion of the innkeeper seems obvious to us, but the would we have done any different? Maybe the question should be: Do we do any different?

Today, Jesus wants access to our very lives. He wants to come into every area of our life, our social life, our marriage, our health, our thoughts, and yes, even our finances. We sometimes think we can retain control of the situation by handling the situation in our own way, but actually the opposite happens. We miss the blessing of the Presence of God and are left with this heavy burden that we weren't meant to bear. We think we must carry it all by ourselves (Matthew 11:28).

When we surrender to the will of God and let Him in, His peace will enter with Him, and there will be no need for anxiety and fear because we know everything is in His capable hands.

When Jesus comes knocking on our heart's door, will we let Him in? The only other alternative is to leave Him outside.

Jesus said, *"Behold, I stand at the door and knock. If anyone hears my voice and opens the door, I will come in to him and eat with him, and he with me." (Revelation 3:20, ESV).*

The Only Begotten Son of God

I was present when each of our children were born. I was utterly amazed that here in my arms was a child I had conceived. This little human being was totally dependent upon my wife and I for even the basics of life. How could this be? Such an honour that I did not deserve, such responsibility I thought, with wonder and amazement. Even though they're my children, they are just as human as I, fully human, not a speck less than I, begotten of me.

Jesus, the eternal Son of God, begotten of God the Father, conceived of the Holy Spirit, became a human being and dwelt among us (Matthew 1:20; John 1:14, 3:16). Jesus is begotten of God. He is God, just as His Father is God. One of his names was Immanuel, which means "God with us" (Matthew 1:23). Some say He was an angel; others say He was just a good man, but God's Word, the Bible, says He was God in human flesh. That's why He had the power to forgive sins. That's why the wise men worshipped Him. That's why Thomas proclaimed to Him *"My Lord and my God!" (John 20:28, ESV)* when he realized Jesus had indeed risen from the dead. That's why the armies of angels rejoiced: *"Glory to God in the highest, and on earth peace among those with whom He is pleased!" (Luke 2:14, ESV).* That's why the wise men bowed down and worshipped Him and gave Him gifts (Matthew 2:11). That's why the apostle John proclaimed of Him, *"In the beginning was the Word, and the Word was with God, and the Word was God." (John 1:1, ESV).* That's why the apostle Paul wrote, *"For in Hm all the fullness of God was pleased to dwell." (Colossians 1:19, ESV).*

May we, together with those of faith from ancient times, also bow down and worship this one and only begotten Son of God with all of our being. Not only during this time of year, but for as long as we are here on this earth and for all eternity!

"For to us a child is born, to us a son is given; and the government shall be upon His shoulder, and His name shall be called Wonderful Counselor, Mighty God, Everlasting Father, Prince of Peace. Of the increase of His government and of peace there will be no end." (Isaiah 9:6–7, ESV).

DECEMBER 21

Celebrate What?

Christmas is almost upon us. It has become a time of great celebration in the Western world. We in the north have the awesome privilege of having a white Christmas with a dreamlike layer of snow on the ground on most Christmas mornings. Leading up to Christmas Day, we see signs in the store windows: Happy Holidays! Season's Greetings! May the Magic of Christmas Be Yours! Sometimes we see a sign that says "Jesus is the Reason for the Season." As we stop and think of it, this is exactly what the Bible tells us. Jesus is the reason for every season. Jesus is the reason we are here. Jesus is the reason for me. Jesus is the reason for the universe. Jesus is the Creator. If He didn't exist, neither would we (John 1:1–5).

Jesus is not only the Creator; He is also God in human flesh. He came for the specific purpose of dying on a wooden cross for the sins of all those who would receive Him (John 1:12; 2 Corinthians 5:15). This is really something to celebrate! All my sins gone! I now can live a life in intimate relationship with the Almighty God. As we contemplate the wonder of the Creator being formed as a child in the womb of the virgin Mary, being born into the human race and becoming one of His creation and ultimately purchasing us back from the pits of hell, we celebrate Jesus, who is called Immanuel (which means God with us)!

The greatest tragedy is to miss the meaning of Jesus Christ's visit to this earth by being distracted by all the trappings of the Christmas season: Santa, Frosty, the gifts, the shopping, the Christmas trees, the turkey dinner, the worries of life. We can miss the real reason why Jesus came, and thus miss Jesus too.

Jesus *"came to seek and to save those who are lost" (Luke 19:10)*. He came to call those who know they are sinners and to save all who will turn to Him and to give us life everlasting (Matthew 9:13).

Do you want something to celebrate not only at Christmas but every day of the rest of your life? Surrender to Jesus, give all your sins, worries, and cares, your very life to Him, and He will set you free to celebrate as you never have before!

"And this is what God has testified; He has given us eternal life, and this life is in his Son. Whoever has the Son has life; whoever does not have the Son does not have life." (1 John 5:11–12).

DECEMBER 22

Little Baby, Big Names

Our First Nations people have a very sophisticated order of leadership among their hereditary chiefs. The youth are encouraged to become involved in the chief system from a very young age, and after gaining knowledge and experience, they might receive a hereditary chief name. Each name has responsibilities and authority attached to it, some to a lesser degree and others more so. Sometimes the chiefs with more responsibility are said to have a big name, others are called wing chiefs, and so on. Before receiving their name, they must put up a potlach in which they produce a large amount of goods and money, after which the existing chiefs, through a detailed ceremony, confer the name upon this person.

We are reminded in God's holy Word, the Bible, especially during the Christmas season, that Jesus was given the names Jesus (Yahweh, the LORD saves) and Immanuel (God with us) by an angel before his birth (Matthew 1:23; Luke 1:31). The coming of Jesus was prophesied through many prophets hundreds, even thousands, of years before He was born to the virgin Mary: *"For a child is born to us, a son is given to us. The government will rest on his shoulders. And he will be called: Wonderful Counselor, Mighty God, Everlasting Father, Prince of Peace." (Isaiah 9:6)*.

The apostles declared, *"There is salvation in no one else! God has given no other name under heaven by which we must be saved." (Acts 4:12)*; *"... that at the name of Jesus every knee should bow, in heaven and on earth and under the earth, and every tongue declare that Jesus Christ is Lord, to the glory of God the Father." (Philippians 2:10–11)*.

How can this all be, a little baby being given the highest names, the very names of God? This is because Jesus is God our Creator, forever pre-existing, who gives every person our life, our breath, our very existence! He spoke everything into existence, and He holds everything together by His mighty power (John 1:1; Colossians 1:17)!

Though we are to respect human authority over us, only God is to be worshipped! The wise men bowed down and worshiped him (Matthew 2:11), even as a baby. How about us, young and old? Will we surrender to Jesus—Immanuel—God with us, and receive Him as our only hope?

"And they fell before the throne with their faces to the ground and worshiped God." (Revelation 7:10).

DECEMBER 23

Born a King

Isn't it interesting that Jesus was born a king. We read in the Gospel of Matthew that the wise men announced to King Herod that a king was born in Bethlehem. Hosts of angels announced His birth, and shepherds went to see Him in the stable (Luke 2:8–20). When the shepherds and wise men saw Him, they bowed down and worshipped Him (Matthew 2:11).

All this celebration happened on earth and also in heaven, because Jesus was the eternal Son of God from eternity past and came into this world as a human being through birth of the virgin, Mary. God's prophets had foretold this event some seven hundred years previously. He came to be a part of His creation that had rebelled against Him so that there would be hope for those who had no hope.

In the book of Revelation, Jesus is called the King of Kings, and the Lord of Lords. In the Gospel of John, He is proclaimed as being God in human flesh and Creator of everything that has been made.

Today God is calling on all people great and small to worship him. We can either bow our knee now in worship and surrender to Him, or we will be compelled to bow the knee at the judgement.

What will we do with this King of kings named Jesus Christ? Let us be wise as the wise men were to bow down in worship.

"Though he was God, he did not think equality with God as something to cling to ... and was born as a human being ... that at the name of Jesus every knee should bow in heaven and on earth and under the earth, and every tongue confess that Jesus Christ is Lord, to the glory of God the Father." (Philippians 2:6, 7b, 10–11).

Will a Manger Do?

I remember when we had the school play, when we re-enacted the coming of the Saviour to this earth. Mary, Joseph, the shepherds, the wise men, and at the centre, baby Jesus in a manger. A manger, a trough for animal feed, in a barn; cows, sheep, goats, and other animals were kept there. This was no place for a baby to be born, let alone a king. Why would the shepherds find Jesus lying in a manger? Yes, there was no room for him in the inn, that is the immediate explanation, but I believe the real explanation is that Jesus, the King of the universe, had the heart of a servant. He came to serve rather than to be served.

'*Though he was God, he did not think of equality with God as something to cling to. Instead, he gave up his divine privileges; he took the humble position as a slave and was born as a human being. When he appeared in human form, he humbled himself in obedience to God and died a criminal's death on a cross." (Philippians 2:6–8).*

When I think of this, it is astounding. This is no play. This is for real! The God of creation, the Author of life, entering this broken world as a little baby, born in a barn, as a servant, living most of His earthly life as a son of a humble carpenter? How can this be? Other world leaders, such as Alexander the Great, Stalin, Hitler, Pol Pot, Mao Tse Tung, ruled as dictators over the people and forced them under their rule. In His own words, Jesus said: *"You know the rulers in this world lord it over their people, and officials flaunt their authority over those under them. But among you it will be different. Whoever wants to be a leader among you must be your servant and whoever wants to be first among you must be become your slave. For even the Son of Man came not be served but to serve others and to give up his life as a ransom for many." (Matthew 20:25–28).*

What is even more astounding is that He is calling those who want to follow Him to be servants, just as He was. How is this possible? I was first in line. Don't I have my rights? I deserve what everyone else is getting! I deserve the best. What? No room in the inn for me?

If we want to be followers of Jesus, we must turn away (repent) from this attitude of privilege and humble ourselves so we too can have the heart of Christ. *"So humble yourselves under the mighty power of God, and at the right time he will lift you up in honor. Give all your worries and cares to God, for he cares about you." (1 Peter 5:6–7).*

If a manger was good enough for the One who made us, it should also be good enough for me.

Room for Jesus

As we consider the Christmas story, we read that Mary *"laid him in a manger, because there was no lodging available for them." (Luke 2:7)*. We often dwell on the obvious conclusion that Jesus was not born in the inn, which would seem the minimal requirement of a place for a woman to give birth. He was rejected, and nobody gave Him any room there.

Then the question comes to mind: When rejected at the inn, where did the Creator of the universe go to be born into the human race? Being the Son of the Living God, you'd think that He would have some pull over His creation to be born into a palace, or at least in a clean, sanitary, private room somewhere. Yet we read that He went to a lowly place and was found wrapped in cloths, lying in a feed trough. This is the place where the shepherds could welcome and greet Him. They would most likely not have been allowed into a palace and would be considered too dirty to come into a sanitary delivery room. Jesus went to the place where those who would recognize Him could come. He met them on their turf.

This was a pattern throughout His whole life. Some of the religious folks of His day accused Him, saying, *"He's a glutton and a drunkard and a friend of tax collectors and other sinners." (Matthew 11:19)*. In fact, He did spend much of His time with these people. He even called Matthew, a tax collector, and Simon, a zealot (an insurgent), to be His disciples. One of His disciples, Judas Iscariot, would betray Him. When asked why He did this, He answered *"I have come to call not those who think they are righteous, but those who know they are sinners." (Matthew 9:13)*. Jesus went to those who would recognize their need of Him, believe in Him, and repent of their sins. He told the religious leaders of His day, *"I tell you the truth, corrupt tax collectors and prostitutes will get into the Kingdom of God before you do." (Matthew 21:31)*.

Today, Jesus has come to meet us on our turf. Do we have room for Jesus in our busy lives? Is He welcome in our heart? Do we realize our absolute desperate need of Him?

Speaking of Himself, Jesus said, *"For the Son of Man came to seek and save those who are lost." (Luke 19:10)*.

The Heart Changer!

Not long after Jesus' birth, a dark side of humanity manifested itself in King Herod, who was jealous of the newborn King Jesus, whose birth the wise men had announced. Herod didn't want anyone to interrupt his rule over others, or even over himself for that matter. He wanted his way and nothing else. His solution was to kill this newborn King of kings. To accomplish this, the Scriptures record that he killed all the boys in and around Bethlehem two years old or younger. The subsequent pain that this caused is expressed in the words: *"A voice was heard in Ramah, weeping and loud lamentation, Rachel weeping for her children; she refused to be comforted, because they are no more." (Matthew 2:18, ESV).*

Has the heart of humanity changed since then? Are we any different? Are we truly honest with ourselves? We need to look at our own hearts. In Canada today, some 100,000 preborn children's lives are cut short annually while still in the womb. Are we really any better than King Herod?

The good part of this piece of history is that Jesus miraculously escaped Herod's plans and went on to willingly offer His life so that people like us could be forgiven! It appears that Herod didn't turn to God for forgiveness, but many like him repented and found forgiveness from God. The prophet Joel addressed the hard hearts of sinful humanity with the following words: *"Yet even now," declares the Lord, "return to me with all your heart, with fasting, with weeping, and with mourning; and rend your hearts and not your garments." Return to the Lord your God, for He is gracious and merciful, slow to anger, and abounding in steadfast love; and He relents over disaster. Who knows whether He will not turn and relent, and leave a blessing behind him, a grain offering and a drink offering for the Lord your God?" (Joel 2:12–14, ESV).*

The heart of God has not changed. Are we willing to let Him change ours?

DECEMBER 27

Wise Men

A group of men came to worship Jesus. They have been called kings and magi and wise men. Much mystery surrounds them because little is mentioned about them. The Bible says, *"And going into the house, they saw the child with Mary His mother, and they fell down and worshiped Him. Then, opening their treasures, they offered Him gifts, gold and frankincense and myrrh." (Matthew 2:11, ESV).*

The Ten Commandments clearly point out that God is the only one we should bow down to or worship (Exodus 20:4–5). The Scriptures mentioned above record that the wise men did both! This would not have been very wise of them if Jesus had not been God! God's Holy Word says of Jesus: *"Who, being in very nature God, did not consider equality with God something to be used to His own advantage; rather, He made Himself nothing by taking the very nature of a servant, being made in human likeness. And being found in appearance as a man, He humbled himself by becoming obedient to death—even death on a cross! Therefore God exalted Him to the highest place and gave Him the name that is above every name, that at the name of Jesus every knee should bow, in heaven and on earth and under the earth, and every tongue acknowledge that Jesus Christ is Lord, to the glory of God the Father." (Philippians 2:6–11, NIV).*

Wise men will bow down and worship the Lord Jesus Christ! What will we do with Jesus in the coming year?

DECEMBER 28

Tested

On January 5, 2024, Alaska Airlines flight 1282 experienced a very serious mid-flight emergency. A door plug blew out of the side of the Boeing 737 Max 9 aircraft at 16,000 ft. All on board faced tragedy and possible death as the plane instantly depressurized, causing a loud bang and strong wind as parts of the adjacent seats sucked out. Even the shirt of a youngster seated nearby was ripped off and followed the door and other debris into a descent to the earth far below.

Thankfully the crew was able to turn the plane around and safely land at the airport of their origin. All escaped with their lives, and only a few experienced minor injuries! What went wrong, so terribly wrong? An investigation revealed loose bolts were found that would have kept the door in place had they been tightened and tested before the airplane was put into service. Obviously, the door plug installation in the aircraft was not properly tested and thus didn't hold up under rigorous flight conditions.

Testing shows how strong and reliable something actually is. This also applies to our person and character. When trials and tribulations come our way, we're being tested to see what we are really made of! God's Word says, *"Consider it pure joy, my brothers and sisters, whenever you face trials of many kinds, because you know that the testing of your faith produces perseverance. Let perseverance finish its work so that you may be mature and complete, not lacking anything." (James 1:2–4, NIV).*

God allows testing to show us the weak points in our lives. Then we can surrender them to Him and have Him give us strength in the place of our weaknesses! If we endure the trials and difficulties of daily life, our character will mature, and we'll be able to persevere even through the most severe testing! Testing is good for us, and we should be thankful that God has allowed these trials and tribulations to mature us, to strengthen us, and develop our character for His glory!

May this be our attitude when we are tested in the years to come!

Facing Our Fears

My grandmother never drove a car or rode a bicycle. My parents informed me that when she was young, she got on a bicycle, fell, and never tried again. Later on, she tried to drive a vehicle, and on her first attempt forgot where the brake pedal was and ran over her rose bush. She never tried driving again. Maybe it was fear of being embarrassed, maybe fear of crashing and getting hurt, but I'm quite sure it was fear that kept her from trying again.

I can understand how she felt, as my first attempt at driving was similar. I couldn't even find first gear and kept stalling the old Austin Healey. It was embarrassing, and the temptation was to give up and quit. After many more attempts and God's help, I was able to learn to drive.

We have many fears: fear of failing, fear of being alone, fear of heights, fear of being embarrassed, fear of darkness. The list is endless, especially if we think we must live this life on our own. We're often paralyzed, or at least limited by fear.

God's Word, the Bible, is very clear that He has a purpose for all who trust in Him. When the Israelites were in captivity, He promised His people: *"'For I know the plans I have for you,' declares the Lord, 'plans to prosper you and not to harm you, plans to give you hope and a future. Then you will call on me and come and pray to me, and I will listen to you.'"* (*Jeremiah 29:11–12 NIV*).

As we surrender in faith to God and allow Him to control our lives, as we grow in our personal relationship with Him, all that is available in Christ Jesus—His love and care for us—becomes more and more evident. We can then proclaim, "I am in the hands of the Almighty Creator. He is my God; there is none other. Surely, He can handle whatever I am facing right now!" With Him in the driver's seat, there's no reason to be immobilized by fear.

As we approach another New Year, may you and I face our fears as we find our confidence in the Almighty God.

"There is no fear in love. But perfect love drives out fear, because fear has to do with punishment. The one who fears is not made perfect in love." (1 John 4:18, NIV).

DECEMBER 30

Little Things—Big Change

Have you ever made a New Year's resolution? I knew a wonderful lady who made a resolution to quit smoking for spiritual, health, and financial reasons. It seemed impossible, as she had smoked for a long time and her husband was also a smoker, not convinced that he wanted to quit! She knew her habit wasn't pleasing to God and that she didn't really need to smoke. It was slowly killing her. As a believer, she asked God for help.

Leaving her last pack and some matches in her pocket, she was determined not to smoke again. Sometimes she would instinctively reach for her cigarettes and remember, "I quit. I don't need this anymore." Other times she became agitated about something and reached for her smokes to calm her, but remembering her resolution, asked God for help. She didn't put a cigarette to her mouth. Though she had many incessant cravings and temptations, she never smoked again, even while her husband continued to smoke right in front of her! God had been faithful by giving her the resolute strength and determined faith, one moment at a time! Step by step she was delivered from this ungodly, unhealthy, and expensive habit.

Does something in your life need to change? Is it something that hinders you in some way? Do you believe this change would honour God? Does it seem too difficult or impossible to change? Do you believe He can give you the strength to change, even little by little? Jesus said, *"If you are faithful in little things, you will be faithful in large ones ..."* *(Luke 16:10).*

After Moses and the Israelites walked through the Red Sea on dry ground, they declared, *"The LORD is my strength and my song; he has given me victory. This is my God, and I will praise him—my father's God, and I will exalt him!" (Exodus 15:2).* God had made a way for them; they only needed to obey, one step at a time. He can also make a way for us!

DECEMBER 31

Redeeming Time

I like to save coupons. These coupons are put safely away, where I plan to keep them until I can redeem them at an opportune time—only to find that some have expired before I was able to cash them in. Coupons once worth a hefty discount or a free sample of a new product could have been redeemed but are now worth nothing, thrown away as fire starter, not worth the paper they're printed on!

In a sense, time is like a coupon, only worth something if it's used before it expires. Good intentions not acted on are only thoughts blown away in the wind, never to have any real substance. The time I knew I should have apologized, the time I ought to have stopped to help someone, the time I felt I needed to talk to someone or just listen but didn't—time unredeemed, thrown away, expired, never to be used again.

Time is a God-given gift to each of us. What will we do with it? We can selfishly live our lives in a way that only pleases us. We can waste away opportunities that we know we're called to respond to. We can foolishly ignore the obvious fact that there is a God and that He has a good and meaningful purpose for our life. Or we can wisely accept God and His purpose for us and thus fulfill what He has created us to be!

Time is limited! Opportunities are great! In this upcoming year, may we seek God and His will for our lives—while there is still time!

"See then that you walk circumspectly, not as fools but as wise, redeeming the time, because the days are evil. Therefore do not be unwise, but understand what the will of the Lord is." Ephesians (5:15–17, NKJV).

ACKNOWLEDGEMENTS

I would like to thankfully acknowledge each person who contributed to the writing of this book. They are many, as no person is an island, and the influence of all those around us has a great impact on us for either good or bad. Sometimes those who meant harm taught me valuable lessons in forgiveness, blessing my enemies, trusting in God rather than man, and the importance of a closer walk with Jesus! On the other hand, I have been blessed with many who helped guide me into faith in God and trust in His Word! It wouldn't be fair to name a few and leave out so many others, but I thank God for each of you who had an influence on my life! But I would be remiss if I didn't name and thank a few obvious ones, whose fingerprints are all over this book.

I am thankful to my parents, though they have passed from this life into the presence of Jesus, who raised me in a solid Christian home. They didn't give up on me, even when I spurned their faith and prayers, sometimes to their face. Yet the Lord answered their prayers, otherwise I would have been lost in my sins, and certainly this book would never have come about!

Thank you, Eunice, the love of my life, for your encouragement throughout this process. You have been the main editor and constructive critic as I attempted to put words to my thoughts. Thank you for your love and patience with me!

Thank you, Ashley, my beautiful granddaughter, for graciously offering a piece of your wonderful artwork to be used for the front cover.

Most of all, I thank my Lord Jesus Christ, who gave up His life to give me eternal life. He took me from a path of darkness and despair to an exciting walk with Him that I cannot help but share with those around me!

Printed in Canada